Business Plans Handbook

Business Plans Handbook

A COMPILATION OF BUSINESS PLANS DEVELOPED BY INDIVIDUALS THROUGHOUT NORTH AMERICA

VOLUME

39

Farmington Hills, Mich • San Francisco • New York • Waterville, Maine
Meriden, Conn • Mason, Ohio • Chicago

Business Plans Handbook, Volume 39

Project Editor: Joseph Palmisano

Composition and Electronic Prepress: Evi Seoud

Manufacturing: Rita Wimberley

WCN: 01-100-101

Gale, a part of Cengage Learning
27500 Drake Rd.
Farmington Hills, MI 48331-3535

ISBN-13: 978-1-4103-2822-9
1084-4473

Printed in Mexico
1 2 3 4 5 6 7 20 19 18 17

Contents

APPENDIXES

Highlights

Business Plans Handbook, Volume 39 (BPH-39) is a collection of business plans compiled by entrepreneurs seeking funding for small businesses throughout North America. For those looking for examples of how to approach, structure, and compose their own business plans, *BPH-39* presents 20 sample plans, including plans for the following businesses:

- Adult Day Care Center
- Bathroom Remodeling Business
- Digital Marketing Agency
- Massage Therapist
- Private Investigator
- Publicist
- Quilt Making Business
- Sealcoating Business
- Temporary Employment Agency
- Yoga Studio

FEATURES AND BENEFITS

BPH-39 offers many features not provided by other business planning references including:

- Twenty business plans, each of which represent an attempt at clarifying (for themselves and others) the reasons that the business should exist or expand and why a lender should fund the enterprise.
- Two fictional plans that are used by business counselors at a prominent small business development organization as examples for their clients. (You will find these in the Business Plan Template Appendix.)
- A directory section that includes listings for venture capital and finance companies, which specialize in funding start-up and second-stage small business ventures, and a comprehensive listing of Service Corps of Retired Executives (SCORE) offices. In addition, the Appendix also contains updated listings of all Small Business Development Centers (SBDCs); associations of interest to entrepreneurs; Small Business Administration (SBA) Regional Offices; and consultants specializing in small business planning and advice. It is strongly advised that you consult supporting organizations while planning your business, as they can provide a wealth of useful information.
- A Small Business Term Glossary to help you decipher the sometimes confusing terminology used by lenders and others in the financial and small business communities.
- A cumulative index, outlining each plan profiled in the complete *Business Plans Handbook* series.
- A Business Plan Template which serves as a model to help you construct your own business plan. This generic outline lists all the essential elements of a complete business plan and their components, including the Summary, Business History and Industry Outlook, Market Examination,

Competition, Marketing, Administration and Management, Financial Information, and other key sections. Use this guide as a starting point for compiling your plan.

- Extensive financial documentation required to solicit funding from small business lenders. You will find examples of Cash Flows, Balance Sheets, Income Projections, and other financial information included with the textual portions of the plan.

Introduction

Perhaps the most important aspect of business planning is simply doing it. More and more business owners are beginning to compile business plans even if they don't need a bank loan. Others discover the value of planning when they must provide a business plan for the bank. The sheer act of putting thoughts on paper seems to clarify priorities and provide focus. Sometimes business owners completely change strategies when compiling their plan, deciding on a different product mix or advertising scheme after finding that their assumptions were incorrect. This kind of healthy thinking and re-thinking via business planning is becoming the norm. The Editor of *Business Plans Handbook, Volume 39 (BPH-39)* sincerely hopes that this latest addition to the series is a helpful tool in the successful completion of your business plan, no matter what the reason for creating it.

This volume, like each volume in the series, offers business plans created by real people. *BPH-39* provides 20 business plans. The business and personal names and addresses and general locations have been changed to protect the privacy of the plan authors.

NEW BUSINESS OPPORTUNITIES

As in other volumes in the series, *BPH-39* finds entrepreneurs engaged in a wide variety of creative endeavors. Examples include an Adult Day Care Center, Commercial Driving School, Pet Sanctuary, Safety Consultant, and Yoga Studio, among others.

Comprehensive financial documentation has become increasingly important as today's entrepreneurs compete for the finite resources of business lenders. Our plans illustrate the financial data generally required of loan applicants, including Income Statements, Financial Projections, Cash Flows, and Balance Sheets.

ENHANCED APPENDIXES

In an effort to provide the most relevant and valuable information for our readers, we have updated the coverage of small business resources. For instance, you will find a directory section, which includes listings of all of the Service Corps of Retired Executives (SCORE) offices; an informative glossary, which includes small business terms; and a cumulative index, outlining each plan profiled in the complete *Business Plans Handbook* series. In addition we have updated the list of Small Business Development Centers (SBDCs); Small Business Administration Regional Offices; venture capital and finance companies, which specialize in funding start-up and second-stage small business enterprises; associations of interest to entrepreneurs; and consultants, specializing in small business advice and planning. For your reference, we have also reprinted the business plan template, which provides a comprehensive overview of the essential components of a business plan and two fictional plans used by small business counselors.

SERIES INFORMATION

If you already have the first thirty-eight volumes of *BPH*, with this thirty-ninth volume, you will now have a collection of over 700 business plans (not including the updated plans); contact information for hundreds of organizations and agencies offering business expertise; a helpful business plan template; more than 1,500 citations to valuable small business development material; and a comprehensive glossary of terms to help the business planner navigate the sometimes confusing language of entrepreneurship.

ACKNOWLEDGEMENTS

The Editor wishes to sincerely thank the contributors to *BPH-39*, including:

- BizPlanDB.com
- Fran Fletcher
- Paul Greenland
- Claire Moore
- Gerald Rekve
- Zuzu Enterprises

COMMENTS WELCOME

Your comments on *Business Plans Handbook* are appreciated. Please direct all correspondence, suggestions for future volumes of *BPH*, and other recommendations to the following:

Project Editor
Business Plans Handbook
Gale, a part of Cengage Learning
27500 Drake Rd.
Farmington Hills, MI 48331-3535
Phone: (248)699-4253
Toll-Free: 800-877-GALE
URL: www.gale.com

Actuarial Consulting Business

Trenton Actuarial Partners LP

21 Green St.
Pittsburgh, PA 15200

Paul Greenland

Trenton Actuarial Partners LP is an independent actuarial consulting practice serving the enterprise risk management market.

EXECUTIVE SUMMARY

Following a 15-year career with a leading insurance company, actuary Sarah Trenton has decided to establish an independent consulting practice with high-growth potential. Trenton Actuarial Partners LP will apply the owner's professional skill and experience as an enterprise risk actuary to the global business market. Specifically, the practice will assist mid-sized consumer packaged goods companies evaluate the risks associated with launching, maintaining, and expanding operations in emerging markets. In addition to Sarah Trenton, the practice will include Chris Parker, an executive with nearly 20 years of global new business development experience.

INDUSTRY ANALYSIS

According to the U.S. Bureau of Labor Statistics, the employment of actuaries is expected to grow at a faster than average rate between 2014 and 2024. During that time frame, an 18 percent growth rate is projected, resulting in the addition of 4,400 new jobs. Enterprise risk management is one key growth driver within the field of actuarial sciences. In addition to rising demand for actuarial services, Trenton Actuarial Partners will benefit from the trend of economic globalization that is occurring within virtually every industry sector.

Consultants like Sarah Trenton and Chris Parker have access to a wide range of industry resources. One helpful organization is the Society of Actuaries (https://www.soa.org). With roots dating back to 1889, this professional association includes some 27,000 actuaries among its membership base. The society's mission is to "advance actuarial knowledge and to enhance the ability of actuaries to provide expert advice and relevant solutions for financial, business and societal challenges." The SOA's members benefit from access to a variety of resources in the areas of education, professional development, and certification.

Another key industry organization is the Society of Risk Management Consultants (http://srmcsociety.org). Established in 1984 through the combination of the Insurance Consultants Society and the Institute of Risk Management Consultants, SRMC has a diverse membership base, including consultants who serve government agencies, non-profit organizations, mid-sized companies, and Fortune 100 organizations. Like Trenton Actuarial Partners, some of SRMC's members specialize in risk identification and enterprise risk management.

MARKET ANALYSIS

In the United States, sales within the consumer packaged goods industry totaled nearly $636 billion in 2015. Sarah Trenton and Chris Parker have decided to target mid-sized consumer packaged goods firms, which may not have in-house expertise in their firm's area of specialization. The partners have conducted a thoughtful analysis and identified 150 top prospects, which they will target with tactics outlined in the Marketing & Sales section of this plan. The firm's top five prospects (by sales) are:

1. McGinty Foods LLC ($1.26 billion)
2. Jamison Consumer Products Inc. ($986 million)
3. Wentworth Weller International Corp. ($657 million)
4. Starborne Apparel ($267 million)
5. Tessa Worldwide ($129 million)

SERVICES

Overview

Capitalizing on the Fortune 500-level experience of its owners, Trenton Actuarial Partners will help consumer packaged goods companies evaluate the plausibility of expanding operations into emerging markets.

Although the needs and situation of each client will be different, the firm will utilize a combination of predictive modeling software, industry research, market analysis, and first-hand knowledge/experience to provide its clients with sound recommendations. These may pertain to a wide range of scenarios, including:

- Establishing a regional sales organization.
- Opening a new manufacturing facility.
- Developing and/or introducing a new product.
- Evaluating tax/government incentives.
- Implementing a security program.

Business actions such as these must be considered in the context of a varying geopolitical, legal, health, economic, societal, and technological risks. Examples include infectious diseases and pandemics, financial volatility, terrorism threats, and the impact of cyber security attacks. Human resources challenges also must be considered, including the ability to hire and retain employees with adequate skill levels.

Process

Trenton Actuarial Partners will provide a free one-hour consultation to all prospective clients. This will provide an opportunity to discuss the prospective client's current situation, business objectives, and growth strategies, and the ways in which the practice can be of assistance. Assuming that a business relationship is of interest, Trenton Actuarial Partners will provide the client with information regarding the practice's fee structure and propose a mutually agreeable block of consulting hours. Finally, the firm will require its clients to sign a consulting agreement that specifies the scope of services to be provided and all related terms and conditions. Trenton Actuarial Partners will sign confidentiality and non-disclosure agreements with its customers.

Fees

In some cases, actuaries who work for large national firms bill more than $500 per hour for their services. Independent consultants may charge anywhere between $150 and $350 per hour based on their particular specialization and industry experience. Because Trenton Actuarial Partners offers a unique blend of highly specialized expertise in both risk management and global business development, and considering the extensive experience of its partners, the firm has established an hourly rate of $300 per hour. In most cases, Trenton Actuarial Partners will agree upon a set block of consulting time for its customers, and will require payment of 50 percent in advance. In the event that a client prefers a retainer arrangement, the firm will negotiate an agreeable arrangement.

OPERATIONS

Location

Trenton Actuarial Partners will maintain operations in Pittsburgh. The partners will commence operations virtually, working from home offices and meeting with clients at their place of business. The owners anticipate that the majority of their clients will be headquartered in major metropolitan areas throughout the United States, requiring extensive business travel. However, they will utilize video chat sessions whenever possible. Trenton and Parker have established a toll-free phone number for the business, allowing prospective and existing customers to contact them at no charge.

Business Structure

Trenton Actuarial Partners has been established as a limited partnership. Sarah Trenton will serve as the firm's general partner, assuming responsibility for its management and partnership obligations. Chris Parker will act as a limited partner, with no management responsibilities. However, his limited partner status will entitle him to a pre-determined share of the firm's profits.

PERSONNEL

Sarah Trenton, General Partner

Sarah Trenton has always had a knack for numbers. An accomplished "mathlete" during her high school years, Trenton earned an academic scholarship to Midwestern University, where she earned an undergraduate degree in actuarial science and began working for a leading insurance company. As required by her profession, Trenton successfully passed a series of professional examinations offered by the Society of Actuaries, obtaining ASA certification after five years. Within seven years, she had achieved fellowship certification in the area of finance/enterprise risk management. After advancing within the organization, Trenton joined the management ranks, but was soon hungry for new challenges. When one of her clients, Chris Parker, approached her about establishing an independent consulting practice, Trenton eagerly embraced the new opportunity.

Chris Parker, Limited Partner

Truly a man of the world, Chris Parker was raised in a military family, giving him opportunities to live in different parts of the world during his youth. His international upbringing enabled him to attend college in the United Kingdom, where he ultimately earned a graduate business degree from the London School of Economics. After beginning his career in marketing, Parker specialized in new business development within the consumer packaged goods industry. As leading global companies began making inroads into emerging markets like Eastern Europe and China, Parker helped his employers execute their expansion plans, gaining invaluable first-hand experience in the process. Over the years, Parker received offers to perform consulting work for colleagues who had joined other organizations. After receiving two lucrative consulting offers, he has decided to pursue the opportunities and use them as the foundation for starting Trenton Actuarial Partners with Sarah Trenton.

Professional & Advisory Support

Trenton Actuarial Partners has established a business banking account with the Bank of Pittsburgh. Herzog & Weller, a business law firm, will provide counsel and assist with client agreements and related matters. Finally, Wauconda Accounting will provide the firm with tax advisement and bookkeeping services.

GROWTH STRATEGY

Trenton Actuarial Partners is fortunate to establish the practice with two clients, whose names are not listed due to confidentiality agreements. Together, these clients have contracted with the firm for the equivalent of 25 hours of weekly billable consulting time through the end of 2017. While working on these projects, Sarah Trenton and Chris Parker will begin marketing the practice to other potential clients, with a goal of securing at least two new clients by the year's end. Annual gross revenues of approximately $375,000 are expected in 2017.

Trenton and Parker have established the following growth targets for their consulting firm's second and third years:

2018: Achieve 35 weekly billable hours and secure at least three additional clients. Generate annual gross revenue of $525,000.

2019: Achieve 45 weekly billable hours and secure at least three additional clients. Generate annual gross revenue of $675,000. Hire an additional limited partner and lease dedicated office space in the Pittsburgh area.

MARKETING & SALES

Because of its highly specialized focus, Trenton Actuarial Partners will rely heavily upon word-of-mouth referrals and networking to grow the business. Additionally, the firm also will use the following tactics as part of its marketing strategy:

1. The use of social media channels, including LinkedIn, to network with potential customers and peers within the risk management field.
2. A media relations strategy that includes outreach to national business publications and media outlets, making the firm's partners available as expert sources for news stories pertaining to risk management/global business topics.
3. A Web site with complete details about the consultancy.
4. An international business blog, with an emerging markets/risk management slant.
5. Printed collateral describing the consultancy (suitable for direct mailings, sales calls, etc.).

6. Writing expert articles about risk management in global markets for industry trade magazines and national business publications.
7. Presentations at business conferences to increase exposure among prospective customers, including leading international business executives.

FINANCIAL ANALYSIS

Following is a breakdown of projected revenue, expenses, and net income for Trenton Actuarial Partners' first three years of operations. Additional financial projections are available upon request.

	2017	2018	2019
Revenue	**$375,000**	**$525,000**	**$675,000**
Expenses			
Salary	$200,000	$250,000	$375,000
Payroll tax	$ 30,000	$ 37,500	$ 56,250
Insurance	$ 5,500	$ 6,000	$ 6,500
Office lease	$ 0	$ 0	$ 15,000
Accounting & legal	$ 7,700	$ 8,300	$ 8,900
Office supplies	$ 700	$ 700	$ 700
Equipment	$ 3,500	$ 2,500	$ 2,500
Marketing & advertising	$ 12,500	$ 13,000	$ 13,500
Telecommunication & Internet	$ 3,250	$ 3,250	$ 3,250
Professional development	$ 1,650	$ 1,750	$ 1,850
Unreimbursed travel	$ 15,500	$ 20,500	$ 25,500
Business meals	$ 5,000	$ 6,000	$ 7,000
Subscriptions & dues	$ 500	$ 500	$ 500
Software licenses	$ 4,500	$ 5,000	$ 5,500
Miscellaneous	$ 500	$ 500	$ 500
Total expenses	**$290,800**	**$355,500**	**$522,450**
Net income	**$ 84,200**	**$169,500**	**$152,550**

Adult Day Care Center

Daycation Senior Care, Inc.

2015 Rocklin Ranch Rd.
Rocklin, CA 95678

Claire Moore

Daycation Senior Care (DSC) is an Adult Day Program (ADP) licensed by the California Department of Social Services. DSC is a community-based, social day care program that provides care to persons 18 years of age or older in need of personal care services, supervision, or assistance essential for sustaining the activities of daily living or for the protection of the individual on less than a 24-hour basis.

EXECUTIVE SUMMARY

Adult day care services are designed to provide care, companionship and certain rehabilitation services for older adults. They also offer relief to care givers allowing them to take time to relax, work or handle personal business.

Adult day care programs strive to delay or prevent institutionalization by offering alternative care in a supportive environment with trained staff. There are two general types of adult day care: social day care and health day care. Social day care provides meals, social activities, and some health services. Adult day health care offers intensive health and therapeutic social services for those with medical conditions that put them at risk of requiring nursing home care.

Costs can vary but tend to range from $30 to more than $100 per day depending on the type of services required. The national average cited by the National Adult Day Services Association is $61 per day. These costs are not usually covered by Medicare insurance but some assistance may be available through state programs such as Medicaid or Veterans Health Administration.

The California Department of Social Services licenses adult day programs (ADPs) as community care facilities. ADP services are not covered by Medi-Cal—the name of California's Medicaid program. They receive funding from Area Agencies on Aging, private fees, and community donations.

Daycation Senior Care (DSC) is an Adult Day Program (ADP) licensed by the California Department of Social Services. DSC is a community-based, social day care program that provides care to persons 18 years of age or older in need of personal care services, supervision, or assistance essential for sustaining the activities of daily living or for the protection of the individual on less than a 24-hour basis.

DSC is a healthy place for seniors to come together, meet new people and socialize with a focus on protective supervision by trained aides, structured activities, health monitoring, meals, out-of-home respite and support for the caregiver. We organize daily activities to keep our members active and involved in their environment. Our friendly and compassionate staff ensures that personalized care is given to each person staying on our campus. We proudly serve the residents of Rocklin, Lincoln, Roseville, Granite Bay, Citrus Heights, Loomis, Newcastle, Fair Oaks, and surrounding areas.

MISSION

Our mission is to enhance quality of life for our participants and their families by providing social activities, supervision, and support with highly trained and certified staff who are committed to our values.

OBJECTIVES

DSC has identified the following objectives to be achieved in its first three years of operation.

- Satisfy all state requirements for operation as an Adult Day Program (ADP) in California.
- Develop a network of volunteers who share our vision of enhancing the quality of life for Placer County seniors and their care givers.
- Recruit, train, and maintain staff that is committed to our values of placing our participants' needs first.

KEYS TO SUCCESS

We have identified the following attributes as key factors in our success:

- Educated and experienced staff
- A commitment to continuous improvement
- Adherence to all state requirements for operation
- Outreach and alliances with organizations that serve our target market

COMPANY SUMMARY

Daycation Senior Care (DSC) is an Adult Day Program (ADP) licensed by the California Department of Social Services. DSC is a community-based social day care program that provides care to persons 18 years of age or older in need of personal care services, supervision, or assistance essential for sustaining the activities of daily living or for the protection of the individual on less than a 24-hour basis.

DSC was created and incorporated in the state of California in 2015 for the purposes of providing quality, affordable day care for adults.

DSC was founded by Ron Hewitt and Jan Jenkins who have worked in eldercare for more than 25 years. DSC is a for-profit, community based program that is designed to fill what we see as an unmet need in the community for a social program that will meet the needs of the socially isolated elder population who need support to maintain an active life while managing the issues related to aging.

COMPANY OWNERSHIP

DSC is structured as a California corporation and is currently owned by Ron Hewitt and Jan Jenkins.

STARTUP SUMMARY

DSC has incurred the following costs of start-up:

Start-up Expense	Cost
Computer/printer/copier/scanner/fax	$ 1,700
Telephone/cell phones	$ 1,475
Laptop computer	$ 550
Storage/filing/shelving	$ 375
Office equipment	$ 350
Office furniture	$ 1,200
Leasehold improvements: fixtures	$12,500
Center furniture: tables, chairs, sofas, television, projector	$ 5,000
Licenses	$ 750
Legal/accounting	$ 2,500
Supplies	$ 575
Advertising	$ 2,550
Software	$ 775
Web site development	$ 2,000
Total start-up expense cost	**$32,300**

COMPANY LOCATION AND FACILITIES

Our location in Rocklin, California is a 3,000 square foot commercial space located in a commercial mall on a main street. There is ample parking and easy access from the nearest interstate. The space includes an office for use by our secretary and staff and a small conference room for meetings and private interviews. There is a large activity room, an area equipped to provide for hair care, a quiet room for naps or reading and a supply room. Storage areas with lockers are also available for clients and staff to store their personal belongings.

DSC has been able to negotiate a very favorable lease that holds the square foot price at $1/sq. ft. for the next three years. The agreement stipulates that all leasehold improvements will remain at the termination of the lease.

The improvements made include: ramps for wheel chair access, a sink for the purposes of providing hair care, additional bathroom facilities, additional lighting, cable and Internet access.

MANAGEMENT TEAM

Ron Hewitt, LCSW, Center Administrator, is responsible for carrying out program responsibilities, supervising the program's operation, coordinating all activities and services, and providing staff orientation and training. Ron is a Licensed Clinical Social Worker in the state of California with 20 years' experience working with children and the elderly.

During his career Ron rose from the ranks of social worker for the Human Services Agency of San Francisco to Manager of Social Work of the Program of All-Inclusive Care for the Elderly (PACE) Social Service department for Los Angeles, California. PACE provides comprehensive medical and social services to certain frail, community-dwelling elderly individuals.

Jan Jenkins, Center Director takes over the duties of Administrator when Mr. Hewitt is absent from the site. Jan is trained as a gerontology social worker. Gerontology social workers help seniors gain a better understanding of the mental and physical complications of getting older and the cultural, social and institutional attitudes accompanying aging. Gerontology social workers use social interventions, clinical interventions and advocacy to help improve the lives of seniors and their families.

Ron Hewitt and Jan Jenkins have over 35 years combined experience in elder care. Our staff consists of CNAs and volunteers committed to our goal of providing the family peace of mind while their loved one attends our day care program.

OTHER TEAM MEMBERS

Todd Jenkins, Attorney: Todd specializes in eldercare issues and estate planning. He will advise DSC in its interactions with customer/members and on creating contracts.

Adele Powers, Bookkeeper: QuickBooks expert and bookkeeper will assist DSC in completing financial statements and the filing of payroll tax forms.

Joe Cahill, CPA: Joe advises DSC on tax and human resource issues. Joe will complete all income tax filings as well as ensure compliance with state regulations for corporations.

Volunteers: DSC has formed a working relationship with local colleges that have programs related to health care. The schools work with DSC to provide interns and volunteers who spend at least 10 hours a week helping members at our location.

Senior Services: DSC works with several companies in Placer County that serve our senior population. We act as an intermediary with these companies to arrange services for our members such as transportation, financial counseling, food and nutrition.

SERVICES

People who attend adult day care usually live either on their own or with a family caregiver. For those seniors who require additional help with typical daily tasks of living, adult day care offers a viable alternative to institutionalization. The social and health activities that adult day care centers provide improve the quality of life for both the attendees and their at-home care givers.

Adult day care services in California are one of two types:

- Adult Day Program (ADP): licensed by the California Department of Social Services
- Adult Day Health Care (ADHC): licensed by the California Department of Public Health

ADP: provide personal care services, supervision or assistance essential for sustaining the activities of daily living or for the protection of the individual on less than a 24-hour basis.

ADHC: therapeutic activities and social services for frail elders or adults with chronic, disabling medical, cognitive or mental health conditions who are at risk for institutional placement.

DSC is an Adult Day Program (ADP) licensed by the California Department of Social Services operating under the statutory authority of Health and Services Code, Chapter 3. As an ADP, we do not qualify for funding nor are we certified by Medi-Cal.

DSC is required to provide the following services as an ADP:

- Individual Plan of Care
- Dietary services
- Meals and snacks
- Personal care and supervision
- Assistance with medication
- Assistance with or provide/arrange transportation

The Benefits of Daycation Senior Care:

- Supervision and a secure environment for senior adults who require it
- A period of respite for the care givers
- Social stimulation and peer support
- Enhanced or maintained level of independence
- Daily activities
- Nutritious meals and snacks

Our activities center is open to the seniors within the community from 7AM to 6PM Monday through Friday and offers:

- Exercises
- Art classes
- Crafts
- Trivia
- Music
- Card games
- Movie screenings
- Family and holiday celebrations
- Sony Wii Video Entertainment Center
- A napping room, comfortable reclining chairs
- Hair care/styling service
- Specialized programming for memory or cognitive losses

PRICES AND PAYMENT

All fees must be paid by participants from their own funds, pension or private insurance.

Medicare does not pay for any kind of adult day care. DSC does not qualify for Medi-Cal or Veterans medical funding. It is possible that veterans could direct Aid & Attendance pensions or Directed Home and Community Based Services Program (VD-HCBS) payments to pay for adult day care. It is up to each participant to apply for and determine what benefits they may qualify for.

DSC currently charges the following fees:

- $85 for Full Day—6 or More Hours
- $67 for Half Day—4 Hours
- $15 Each Additional Hour

A full day or half day includes lunch. Snacks are included: a snack is served each morning and afternoon.

INDUSTRY DESCRIPTION

The number of adults age 65 and older is expected to rise to 55 million by 2020. About 38 percent of older adults have some type of disability and this number will increase as the population increases. According to the National Adult Day Services Association (NADSA) there were about 5,685 programs operating in the U.S. in 2014, up from 4,600 in 2010. NADSA participated with Met Life in a survey of adult day care programs in 2010.

Survey results indicated that nearly 80 percent of care centers had a nursing professional on staff, nearly 50 percent had a social work professional on staff and about 60 percent offered case management services. About half of the centers offered physical, occupational, or speech therapy.

Today, about 90 percent of centers offer cognitive stimulation programs while about 80 percent provide memory training programs. More than 75 percent offer educational programs.

The 2010 Met study showed that 27 percent of centers reported private for-profit status compared to 22 percent in 2002. This may be indicative of the financial health of the industry and an expected evolution as adult day care centers become more sophisticated and focused on medical services.

Over 80 percent of participants attend full days and 46 percent attend five days per week thus enabling family caregivers the ability to remain employed. Most centers (70 percent) offer caregiver support programs that include education, support groups and counseling.

Trends in the adult day care industry indicate the following:

- An increase in disease-specific programs to address chronic conditions such as diabetes, mental illness and physical disability
- An increased focus on prevention and health maintenance with physical activity programs

NADSA recommends a minimum staff-to-participant ratio of one-to-six. If participants require a higher level of care, for example participants with dementia, the ratio should be closer to one-to-four.

The average participant is a white woman age 65 years or older with dementia, hypertension or a physical disability requiring assistance with the activities of daily living, and in need of medication management. She typically receives care primarily from an adult child.

MARKET ANALYSIS

According to the California Department of Aging, California currently comprises 12 percent of the nation's population and this will increase to 14 percent by 2020. The California elderly population is expected to grow more than twice as fast as the total population. The growth rate of those aged 85 and over in Placer County is projected to be more than 200 percent. As of 2015 there were 50,506 homes in Placer County with one or more people age 60 and over.

Placer County encompasses 1,506 square miles and is located 80 miles northeast of San Francisco, California. The County is part of the Sacramento Region which includes the Counties of El Dorado, Sacramento, Sutter, Yolo and Yuba. It is home to a population numbering 348,432. The median age of residents is 40. Persons 65 years and over comprised 18.5 percent of the population.

Average household income is $93,615 and median household income is $76,541. Incomes have increased by 33 percent since the year 2000.

Recent growth in Placer County has been fueled by the relocation of large companies such as Hewlett-Packard from the Bay Area. The growth rate of Placer County is second among all California counties.

Many of Placer County's population of working adults are responsible for the health and safety of elderly relatives. As our population of baby boomers ages, the challenge of balancing career and care giving will continue to be a fact of life for this demographic.

MARKET SEGMENTATION

Adult day care health services are appropriate for adults who require intense, specialized oversight, care and rehabilitation for conditions such as strokes and dementia.

There are few organizations in Placer County that specialize in social day care for adults. DSC will focus on providing social day care that includes activities that foster prevention and health maintenance.

The national average for a one-bedroom apartment in an assisted living facility is $3,450 per month according to Genworth Financial's Cost of Care Survey. A semi-private room in a nursing home costs an average of $6,200 per month. An in-home health aide charges $19 per hour on average.

In contrast, Daycation charges a fee of $85 per day or $14.12 per hour for a six-hour day.

COMPETITION

We found other adult day care facilities in our area:

Name	Location	Services
AD Experiences	Rocklin	Specialized program of speech therapy
Craig Cares	Roseville	In home care
Roseville Adult Center	Roseville	Programs related to vocational training, daily living practices, cognitive growth and mobility training
Seniors First	Auburn, Lincoln	Social day care: Auburn: two days/week from 9am to 1pm; Lincoln: four days a week from 9am to 1pm

Because many Placer County residents work in the city of Sacramento, we also researched adult day care services located in Sacramento.

Name	Location	Services
Triple R Adult Day Program	Midtown Sacramento	Specializes in dementia care for moderate to severe memory loss
Altamedix	Sacramento	Helping adults with chronic medical, cognitive or mental health conditions
Health for All	Sacramento	Adult day health center providing medical, nursing, physical therapy, speech therapy and social activities

Our target market is adults who are responsible for the care of an adult who is experiencing a decrease in their social, physical, and mental functioning and who requires supervision, assistance with medication, physical and mental activities, and minimal therapeutic care. Our ideal participant is an adult who is socially isolated at home during the day due to age, physical or cognitive impairment, or minor disability.

We are conveniently located to residents of Placer County as our location is central and near a major freeway into Sacramento. By working with organizations such as Seniors First, a non-profit organization in Auburn, we help our participants to arrange door-to-door transportation to and from our location.

MARKETING STRATEGY

Our ideal customer possesses the following characteristics:

- A working adult whose income is at least $75,000 per year.
- Seeking supervised day care for an adult in need of social activities, some medical and nutrition supervision and minor cognitive and memory therapy.
- Lives or works within our service area.

DSC will employ a marketing campaign directed at those who are seeking care for another adult. Marketing strategies will include:

- Listings on Caring.com, AgingCare.com, Angie's List, SeniorCare.com and ElderCareResourcesSacramento.com, PlacerNetworkofCare.org, SeniorCareLink.org, and CommunityWarVets.org
- Maintenance of a web site that provides outreach to potential customers and tools to help them connect with us and our services
- Advertisements in print publications such as the *Sacramento News and Reviews, The Sacramento Business Journal, The Sacramento Bee* and the *Placer Herald*
- A monthly open-house event for the public which will be listed on online community calendars for cities in our service area
- Brochures and flyers advertising our services to be placed at key locations such as: local churches, medical clinics and pharmacies

MARKETING OBJECTIVES

DSC has identified the following marketing objectives:

- Establish relationships with estate and eldercare attorneys and long-term care insurance providers within our targeted market for the purpose of cross-marketing.
- Create an online presence that provides exposure for our brand, educates the public and allows for contact from the public.
- Our site will gather information from other sources in order to educate the public on the subject of eldercare.

Other marketing strategies will include maintenance of an informational web site that contains articles on benefits of adult day care and a calendar of activities at our location. The web site will include a contact form that can be used to send us inquiries and schedule a guided tour of our facility. All contact submissions will receive a response on the next business day.

MILESTONES

Task	End Date
Check business name, register name	6/5/2015
Begin business plan	7/1/2015
Form corporation, obtain IRS EIN	8/5/2015
Open corporate bank accounts	8/15/2015
Secure Adult Day Program (ADP) license	8/15/2015
Secure health permit	9/16/2015
Secure business license	9/16/2015
Finalize lease agreement	10/1/2015
Begin leasehold improvements	10/15/2015
Complete inspection by Calif. Dept. Social Services	11/15/2015
Complete leasehold improvements	11/30/2015
Recruit employees	12/1/2015
Begin work on web site	12/1/2015
Purchase and install furniture and equipment	12/2/2015
Complete health/safety inspections	12/15/2015
Complete business plan	12/31/2015
Begin operations	1/15/2016

PERSONNEL PLAN

Typical staffing in adult day care programs includes the following:

- Activity director
- Center director
- Assistants to activity director
- Office staff: secretary, bookkeeper

Personnel Plan	Year 1	Year 2	Year 3
Ron Hewitt, Center Administrator	$ 36,000	$ 46,000	$ 56,000
Jan Jenkins, Center Director	$ 36,000	$ 46,000	$ 56,000
Certified nurse assistant 1	$ 16,000	$ 18,000	$ 20,000
Certified nurse assistant 2	$ 16,000	$ 18,000	$ 20,000
Certified nurse assistant 3 (part-time)	$ 8,000	$ 9,000	$ 10,000
Certified nurse assistant 4 (part-time)	$ 8,000	$ 9,000	$ 10,000
Activity assistant	$ 18,000	$ 20,000	$ 22,000
Receptionist/secretary	$ 24,000	$ 24,000	$ 26,000
Assistant to administrator	$ 24,000	$ 24,000	$ 26,000
Assistant center director	$ 24,000	$ 24,000	$ 26,000
Total people	**10**	**10**	**10**
Total payroll	**$210,000**	**$238,000**	**$272,000**

FINANCIAL PLAN

Projected Profit and Loss Statement

Revenue	Year 1	Year 2	Year 3
Day care fees	$365,000	$435,000	$495,000
Cost of goods sold:			
Supplies: Food, sundries, cleaning	$ 54,750	$ 65,250	$ 74,250
Service payroll	$138,000	$146,000	$ 160,000
Total cost of sales	**$192,750**	**$211,250**	**$234,250**
Gross profit	$172,250	$223,750	$260,750
Gross profit %	47%	51%	53 %
Expenses			
Admin. payroll	$ 72,000	$ 92,000	$112,000
Depreciation	$ 2,315	$ 2,315	$ 2,315
Payroll taxes/benefits	$ 31,500	$ 35,700	$ 40,800
Office supplies	$ 450	$ 500	$ 600
Web site maintenance	$ 350	$ 350	$ 350
Insurance	$ 3,000	$ 3,000	$ 3,000
Dues & subscriptions	$ 650	$ 750	$ 900
Continuing education	$ 800	$ 800	$ 800
Computers & software	$ 500	$ 500	$ 500
Marketing	$ 5,500	$ 6,000	$ 4,000
Licenses	$ 450	$ 450	$ 450
Telephone/Internet services	$ 2,400	$ 2,400	$ 2,400
Utilities	$ 4,000	$ 4,200	$ 4,200
Professional dues	$ 475	$ 475	$ 475
Subscriptions	$ 350	$ 350	$ 350
Rent	$ 36,000	$ 36,000	$ 36,000
Repairs, cleaning, maintenance	$ 8,500	$ 8,500	$ 8,500
Legal/accounting	$ 3,400	$ 3,200	$ 3,200
Other expenses	$ 1,000	$ 1,000	$ 1,000
Total operating expenses	**$173,640**	**$198,490**	**$221,840**
Net profit before taxes	**($ 1,390)**	**$ 25,260**	**$ 38,910**
Income tax		$ 3,789	$ 5,837
Net profit	**($ 1,390)**	**$ 21,471**	**$ 33,073**
Net profit/sales	**−1%**	**10%**	**13%**
Average monthly break even revenue	**$ 26,200**		
Assumptions:			
Average percent variable cost	**49%**		
Estimated monthly fixed costs	**$ 13,287**		

Projected Balance Sheet	Year 1	Year 2	Year 3
Current assets			
Cash	$ 9,575	$23,561	$48,449
Accounts receivable	$ 3,200	$ 3,000	$ 3,500
Other current assets	$ 5,000	$15,000	$25,000
Total current assets	**$17,775**	$41,561	$76,949
Long term assets			
Leasehold improvements	$12,500	$12,500	$12,500
Center furniture	$ 5,000	$ 5,000	$ 5,000
Office furniture	$ 5,650	$ 5,650	$ 5,650
Less accumulated depreciation	$ 2,315	$ 4,630	$ 6,945
Total long-term assets	**$20,835**	**$18,520**	**$16,205**
Total assets	**$38,610**	**$60,081**	**$93,154**
Current liabilities			
Accounts payable			
Current maturities	$ —	$ —	$ —
Other current liabilities	$ —	$ —	$ —
Total current liabilities	$ —	$ —	$ —
Long-term liabilities	$ —	$ —	$ —
Total liabilities	$ —	$ —	$ —
Capital			
Paid in capital	$40,000	$40,000	$40,000
Retained earnings		$ (1,390)	$20,081
Earnings	$ (1,390)	$21,471	$33,073
Total capital	**$38,610**	**$60,081**	**$93,154**
Total liabilities and capital	**$38,610**	**$60,081**	**$93,154**

Bathroom Remodeling Business

Benson Brothers Bathroom Remodeling LLC

2185 Division Ave., Ste. 369
Prestwick, PA 18339

Paul Greenland

Benson Brothers Bathroom Remodeling LLC is located near Philadelphia, in the community of Prestwick.

EXECUTIVE SUMMARY

Benson Brothers Bathroom Remodeling LLC is located near Philadelphia, in the community of Prestwick. The business is being established by Peter Benson, a former carpenter, and his brother Steve, an independent plumber. Peter's construction and installation experience, combined with Steve's plumbing expertise, will provide the foundation for a successful bathroom remodeling operation. The following business plan outlines the Bensons' strategy for establishing and growing their business.

INDUSTRY ANALYSIS

According to the National Kitchen & Bath Association (NKBA), a leading trade association, consumers in the United States were expected to spend approximately $13 billion on 2.5 million bathroom remodeling projects in 2016. This figure does not include an estimated 2.8 million bathroom installations in the new construction market, replacement/repair projects, or projects in non-residential buildings like offices and hospitals. Among the aforementioned 2.5 million projects, it was estimated that about half would be managed by professionals like Benson Brothers Bathroom Remodeling.

With roots dating back to 1963, the non-profit NKBA (www.NKBA.org) serves approximately 14,000 industry players from all corners of the kitchen and bath industry. With a mission "to inspire, lead and empower the kitchen and bath industry through the creation of certifications, marketplaces and networks," NKBA offers a variety of resources to its members, including the Kitchen & Bath Industry Show.

MARKET ANALYSIS

Benson Brothers Bathroom Remodeling is located near Philadelphia, in the community of Prestwick. The business will serve customers in the broader Philadelphia area, which features many older and higher-end homes, providing significant growth opportunities.

According to market research data obtained at the Prestwick Public Library, the Philadelphia area included 617,139 housing units in 2016, 91.5 percent of which were occupied. Between 2010 and 2021, the number of occupied units was projected to increase 3.9 percent.

Benson Brothers Bathroom Remodeling will market its services to owners of homes with a value of $150,000 or more. According to the aforementioned market research data, the business's target market (by home value) breaks down as follows:

- $150,000—$199,999 (15.9%)
- $200,000—$299,999 (17.9%)
- $300,000—$399,999 (5.9%)
- $400,000—$499,999 (3.0%)
- $500,000—$749,999 (2.0%)
- $750,000—$999,999 (0.8%)
- $1,000,000 or more (0.6%)

Additionally, the vast majority of homes in the business's primary market area are older construction:

- Before 1939: (39.6%)
- 1940-1949: (15.3%)
- 1950-1959: (17.1%)
- 1960-1969: (10.5%)
- 1970-1979: (6.3%)
- 1980-1989: (3.5%)
- 1990-1999: (2.6%)
- 2000-2004: (4.0%)
- 2005+: (0.7%)

SERVICES

Benson Brothers Bathroom Remodeling offers full-service bathroom remodeling, renovation, and installation services. Beyond general bathroom projects, Benson Brothers Bathroom Remodeling will offer specialized products and services (e.g., walk-in bathtubs, grab-bars, etc.) for older and disabled individuals who wish to remain independent in their homes.

Process

When working with prospective customers, the owners will take the following approach:

1. Benson Brothers Bathroom Remodeling will offer a free one-hour consultation to all prospective customers. This will provide an opportunity for the owners to showcase their expertise and establish a rapport with individuals who are considering a bathroom remodeling project. During the consultation, the Bensons will gain a clear understanding of the prospective customer's objectives, desires, and, most importantly, budget.
2. Following the consultation, the Bensons will develop a detailed proposal. Using a leading architectural design software application, several different configurations/layouts will be developed for

the customer, along with a selection of different products and material choices (e.g., tiles, fixtures, hardware, lighting, windows, etc.) at varying price points.

3. At the customer's convenience, Benson Brothers Bathroom Remodeling will present the project proposal to them. In addition to leaving behind color print-outs, product samples, and related literature, the Bensons also will use a tablet computer to show 3-D renderings of their recommended configurations/layouts.
4. Once the prospective customer has had a suitable amount of time to consider the proposal, the owners will use their feedback to develop a detailed time-and-cost estimate.
5. Upon acceptance of the estimate, a 50 percent deposit will be required, with the remainder due upon project completion.
6. Benson Brothers Bathroom Remodeling will then handle all aspects of the project, from obtaining local permits and ordering materials to obtaining approvals from building inspectors. Throughout the project, the owners will go to great lengths to keep the lines of communication open with customers, ensuring their satisfaction and keeping them apprised of any potential delays.

Customer satisfaction is Benson Brothers Bathroom Remodeling's number one priority. The owners will do whatever it takes to ensure that their customers not only love their new bathroom, but are willing to recommend the business to their friends and family. As part of their commitment to customer satisfaction, the owners will provide a three-year warranty on all workmanship.

OPERATIONS

Business Structure

Benson Brothers Bathroom Remodeling is organized as a limited liability company in the Commonwealth of Pennsylvania. This business structure provides liability protection, without the complexities associated with a corporation. The Benson brothers used a popular online legal document service to form their LLC as cost-effectively as possible.

Suppliers

Benson Brothers Bathroom Remodeling will work with many leading suppliers, providing its customers with a broad range of options. These include, but are not limited to:

- Acryline Air Tubs
- Air King Ventilation
- Best-Bath Systems
- Brizzo Faucets
- Broan-NuTone, LCC
- Brondell
- Cardinal Shower Doors
- Central Cabinetry
- Coverquik Tiles
- Daltile Corporation
- Danze Faucets
- Delta Faucets

- Ellas Walk-in Baths
- Fantech, Inc.
- Healthcraft Products
- Jaclo Plumbing
- Lewis Plumbing
- Lifespan Closets
- Living Spaces LLC
- Midwest Bathing Systems
- Mirage Glass Tile
- Moen
- Mountain Hardware
- Northwestern Stone
- Onyx Collection
- Peterson Wood Products
- Precision Knob Company
- Rev-A-Shelf
- Safety Bath Door Inserts
- Safeway Tub Step
- Sea Gull Lighting Products, Inc.
- Sentrels Bath Systems
- Shower Buddy
- Western Lighting Corp.

Tools

The owners will need the following tools to begin operations:

- Air compressor
- Biscuit joiner
- Caulk guns
- Caulk removal tools
- Chalk lines
- Chisels
- Circular saws
- Clamps
- Compound double bevel miter saw
- Cordless drills
- Drill bits
- Ear protection

- Extension cords
- Flashlights
- Grinder
- Hammers
- Jigsaws
- Levels
- Miter saw stand
- Nail gun
- Orbital sander
- Palm sander
- Pipe wrenches
- Portable tablesaw
- Portable work lights
- Putty knives
- Reciprocating saws
- Rotary cutting tool
- Router
- Safety glasses
- Screwdrivers
- Squares
- Utility knives

Supplies

In addition, an inventory of the following items will be needed on an ongoing basis:

- Bolts
- Nails
- Pipe compound
- Rags
- Sandpaper
- Screws
- Silicone caulk
- Steel wool
- Solvent

Location

Benson Brothers Bathroom Remodeling has identified an ideal location that is available for lease. Located in the city's manufacturing district, the climate-controlled facility includes a small staging/ storage space where deliveries can be received from suppliers and inspected for damage prior to installation. The space is large enough for the owners to store their work van and trailer after hours.

A small office space with telephone/Internet access is included. As the business grows, the building owner has larger units for lease should additional space be required.

Hours of Operation

Although Benson Brothers Bathroom Remodeling will be as accommodating as possible, the owners typically will work on bathroom remodeling projects between the hours of 7:00 a.m. and 6:00 p.m., Monday through Saturday. Through their Internet service provider, the Bensons have obtained a business phone number that will ring at their office, and on a designated smartphone, enabling them to accept calls from suppliers and customers while they are out in the field.

PERSONNEL

Benson Brothers Bathroom Remodeling is being established by brothers Peter and Steve Benson.

Peter Benson

A graduate of Philadelphia Area Technical College, Peter began his career as a carpenter, working on residential construction projects. During the Great Recession, when new construction came to a screeching halt, Benson was fortunate to find work as an installer with AAA Bathroom Systems, a specialist in upscale bathroom installations. After witnessing the income potential and market demand within this lucrative niche, Benson has decided to establish his own business in partnership with his brother.

Steve Benson

Steve Benson is an independent plumber in the Philadelphia area. After working for a local plumbing services company for many years, Steve went into business for himself five years ago. Although he has grown his customer base, Steve has been seeking a differential that will enable him to stand out in the marketplace. In addition, he would like to establish a business that is scalable, and where he eventually can function as a business owner instead of a service provider.

The owners are confident that Steve's plumbing expertise, combined with Peter's construction and installation experience, will provide the foundation for a successful bathroom remodeling business. Because remodeling work and running a business are two entirely different things, the brothers have taken advantage of a small business management certificate program at their local community college, giving them fundamental knowledge and helping them to avoid common pitfalls and mistakes when starting their new venture.

Independent Contractors

Benson Brothers Bathroom Remodeling will develop a network of reliable independent contractors, providing them with operational scalability and outside expertise when needed. These include carpenters, plumbers, electricians, and installers.

Professional & Advisory Support

Benson Brothers Bathroom Remodeling has established a business banking account with Greater Pennsylvania Bank, including a merchant account for accepting credit card payments. Tax advisement is provided by Bruce Evans Tax Service.

GROWTH STRATEGY

Year One: Begin operations with financial capital of $25,000. Concentrate on establishing Benson Brothers Bathroom Remodeling as a trusted business in the local market. Complete 20 bathroom remodeling projects. Generate gross sales of $400,000 and net profits of $60,000. Begin developing a network of reliable subcontractors for operational scalability.

Year Two: Complete 25 bathroom remodeling projects. Generate gross sales of $500,000 and net profits of $75,000. Continue to develop the business's subcontractor network. Recoup owners' startup funding ($35,000) and repay $25,000 family loan.

Year Three: Complete 30 bathroom remodeling projects. Generate gross sales of $600,000 and net profits of $90,000. Begin formulating plans to add two additional full-time installers (forming a second crew) and a part-time administrative assistant during year four.

MARKETING & SALES

Benson Brothers Bathroom Remodeling has identified several marketing and sales tactics to support its growth strategy, including:

1. A brochure describing the business and the services it provides, which can be distributed to prospective customers and business partners.
2. A listing in several online home improvement and remodeling directories.
3. An SEO-optimized Web site with complete details about the business and its services and testimonials from satisfied customers.
4. A bathroom remodeling blog, offering tips for do-it-yourselfers and prospective customers alike.
5. A quarterly aging-in-place-focused guest column in the *Philadelphia Senior Beacon*, a free newspaper that is distributed to senior citizens in the Philadelphia market.
6. A YouTube channel showcasing select projects and providing ideas and inspiration to prospective customers.
7. A Facebook page, where the owners can share links to content from their YouTube channel and blog, and encourage word-of-mouth referrals from satisfied customers.
8. Graphics (brand identity and contact information) on the business's service vans and trailers.
9. A monthly e-newsletter for both existing and prospective customers, providing yet another channel for showcasing innovative projects, discussing new products and trends, and addressing common bathroom remodeling questions and concerns.
10. A half-page advertisement in the quarterly lifestyle magazine, *Philadelphia Living.*
11. A customer referral program, rewarding former customers with a $150 Visa Gift Card for each successful referral they make.
12. Membership in the local Chamber of Commerce and Better Business Bureau to build and enhance credibility.
13. A monthly direct mail campaign to homeowners in the business's target market who match the criteria in the Market Analysis section of this plan. The mailing will include a discount voucher, good for 60 days, as an incentive.
14. Sales calls to local and regional aging-in-place consultants to encourage referrals for senior citizens who are modifying their homes.

LEGAL

Benson Brothers Bathroom Remodeling is bonded and insured, and will adhere to all local, state, and federal building codes and construction laws. Permits are secured from the local building department for all projects, and the owners will consult with building inspectors to obtain all necessary approvals.

FINANCIAL ANALYSIS

According to the National Kitchen & Bath Association, in 2016 about half of bathroom remodeling jobs were expected to fall within the $10,000-$30,000 price range. Based on this information, as well as the owners' knowledge of the local market, Benson Brothers Bathroom Remodeling estimates that, on average, most of its projects will cost approximately $20,000.

Overhead and expenses will impact the profits that Benson Brothers Bathroom Remodeling can expect from each job. These include costs for materials, permits, labor, haul-away/disposal, subcontractors (if needed), facility lease, and vehicles. Based on their calculations and conversations with other industry players, the owners anticipate that overhead will represent approximately 25 percent of projected first-year gross sales. Additionally, the Bensons expect an average profit margin of 15 percent. Due to heightened competition, profit margins typically are smaller in larger metropolitan areas. In a smaller market, profit margins of 20 percent are realistic.

The owners will incur initial startup costs of about $35,000:

Start-up Expense	Cost
Advertising	$ 3,000
Miscellaneous	$ 500
Accounting	$ 700
Legal	$ 600
Office supplies	$ 400
Tools & equipment	$15,550
Office equipment	$ 500
Vehicle	$ 9,250
Trailer	$ 4,500
Total cost	**$35,000**

The Benson brothers will each contribute $17,500 toward the above costs. In addition, they are seeking a family loan from their father in the amount of $25,000, to provide cash flow for initial operations.

Additional financial projections are available upon request.

Before/After School Program

Bedford Before & After Care Inc.

22 Williams Ave.
Bedford, CO 76664

Paul Greenland

Bedford Before & After Care serves families with children in kindergarten through fifth grade who need flexible childcare options before and after school.

EXECUTIVE SUMMARY

Stanley and Lorraine Miller recently retired from 35-year elementary school teaching careers. Although they have filled in as substitute teachers on occasion, and volunteered their time as tutors, the Millers miss the opportunity to engage with young students on a regular basis and lead them in group activities. Recently, they learned that a new private school was being established at their church, and that the new entity was in need of a before/after school program to meet the needs of students with busy working parents. After meeting with the principal, Stanley and his wife, Lorraine, have agreed to establish and run a dedicated program that not only will serve the students of Bedford Lutheran School, but also compete with a program operated by another provider at a nearby public elementary school.

Bedford Lutheran School has agreed to make its facilities, including a large fellowship hall, gymnasium, an outdoor playground, available to the Millers, along with access to an inventory of sports/playground equipment, games, and arts and crafts supplies. In exchange, the Millers will share a mutually agreed-upon portion of the program's revenue with Bedford Lutheran. The following business plan outlines the Millers' strategy for growing the program during its first years of operations.

MARKET ANALYSIS

Market Overview

Bedford Before & After Care is located in Bedford, Colorado. The market is mainly served by the Bedford Public School District, which includes 9 elementary schools (K-5), two middle schools (grades 6-8), two high schools, and several special schools, including one for children with special needs.

In 2015 the Bedford population totaled approximately 85,000. This figure was expected to increase 10 percent by 2020, at which time the population is projected to reach roughly 93,500. In keeping with this population growth, the number of families with young children also is expected to rise. For example, the 5-14 population segment, which totaled 10,032 in 2015, is expected to increase 13 percent by 2020, totaling 14,984.

Along with growth in the number of school-age children is an increase in the number of high-income households. Households with incomes ranging from $75,000-$99,999 (4,304 in 2015) are expected to grow 2.5 percent by 2020, reaching 4,417. Households with incomes between $100,000 and $149,999 (5,032 in 2015) are projected to increase 12.7 percent by 2020, totaling 5,671. Finally, households with incomes above $150,000 (2,454) are projected to increase 14.4 percent, reaching 2,807.

Target Markets

Bedford Before & After Care serves families with children in kindergarten through fifth grade who need flexible childcare options before and after school.

Competition

Bedford Before & After Care will serve as the only before/after school care provider at Bedford Lutheran School. When Bedford Before & After Care opens its program to families outside of Bedford Lutheran, its greatest source of competition will be A-1 Care, a program operated by a leading community service organization. A-1 Care serves all of the public schools in Bedford, including Thompson Elementary School, which is located directly across the street from Bedford Lutheran School/Bedford Before & After Care.

SERVICES

Bedford Before & After Care serves families with children in kindergarten through fifth grade who need flexible childcare options before and after school. The organization provides children with stimulating, age-appropriate individual and group activities in a safe, nurturing environment, under the supervision of a trained staff and the leadership of two experienced educators.

Program participants can choose from three options (before school, after school, or both). During the business's first year of operations, services will be available on school days only. Plans to expand the program are detailed in the Growth Strategy section of this plan.

Bedford Before & After Care will maintain a staff-to-participant ratio of 1:15 at all times. Depending on weather conditions, Bedford Before & After Care provides a curriculum that includes both indoor and outdoor games and activities, such as:

- Basketball
- Freeze Tag
- Kickball
- Knock Hockey
- Leap Frog
- Obstacle courses
- Parachute
- Playground equipment
- Red Light, Green Light 1-2-3
- Red Rover
- Relay races
- Soccer

Indoor activities are arranged into dedicated activity centers, where children can engage in the following:

- Arts and crafts
- Board games
- Homework help
- Music
- Playacting (e.g., puppet shows, etc.)
- Reading
- Storytelling

The program includes a 30-minute block of time when children participate in a quiet activity (toward the end of the session).

Morning and afternoon sessions both include time for a healthy snack and beverage.

Cost

The following fee structure has been developed for Bedford Before & After Care:

1. Before School Session: $325/month
2. After School Session: $450/month
3. Before/After School Sessions: $575/month

Parents will be subject to a $15 late pick-up fee for the first 15 minutes after the program closes, after which time they will be subject to a fee of one dollar per minute. Frequent late pick-ups are grounds for elimination from the program.

Enrollment

Parents interested in enrolling their children for Bedford Before & After Care can do so online, through the program's Web site, or by completing a series of paper forms available at the office of Bedford Lutheran. The program charges a $25 (non-refundable) registration fee.

OPERATIONS

Equipment & Supplies

Bedford Before & After Care has access to the following equipment and supplies for its operations:

- Acrylic paint
- Basketballs
- Beads
- Board games (10-15)
- Buttons
- Cardstock paper
- Clay (nondrying)
- Colored chalk
- Construction paper
- Cookie cutters

- Cornstarch
- Cotton balls
- Cotton swabs
- Craft sticks
- Crayons
- Disposable cups and plates
- Dry erase markers
- Felt
- Food dye
- Glitter
- Glue gun
- Glue sticks
- Graph paper
- Hole punch
- Jump ropes
- Magnetic tape
- Oil pastels
- Old parachute
- Packing tape
- Paint brushes
- Paint pens
- Paint shirts
- Pencil sharpener
- Pencils, colored
- Pencils, regular
- Permanent markers
- Pipe cleaners
- Plastic cones
- Play Dough
- Playground balls
- Pom-Poms
- Popsicle sticks
- Ribbon
- Rubber bands
- School glue
- Shaving cream

- Soccer balls
- Sponges
- Stapler
- Stickers
- Straws
- Tablecloth
- Tempera paint
- Washable markers
- Watercolor paints
- White paper
- Yarn

Business Structure

Bedford Before & After Care is organized as an S Corporation in the state of Colorado. This business structure will provide the owners with certain tax and liability advantages. The Millers will operate the business as a joint venture with Bedford Lutheran School, sharing revenue on a 50-50 basis. The owners worked with a local business attorney to establish their Corporation and draft an agreement outlining the terms of their revenue-sharing arrangement with Bedford Lutheran.

Hours of Operation

Bedford Before & After Care will maintain the following hours of operation:

- Before School (6:25 AM-9:05 AM)
- After School (3:25 PM-6:35 PM)

Although the schedule is subject to change, the first 30 minutes of each program will include unstructured playtime as children sign in. Group leaders will then take children through structured indoor and/or outdoor activities, followed by snack time. The last 30 minutes of the morning program will be dedicated to dismissal preparation (either for release to Bedford Lutheran classes or bus pick-up from Thompson Elementary School). The last 30 minutes of the after school program typically will include quiet time where students work on a structured indoor activity or homework, prior to parent pick-up.

Policies & Procedures

The Millers have consulted with before/after school program operators in other markets, as well as school administrators and a local attorney, to develop a policy and procedure manual for Bedford Before & After Care that includes the following:

- Allergy Action Plans
- Behavior & Discipline
- Drop-off/Pick-up Procedures
- Emergency Response
- Food Allergy/Intolerance Health Care Provider Statement
- Illness & Injuries
- Individual Care Plans
- Medication Treatment Forms

- Parent/Staff Communication
- Payments & Fees
- Personal Belongings (e.g., not bringing valuables or toys to the program)
- Staff-to-Student Ratios

PERSONNEL

Stanley and Lorraine Miller recently retired from 35-year careers as elementary school teachers. Although they have filled in as substitute teachers on occasion, and volunteered their time as tutors, the Millers miss the opportunity to engage with young students on a regular basis and lead them in group activities. Stanley and Lorraine have agreed to establish and run a dedicated program that not only will serve the students of Bedford Lutheran School, but also compete with a program operated by another provider at a nearby public elementary school.

Stanley and Lorraine both hold Master's degrees in education. They have underground criminal background checks and are current in first aid and CPR training. Additionally, the Millers have the qualities that are necessary for success as before/after school program operators. Specifically, they:

- are strong planners
- are extremely organized
- are able to multi-task
- possess exceptional written and oral communication skills
- have a genuine appreciation of/love working with children
- are natural leaders
- have extensive experience leading programs for/working with young children
- are able to adapt to various situations quickly
- are extremely dependable

Support Staff

Bedford Before & After Care will begin operations with Stanley and Lorraine Miller as the sole employees. As the business grows, additional staff will be added to maintain a staff-to-student ratio of 1:15 at all times. When it eventually reaches maximum capacity, the program will be able to accommodate up to 80 children. Based on the projections outlined in the Growth Strategy section of this plan, the Millers anticipate the need to hire an additional staff member during the third year of operation.

In order to provide program coverage when the Millers are not available, Bedford Lutheran School has identified four teachers who are willing to fill in when needed. Like the Millers, they have undergone criminal background checks, are experienced educators, and have up-to-date first aid and CPR training. When these additional support personnel are needed, the Millers will compensate them on an hourly basis ($15/hour) as independent contractors.

Professional & Advisory Support

Bedford Before & After Care has established a business banking account with Bedford Community Bank, including a merchant account for accepting credit card payments. Tax advisement is provided by Bedford Tax Advisors PC.

GROWTH STRATEGY

Year One: Establish Bedford Before & After Care as a before/after school program serving the students of Bedford Lutheran School. Achieve total enrollment (across all sessions) of approximately 30 students.

Year Two: Expand Bedford Before & After Care to also serve the students of a nearby public elementary school, in addition to Bedford Lutheran School families. Increase total enrollment (across all sessions) to approximately 40 students.

Year Three: Hire a third staff member to accommodate additional enrollment and maintain a 15:1 staff-to-student ratio. Increase total enrollment (across all sessions) to approximately 60 students.

Year Four: Add coverage on non-school days (e.g., institute days, select holidays such as Presidents' Day, etc.). Hire a fourth staff member. Increase total enrollment (across all sessions) to approximately 80 students. Reach maximum capacity levels in both before and after school sessions.

Year Five: Add a summer day program. Hire a fifth staff member. Consider selling ownership stake in the business to joint venture partner (Bedford Lutheran School) or an outside party, or hiring an outside director to oversee the program.

The following table provides a snapshot of Bedford Before & After Care's growth projections for the first five years of operations:

Sessions	2017	2018	2019	2020	2021
Before school	6	10	15	20	20
After school	8	10	15	20	20
Before/after school	15	20	30	40	40
Non-school days	0	0	0	30	40
Summer	0	0	0	0	30

MARKETING & SALES

Bedford Before & After Care has developed a marketing plan that relies upon the following main tactics:

1. Printed collateral describing the program for distribution to parents of prospective participants and referral sources.
2. A page on the Bedford Lutheran School Web site.
3. Participation in Bedford Lutheran School open houses and information presentations.
4. Participation in events sponsored by the Bedford Neighborhood Association (e.g., neighborhood carnival, association meetings, etc.).
5. A regular advertisement in the Bedford Lutheran School newsletter.
6. Beginning in the second year, semi-annual direct mailings to households with children who attend neighboring Thompson Elementary School.

FINANCIAL ANALYSIS

Following are revenue projections for Bedford Before & After Care's first three years of operations:

Sessions	2017	2018	2019
Before school	$ 23,400	$ 39,000	$ 58,500
After school	$ 43,200	$ 54,000	$ 81,000
Before/after school	$103,500	$138,000	$207,000
Total revenue	**$170,100**	**$231,000**	**$346,500**

The Millers will operate the business as a joint venture with Bedford Lutheran School, sharing revenue on a 50-50 basis. The school will provide its facilities and cover necessary supplies and equipment, while the Millers will provide administrative and operational oversight. Additional financial projections are available upon request. Bedford Before & After Care and Bedford Lutheran School also have agreed to share marketing expenses, which will be minimal during the first year, on a 50-50 basis. Projected expenses for independent contractors, which will be paid solely by the Millers, are expected to account for approximately 15 percent of revenue annually.

Additional financial statements are available upon request.

Bread Bakery

Breadcrafter

8900 Green Lake Rd.
Port Hanover, MI 49333

This business plan is a tightly constructed, succinct consideration of all factors relevant to launching this bakery. From rent charges to competition and seasonal changes to costs per loaf, this plan has not left anything out, all without being overly verbose. This exemplary plan is very focused and complete, which will help the business stay on course.

This business plan appeared in ***Business Plans Handbook, Volume 5.*** *It has been updated for this volume.*

EXECUTIVE SUMMARY

Awareness of high quality baked goods is on the rise. Good bread is a rare combination of nutrition, convenience, and luxury. Today's consumer has less time to create wholesome, handmade bread, but increasingly appreciates the nutritional and sensory benefits it provides. Good bread provides fiber and carbohydrates in a convenient, low fat form that is portable and delicious. Good bread never goes out of style.

Breadcrafter will produce and sell high quality, handmade breads to the residents and tourists of Port Hanover and Freeman County. The Company will focus on European Style, naturally leavened breads and baguettes made with high quality ingredients. Breads will be baked and sold at a storefront facility using a 4 deck, steam injected bread oven. Labor saving devices will allow the proprietor to run the entire operation with the help of two part-time, seasonal employees.

Breadcrafter's main competition includes a health food store, three pastry shops and three supermarkets in the Port Hanover area. Its advantage lies in the high quality of its products due to specialization and artisan manufacturing. The main marketing focus will be an eye-catching sign, the scent of fresh bread wafting out of the storefront, and periodic printed advertisements. The company will sample its products liberally.

After establishing the operation, the company will explore the possibility of making takeout sandwiches. Delivering wholesale bread and baked goods to area restaurants and specialty retailers will also be considered. Gluten-free recipes are being explored but will only be considered if the quality and taste meet or exceed our current offerings.

The company is founded by Kevin Richards, an artisan baker currently baking breads and pastries for Toothsome Foods Company in Port Hanover, Michigan. Kevin has spent the last two years building the TFC program from the ground up. His wife Renee Richards is also a bread baker, having baked for one year at the Grainery Food Co-op, Breadcrafter's chief competitor. Together they bring a wealth of practical experience and a realistic market sense to the company.

Breadcrafter is currently seeking $80,500 in loans to get the business underway. Major costs include equipment purchases, shop rent, ingredient purchases, site modifications, and marketing, which total $70,150. Projected sales for the first three months, based on market and competition studies, will total $47,250. Total operating expenses and cost of sales will leave an average profit of $5,450 per month.

Opening day is scheduled for July 1, 2016. While Breadcrafter has the potential for high growth, the first three years will be spent establishing company financial stability and increasing market share.

THE COMPANY

Breadcrafter will be created to serve the Port Hanover community by exploiting the need for a good bread bakery. It will offer a variety of high quality, European and American style artisan breads, baked fresh in its storefront bakery.

The company's immediate goals are to achieve start up by July 1, 2016, in time to capitalize on the lucrative summer tourist season. It will start with the proprietor, Kevin Richards, as baker and manager with the help of two part time employees. The company should gross over $115,000 in its first year. Long-term goals include the addition of a takeout sandwich store to the storefront, wholesale bread sales within one year, and the possible addition of gluten-free options.

Kevin Richards, the proprietor and baker, is the creator of Breadcrafter. For four years, he has been employed at Toothsome Foods Company, a specialty foods manufacturer in Port Hanover, Michigan. His experience as a Production Supervisor and as a Research & Development Cook bring a sense of production realities and technical savvy to the company. As the driving force behind TFC's current Handmade Bread program, Kevin has two years practical experience with sourdough breads. He holds a BA in English Literature from the University of Michigan.

Renee Richards, Kevin's wife, also has bread-baking experience. She baked bread at the Grainery Food Co-op in Port Hanover, Michigan for one year, and she contributes a keen sense of the bread market. She also contributes retail sales experience accrued through several retail jobs around Port Hanover.

The company is in the process of securing $80,500 in startup financing.

PRODUCTS

Breadcrafter's breads will stand out from the competition due to their uniqueness and outstanding quality. Most of the breads are European in style, including Sourdough, Miche (a traditional French whole wheat bread), and Sourdough Rye. These breads are made by the sourdough method, which uses no added yeast. This method imparts a rich flavor, which can be tangy or mild, as well as a toothsome inner crumb and a crackly crust. By using this method, a skilled baker can create truly delicious breads without added fats or sugars, making many of Breadcrafter's products 100% fat free. Sourdough breads also have an extended shelf life, remaining fresh for days without the use of preservatives. Breadcrafter will also offer specialty breads, which will be made in the sourdough way with the addition of such luxurious ingredients as Parmigiana cheese with fresh ground pepper and dried Michigan cherries with roasted pecans. Spent Grain Bread, made with barley leftover from beer brewing, is another unique product that Breadcrafter will offer. Two varieties of French style baguettes will be offered fresh daily, a high demand product that is available nowhere else in the area. Breadcrafter will also produce White and Wheat Sandwich Breads with soft crust and a tender crumb for traditional American-style sandwiches. As the needs of the customer change, so will the lineup of Breadcrafter's products. The bakery equipment is chosen with versatility in mind.

After establishing the business, Breadcrafter will research the possibility of producing sandwiches to increase revenues. This investment would require approximately $1,725 for the purchase of equipment and ingredients. The company will also pursue wholesale contracts. Toothsome Foods Company has indicated interest in a contract to produce two Christmas products on a per loaf basis, Cherry Chocolate Fruitcake and Midwest Christmas Stollen. These products can help generate revenue in the slower autumn months. The proprietor will also consider producing some of Toothsome Foods' current lineup of Handmade Breads on a wholesale basis. Finally, Breadcrafter will explore gluten-free options to meet the growing demand for such products, but will only add the them if a recipe that meets or exceeds our quality and taste standards can be developed.

A self-serve beverage cooler filled with soft drinks will also help increase revenue, as will the sale of fresh brewed coffee.

PRODUCTION

Production of sellable breads is projected to begin on July 1, 2016. Raw ingredients will be ordered for bi-weekly delivery from North Farm Co-op and Sysco Inc., at which time a two-week production schedule will be drawn up by Kevin Richards, the proprietor/baker. Ingredients will be stored in a dry storage area and in a walk in cooler (already on the proposed premises). Rent of the facility will be $1,200 per month with utility costs running approximately $835/month.

Scheduling will begin with three large bakes per week (M, T, TH) and two small bakes (W/F). Due to the extended shelf life of sourdough breads, product can be sold for two days before staling. Each bake day the baker will bake breads in a deck oven. The oven provides intense, even heat and a controllable amount of steam injection, allowing tremendous control of crust crispness. Everything from soft white sandwich breads to thick crusted, dense savory breads to sweet baked goods can be perfectly baked in this oven. While breads are baking, the baker will begin mixing the long fermenting doughs to be baked off the next day. Labor saving equipment including a dough divider and a bread moulder makes this possible. Hot breads will begin coming out of the oven by 7:00 AM, and all baking will be finished by 10:00 AM.

The storefront will open at 9:00 AM and close at 6:00 PM Monday through Friday. Saturday hours will be 9:00 AM to 4:00 PM for sales only. Part time employees will work the counter and assist with store maintenance during peak hours while the baker is baking. A beverage cooler and coffee machine will encourage convenience sales at the register.

Breadcrafter will economize on bookkeeping costs by handling its payroll duties in-house. A professional accountant will handle year-end bookkeeping.

MARKET

The specialty bread market is about to experience enormous growth. Throughout the country, small bakeries are appearing at an increasing rate. Chain stores, such as Great Harvest Bread Company, are experiencing tremendous growth by capitalizing on the wholesome appeal of fresh baked loaves. According to the Bread Baker's Guild of America, a trade organization, membership increased 40% between 2014 and 2015. As people become more aware of its healthy nutritional profile, good bread becomes even more attractive.

There is currently only one source for artisan breads in Port Hanover, Toothsome Foods Company, where the proprietor learned to bake. Market tests performed in the summer of 2015 by Toothsome Foods Company showed strong demand for the product, no price resistance and the need for a more frequent and visible presence. As a pilot program with no promotion in the summer of 2015,

Toothsome Foods Company was able to sell all available loaves (20-30 per bake, two bakes per week) all summer long. Even without the benefit of window signage or a consistent delivery schedule, Kevin Richards and TFC have developed a loyal following of regular buyers that continues to grow.

The Millwright Bakery in Maple, Michigan, a similar operation to Breadcrafter, currently bakes 200-700 loaves a day for wholesale in the Connor City Area. This bakery has been open since November 2015 and has not yet experienced a summer tourist influx. It has stopped taking on new accounts for fear of exceeding its production capacity during that season. Millwright finds the Port Hanover area very attractive, but delivery from Maple is impractical. This summer season will bring Millwright a large influx of cash, and they will almost certainly consider establishing a bakery in Port Hanover if none yet exists.

Breadcrafter will set up its storefront bakery in the Green Lake Shopping Center. The center is conveniently located on one of the busiest arteries to and from Port Hanover. It has plenty of parking and is easily accessible from the road. The shopping center currently contains a successful, higher-end grocery store, a successful liquor convenience store, and a donut bakery that also sells country clutter handicrafts. The shopping center is currently a destination for people seeking gourmet foods. These people will appreciate Breadcrafter's products. There is very little market overlap between Breadcrafter and the donut shop, and the two could exist in synergy.

Pricing of artisan type breads around Port Hanover currently ranges from $2.75 per loaf (Grainery Whole Wheat) to $6.50 per loaf (Toothsome Foods Pesto Bread). Breadcrafter's products will range in price from $2.60 (Sourdough Baguette) to $5.25 (Pepper Parmesan Loaf).

COMPETITION

Grainery Food Co-op

Breadcrafter's primary competitor. The Grainery currently has a customer base that regularly buys whole grain breads. These customers are interested in healthy foods, and they will appreciate the attractive nutritional profile of our products. Due to under capitalization, the Grainery will have trouble responding to the quality advantage our equipment and methods provide. Many potential customers are reluctant to patronize the Grainery, perceiving its patrons and employees as "too liberal." True or not, these customers may feel more comfortable at Breadcrafter. Renee Richards, the proprietor's wife, was formerly a Grainery bread baker. She knows their business well.

Helmut's Pastry Shop

An established bakery specializing in pastries and doughnuts. They have a capable facility. Due to heavy investment in pastry equipment and relatively small bread sales, they are unlikely to react strongly to our presence.

Twin's Bakery

Very similar to Helmut's.

The Coffee Mug

Specializing in donuts, pastries, and country clutter handicrafts. They sell some lower-quality breads. Major risk is their location, right next door to Breadcrafter's prospective site. This risk could also be an asset, bringing bakery customers in search of better bread to Breadcrafter.

Fred's Markets

Large supermarket with in-store bakery. Fred's offers non-scratch, relatively low-quality breads and pastries at very low prices. Their largest advantage, other than price, is the convenience of one-stop shopping. There is some possibility of future wholesale distribution of our products.

Daley's Supermarkets

Very similar to Fred's.

Taylor's

Similar to Fred's and Daley's, but smaller. Higher possibility of future wholesale distribution.

Toothsome Foods Company

Downtown specialty foods retailer. Current employer of Breadcrafter's proprietor. TFC has a small, undercapitalized bread program. Due to the absence of the baker, they are unlikely to compete. Proprietor will offer to buy some of the bakery equipment. Future wholesale distribution of contract products is a strong possibility.

Breadcrafter's production capacity will be an advantage over the specialty stores. Product specialization will be an advantage over the pastry shops and supermarkets. Breadcrafter's product quality will be an advantage over all local competitors.

MARKETING

Breadcrafter will sell its products to new and repeat customers from its storefront in the Green Lake Shopping Center, located on the busy stretch of M-17 between Port Hanover and Crescent Heights, Michigan. A large, tasteful, storefront sign will catch the attention of passing motorists. The smell of bread as it comes from the oven will bring customers in from the parking lot. Breadcrafter will offer a sample of fresh baked bread to anyone who comes into the store.

Breadcrafter's products will be truly unique in the marketplace. The look, feel and taste of its breads, when compared to the competition, will underscore their quality and value. Many of the products, such as Pepper Parmesan Bread and Sourdough Baguettes, will not be available anywhere else. Breadcrafter will also actively encourage customer satisfaction. Our product line will react to the needs and desires of the customer, thereby encouraging repeat and word-of-mouth sales. As a small, hands-on facility, Breadcrafter will have the freedom to react quickly and accurately to changes in the market. Due to its uniqueness and convenient location, Breadcrafter will become a destination for food lovers.

Printed advertisements, which will run opening week, will highlight bread as an everyday product, to be purchased fresh on a weekly or daily basis. More printed advertisements will run Labor Day weekend and during the Christmas season. Costs for these advertisements will be approximately $230 each.

RISKS

The major risk to any Port Hanover area retail operation is the seasonality of the customer base. Breadcrafter will address this problem by opening at the height of the lucrative summer season. This will give the company a good supply of working capital to help with the startup period. The company will market itself primarily to the year-round population. Contract products prepared for Toothsome Foods Company will bring in cash during the slow fall season. Unless strong demand shows a need, labor will be eliminated in the slower seasons and advertising will be minimal. Depending on available cash after Christmas, Breadcrafter will contemplate adding a sandwich bar to serve local shoppers and employees. Gluten-free options will be explored as an expansion of our current product line. There is high demand for a good-tasting, quality product, but we don't want to rush an offering that will disappoint.

Breadcrafter will budget $11,270 in cash reserves as a cushion to help weather the startup period.

FINANCES

(Personal Income Statement removed for privacy.)

Start Up Costs

Equipment—$52,900

Materials—$5,175

Rent (2 Months)—$2,415

Site modification—$5,750

Signage, stationary, etc.—$1,150

Consultation—$1,150

Supplies—$690

Cash reserves—$11,270

Total Start Up Costs—$80,500

The company is in the process of securing financing for startup. The proprietor currently has $23,000 from private sources and is seeking $57,500 in additional bank loans.

OPERATING COSTS

Payroll

Two part-time employees will be hired to start working on opening day. They will be retained until Labor Day weekend unless strong sales show a further need for them. In the fall, winter and spring, the proprietor and his wife will be the only staff required. Employees will be paid $8.90 per hour, and will work a combined total of 20 hours per week. Wage expenditures will be $813 a month with additional payroll taxes running $82, for a total expenditure of $895.

Rent

The Green Lake storefront currently under consideration rents for $1,200 a month.

Utilities

Heat and electric bills for Jordan Galleria, a downtown storefront of approximately the same dimensions required by Breadcrafter, totals $260 at the height of the winter heat season. Taking into account walk in and reach in cooler use, a figure of $400 is a reasonable estimated monthly average.

The bread oven will be run four hours per day on busy bake days. Conversations with other bakery owners have indicated that a 4-deck oven consumes $4.60 of gas per hour, for a total of $394 per month at maximum capacity.

A total figure of $835 per month is a reasonable estimated monthly average.

Advertising

Breadcrafter will run an advertisement in the *Port Hanover News Review* during opening week. Another advertisement will run Labor Day weekend. Total advertisement expenditures will run $230 per month. The *News Review* is known to do spotlight stories on new Port Hanover businesses and Breadcrafter will take advantage of this publicity.

Advertising expenditures will be kept to a minimum in the fall, winter and spring. The company will rely on community service functions, liberal sampling, and word-of-mouth to reach new customers.

Repair and Maintenance

The estimated maintenance cost for the first month is $575. From there it gradually diminishes to $230 a month for the remainder of the year. After the first of the year, maintenance estimates are reduced to $115 a month.

Insurance

A Business Owner's Policy, covering contents, liability, and some loss of income, will cost $460-$575 a year for Breadcrafter, as quoted by Sam Williams of Port Hanover Insurance. Worker's Comp will run $2.59 for every $100 paid. Breadcrafter has budgeted $58 a month in general insurance and $23 a month in Worker's Comp. Health Insurance premiums for the proprietor and his family will run $285 per month.

Taxes and Licenses

The company has budgeted $175 a month on miscellaneous taxes and licenses.

General Supplies

General supplies will consist mainly of bread bags, which cost $.06 each for paper and $.03 each for plastic. The customer will choose bag material, which affects the quality of the crust in storage. These prices have been included in the cost of sale of each loaf. Cleaning and maintenance supplies will total no more than $60 per month. Breadcrafter has budgeted $145 per month as a conservative figure.

Professional Fees

Professional fees after startup will be kept to a minimum. The proprietor will perform all the necessary filing and bookkeeping chores required except year-end tax filing and calculation of depreciation. The company has budgeted $375 in January and $375 in March to cover these needs.

Miscellaneous

Breadcrafter has budgeted $140 per month to cover miscellaneous expenses.

Proposed Baking Materials Requirements

Ingredients	Amount	$/unit	Total
GW flour	2200.0	0.46	1012.00
Unbl wht flour	1200.0	0.63	756.00
Beverages	1200	0.48	576.00
Dried cherries	80	6.33	506.40
All purpose	1000	0.53	530.00
Parmigiana cheese	80	5.75	460.00
WW flour daily	800	0.56	448.00
Pecan halves	30	6.33	165.00
Coffee	20	9.2	190.00
Yeast	50	2.16	108.00
Powdered milk	50	1.93	96.50
Fennel seeds	24	3.08	73.92
Lecithin	10	5.75	57.50
Rye flour	100	0.56	56.00
Canola oil	70	0.77	53.90
Flax seeds	20	2.29	45.80
Sunflower seeds	50	0.90	45.00
Sesame seeds	12	2.78	33.36
Sugar	50	0.52	26.00
Pepper	5	4.95	24.75
Sea salt	100	0.24	24.00
Cracked wheat	25	0.53	13.25
Baking powder	5	1.39	6.95
Half n half	2	2.3	4.60
Total			**$5312.93**

Proposed Equipment Requirements

	Quantity	Price ea.	Total
Oven, Snorr	1	20,700	20,700
Divider, Snorr	1	4,600	4,600
Mixer, ASF	1	4,600	4,600
Moulder, Snorr	1	2,760	2,760
Bannetons, FBM	60	35	2,100
Loader, Snorr	1	1,725	1,725
Loaf pans	100	11.50	1,150
Bread slicer, used	1	1,090	1,090
Pan racks, Snorr	6	160	960
Cooling racks, Snorr	2	700	1,400
Software upgrades	1	575	575
Triple sink, Louie	1	450	450
Heavy scale, McMaster-Carr	1	450	450
Maple bench, materials	1	450	450
Small loaf pans	100	4.50	450
Countertop mixer	1	1,200	1,200
Flour bins	3	150	450
Sheet pans	40	10	400
Food processor	1	300	300
Cash register	1	300	300
Coffee maker	1	300	300
Books			60
Bread boards	40	5	200
Baskets	100	2.5	250
Chest freezer, used	1	230	230
Coffee mill	1	230	230
Baker's canvas, MTR, FBM	2	115	230
Oven peels	2	90	180
Garbage disposal	1	175	175
15 in. skillet	1	120	120
Garbage cans	3	46	138
Handsink, Louie's	1	115	115
Gm./oz. scale	1	175	175
Faucets	2	50	100
Used range	1	115	115
Counter, used	1	115	115
File cabinet, 4-drawer	1	115	115
7 qt. saucepan	1	100	100
Bread knives	4	23	92
Mop bucket, MacMaster	1	92	92
Timer	2	40	80
Dough tubs	5	12	60
Oven thermometer	1	46	46
1 qt. saucepan	1	46	46
Mop heads	10	3.5	35
Coffee pots	6	6	36
Whisks	4	7	28
Lames	2	14	28
Thermometers	2	10	20
Wooden spoons	5	4	20
Measuring cups	5	4	20
Dough knives	3	7	21
Oven mitts	4	4	16
Spoonulas	3	6	18
Sieve	1	17	17
Dough scrapers	3	4	12
Ladles	3	4	12
Pastry brushes	2	6	12
Brooms	1	10	10
Dustpans	1	10	10
Mop	1	10	10
Pastry brush 1½ in.	2	5	10
Sifter	1	5	5
Measuring spoons	1	5	5
Total			**$49,820**

Miscellaneous Requirements

Supplies	Amount	$/# unit	Total
Paper bags	4000	$ 0.06 ea.	$240.00
Plastic bags	2000	$ 0.02 ea.	$ 40.00
Register tape	1	$ 23.00 cs.	$ 23.00
Bleach	6	$ 1.50	$ 9.00
Hand soap	4	$ 6.60 cartridge	$ 26.40
Floor soap	45	$ 0.48 pkt.	$ 21.60
Kitchen soap	4	$10.00 5 qt.	$ 40.00
Plastic film	2	$23.77 roll	$ 47.54
Aluminum foil	1	$55.37 roll	$ 55.37
Stationary	1	$ 57.50 cs.	$ 57.50
Purchase orders	1	$ 23.00 cs.	$ 23.00
Receipt pads	1	$ 23.00 cs.	$ 23.00
File folders	1	$ 23.00 cs.	$ 23.00
Garbage bags	312	$ 0.36 ea.	$112.32
Paper cups	1000	$ 0.03 ea.	$30.00
Total			**$771.73**

Bread Cost/Profit Analysis

Sourdough loaf: Scale at 24 oz. 20 breads

Ingredient	Price	Weight	Cost	Percent
Unbleached white	$0.56	15.15 lb.	$8.48	47.34%
Water	$0.01	12.75 lb.	$0.15	39.83%
Gold & White flour	$0.46	3.79 lb.	$1.74	11.85%
Salt	$0.16	0.31 lb.	$0.05	0.98%
		32.00 lb.	$10.42	100.00%

Ingredient total: $10.42
Yield: 20
Unit cost: $0.52
Bag: $0.06
Retail: $4.55
Net: $3.97

Whole wheat: Scale at 24 oz. 30 breads

Ingredient	Price	Weight	Cost	Percent
Water	$0.01	18.26 lb.	$0.18	38.85%
Gold & White flour	$0.46	14.17 lb.	$6.52	30.15%
Whole wheat flour	$0.53	14.17 lb.	$7.51	30.15%
Salt	$0.16	0.40 lb.	$0.06	0.86%
		47.00 lb.	$14.27	100.00%

Ingredient total: $14.27
Yield: 30
Unit cost: $0.48
Bag: $0.06
Retail: $4.55
Net: $4.01

Sourdough baguette: Scale at 12 oz. 30 breads

Ingredient	Price	Weight	Cost	Percent
Unbleached white	$0.56	10.65 lb.	$5.96	47.34%
Water	$0.01	8.96 lb.	$0.09	39.83%
Gold & White flour	$0.46	2.67 lb.	$1.23	11.85%
Salt	$0.16	0.22 lb.	$0.04	0.98%
		22.50 lb.	$7.32	100.00%

Ingredient total: $7.32
Yield: 30
Unit cost: $0.24
Bag: $0.06
Retail: $2.60
Net: $2.30

Seed baguette: Scale at 24 oz. 30 breads

Ingredient	Price	Weight	Cost	Percent
Gold & White flour	$0.46	9.58 lb.	$4.41	41.59%
Water	$0.01	8.08 lb.	$0.08	35.06%
Whole wheat flour	$0.53	3.22 lb.	$1.71	13.99%
Sunflower seeds	$1.37	1.20 lb.	$1.64	5.21%
Sesame seeds	$3.16	0.37 lb.	$1.17	1.62%
Fennel seeds	$2.71	0.19 lb.	$0.51	0.82%
Salt	$0.16	0.18 lb.	$0.03	0.78%
Dark sesame oil	$1.97	0.11 lb.	$0.22	0.48%
Poppy seeds	$4.89	0.10 lb.	$0.49	0.46%
		23.04 lb.	$10.26	100.00%

Ingredient total: $10.26
Yield: 30
Unit cost: $0.34
Bag: $0.06
Retail: $2.75
Net: $2.35

Bread Cost/Profit Analysis [CONTINUED]

Pepper parmesan: Scale at 24 oz. 20 breads

Unbleached white	$0.56	12.84 lb.	$7.19	40.13%
Water	$0.01	10.81 lb.	$0.11	33.77%
Parmesan	$3.45	4.24 lb.	$14.63	13.25%
Gold & White flour	$0.46	3.21 lb.	$1.48	10.04%
Pepper	$4.83	0.64 lb.	$3.09	1.99%
Salt	$0.16	0.26 lb.	$0.04	0.82%
		32.00 lb.	$26.54	100.00%

Ingredient total: $26.54
Yield: 20
Unit cost: $1.33
Bag: $0.06
Retail: $5.25
Net: $3.86

Sourdough rye: Scale at 24 oz. 20 breads

Water	$0.01	12.43 lb.	$0.12	38.88%
Gold & White flour	$0.46	11.57 lb.	$5.32	36.20%
Rye flour	$0.56	5.79 lb.	$3.24	18.10%
Whole wheat flour	$0.53	1.91 lb.	$1.01	5.96%
Salt	$0.16	0.28 lb.	$0.04	0.86%
		31.97 lb.	$9.73	100.00%

Ingredient total: $9.73
Yield: 20
Unit cost: $0.49
Bag: $0.06
Retail: $4.55
Net: $4.00

Beverage Cost/Profit Analysis

	Cost	Retail	Profit
Coke Classic	$0.40	$1.00	$0.60
Sprite	$0.40	$1.00	$0.60
Diet Coke	$0.40	$1.00	$0.60
Minute Maid	$0.40	$1.00	$0.60
Naya	$0.60	$1.45	$0.85
Fruitopia	$0.74	$1.45	$0.71
Tea	$0.40	$1.00	$0.60
Avg.	**$0.48**	**$1.13**	**$0.65**
Frontier Organic Coffee, incl. shipping			$/#
Mexican Altura			$8.10
Decaf			$10.35

Production Schedule—July

Product	Retail	Raw	Mon	Tues	Wed	Thurs	Fri/Sat	Revenue	Cost
Sour	$4.55	0.63	20	20	0	30	0	$ 318.50	$ 44.10
Miche	$4.55	0.58	20	20	0	30	0	$ 318.50	$ 44.10
Sour rye	$4.55	0.58	10	30	0	0	0	$ 182.00	$ 23.20
White	$4.00	0.63	20	20	20	20	30	$ 440.00	$ 69.30
Wheat	$4.00	0.63	20	20	20	20	30	$ 440.00	$ 69.30
Cherry pecan	$5.25	1.44	10	20	0	0	0	$ 157.50	$ 43.20
Pepper parm	$5.25	1.73	10	20	0	0	0	$ 157.50	$ 43.20
Spent grain	$4.55	1.15	10	30	0	0	0	$ 182.00	$ 46.00
Baguette	$2.60	0.29	30	30	30	30	40	$ 416.00	$ 46.40
Seed bag	$2.75	0.41	30	30	30	30	40	$ 440.00	$ 65.60
Total			**180**	**240**	**100**	**160**	**140**	**$3,052.00**	**$494.40**
Beverages	$1.13	0.48	60	40	40	40	120	$ 339.00	$144.00
Other	$ 0	0	0	0	0	0	0	$ 0	$ 0
Average Daily Units									
Bread	137								
Beverage	50								
Other	0								

Production Schedule—August

Product	Retail	Raw	Mon	Tues	Wed	Thurs	Fri/Sat	Revenue	Cost
Sour	$4.55	0.63	20	20	0	30	0	$ 318.50	$ 44.10
Miche	$4.55	0.58	20	20	0	30	0	$ 318.50	$ 44.10
Sour rye	$4.55	0.58	10	30	0	0	0	$ 182.00	$ 23.20
White	$4.00	0.63	20	20	20	20	30	$ 440.00	$ 69.30
Wheat	$4.00	0.63	20	20	20	20	30	$ 440.00	$ 69.30
Cherry pecan	$5.25	1.44	10	20	0	0	0	$ 157.50	$ 43.20
Pepper parm	$5.25	1.73	10	20	0	0	0	$ 157.50	$ 43.20
Spent grain	$4.55	1.15	10	30	0	0	0	$ 182.00	$ 46.00
Baguette	$2.60	0.29	30	30	30	30	40	$ 416.00	$ 46.40
Seed bag	$2.75	0.41	30	30	30	30	40	$ 440.00	$ 65.60
Total			**180**	**240**	**100**	**160**	**140**	**$3,052.00**	**$494.40**
Beverages	$1.13	0.48	60	40	40	40	120	$ 339.00	$144.00
Other	$ 0	0	0	0	0	0	0	$ 0	$ 0
Average Daily Units									
Bread	137								
Beverage	50								
Other	0								

Production Schedule—September

Product	Retail	Raw	Mon	Tues	Wed	Thurs	Fri/Sat	Revenue	Cost
Sour	$4.55	0.63	20	0	0	0	20	$ 182.00	$ 25.20
Miche	$4.55	0.58	20	0	0	0	20	$ 182.00	$ 25.20
Sour rye	$4.55	0.58	0	0	0	0	0	$ 0	$ 0
White	$4.00	0.63	20	0	20	0	30	$ 280.00	$ 44.10
Wheat	$4.00	0.63	20	0	20	0	30	$ 280.00	$ 44.10
Cherry pecan	$5.25	1.44	10	0	0	0	10	$ 105.00	$ 28.80
Pepper parm	$5.25	1.73	10	0	0	0	10	$ 105.00	$ 34.60
Spent grain	$4.55	1.15	10	0	0	0	20	$ 136.00	$ 34.50
Baguette	$2.60	0.29	20	20	20	20	30	$ 286.00	$ 31.90
Seed bag	$2.75	0.41	20	20	20	20	30	$ 302.50	$ 45.10
Total			**150**	**40**	**80**	**40**	**200**	**$1,858.50**	**$ 313.50**
Beverages	$1.13	0.48	30	20	20	20	60	$ 169.50	$ 72.00
Other	$5.25	3.45	0	200	0	200	0	$2,100.00	$1,380.00

Average Daily Units

Bread	85
Beverage	25
Other	67

Production Schedule—October

Product	Retail	Raw	Mon	Tues	Wed	Thurs	Fri/Sat	Revenue	Cost
Sour	$4.55	0.63	20	0	0	0	20	$ 182.00	$ 25.20
Miche	$4.55	0.58	20	0	0	0	20	$ 182.00	$ 25.20
Sour rye	$4.55	0.58	0	0	0	0	0	$ 0	$ 0
White	$4.00	0.63	20	0	20	0	30	$ 280.00	$ 44.10
Wheat	$4.00	0.63	20	0	20	0	30	$ 280.00	$ 44.10
Cherry pecan	$5.25	1.44	10	0	0	0	10	$ 105.00	$ 28.80
Pepper parm	$5.25	1.73	10	0	0	0	10	$ 105.00	$ 34.60
Spent grain	$4.55	1.15	10	0	0	0	20	$ 136.00	$ 34.50
Baguette	$2.60	0.29	20	20	20	20	30	$ 286.00	$ 31.90
Seed bag	$2.75	0.41	20	20	20	20	30	$ 302.50	$ 45.10
Total			**150**	**40**	**80**	**40**	**200**	**$1,858.50**	**$313.50**
Beverages	$1.13	0.48	30	20	20	20	60	$ 169.50	$ 72.00
Other	$5.75	3.10	0	0	0	75	75	$ 835.00	$465.00

Average Daily Units

Bread	85
Beverage	25
Other	25

Commercial Driving School

The Trucking Academy (TTA)

69078 Woodward Ave.
Pontiac, MI 48341

Zuzu Enterprises

The Trucking Academy (TTA) provides the highest standard of education and preparedness in the transportation industry by including a combination of classroom, field, and road instruction. Each student is equipped with the knowledge and the professional skills to start a successful, lucrative career as a licensed truck driver, because we realize that your *success is* our *success.*

COMPANY OVERVIEW

TTA will provide classroom education and practical, hands-on training needed to obtain a commercial driving license.

All training will include:

- Hands-on time driving a truck, both at our practice facility and on the road
- Map reading, trip planning and compliance with Department of Transportation laws
- Backing, turning and hooking/unhooking a trailer
- Advanced truck driving techniques such as skid avoidance and recovery
- Other emergency actions for special situations such as a break away trailer or hydroplaning
- Top-notch practice equipment and facilities, including spacious classrooms and computer labs, specially designed field-driving courses and late-model tractor-trailers exclusively for student training
- 3- to 4-week classes that focus on CDL training and CDL license exam preparation
- On-site testing
- On-site recruiters
- Job placement assistance
- Financial assistance for those who qualify

MISSION

The Trucking Academy (TTA) provides the highest standard of education and preparedness in the transportation industry by including a combination of classroom, field, and road instruction. Each student is equipped with the knowledge and the professional skills to start a successful, lucrative career as a licensed truck driver, because we realize that *your* success is *our* success.

INDUSTRY OUTLOOK

Job Description

Heavy and tractor-trailer truck drivers transport goods from one location to another. Most tractor-trailer drivers are long-haul drivers and operate trucks with a gross vehicle weight (GVW) capacity exceeding 26,000 pounds. These drivers deliver goods over intercity routes, sometimes spanning several states.

Heavy and tractor-trailer truck drivers typically do the following:

- Drive long distances
- Report to a dispatcher any incidents encountered on the road
- Follow all applicable traffic laws
- Inspect their trailers before and after the trip, and record any defects they find
- Maintain a log of their working hours, following all federal and state regulations
- Report serious mechanical problems to the appropriate personnel
- Keep their trucks and associated equipment clean and in good working order

Working as a long-haul truck driver is a major lifestyle choice because these drivers can be away from home for days or weeks at a time. They spend much of this time alone. Driving a truck can be a physically demanding job as well. Driving for many hours in a row can be tiring, and some drivers must load and unload cargo.

Most heavy tractor-trailer drivers work full time. The Federal Motor Carrier Safety Administration regulates the hours that a long-haul truck driver may work. Drivers may not work more than 14 straight hours, comprising up to 11 hours spent driving and the remaining time spent doing other work, such as unloading cargo. Between working periods, drivers must have at least 10 hours off duty. Drivers also are limited to driving no more than 60 hours within 7 days or 70 hours within 8 days; then drivers must take 34 hours off before starting another 7- or 8-day run. Drivers must record their hours in a logbook. Truck drivers often work nights, weekends, and holidays.

Income Potential

Heavy and Tractor-trailer Truck Drivers

2015 median pay	$40,260 per year $19.36 per hour
Typical entry-level education	Postsecondary nondegree award
Work experience in a related occupation	None
On-the-job training	Short-term on-the-job training
Number of jobs, 2014	1,797,700
Job outlook, 2014–24	5% (As fast as average)
Employment change, 2014–24	98,800

The median annual wage for heavy and tractor-trailer truck drivers was $40,260 in May 2015. This amount varies based on the specific type of industry worked; the median annual wages for heavy and tractor-trailer truck drivers in the top industries in which they worked were as follows:

General freight trucking: $42,320

Specialized freight trucking: $40,840

Wholesale trade: $39,500

Drivers of heavy trucks and tractor-trailers usually are paid by how many miles they have driven, plus bonuses. The per-mile rate varies from employer to employer and may depend on the type of cargo and the experience of the driver. Some long-distance drivers, especially owners-operators, are paid a share of the revenue from shipping.

Income potential also varies by location. While the median pay across the U.S. was $40,260 in 2015, truck drivers in the state of Michigan earned slightly less, with a median pay of $38,600.

Location	Pay Period	2015				
		10%	25%	Median	75%	90%
United States	Hourly	$ 12.62	$ 15.71	$ 19.36	$ 24.13	$ 29.81
	Yearly	$26,200	$32,700	$40,300	$50,200	$62,000
Michigan	Hourly	$ 12.70	$ 15.50	$ 18.54	$ 23.21	$ 28.75
	Yearly	$26,400	$32,200	$38,600	$48,300	$59,800

Employment Projections

Employment of heavy and tractor-trailer truck drivers is projected to grow 6 percent from 2014 to 2024, about as fast as the average for all occupations. As the economy grows, the demand for goods will increase and more truck drivers will be needed to keep supply chains moving.

The economy depends on truck drivers to transport freight and keep supply chains moving. As the demand for goods increases, more truck drivers will be needed. Trucks transport most of the freight in the United States, so, as households and businesses increase their spending, the trucking industry will grow.

The number of heavy trucks on the road has not reached prerecession levels, despite the increasing demand for freight transportation. To meet the demand, companies are starting to invest in new trucks that are more fuel efficient and easier to drive. For example, some new heavy trucks are equipped with automatic transmissions, blind-spot monitoring, and variable cruise control.

Demand for truck drivers is expected to remain strong in the oil and gas industries as more drivers are needed to transport materials to and from extraction sites.

The market for truck drivers in the state of Michigan is expected to grow at double the national average, boding well for students at graduates of TTA.

	Employment		Percent Change	Projected Annual Job Openings
	2014	2024		
United States				
Heavy and tractor-trailer truck drivers	1,797,700	1,896,400	+6%	40,450
Michigan				
Heavy and tractor-trailer truck drivers	54,330	60,750	+12%	1,570

Heavy and tractor-trailer truck drivers held about 1.8 million jobs in 2014. The industries that employed the most heavy and tractor-trailer truck drivers were as follows:

General freight trucking: 33%

Specialized freight trucking: 13%

Wholesale trade: 11%

Licenses, Certifications, and Registrations

All long-haul truck drivers must have a commercial driver's license (CDL). Qualifications for obtaining a CDL include passing both a knowledge test and a driving test. States have the right to refuse to issue a CDL to anyone who has had a CDL suspended by another state.

Drivers can get endorsements to their CDL that show their ability to drive a specialized type of vehicle. Truck drivers transporting hazardous materials (HAZMAT) must have a hazardous materials endorsement. Getting this endorsement requires passing an additional knowledge test and a background check.

Federal regulations require random testing of on-duty truck drivers for drug or alcohol abuse. In addition, truck drivers can have their CDL suspended if they are convicted of driving under the influence of alcohol or drugs or are convicted of a felony involving the use of a motor vehicle.

MARKET ANALYSIS

With 55 schools, there is significant competition in the transportation education industry in Michigan. We will remain competitive through pricing and our exceptional training and job placement services.

Trucking Schools in Michigan

Total schools: 55

Undergraduate programs: 20

Graduate programs: 8

Average acceptance rate: 70%

Average tuition cost: $7,347

Average loan amount: $5,461

Average scholarship award: $2,223

Average classroom size: 20 students

CDL LICENSES AND REQUIREMENTS

Since April 1992, all drivers have been required to have a CDL in order to drive a Commercial Motor Vehicle. Tractor-trailers require advanced skills and knowledge above and beyond those required to drive a car or other lightweight vehicle. There are two types of CDL licenses, Class A and Class B.

Class A CDL License:

The Class A is needed to operate any combination of vehicles with a GVWR of 26,001 or more pounds provided the GVWR of the vehicle(s) being towed is in excess of 10,000 pounds.

- Vehicles requiring a Class A CDL license are primarily tractor-trailers.

Class B CDL License:

The Class B is needed to operate any single vehicle with a GVWR of 26,001 or less pounds or any such vehicle towing a vehicle not in excess of 10,000 pounds. Vehicles requiring a Class B CDL license may include:

- Cars with trailers, buses (regardless of size), passenger vans and motorhomes
- Standard-sized dump trucks, tow trucks, cement mixers and garbage trucks
- Delivery trucks and utility trucks
- Any single vehicle with GVWR of 26,001 pounds or more that is not towing an excess of 10,000 pounds GVWR

States are able to issue a CDL license only after a written and driving test have been given by the state or approved testing facility.

CLASSES

TTA offers two main classes, the entry level tractor trailer training and professional tractor trailer training. The entry level class runs for 4 weeks full-time or 10 weeks part-time and offers the basic, minimum training that we find is necessary to be a successful truck driver and pass the CDL exam. The professional program is more extensive, lasting 18 weeks. The additional time allows us to cover topics more in-depth, including business skills and additional driving practice. Whatever class is chosen, it is important to train for your CDL exam because the test itself can be extremely difficult to pass without the proper training and many carriers won't hire a candidate without proper training, even if you've passed the CDL exam.

Entry Level Tractor Trailer Training Program

This course is designed to prepare students for the minimum entry-level requirements for obtaining their Class A CDL certificates. Students will receive classroom, lab, range, and road instruction throughout the duration of the course. Graduates have the opportunity to be placed with a preferred major national trucking company and will enter into on-the-job training.

Professional Tractor Trailer Training Program

This course is designed for those who have little to no experience with truck driving or CDL training. Students will gain extensive knowledge about the transportation industry. Learning the necessary skills to manage the business aspect of the transportation industry, along with the practical application for effectively operating a class A vehicle are invaluable parts of becoming a successful professional truck driver. Graduates of this program have gone into entry-level positions as heavy truck drivers, tractor-trailer drivers, and owner operators.

Continuing Education Courses

Individuals that already hold a CDL Class A or B license and have not driven for a period can enroll into our customized refresher program to get them ready to go back on the open road. Our refresher program can be custom tailored to each individual's needs.

All classes will include:

- Hands-on time driving a truck, both at our practice facility and on the road
- Map reading, trip planning and compliance with Department of Transportation laws
- Backing, turning and hooking/unhooking a trailer
- Advanced truck driving techniques such as skid avoidance and recovery

- Other emergency actions for special situations such as a break away trailer or hydroplaning
- Top-notch practice equipment and facilities, including spacious classrooms and computer labs, specially designed field-driving courses and late-model tractor-trailers exclusively for student training
- On-site testing
- On-site recruiters

OTHER SERVICES

Job Placement

We strive to provide the very best services to our current students and graduates of our program by maintaining an exclusive job placement program. All enrolled students complete a job placement questionnaire and interview during their training courses to ensure applications are accurately completed and submitted for review. All graduates are encouraged to utilize TTA's career guidance department throughout their lifetime and we also take a proactive approach by notifying our former students about new and exciting employment opportunities.

We have aligned ourselves with many of the top transportation companies in the country, and have long-standing partnerships with many organizations. As such, our database of job openings is extensive and comprehensive. Some partnerships include the following:

- C.R. England
- U.S Xpress
- TMC
- Universal Truckload

Veterans Programs

TTA is approved by the Michigan State Approving Agency for the training of VA students and other eligible beneficiaries.

ADMISSIONS

To be eligible for enrollment at TTA, applicants must meet the following requirements. Applicants must:

- have a valid Michigan driver's license
- be eligible for a Class A CDL upgrade through the state of Michigan
- be at least 21 years of age
- pass a Department of Transportation physical and drug screen
- pass the Secretary of State Temporary Instruction Permit written test, which requires basic reading and writing of the English language

Applicants with a negative driving record or felony history (as listed below) should be advised that finding employment in the transportation industry might be difficult; obtaining a letter of pre-employment prior to enrollment is highly recommended before entry.

- DWI or DUI within the past 5 years

- Felony within the past 7 years
- Careless or reckless driving within the past 3 years
- At fault accident in the past 1 year

SCHEDULE

The current class schedule is listed below.

Entry Level Tractor Trailer Training Program (4/10 weeks)

Full Time Students: 8:00a.m.—4:30p.m., Monday through Friday for 4 weeks

Weekend Students: 8:00a.m.—4:30p.m., Saturday and Sunday for 10 weeks

Professional Tractor Trailer Training Program (18 weeks)

Weeks 1-4: 8:00a.m.—6:00p.m., Monday through Friday

Weeks 5-6: 8:00a.m.—3:30p.m., Monday through Friday

Week 7-12: 10:30a.m.—6:00p.m., Monday through Friday

Week 13-15: 8:00a.m.—3:30p.m., Monday through Friday

Week 16-18: 7:00a.m.—1:30p.m., Monday through Friday

STAFF

David James—President/Instructor

David James has been in the trucking industry for more than 20 years, with extensive experience as both a driver and an instructor. He started TTA 2 years ago and serves as both President and instructor.

Austin Peyrolo—Vice President/Instructor

Austin Peyrolo, Vice President/Instructor, has 15 years' experience in the trucking industry, including 7 years as an instructor.

Mike Hamilton—Instructor

Mike Hamilton is employed as a part-time instructor with TTA. He has 5 years' experience as a driving instructor and experience driving all types of trucks.

Eva Denaji—Admissions/Job Placement Coordinator

Eva Denaji serves as both admissions and job placement coordinator. She has previous, related experience at Oakland Community College.

SUCCESS RATES

TTA has achieved impressive rates of success over the past 2 years of operations. Statistics include:

Student completion rate—94%

License exam pass rate—96%

Job placement rate—91%

Student satisfaction survey results—98%

We are proud of our success and the fact that current and prospective students can be confident in the quality of their education and the value they are receiving for their money.

ACCREDITATION

TTA is accredited by the Council on Occupational Education, a national institutional accrediting agency for the accreditation of non-degree-granting and applied associate degree-granting postsecondary occupational education institutions. It is recognized by the U.S. Secretary of Education as a reliable authority on the quality of education offered by the institutions it has accredited.

FEES

Tuition costs include all books and supplies. Career guidance and job placement assistance are also provided to students and graduates at no extra charge. Students are responsible for travel, meals, housing (if required) and incidental expenses not directly related to training.

Trucking companies may offer reimbursement for truck driver training programs. Many trucking companies will pre-hire students and reimburse their training costs as long as that company employs them.

Entry Level Tractor Trailer Training Program

Tuition: $3999

Registration: $25

Road Test: $100 ($100 fee for all additional road tests taken)

Drug Test: $45

D.O.T Physical: $75

Temporary Instruction Permit: $60 (operator's license), $25 (chauffeurs license)

License Conversion Fee: $18

Total: $4,322

Professional Tractor Trailer Training Program

Tuition: $7999

Registration: $25

Road Test: $100 ($100 fee for all additional road tests taken)

Drug Test: $45

D.O.T Physical: $75

Temporary Instruction Permit: $60 (operator's license), $25 (chauffeurs license)

License conversion fee: $18

Total: $8,322

Financing

Financing is available to those who qualify, as well as grants and state-funded tuition assistance such as:

- Michigan Works
- WIA
- TAA
- TARFF
- Other

Courier Service

Courier Express

57961 Hwy. 82 W
Tifton, GA 31793

Fran Fletcher

Courier Express is a courier service located in Tifton, Georgia. It is owned and operated by Hugh Giles. Courier Express will provide same-day courier services to businesses within a 100-mile radius of Tifton. This will include the cities of Douglas, Valdosta, Albany, and all areas in between.

EXECUTIVE SUMMARY

Courier Express is a courier service located in Tifton, Georgia. It is owned and operated by Hugh Giles. Courier Express will provide same-day courier services to businesses within a 100-mile radius of Tifton. This will include the cities of Douglas, Valdosta, Albany, and all areas in between. The business will operate Monday through Friday 8 a.m.—6 p.m., but will offer after-hours and weekend pick-ups by appointment.

Mr. Giles has 15 years of experience in the car parts industry. While working in retail, he noticed that there was a need in the area for a fast and reliable courier service that offered same-day service. Mr. Giles is starting Courier Express to meet this business need in South Georgia.

The following types of businesses are the target market for Courier Express:

- Businesses with multiple locations that need to transport goods between stores
- Agricultural-based businesses that need test samples transported to the appropriate testing lab
- Banks that need legal documents delivered to another branch
- Legal offices that need documents delivered to another firm
- Big box office suppliers

Mr. Giles will perform administrative duties, contact potential customers, field customer calls, dispatch drivers, and transport packages when needed. He plans to hire two drivers with clean driving records in the beginning, and will add more drivers as business volume increases.

There are two other businesses in the area providing similar services. Mr. Giles is confident that Courier Express will stand out from its competitors by transporting a variety of items instead of specializing. The company will highlight the following to set itself apart from the competition:

- Reliability
- Availability of services

- Fair pricing/volume discounts
- Variety of items transported

Courier Express will initially advertise through newspaper ads and by reaching out to potential customers by phone. Referrals will be crucial, and Mr. Giles will work hard to gain the respect of clients by providing fast, friendly, and affordable service.

Conservative estimates reveal that Courier Express will generate profits during the first few months and will experience an increase in both expenses and income in subsequent months.

Mr. Giles is seeking a business line of credit in the amount of $30,250 to finance this venture. Financing will cover start-up fees and three months of expenses. Mr. Giles plans to repay the line of credit within two years.

COMPANY DESCRIPTION

Location

Courier Express is located in Tifton, Georgia. The business is in close proximity to the Interstate that runs north and south and is located on a major U.S. highway that runs eat and west. This will enable the company to travel easily in all directions.

Hours of Operations

Monday—Friday, 8 AM—6 PM

After Hours (appointment only)

Saturday (appointment only)

Sunday (appointment only)

Personnel

Hugh Giles (Owner)
Mr. Giles has 15 years of experience working in the auto parts industry. He will contact potential customers, dispatch drivers, manage billing, and provide courier services as needed.

Drivers
Two full-time drivers with clean driving records will be hired to help provide courier services. Additional drivers may be hired as business volume increases.

Products and Services

Services
Courier Express will transport the following:

- Legal/bank documents
- Office supplies
- Auto parts
- Commodity lab samples (peanuts, corn)
- Miscellaneous items

MARKET ANALYSIS

Industry Overview

Tifton is centrally located in South Georgia. This will enable Courier Express to provide services to businesses in Douglas, Valdosta, Albany, and smaller cities in between. There are numerous banks, peanut shelling facilities, pecan processing, chicken processing, and auto parts stores that will provide an adequate customer base for the business.

Target Market

The target market for Courier Express will be businesses in the area who need documents or products delivered within a 100-mile radius of Tifton. Courier Express will target peanut shellers requiring 50-pound samples to be transported to food testing labs, banks who have multiple branches throughout South Georgia, auto parts stores, and office supply stores.

Competition

There are currently two similar services being offered in Tifton at this time. The first courier specializes in transporting lab samples from medical clinics to testing laboratories. The second specializes in transporting office supplies within a 30-mile radius of Tifton.

1. Deliver To You, 648 Tenth St., delivers office supplies for a big box office retailer
2. Lab Transport Service, 4836 Carpenter Rd., transports lab samples for area medical clinics

GROWTH STRATEGY

The overall growth strategy of the company is to gain a reputation for fast, convenient delivery of products and documents. Courier Express wishes to achieve strong financial growth during the first year of operation. Mr. Giles already has clients in mind, but will constantly try to locate new clients and industries in need of courier services. Mr. Giles plans to hire additional drivers as business volume increases.

Sales and Marketing

The company's marketing plan consists of contacting businesses to let them know that the courier service is available and that the prices are competitive. The first couple of weeks, Mr. Giles will call companies in Tifton, Douglas, Valdosta, and Albany that would benefit from the courier service. He will follow up these phone calls by e-mailing information packets.

According to the Small Business Development Center, referrals serve as an important advertising method. Referrals will be extremely important to the company's marketing strategy once the business is established. In addition to referrals, Mr. Giles thinks that it is very important to let people know about his business through advertising. Mr. Giles has identified key advertising avenues and tactics to bring in customers while building a reputation for quality.

Courier Express will focus marketing materials on the following:

- Same day delivery
- Express same day delivery

Advertising

Initial advertising will include placing ads in the following area newspapers:

- *Tifton Gazette*
- *Douglas Enterprise*

- *Valdosta Times*
- *Albany Herald*

In addition to advertising, the company will join the Tifton Chamber of Commerce and will e-mail information packets to potential customers.

FINANCIAL ANALYSIS

Start-up Costs

Estimated Start-up Costs

Business license	$ 250
Insurance	$ 500
Initial advertising	$1,000
Camper top for trucks	$7,500
Total	**$9,250**

Pricing Strategy

Prices for Services

Service	Price
Documents	$50
Misc. products under 30 lbs.	$30
Misc. products over 30 lbs.	$50
Office supplies	$50
Commodity lab samples	$30

A minimum courier charge of $50 may apply. Volume discounts are available.

Estimated Monthly Expenses

Loan payment	$ 900
Phone/Internet	$ 200
Advertising	$ 300
Insurance	$ 400
Wages for Mr. Giles (est.)	$2,600
Wages for employees (est.)	$3,000
Total	**$7,400**

Profit/Loss

Mr. Giles takes a conservative approach and estimates that until his business is established, he will deliver approximately 250 lab samples per week at a volume discounted rate of $15 each, 10 car parts per week at a discounted rate of $15 each, and 10 financial/legal documents per week at a rate of $50 each. The courier surcharge is not included in the profit estimation.

Mr. Giles expects monthly expenses to remain steady at $7,400, at least for the first 6 months. The company estimates that there will be a 3% increase in expenses and a 5% increase in income over the next 6 months.

Mr. Giles expects to make a profit the first month, and expects the profits to steadily increase as the business becomes established.

Estimated Profits Years 1–2

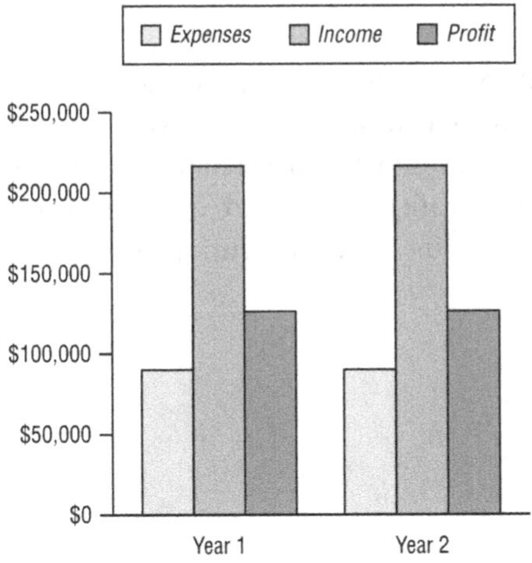

Estimated Profits Months 1–6

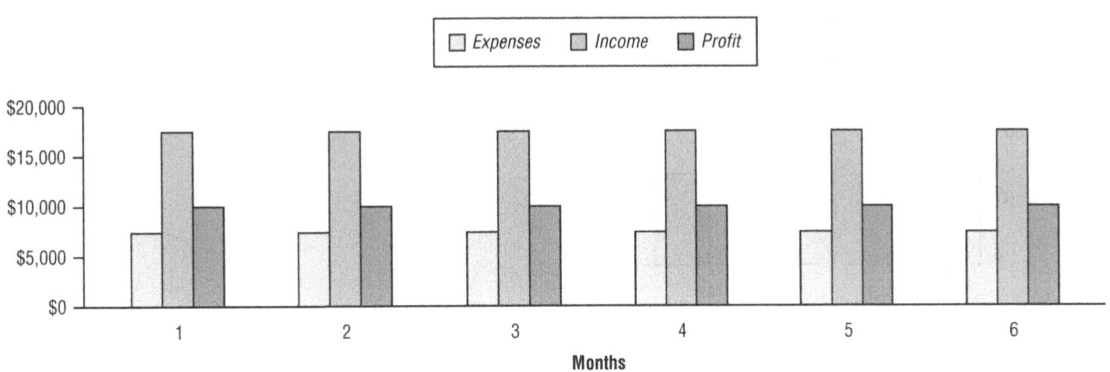

Estimated Profits Months 7–12

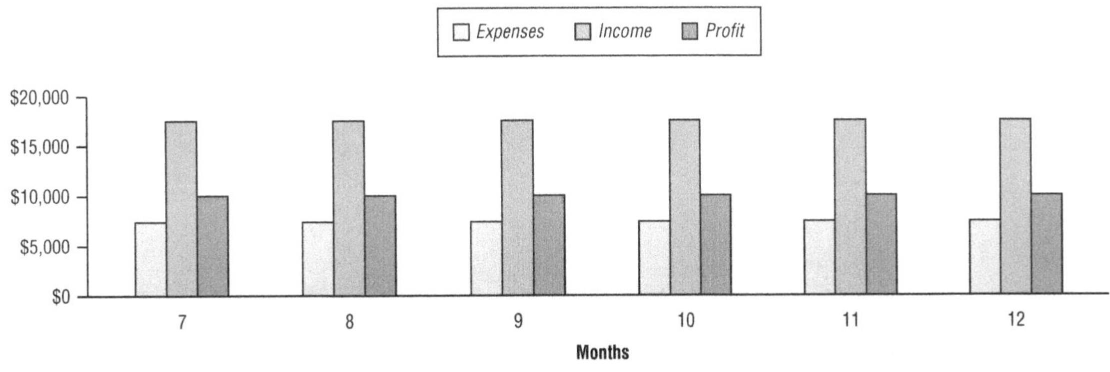

Mr. Giles conservatively estimates that his income and expenses will remain steady in the second year.

Financing

Mr. Giles would like to obtain a business line of credit for $30,250, the amount needed to cover the start-up costs and expenses for the first three months of operation. Mr. Giles will use his home as collateral for the line of credit. He has budgeted $900 per month for loan repayment, but will pay a lump sum on the loan (approximately 10% of annual profit) at the end of each year. If profit projections are met, Mr. Giles will be able to pay off the line of credit during the second year of operation.

Loan Repayment Plan

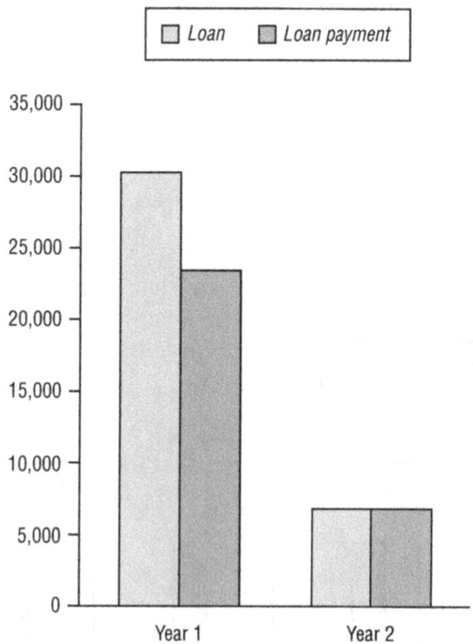

Court Reporting Business

Williamston Reporting LLC

5736 Market St., Ste. 3
Wilmington, DE 19800

Paul Greenland

Williamston Reporting LLC is an independent court reporting service targeting law firms, corporations, government agencies, and the hearing-impaired.

EXECUTIVE SUMMARY

Court reporters play a critical role in the judicial system by providing detailed transcription of legal proceedings. These include exact, word-for-word accounts of administrative hearings, depositions, and trials. While many court reporters are employed directly by the court system, including local, state, and federal courts, significant opportunities exist for independent contractors. Lucrative freelance assignments for court reporters exist both within and beyond the judicial system. Led by experienced court reporter Monica Williamston, Williamston Reporting LLC is a newly established independent court reporting service that serves four main target markets: law firms, businesses/corporations, government agencies, and the hearing-impaired.

INDUSTRY ANALYSIS

Court reporters have access to a wide range of resources specific to their profession, including membership in the National Court Reporters Association (www.ncra.org), which "promotes excellence among those who capture and convert the spoken word to text and is committed to supporting every member in achieving the highest level of professional expertise."

Since 1935, the organization has offered members of variety of certifications, including:

- Registered Professional Reporter (RPR)
- Registered Merit Reporter (RMR)
- Registered Diplomate Reporter (RDR)
- Certified Realtime Reporter (CRR)
- Certified Realtime Captioner (CRC)
- Certified Legal Video Specialist (CLVS)

In addition, other useful industry associations (which also offer certification opportunities) include the American Association of Electronic Reporters & Transcribers (www.aaert.org) and the American Guild of Court Videographers (https://agcv.com). Finally, many court reporters also belong to organizations that are specific to the state in which they work.

MARKET ANALYSIS

Freelance opportunities for court reporters exist within the judicial system, where law firms utilize their services for things such as pretrial depositions. However, additional opportunities exist in many other areas, including the corporate sector, where reporters are used to provide detailed accounts of business and board meetings. Additionally, government agencies also work with independent court reporters to obtain transcripts of different types of proceedings. Finally, a growing and potentially lucrative niche for experienced professionals is the provision of Communication Access Real-Time Translation (CART) for the hearing impaired, as well as closed captioning for television programming. Markets with the greatest opportunities include major metropolitan areas with busy court systems and large concentrations of businesses and industries.

Target Markets

Williamston Reporting is located in Wilmington, Delaware. In 2016 Wilmington had a population of about 73,000 people. The city's more than 4,500 businesses provided employment for approximately 77,500 workers. Utilizing a business database at her local library, Monica Williamston has identified several key industry sectors, along with numbers of related establishments, that hold the greatest opportunity for her business, including:

Finance, Insurance, & Real Estate

- Depository Institutions (56)
- Holding and Other Investment Offices (218)
- Insurance Agents, Brokers and Service (44)
- Insurance Carriers (15)
- Nondepository Credit Institutions (18)
- Real Estate (153)
- Security & Commodity Brokers, Dealers, Exchanges & Services (66)

Public Administration

- Administration of Economic Programs (16)
- Administration of Environmental Quality and Housing Programs (6)
- Administration of Human Resource Programs (11)
- Executive, Legislative & General Government, Except Finance (28)
- Justice, Public Order and Safety (58)
- National Security and International Affairs (5)
- Public Finance, Taxation and Monetary Policy (7)

Transportation, Communications, Electric, Gas, & Sanitary Services

- Communications (32)
- Electric, Gas and Sanitary Services (29)
- Local, Suburban Transit & Interurban Highway Passenger Transport (5)

- Motor Freight Transportation (25)
- Pipelines, Except Natural Gas (1)
- Railroad Transportation (2)
- Transportation Services (38)
- Transportation by Air (6)
- United States Postal Service (2)
- Water Transportation (3)

In addition to businesses, the owner has determined that there are more than 2,000 attorneys practicing in the local market. According to the publication *U.S. News & World Report,* several law firms rank as leaders in the Wilmington area, including:

- Grant & Eisenhofer P.A.
- Hartnett & Hartnett
- Hudson & Castle Law LLC
- J. R. Julian, P.A.
- Landis Rath & Cobb LLP
- Morris James Wilson Halbrook & Bayard, P.A.
- Old Capital Law Firm
- Pazuniak Law Office
- Shanley & Associates
- Weik, Nitsche, Dougherty & Galbraith
- Chimicles & Tikellis LLP
- Kelleher & Laffey
- Knepper & Stratton
- Pinckney, Weidinger, Urban and Joyce LLC
- Tarabicos Grosso, LLP

Competition

Williamston Reporting will face competition from the following court reporting services:

- James DeCrescenzo Reporting, LLC
- Basye Santiago Reporting
- Wilcox & Fetzer, Ltd.
- Hawkins Reporting Service
- National Court Reporters
- Huseby, Inc.
- Veritext
- Professional Court Reporting & Video
- Miller Verbano Reporting, LLC
- Karasch & Associates

Although the market is already home to several established providers, the owner is confident that there is significant demand for the services she will provide. Monica Williamston will seek to differentiate her court reporting service by focusing heavily on Communication Access Real-Time Translation (CART) and real-time captioning which, according to the U.S. Department of Labor, hold the greatest opportunities for industry participants through 2024.

SERVICES

Williamston Reporting will provide a variety of services, including:

- Court Reporting (Business and Legal)
- Electronic Transcription
- Video Reporting/Editing

These services will be offered for a variety of situations, such as:

- Arbitration
- Board Meetings
- Bond Meetings
- Budget Meetings
- Business Meetings
- Convention Board Meetings
- Depositions
- Disciplinary Hearings
- Mediations
- Municipal Hearings
- Stockholder Meetings
- Union Hearings

In addition, the owner also will provide real-time captioning for hearing impaired and deaf individuals, in both individual and group settings, including on-site or remote stadium captioning for conferences, educational sessions, and seminars.

Fees

Generally speaking, Williamston Reporting charges several different types of fees for its services, including:

1. Appearance Fees: $65/hour (half day); $125 (full day) for depositions; board meetings, arbitrations, other legal proceedings ($225)
2. Page Fees/Original Transcript (25 lines/page; 50-65 characters/line): $3.50-$4.25
3. Page Fees/Transcript Copy: $2.25-$3.00
4. Other Fees: Additional charges will be assessed for things like late cancellations; shipping & handling; rush jobs (40-100% additional charge), etc.

OPERATIONS

Location

Williamston Reporting initially will operate as a home-based business. Monica Williamston has established a dedicated home office that she will use exclusively for business purposes. When not providing services remotely, Williamston will travel to her client's location to provide services on-site. Williamston will communicate with customers via her smartphone, allowing her to be as responsive as possible when out in the field.

Equipment

In addition to general office equipment, Williamston Reporting will require the following equipment ($13,450) in order to provide court reporting services:

- Full Translation Professional Software ($2,300)
- Digital Wireless Microphone System ($350)
- Travel Desk Mobile Workstation ($250)
- Infinity II Traditional CART with LCD ($4,200)
- Stenograph Diamante Pro Writer ($3,000)
- HP LaserJet ($2,500)
- Tablet Computer ($850)

Business Structure

Williamston Reporting is organized as a limited liability company in the state of Delaware, providing liability protection without the complexity of a corporation. A local attorney was used to establish the LLC.

PERSONNEL

Monica Williamston, RMR, CRC

A court reporter with 15 years of experience, Monica completed her court reporting training in Massachusetts, where she earned an associate's degree from Eastern Community College. After working in local courts for five years, Monica proceeded to serve as a court reporter in New York, where she worked in the state court system.

After initially receiving certification as a Registered Professional Reporter (RPR) from the National Court Reporters Association, Monica demonstrated her advancement within the profession by passing the Registered Merit Reporter (RMR) exam and earning a certification held by a select group of her peers nationwide. In addition, Monica also holds the Certified Realtime Captioner (CRC) credential from the NCRA. Currently, she is looking to expand her capabilities by pursuing certification as a Certified Legal Video Specialist (CLVS).

Monica has the attributes necessary for success as an independent court reporter. In addition to a high degree of self-discipline and excellent time management skills (qualities needed to be successful in any small business), she possesses exceptional writing and listening skills and is capable of concentrating for extended periods of time.

Professional & Advisory Support

Williamston Reporting has established a business banking account with Great Delaware Bank, including a merchant account for accepting credit card payments. Tax advisement is provided by Lawrence J. Wakefield & Associates.

GROWTH STRATEGY

The following three-year growth strategy has been developed for Williamston Reporting:

Year One: Establish Williamston Partners in the Wilmington area. Generate gross revenue of $60,000 and recoup the owner's initial capital investment. Generate approximately 70 percent of sales from legal court reporting, 20 percent from the business community, and 10 percent from real-time captioning for the hearing impaired. Initially limit services to traditional court reporting and real-time captioning.

Year Two: Continue to increase awareness about Williamston Reporting in the local market. Achieve Certified Legal Video Specialist (CLVS) certification and begin offering video reporting and editing services. Generate $80,000 in sales (55 percent from legal court reporting, 25 percent from the business community, 15 percent from real-time captioning for the hearing impaired, and 5 percent from video reporting/editing).

Year Three: Intensify marketing efforts specific to real-time captioning and video reporting/editing. Increase sales to $100,000 (40 percent from legal court reporting, 30 percent from the business community, 20 percent from real-time captioning, and 10 percent from video reporting/editing). Begin investigating the possibility to expand the business by hiring another court reporter.

MARKETING & SALES

A marketing plan that incorporates the following tactics has been established:

1. Listing in online directories, including www.stenosearch.com.
2. Registration with social service agencies and directories serving the deaf and hearing impaired community.
3. Letters and sales calls to venues (e.g., arenas, churches, convention centers, etc.) in need of real-time captioning services for the deaf and hearing-impaired.
4. Registration with the General Services Administration (www.GSA.gov) to become a vendor to local, state, and federal government agencies through the GSA Schedules program.
5. The use of social media channels, including LinkedIn, to network with potential customers and peers within the court reporting field.
6. A brochure providing information about the owner, and a detailed listing of services offered.
7. Stationery (e.g., business cards, envelopes, letterhead).
8. Membership in the Wilmington Delaware Chamber of Commerce.
9. A Web site with complete details about Williamston Reporting.
10. Quarterly direct mailings, consisting of an introductory letter and the aforementioned brochure, to law firms in the Wilmington area, as well as businesses in the categories outlined in the Market Analysis section of this plan. The owner will begin by targeting companies in each category whose

revenues are in the top quartile. A mailing list based on Williamston Reporting's criteria has been obtained from a reputable list broker.

11. Networking at industry conferences attended by prospects in the legal, government, and business communities.

FINANCIAL ANALYSIS

Following is a breakdown of Williamston Reporting's projected revenue, expenses, and net income for its first three years of operations. Additional financial projections are available upon request.

	2017	2018	2019
Revenue			
Court reporting/legal	$42,000	$44,000	$ 40,000
Court reporting/business	$12,000	$20,000	$ 30,000
Real-time captioning	$ 6,000	$12,000	$ 20,000
Video reporting/editing	$ 0	$ 4,000	$ 10,000
Total revenue	**$60,000**	**$80,000**	**$100,000**
Expenses			
Salary	$30,000	$50,000	$ 60,000
Payroll taxes	$ 4,500	$ 7,500	$ 9,000
Professional liability insurance	$ 2,800	$ 3,000	$ 3,200
Accounting & legal	$ 900	$ 700	$ 700
Office supplies	$ 650	$ 750	$ 850
Equipment	$14,000	$ 500	$ 500
Marketing & advertising	$ 2,500	$ 3,500	$ 4,500
Telecommunications & Internet	$ 950	$ 950	$ 950
Maintenance & repair	$ 250	$ 500	$ 500
Travel	$ 2,000	$ 3,000	$ 4,000
Miscellaneous	$ 500	$ 600	$ 700
Total expenses	**$59,050**	**$71,000**	**$ 84,900**

Digital Marketing Agency

Denton Digital Inc.

51 Redington Ave.
Minneapolis, MN 55400

Paul Greenland

Denton Digital Inc. is the digital marketing solution of choice for small- and medium-sized retailers.

EXECUTIVE SUMMARY

For many businesses, successfully engaging in digital marketing can be the difference between success and failure. The words "digital marketing" can evoke varying degrees of anxiety among business owners and managers—especially those who are not versed in technology. One main reason is the sheer number of things that digital marketing encompasses. Most businesses engage in at least a few forms of digital marketing, but they may do so haphazardly, without an overarching strategy.

Denton Digital Marketing Inc. is the digital marketing solution of choice for small- and medium-sized retailers. The firm works with clients that wish to engage in digital marketing, but need some guidance getting started and developing the right approach. Denton Digital is the brainchild of Katrina Denton, who has decided to establish her own digital marketing firm with partners Jim Erickson, Rick Fallgate, and Sonya Brown. All three are experienced marketers who have worked for leading retailers. Each partner brings a solid base of fundamental marketing expertise to the firm, along with specialized expertise in a specific discipline.

INDUSTRY ANALYSIS

The digital marketing industry is relatively young, having evolved with the World Wide Web since the mid-1990s. Since that time, online marketing has evolved from static Web sites, many of which were not effectively integrated with retailers' legacy back-end systems, to highly sophisticated digital marketing initiatives targeting consumers through multiple channels (e.g., Web, social, e-mail, mobile, etc.) based on their shopping habits and preferences.

Industry Resources

Digital marketers have access to numerous resources that provide access to best practices and information regarding emerging trends and strategies. One in particular is the American Marketing Association (https://www.ama.org). Also known as the AMA, the association bills itself as the "essential community for marketers." In addition to journals, newsletters, training opportunities, and events that focus on marketing in general, the AMA offers specific resources pertaining to digital marketing, covering topics such as programmatic buying, online research, social media, and mobile marketing.

Beyond leading national associations like the AMA, digital marketers also have access to resources at the state and local level. For example, Denton Digital is a member of the Minnesota Interactive Marketing Association (https://www.mima.org), which claims to be the nation's oldest interactive marketing association. Like the AMA, its membership includes individuals from a variety of backgrounds, including designers, writers, executives, technologists, and consultants.

Regardless of their geographic focus, organizations such as these provide excellent opportunities for networking and collaboration in a field that is constantly changing and evolving.

MARKET ANALYSIS

Market Overview

Denton Digital specializes in working with mid-market (e.g., small and medium enterprises) clients in the retail industry. Its typical customer has less than 200-500 employees and revenue in the range of $35 million-$500 million. According to the November 2016 *Worldwide Semiannual Small and Medium Business Spending Guide* from the research firm IDC technology spending among small and medium-sized businesses reached $564 billion in 2016, including investments in software applications in areas such as customer relationship management and content. By the year 2020, this figure is expected to reach $668 billion. As general technology-related spending increases among its ideal customers, Denton Digital will be in a strong position to help them make the most effective and strategic use of their investments.

Prospects

Based on the partners' knowledge of the retail market, a list of approximately 325 up-and-coming small and mid-sized retailers has been compiled. These have been further divided into three tiers of prospects (list available upon request). These prospects will be the focal point of the strategies outlined in the Marketing & Sales section of this plan.

Competition

Denton Digital will compete in a market that already includes several successful digital marketing agencies, including:

- UPTOWN Co.
- Whip Co.
- Firestorm LLC

In addition, competition also will come from traditional advertising and marketing agencies that provide digital services. However, Denton Digital's specialization in retail will provide it with a unique differential over its competitors. This is especially true considering the partners' collective experience working for leading retailers such as Kohl's, Target, and Macy's.

SERVICES

Denton Digital is a firm believer that every marketing plan needs to include a digital strategy. Most businesses engage in at least a few forms of digital marketing, but they may do so haphazardly, without an overarching strategy. As the digital marketing solution of choice for small and medium-sized retailers, Denton Digital collaborates with small- and medium-sized businesses that wish to engage in digital marketing, but need some guidance getting started and developing the right approach.

Because digital marketing is one component of a company's broader marketing strategy, Denton Digital will begin all client relationships by spending time to understand and discover its client's overall marketing strategy. If a client has an existing marketing plan, reviewing it will be the first priority.

For clients who have not devoted enough attention in this area, Denton Digital will attempt to guide the client through the process of developing an overall marketing plan. This way, the client will have a clear understanding of their target customers, the unique selling proposition (USP) that sets them apart from their competitors, and the key marketing objectives supporting their overall business goals. With these fundamental elements in place, the client will then be in a position to consider the right tactical mix of traditional and digital marketing.

Traditional Services

Denton Digital provides its customers with traditional marketing agency services such as:

- Advertising
- Branding
- Copywriting
- Illustration
- Media Buying
- Planning
- Videography

Digital Services

The firm also offers a full complement of digital marketing services, including:

- Analytics & Reporting
- Animation
- Business Listing Management
- Content Creation
- Content Management Systems
- Code Analysis and Debugging
- Customer Relationship Management (CRM)
- Database/Back-end Development
- E-commerce
- E-Mail Marketing
- Hosting Management
- Mobile Marketing
- Mobile/Web App Design & Development
- Online Advertising Placement
- Prototyping
- Reputation Management

- Search Engine Marketing (SEM)
- Search Engine Optimization (SEO)
- Social Media Marketing
- User Interface Design
- Web Design

Technologies

Denton Digital has experience with multiple programming languages and technology platforms, including:

- CSS3
- HTML5
- JavaScript
- Object Oriented Programming
- PHP/MySQL

Process

Once Denton Digital has a clear understanding of its client's marketing plan and objectives, one of the firm's partners will serve as the primary contact for the client. Because all four partners are experienced marketers, each is equally skilled at helping clients with marketing fundamentals. However, each partner also has a unique digital marketing skill set that may make them the most suitable primary contact for a given customer.

Working together, the partner will recommend digital strategies to help the client achieve stated objectives. Based on these strategies, specific tactics will be recommended. For example, a client already may have an excellent Web site, but would benefit from a content management system that makes it easier to update existing content and publish new content. Other clients may need assistance identifying a new e-commerce platform, because older legacy systems no longer meet their needs in areas like mobile commerce. In some cases, assistance may be needed to increase customer engagement through the development of a social media presence. Finally, a customer's strategy may call for search engine optimization initiatives or the development of video content.

Regardless of the tactical mix, Denton Digital will provide its customers with solid recommendations based on their strategies. Working together, the firm will help its customers to prioritize tactics based on available resources. Finally, the firm will provide a detailed time and cost estimate, providing clients with a clear picture of development and execution time frames.

Denton Digital will attempt to maintain its relationship with clients following the conclusion of all development work. With this in mind, the partners not only will make every effort to ensure that their clients are completely satisfied, but also that their digital marketing strategies are working in the short- and long-term. Digital marketing is a moving target, and frequent evaluation adjustment is often needed.

OPERATIONS

Facility & Location

Denton Digital is located at 51 Redington Avenue in Minneapolis, Minnesota. The firm is located in a historic house that has been renovated for office use. The partners have secured a competitive lease for this unique space, which includes areas for offices, meetings, and recreation/relaxation. The house is conveniently located near downtown, providing easy access to a healthy staple of clients, and also to highway and air transportation when business travel is required.

Payment & Fees

Denton Digital's services will range anywhere from $100 to $200 per hour, averaging approximately $150 per hour. The firm will consider slightly lower rates for customers who are agreeable to a retainer arrangement. Denton Digital will provide customers with a detailed time and cost estimate for all projects, and will request advance payment ranging from 33 percent to 50 percent. A standard fee agreement has been created with the assistance of a local business attorney.

PERSONNEL

Denton Digital Marketing is the brainchild of Katrina Denton, who has decided to establish her own digital marketing firm with partners Jim Erickson, Rick Fallgate, and Sonya Brown. All four are experienced marketers who have experience working for leading retailers.

Katrina Denton, President

Focus: Digital Strategy

Katrina has worked in the retail industry for more than 20 years. Her career began in traditional marketing and advertising roles, but transitioned to e-commerce in 2002. She gained valuable experience developing e-commerce strategies for several major big-box retailers that involved e-mail marketing, mobile marketing, SEO, and more. In addition to an MBA from the University of Minnesota, Katrina also has pursued additional courses in interactive marketing.

Jim Erickson, Partner

Focus: Web & Database Development

Jim has extensive experience on the agency side, having worked for several Web development firms over the past 15 years. In those roles, Jim focused on developing e-commerce sites, mainly for small- and medium-sized retailers. In addition to exceptional design and layout abilities, he is a gifted coder who has worked extensively with a variety of CMS systems, as well as frameworks made with PHP and JavaScript. Jim holds an information technology degree from Minnesota State University, as well as a graphic design degree from Central Institute of Technology.

Rick Fallgate, Partner

Focus: Social Media

Rick's career began in customer relations for a leading retailer. In that role, he handled the development of traditional customer satisfaction programs. When social media exploded in popularity, Rick was well-positioned to begin focusing exclusively in this area. Through the application of his traditional customer relations experience, Rick began developing social strategies for his employer that took customer engagement and satisfaction to new heights. He now brings this expertise to Denton Digital. Rick holds an undergraduate business degree from Central State University.

Sonya Brown, Partner

Focus: Content Strategy & Development

Sonya began her career in media relations, writing press releases and proactively securing positive news coverage for her employers. Eventually, she transitioned into management, overseeing communications from a higher level and helping her employers to develop and share content in new and interesting ways. With her experience, Sonya will serve as Denton Digital's "chief storyteller." In addition to developing content for clients, she also will oversee outside resources (including freelance writers, editors, illustrators, and videographers) that will help in the execution of content development projects. Sonya earned an undergraduate journalism degree from Northwestern University in Chicago.

Support Staff

Denton Digital will begin operations with one full-time administrative assistant. The business will evaluate the addition of in-house professionals (programming, graphic design, and content development) during its second and third years of operations, based on business growth.

Independent Contractors

Denton Digital has developed a network of reliable independent contractors who can provide services such as animation, writing, editing, proofreading, illustration, photography, graphic design, database development, project management, and videography. These resources will provide the agency with operational scalability and specialized expertise when needed.

Professional & Advisory Support

After careful consideration, Denton Digital has identified a certified public accountant whose firm will provide bookkeeping and tax advisory services for the business. In addition, a relationship also has been established with a local business attorney and insurance agent. Finally, Denton Digital has established a commercial checking account with the Bank of Minneapolis.

GROWTH STRATEGY

Denton Digital is fortunate to begin operations with several clients and digital marketing projects, which its partners have obtained through their respective industry contacts. The firm has established the following targets for its first three years of operations:

Year One: Begin operations with two new clients and startup capital of $100,000 provided by the four partners. Secure eight new clients and achieve the equivalent of 3,840 billable hours for the year. Generate net income of $51,900 on revenue of $524,100.

Year Two: Fully recoup the owners' collective startup investment midway through the year. Secure 10 new clients and achieve the equivalent of 4,800 billable hours for the year. Generate net income of $95,050 on revenue of $624,950. Based on demand, expand staff through the addition of an additional in-house programmer and graphic designer.

Year Three: Secure 12 new clients and achieve the equivalent of 5,760 billable hours for the year. Generate net income of $108,200 on revenue of $755,800. Continue to expand staff through the addition of an in-house content developer.

MARKETING & SALES

Denton Digital's marketing and sales efforts will emphasize its position as "The digital marketing solution of choice for small- and medium-sized retailers." Supported by a unique brand identity, the company's marketing approach will involve the following tactics:

1. As a digital marketing firm, the company realizes that its own online presence is a reflection of its capabilities, and in many ways the nucleus of its marketing strategy. With this in mind, Denton Digital will invest heavily in ***digital and interactive marketing*** to reach prospective customers. Its traditional and mobile Web sites will showcase the firm's range of skills and expertise, especially in

highly visual categories such as animation, branding, copywriting, design, videography, and content development. The company also will have a strong and active presence on all major social media platforms, including Twitter, YouTube, LinkedIn, and Facebook.

2. Denton Digital will employ ***"lead magnet" tools*** that provide prospects with valuable content (e.g., free digital marketing checklists, reports, white papers, case studies, etc.) in exchange for their contact information. This will enable the firm to build a proprietary prospect database that can be used for e-mail marketing efforts. By staying visible with prospects on a regular basis, Denton Digital seeks to be top-of-mind when digital marketing solutions are needed.
3. In addition, the firm will pursue ***networking opportunities*** through membership in specific industry-focused online groups.
4. Denton Digital's partners also will share their knowledge and expertise by ***writing guest articles*** for marketing publications and blogs.
5. The firm's partners have identified a short list of key industry trade shows attended by retailers. Beyond simply attending these shows, the partners also will ***pursue speaking engagements*** to position the firm as a thought leader and provide opportunities to showcase its work through case study examples.
6. Finally, Denton Digital will put a major emphasis on ***word-of-mouth referrals.*** At the beginning of all client relationships, the partners will tell clients that, at the end of a given project, they will request a testimonial (which can be used in marketing efforts) and a referral to one of their colleagues. If the client is not completely satisfied and willing to do this, the partners will attempt some form of service recovery, pursuing a goal of total customer satisfaction.

FINANCIAL ANALYSIS

Following is a breakdown of projected revenue, expenses, and net income for Denton Digital's first three years of operations. The owners anticipate that 60 percent of revenue will come from hourly billings, followed by retainers (30%), and other sources (10%) such as speaking fees and sales of reports, white papers, etc. Additional financial projections are available upon request.

	2017	2018	2019
Revenue			
Retainers	$172,800	$216,000	$259,200
Hourly billings	$345,600	$432,000	$518,400
Other	$ 57,600	$ 72,000	$ 86,400
Total revenue	**$576,000**	**$720,000**	**$864,000**
Expenses			
Salary	$275,000	$325,000	$400,000
Payroll tax	$ 41,250	$ 48,750	$ 60,000
Independent contractors	$144,000	$180,000	$216,000
Insurance	$ 1,400	$ 1,500	$ 1,600
Office lease	$ 18,000	$ 18,000	$ 18,000
Accounting & legal	$ 2,500	$ 2,500	$ 2,500
Office supplies	$ 700	$ 700	$ 700
Equipment	$ 3,500	$ 2,500	$ 2,500
Marketing & advertising	$ 20,000	$ 25,000	$ 30,000
Telecommunications & Internet	$ 2,500	$ 2,500	$ 2,500
Professional development	$ 1,250	$ 1,500	$ 2,000
Unreimbursed travel	$ 8,500	$ 10,000	$ 11,500
Business meals	$ 1,500	$ 2,000	$ 2,500
Subscriptions & dues	$ 500	$ 500	$ 500
Software licenses	$ 3,000	$ 4,000	$ 5,000
Miscellaneous	$ 500	$ 500	$ 500
Total expenses	**$524,100**	**$624,950**	**$755,800**
Net income	**$ 51,900**	**$ 95,050**	**$108,200**

Mailing List Broker

A-List Medical Marketing LLC

2007 4th Ave. W
Bellevue, WA 98005

Paul Greenland

A-List Medical Marketing LLC is a business-to-business mailing list broker specializing in the healthcare market.

EXECUTIVE SUMMARY

Large corporations have the luxury of running branding and image advertising campaigns that require massive budgets to sustain over long periods of time, with results that can be difficult or impossible to measure. Comparatively, a direct-response approach provides marketers with a highly targeted and cost-effective means of reaching customers who need their products or services. Traditional postal mailings and e-mailings, used alone or in combination, continue to be highly effective direct marketing tactics.

To be successful, marketers must have solutions that are in demand, a clearly defined target market, a compelling message, and importantly, a high-quality list of prospects. The absence of any one of these elements can have a negative impact on the success of a direct marketing campaign. A-List Medical Marketing LLC is a business-to-business (B2B) mailing list broker. Working in partnership with a variety of mailing list owners and data sources (trade and professional associations, industry publications, business directories, conference/trade show firms, government agencies, etc.), the company purchases data at wholesale and compiles mailing lists based on its customers' unique specifications and requirements.

There are many different types of mailing list brokers, offering either business-to-consumer (B2C) lists, business-to-business lists, or both. Some are broad in focus, while others provide highly specialized types of industry lists. Because of its owners' professional background, A-List Medical Marketing will concentrate its services in the B2B category, concentrating mainly in the medical/healthcare sector.

INDUSTRY ANALYSIS

Although direct mail has been declining as more marketers pursue digital strategies, in 2016 the Direct Marketing Association (DMA) indicated that approximately 57 percent of all mail volume was still attributed to direct mail. So-called "omni-channel" marketers continued to include direct mail in their arsenal, in combination with other tactics. For example, traditional postal mailings continue to be an important part of the marketing mix within integrated campaigns that also include social media, Web, e-mail marketing, and print/online advertising elements. Adding to the appeal of direct mail is its measurability. The most successful marketers incorporate a call-to-action in their direct mail campaigns, encouraging recipients to respond in some way, such as requesting a free consultation, signing up for a free report or newsletter, or opting into a mailing list. Additionally, technologies such as variable data printing allow marketers to customize high-quality, four-color marketing pieces and boost responsiveness.

The DMA (https://thedma.org) is a leading resource for industry players, billing itself as "the world's largest trade association dedicated to advancing and protecting responsible data-driven marketing." With roots dating back to 1917, the DMA includes thousands of non-profit organizations and leading companies among its members.

MARKET ANALYSIS

Because of its owners' professional background, A-List Medical Marketing will concentrate its services in the B2B category, mainly in the healthcare sector. Specifically, the company will focus on helping pharmaceutical companies and surgical equipment/medical device and supplies manufacturers market their goods to healthcare services providers throughout the United States and its territories.

Following is a detailed description of the manufacturers/service providers that A-List Medical Marketing will target for mailing list rental services. In addition, the company also will compile and sell mailing lists among companies in these categories (e.g., to businesses that supply ingredients and materials to one another for manufacturing, etc.).

Target Markets (Manufacturers)

- Abdominal Supports
- Absorbents
- Artificial Limbs
- Collars
- Colonic Therapy Apparatus & Supplies
- Drugs
- First Aid Supplies
- Foot Appliances
- Health Care Apparel
- Hospital Equipment & Supplies
- Masks Protective
- Metallurgists Equipment & Supplies
- Orthopedic Appliances
- Prosthetic/Surgical Appliances
- Oxygen Therapy Equipment
- Physical Therapy Equipment
- Respirators
- Safety Equipment & Clothing

- Shoes, Orthopedic
- Sterilizing Apparatus
- Surgical Appliances
- Surgical Dressings
- Surgical Instruments
- Vitamin Products
- Wheel Chairs
- Whirlpool Bath Equipment & Supplies
- X-Ray Apparatus & Supplies

A-List Medical Marketing will connect manufacturers with the following providers of healthcare services:

- Ambulance Services
- Ambulatory Health Care Services
- Blood and Organ Banks
- Chiropractors
- Dentists
- Diagnostic Imaging Centers
- Freestanding Ambulatory Surgical and Emergency Centers
- General Medical and Surgical Hospitals
- HMO Medical Centers
- Home Health Care Services
- Kidney Dialysis Centers
- Medical Laboratories
- Mental Health Practitioners (except Physicians)
- Miscellaneous Health Practitioners
- Nursing Care Facilities
- Optometrists
- Outpatient Care Centers
- Outpatient Mental Health and Substance Abuse Centers
- Physical, Occupational and Speech Therapists, and Audiologists
- Physicians (except Mental Health Specialists)
- Physicians, Mental Health Specialists
- Podiatrists
- Psychiatric and Substance Abuse Hospitals
- Specialty (except Psychiatric and Substance Abuse) Hospitals

Competition

A-List Medical Marketing's primary competitor will be MedicaMarket Worldwide LLC, which has a similar focus. In addition, three other national mailing list brokers also offer healthcare mailing list services, although they focus in other areas as well. These include: J Petersburg & Associates List Company Inc., TopData Corp., and Foster Hill Direct Reach Marketing Inc.

A-List Medical Marketing will leverage (1) its highly specialized focus, (2) its owners' collective 85 years of experience in healthcare marketing and materials management, and (3) highly personalized service to differentiate itself from these competitors.

SERVICES

When contacted by a prospective customer, A-List Medical Marketing will make every effort to convert the prospect into a customer (and hopefully a long-term customer). This will be accomplished by listening to the prospect and helping them to clearly identify their direct marketing objectives. Based on the owners' personal experience, prospects are often turned off by list brokers who do not present them with options based on their specific requirements. This results in unnecessary back-and-forth communication and wasted time on the part of the prospect, list broker, and list owner.

Once objectives and expectations are clearly understood, A-List Medical Marketing will get to work, contacting one of several trusted list owners to identify the very best data for the prospect's campaign. Then, one of A-List Medical Marketing's list specialists will share options and costs with the prospect. Multiple variables can impact the cost of a mailing list, including the number of "selects" or fields. Lists with more data (especially e-mail addresses) typically carry a higher cost. Additionally, lists that will be utilized multiple times also can be more expensive.

Mailing lists can include an incredibly wide array of selects beyond typical ones such as contact name, company name, address, city, state, and ZIP code. For example, lists may contain data regarding metropolitan statistical area (MSA), latitude, longitude, census block group, census tract, credit score, stock exchange/ticker symbol, industry category, employment size, location size, sales volume, year founded, and more.

Although cost varies depending on the aforementioned variables, as well as list owner charges, postal mail-only lists typically are available for about $75 per 1,000 records, with a $200 minimum. E-mail only lists cost $90 per 1,000 records, with a $700 minimum, while lists that include both e-mail and postal mail addresses cost $130 per 1,000 records, and also carry a $700 minimum.

Most of A-List Medical Marketing's list owners require that e-mail address lists be sent via a commercial third-party whose servers are "white listed" and comply with all CANSPAM laws. However, postal mail lists typically are provided directly to the customer in a comma-separated value (CSV) format. These then can be provided to a letter shop/mail house that handles preparation and sending of the actual mailing. A-List Medical Marketing takes great pains to determine the quality of its mailing list sources, ensuring that they are updated continuously and "scrubbed" on a regular basis to remove outdated information using the National Change of Address (NCOA) database.

Once a prospect becomes a customer, A-List Medical Marketing will provide them with a simple mailing list agreement outlining terms and conditions pertaining to use of the list and payment. The company will require all customers to pay for their list in advance via credit card.

OPERATIONS

Location

A-List Medical Marketing will operate as a virtual business. Its owners will each maintain dedicated home offices. However, the business's headquarters address will be the home of President Sarah Laxton.

Business Infrastructure

Although it operates virtually, A-List Medical Marketing has established a toll-free number for the business, along with dedicated extensions for its main "departments" (billing and customer support). In addition, existing customers can enter an extension to reach either one of the owners directly. Customers who select "billing" will be transferred to a dedicated representative at Redbird Accounting, the company's billing, bookkeeping, and accounting service provider. Customers who select "customer support" will be directed to the owners' shared virtual assistant, Tammy Rockwell, who will ensure that their needs are met quickly and efficiently.

In addition, A-List Medical Marketing also has secured a dedicated Internet domain name. The owners created a professional-looking Web site at a minimal cost using a popular online Web hosting company. As part of a relatively inexpensive monthly subscription, A-List Medical Marketing's employees have access to cloud-based file sharing, virtual meeting capabilities, Exchange e-mail/calendar tools, and more. Finally, A-List Medical Marketing has the ability to track expenses virtually and accept credit card payments through a subscription to a cloud-based accounting software service.

Business Structure

A-List Medical Marketing is organized as a limited liability company in the state of Washington, providing the owners with affordable liability protection. A well-known online legal document service was used to cost-effectively establish the LLC.

PERSONNEL

Sarah Laxton, President

An experienced healthcare marketing executive, Sarah Laxton has worked for several large pharmaceutical companies over the years, overseeing massive consumer advertising campaigns for a number of blockbuster drugs. She later started managing campaigns that targeted prescribing physicians, allowing her to develop extensive business-to-business direct marketing expertise. Following the merger of her employer with another pharmaceutical company, Laxton was laid off from her marketing director position, but was given a generous severance package. She is capitalizing on this time of transition, and her entrepreneurial spirit, to establish A-List Medical Marketing in partnership with John Churchville.

John Churchville, Vice President

Prior to establishing A-List Medical Marketing, John Churchville worked in the field of healthcare materials management for a leading health system in Portland, Oregon. In that role, he oversaw purchasing for three hospitals, a network of 26 clinics, a home healthcare agency, an outpatient rehabilitation center, and a large employee daycare facility. John developed close working relationships with many vendors and suppliers, and was successful in negotiating contracts that significantly benefited his organization's bottom line. After 28 years in materials management, Churchville is now semiretired and ready to put his industry expertise to work for A-List Medical Marketing. Churchville earned an MBA from Mountain Hills University.

Personnel Plan

Initially, Laxton and Churchville will be A-List Medical Marketing's sole employees. After breaking even during the second year of operations and accumulating enough profit, the owners will evaluate the addition of a third list specialist, probably during the business's fourth year of operations. This position will be partially commission-based.

Professional & Advisory Support

A-List Medical Marketing has established a business banking account with Bellevue Community Bank. Tax advisement is provided by Redbird Accounting. In addition, the company has partnered with virtual assistant Tammy Rockwell, who can provide their growing business with cost-effective, scalable administrative support.

GROWTH STRATEGY

Year One: Establish A-List Medical Marketing as a virtual B2B mailing list broker in the healthcare industry with an initial investment of $30,000. Achieve brokerage commissions of $160,000 and net income of $17,600.

Year Two: Increase brokerage commissions at a compound annual rate of approximately 20 percent over the previous year. Break even during the early part of the year, recouping startup costs. Generate net income of $15,650 on commissions of $192,000.

Year Three: Increase brokerage commissions at a compound annual rate of approximately 20 percent over the previous year. Generate net income of $20,100 on commissions of $230,400. Use accumulated profits to hire a third list specialist during year four.

MARKETING & SALES

A-List Medical Marketing will focus heavily on digital and direct marketing to reach prospects for its list rental services.

In partnership with a local marketing agency, the company has developed a unique brand identity to help its name stand out in the marketplace. A-List Medical Marketing will showcase its brand identity on a robust Web site that is search engine optimized. The company's site will keep its contact information highly visible on all pages, along with opportunities for prospects to engage in a live chat with an available associate (one of the owners or their virtual assistant) during regular business hours. Another feature of the site will be an intake form, which prospects can use to request lists based on their objectives, campaign parameters, and unique requirements. A-List Medical Marketing will then respond to this request within one business day.

Additionally, A-List Medical Marketing will employ targeted online advertising approaches using social channels such as LinkedIn.

Significantly, the company will employ print, digital, and direct marketing strategies to reach the readers of leading publications to which its prospects subscribe. These may include:

- *American Journal of Health-System Pharmacy*
- *BioSupply Trends Quarterly*
- *Drug Topics*
- *IN VIVO*

- *Medical Design Briefs*
- *Medical Device & Diagnostic Industry*
- *Medical Product Outsourcing*
- *MedicalDeviceSummit.com*
- *Monthly Prescribing Reference*
- *Pharmaceutical Representative*
- *Pharmacy Practice News*
- *Pharmacy Times*
- *Pharmacy Today*
- *The Medical Letter on Drugs & Therapeutics*
- *The MedTech Strategist*
- *Today's Medical Developments*
- *U.S. Pharmacist*

Finally, A-List Medical Marketing has purchased a cost-effective tradeshow display, which will be used to exhibit at select industry shows (many of which are sponsored by the aforementioned publications).

FINANCIAL ANALYSIS

Sarah Laxton will contribute 66 percent of the startup cost required for A-List Medical Marketing ($20,000), while John Churchville will contribute the remaining 33 percent ($10,000). The owners anticipate that they will recoup their investments and break even during the early part of the business's second year of operations.

Following is a breakdown of projected revenue, expenses, and net income for A-List Medical Marketing's first three years of operations. The owners have based their sales figures on an average brokerage commission of 20 percent. Additional financial projections are available upon request.

	2016	2017	2018
Revenue			
Revenue (brokerage commissions)	$160,000	$192,000	$230,400
Expenses			
Salary	$ 90,000	$110,000	$130,000
Payroll tax	$ 13,500	$ 16,500	$ 19,500
Insurance	$ 450	$ 500	$ 550
Accounting & legal	$ 2,500	$ 3,000	$ 3,500
Office supplies	$ 400	$ 450	$ 500
Software licenses	$ 850	$ 850	$ 850
Marketing & advertising	$ 20,000	$ 25,000	$ 30,000
Virtual assistant	$ 10,000	$ 15,000	$ 20,000
Internet services	$ 1,050	$ 1,150	$ 1,250
Telecommunications	$ 2,500	$ 2,750	$ 3,000
Subscriptions & dues	$ 650	$ 650	$ 650
Miscellaneous	$ 500	$ 500	$ 500
Total expenses	**$142,400**	**$176,350**	**$210,300**
Net income	**$ 17,600**	**$ 15,650**	**$ 20,100**

Massage Therapist

Professional Massage Services

16800 Southfield Rd.
Beverly Hills, MI 48025

Zuzu Enterprises

Haley Rosseau is a certified massage therapist with two years' experience in the field. She is starting her own massage therapy business, Professional Massage Services, and plans to see clients through two outlets: space she has rented in a local, busy salon, and offsite in people's homes and offices.

EXECUTIVE SUMMARY

Massage therapists treat clients by using touch to manipulate the muscles and other soft tissues of the body. With their touch, therapists relieve pain, help heal injuries, improve circulation, relieve stress, increase relaxation, and aid in the general wellness of clients.

Haley Rosseau is a certified massage therapist with two years' experience in the field. She is starting her own massage therapy business and plans to see clients through two outlets: space she has rented in a local, busy salon, and offsite in people's homes and offices.

MASSAGE THERAPY

According to the *Occupational Outlook Handbook* published by the Bureau of Labor Statistics, massage therapists treat clients by using touch to manipulate the muscles and other soft tissues of the body. With their touch, therapists relieve pain, help heal injuries, improve circulation, relieve stress, increase relaxation, and aid in the general wellness of clients.

Massage therapists typically do the following:

- Talk with clients about their symptoms, medical history, and desired results
- Evaluate clients to locate painful or tense areas of the body
- Manipulate muscles and other soft tissues of the body
- Provide clients with guidance on stretching, strengthening, overall relaxation, and how to improve their posture
- Document clients' conditions and progress

Massage therapists use touch to treat clients' injuries and to promote the clients' general wellness. They use their hands, fingers, forearms, elbows, and sometimes feet to knead muscles and soft tissues of the body.

Massage therapists may use lotions and oils, and massage tables or chairs, when treating a client. A massage can be as short as 5–10 minutes or could last more than an hour.

Therapists talk with clients about what they hope to achieve through massage. Massage therapists may suggest personalized treatment plans for their clients, including information about additional relaxation techniques to practice between sessions. The type of massage given typically depends on the client's needs and physical condition. For example, therapists may use a special technique for elderly clients that they would not use for athletes.

Because therapists work by appointment in most cases, their schedules and the number of hours worked each week vary considerably. Moreover, because of the strength and endurance needed to give a massage, many therapists cannot perform massage services 8 hours per day, 5 days per week.

INDUSTRY ANALYSIS

Quick Facts: Massage Therapists

2015 median pay	$38.040 per year $18.29 per hour
Typical entry-level education	Postsecondary nondegree award
Work experience in a related occupation	None
On-the-job training	None
Number of jobs, 2014	168,800
Job outlook, 2014–24	22% (Much faster than average)
Employment change, 2014–24	36,500

Massage therapists held about 168,800 jobs in 2014. About half of massage therapists were self-employed in 2014.

Employment of massage therapists is projected to grow 22 percent from 2014 to 2024, much faster than the average for all occupations. Continued growth in the demand for massage services will lead to new openings for massage therapists. Michigan is expected to grow at 21 percent for the same time period.

	Employment			
	2014	2024	Percent Change	Projected Annual Job Openings
United States				
Massage Therapists	168,800	205,200	+22%	4,900
Michigan				
Massage Therapists	3,110	3,750	+21%	90

As an increasing number of states adopt licensing requirements and standards for therapists, the practice of massage is likely to be respected and accepted by more people as a way to treat pain and to improve overall wellness.

Similarly, as more healthcare providers understand the benefits of massage, demand will likely increase as these services become part of treatment plans. However, demand in healthcare settings will be tempered by limited insurance coverage for massage services.

Massage also offers specific benefits to particular groups of people whose continued demand for massage services will lead to overall growth for the occupation. For example, many sports teams hire massage therapists to help their athletes rehabilitate from injuries and to relieve or manage pain.

The number of massage clinic franchises has increased in recent years. Many franchised clinics offer more affordable massages than those provided at spas and resorts, making massage services available to a wider range of customers.

However, demand for massage services may be limited by the overall state of the economy. During tough economic times, both the number of people who seek massage therapy and the frequency of their massages may decline.

In states that regulate massage therapy, opportunities should be available to those who complete formal programs and pass a professionally recognized exam. However, new massage therapists should expect that it can take time build a client base.

Because referrals are an important source of work for massage therapists, marketing and networking may help increase the number of job opportunities. Joining a professional association also can help build strong contacts and further increase the likelihood of steady work. In addition, massage therapists may be able to attract a wider variety of clients by completing education programs in multiple modalities.

MARKET ANALYSIS

Target Markets

Professional Massage Services will operate in the Metropolitan Detroit area with salon services being offered in Beverly Hills, Michigan. Beverly Hills is a mere 4 square miles and has a population of just over 10,000 people. The population is highly educated, with nearly 90% of residents having some college education to advanced degrees; this equates to a median household income of nearly $110,000 and more than half of all residents making a minimum of $100,000 per year. Nearly 20% of the population earns $200,000 or more.

Beverly Hills is also located within a very short drive of other affluent cities, including: Birmingham, Berkley, Franklin, and Bloomfield Township.

House calls may be done anywhere in the metropolitan area, with concentration being in Beverly Hills, Birmingham, Berkley, Franklin, Troy, Bloomfield Hills, Bloomfield Township, West Bloomfield, Farmington Hills, and Royal Oak.

Competition

While there are numerous salons offering massage service in the area, the Amelie Salon and Spa is a well-known and highly popular spa in the area with a loyal and dedicated client base. In addition, very few certified massage therapists in the area are willing to travel to the client's home or business for personalized, convenient appointments.

SERVICES

Swedish Massage

A traditional Swedish massage includes gliding, kneading, tapping and stretching techniques, which are applied with focus on returning blood and oxygen to the heart by improving circulation and relieving tension. This type of massage is gentle enough to be right for everyone.

Deep Tissue Massage

When soft tissue massage is not enough to get rid of deeper tensions, a therapeutic deep tissue or sports massage may be necessary. These types of massage include deeper pressure, a wide range of stretches and massage to the target specific, aching muscles.

Prenatal Massage

Prenatal massage can be extremely beneficial for both a mom-to-be or a brand-new mom. Pregnancy, hormones, and child birth cause major changes to the entire body and those aches and pains need to be addressed.

Reflexology

Reflexology massage focuses on pressure points in the hands and feet, which correspond to all the organs in the body. An ancient art, this type of massage is very therapeutic and relaxing for the entire body.

Hot Stone Massage

Hot stone massage is a type of heat therapy using carefully warmed lava stones which are placed on specific acupressure points. This direct heat relieves stress and tension in the body.

Chair Massage

Chair massage keeps you in a seated, inclined position and is a relatively fast option when you're sore and only have a few minutes. As it requires no lying down or disrobing, this is a perfect option for those pressed for time but looking for relief from aches and pains.

PRICING STRUCTURE

The pricing structure for offsite treatments is slightly higher to accommodate travel time and expenses. In addition to the salon prices listed below, offsite treatments incur an additional $10-$30 fee, based on location.

Swedish Massage

60 minutes: $65

90 minutes: $95

Deep Tissue Massage

60 minutes: $65

90 minutes: $95

Prenatal Massage

60 minutes: $65

90 minutes: $95

Reflexology

40 minutes: $60

Hot Stone Massage

60 minutes: $90

90 minutes: $125

Chair Massage

$1.00 per minute

EQUIPMENT

Professional Massage Services will need to procure the following equipment:

Massage table with accessories—$1,500

Massage table, portable, with carry case—$900

Massage chair, portable, with carry case—$500

Oils and lotions, variety—$250

Hot stone warmer and various stones—$300

Sheets and covers—$100

Towels—$100

Aromatherapy diffuser and oils—$175

Robes/slippers—$250

Cleaning supplies—$150

Towel warmer—$200

iPod and portable speaker—$250

Total—$4,675

MARKETING

Social Media & Web

The salon will feature the services of Professional Massage Services on its website and social media accounts. Full descriptions, pricing, and appointment booking options will be available. In addition to this, Professional Massage Services will create its own online presence that features its available offsite services as well as wellness tips and promotions.

Advertising

Business cards with contact information will be printed and available at the salon and to all customers. Client referral programs will encourage current clients to relate their experiences to friends and family and encourage word-of-mouth advertising.

EDUCATION/CERTIFICATION

Haley Rosseau graduated from Rochester High School before continuing her education at Naturopathic School of the Healing Arts in Ann Arbor. A Michigan Board of Massage Therapy approved education program, this course included both classroom study and hands-on practice of massage techniques. The program covered subjects such as anatomy; physiology; kinesiology; pathology; business management; and ethics. The cost of this training was nearly $10,000, including books and fees. It included a clinical internship at New Life Energies as well as more than 670 hours of training.

Haley Rosseau is also licensed by the State of Michigan, Department of Licensing and Regulatory Affairs, Bureau of Professional Licensing, Board of Massage Therapy. This licensure required graduation from an approved massage therapy program and passing the Federation of State Massage Therapy

Board's Massage and Bodywork Licensing Examination (MBLEx). Therapists also had to pass a criminal background check, file a fingerprint report, have liability insurance, and be certified in cardiopulmonary resuscitation (CPR). Continuing education credits and periodic license renewal are also required.

ASSOCIATIONS

Haley Rosseau is a member of the American Massage Therapy Association, a nonprofit, professional association created in 1943 by massage therapists, for massage therapists. Its mission is to serve its members while advancing the art, science and practice of massage therapy. The association requires its members to abide by its Code of Ethics and Standards of Practice.

INSURANCE

The AMTA Professional Membership includes broad liability insurance for massage therapists to protect from covered losses. Coverage includes:

- Up to $2 million per occurrence/$6 million aggregate for professional liability, general liability, products and personal injury
- Hot stone massage coverage is included at no extra cost

FINANCIAL ANALYSIS

Start-Up Costs

Equipment—$4,675

Advertising—$250

Rental deposit—$500

Insurance—$500

Auto decals—$500

Business cards—$100

Total—$6,525

Monthly Costs

Rent—$500

Consumables (oils, lotion, etc.)—$100

Maintenance/replacement—$50

Advertising—$50

Total—$700

Travel expenses are not included in the monthly totals because they will be offset by the additional travel charges.

Earnings

The median annual wage for massage therapists was $38,040 in May 2015. The lowest 10 percent earned less than $18,860, and the highest 10 percent earned more than $74,860. Most massage therapists earn a combination of wages and tips. Michigan showed higher than average median wages, with $46,700 in May 2015.

Location	Pay Period	2015 10%	25%	Median	75%	90%
United States	Hourly	$ 9.07	$ 12.19	$ 18.29	$ 27.01	$ 35.99
	Yearly	$18,900	$25,400	$38,000	$56,200	$74,900
Michigan	Hourly	$ 9.14	$ 14.16	$ 22.47	$ 29.25	$ 33.79
	Yearly	$19,000	$29,500	$46,700	$60,800	$70,300

Professional Massage Services anticipates it will meet the Michigan median income of $46,700 for massage therapists in the second year of operations. At an average cost of $65 per hour (not including tip), this would equate to 15 massages per week, less costs.

Pet Sanctuary

Pawsome Pet Sanctuary

2553 Vernon Rd.
Roseville, CA 95747

Claire Moore

Pawsome Pet Sanctuary (PPS) is a nonprofit 501(c) (3) volunteer-based animal welfare organization dedicated to rescuing homeless dogs and cats from overcrowded shelters. By working with a network of volunteer advocates, foster caregivers, local veterinarians, trainers and shelters, PPS can rescue hundreds of animals every year.

EXECUTIVE SUMMARY

According to the American Society for the Prevention of Cruelty to Animals (ASPCA) approximately 7.6 million companion animals enter animal shelters nationwide every year. Of those, approximately 3.9 million are dogs and 3.4 million are cats. Each year, approximately 2.7 million animals are euthanized (1.2 million dogs and 1.4 million cats). About 2.7 million shelter animals are adopted each year (1.4 million dogs and 1.3 million cats).

Pawsome Pet Sanctuary (PPS) is a nonprofit 501(c) (3) volunteer-based animal welfare organization dedicated to rescuing homeless dogs and cats from overcrowded shelters. By working with a network of volunteer advocates, foster caregivers, local veterinarians, trainers and shelters, PPS can rescue hundreds of animals every year.

We provide these animals with care and temporary homes until we can place them into their permanent homes. We also serve as a resource to our community by providing information on pet ownership, including resources for spay/neuter, positive behavior training, nutrition, and veterinary care. We believe that no animal should be mistreated and are working towards the day when no companion animal is euthanized for lack of a home.

We also believe that adoption is not the only solution to pet overpopulation and the high rates of animal euthanasia. Therefore, we are also dedicated to the process of outreach and education to encourage and assist spaying and neutering of companion animals.

MISSION STATEMENT

The mission of Pawsome Pet Sanctuary is to prevent cruelty to animals by promoting humane standards through education and example, to provide care and shelter for homeless animals, and to provide the best possible care for the animals while in our custody and finding them new permanent, loving homes. Our main goal is to aid in the reduction of domestic animal overpopulation.

BOARD OF DIRECTORS

The Board of Directors of PPS consists of three individuals who are from varying backgrounds yet are united in their dedication to the cause of animal welfare in Placer County.

- **President of the Board:** Guy Anderson has an extensive background in fundraising and grant writing.
- **Secretary:** Milly Powers is the board secretary and has been employed as a paralegal for the Placer Superior Court for the past ten years.
- **Treasurer:** Karen Williams is the board treasurer and is retired from her profession as a licensed CPA.

PPS also has several Members who contribute their time in managing specific programs within the organization.

- **Members include:** Carol McIntyre, Kathy Simon, Sara Dant, Sam Ferris
- The PPS Center Manager is Mary Perrault; Executive Director is Penny Anderson.

Another important and vital aspect of PPS is our association with local veterinarians and a spay/neuter clinic. These organizations have agreed to provide necessary services to our animals at a reduced rate.

HISTORY

Pawsome Pet Sanctuary was founded in 2010 by Mary Perrault and a small band of supporters who envisioned a no-kill, non-profit animal rescue shelter to serve Placer County. After acquiring acreage in the Sierra Foothills of Placer County, Mary became aware of the constant population of feral cats that roam the area. What began as a quest to help manage the population of feral animals in her area evolved into a larger goal of helping all companion animals in Placer County that need a loving home.

Our goal is to help homeless and abused cats and dogs to find a safe living environment be it in a private home or in a sanctuary.

Our facility began in a 1,600-square foot, dedicated single-wide mobile home that is situated on acreage owned by Mary Perrault and her husband. As the years have passed modifications have been made to the facility to add in-door/outdoor animal housing and runs that provide shelter and recreation space for the animal residents. It also allows us to showcase the animals for adoption. We have added office space and expanded our medical services area.

PPS leases one acre of space from Mary Perrault but it owns the building, furnishings and leasehold improvements.

We care for about 350 cats and dogs each year. Our areas of focus include:

- Animals that have been abused.
- Animals at local shelters that are going to be euthanized.
- Animals that are abandoned or whose owners can no longer care for them.

The animal either resides permanently at our facility, is housed with a foster volunteer until it can be adopted, or is adopted into a forever home.

Our "no-kill" philosophy means that animals rescued and formally accepted as a "Pawsome cat or dog" will not be euthanized by PPS unless a condition develops in which there is no hope for recovery and/or quality of life. If adoption is not possible, the animal will receive love, compassion, and care for its lifetime.

Because our philosophy is to help those who cannot help themselves, we do not accept animals surrendered by individuals but refer them to their local animal shelter. Our rescue efforts are focused primarily on the categories outlined above.

While we are committed to helping at-risk animals at shelters to find a forever home, we also believe that the best way to stem the tide of homeless pets is with a comprehensive spay/neuter program. We work with Placer County Animal Services (PCAS), our county animal shelter as well as two veterinarian clinics and Auburn Animal Spay & Neuter Clinic (low-cost clinic) to provide members of our community with free and low-cost spay and neuter services.

ORGANIZATIONAL STRUCTURE

PPS is organized exclusively for charitable and educational purposes related to companion animal rescue. The organization is not-for-profit and obtained 501(c)(3) status from the IRS in 2011. We are committed to fiscal responsibility and conduct independent audits in compliance with state law.

Penny Anderson serves as the executive director of PPS, running the day-to-day operations. Ms. Anderson's position is one of our few paid positions. Other paid staff include: an office manager/bookkeeper and two part-time animal care staff.

In addition, the organization has a volunteer staff consisting of one records manager, two surrender prevention counselors, two adoption coordinators, two foster coordinators, three medical coordinators, one volunteer coordinator, one facility director, two event coordinators (for adoption events), one fundraising coordinator, an animal training specialist, and one grants coordinator.

SERVICES

Our primary purpose is outreach and education to encourage the community to spay and neuter companion animals and to assist them in accomplishing that goal.

Our primary service is fostering and placement of cats and dogs in the community. While cats comprise the majority of our fosters/adoptions, PPS also cares for dogs, and we have taken rabbits, ferrets and other creatures as the need has arisen. We find it easier to specialize in cat care as opposed to other animals which require more care and more personal attention.

We also offer basic medical care to our foster animals. Our medical volunteers undergo training from our nurse volunteers and a few have had formal veterinary assistance training. Two of our volunteers are trained nurses and conduct blood testing.

We document all services in a specialized database that lets us track the progress of each animal. All follow-up services including any post-operative care will be referred to one of our associated veterinarians.

PPS has established a working relationship with two local veterinarians whereby we give an adopter a voucher for a free or reduced rate on their initial visit after adoption. By doing this we hope to encourage the pet owners to maintain an ongoing relationship with their veterinarian thus improving the lives of the animals in their care.

PPS either provides or facilitates the following services to Placer County.

- Testing for common diseases
- Behavior assessment
- Vaccinations

- Flea treatment
- Help in obtaining spay/neuter services for companion animals
- Microchip
- Necessary medical care for our foster animals
- Advice and information on resources to help owners keep their pets
- Post-adoption counseling
- Temporary foster care for homeless and abandoned animals before placing them in safe, caring, forever homes
- Continuing care for animals that cannot be placed in homes
- Assistance for seniors and others who need help in obtaining veterinary services for their animals
- Education in the humane treatment of animals

Animals typically come to PPS from shelters and have already received medical attention, been altered, and micro-chipped. Our focus for these animals is to present them in our adoption venues in order to find them a permanent home. We continue any basic medical care that may be needed and, when specialized care is required, the animal is serviced by one of our associated veterinarians.

At times an animal that has been abandoned, found and then taken to a shelter is evaluated and referred to us directly. So far we have never declined a request for intake. Depending on what the animal requires we will continue with any medical protocol that they need. In most cases the shelter agrees to sponsor the animal and reimburse PPS for its preliminary medical care. We maintain medical records on each animal and bill shelters monthly for reimbursement.

Animals will either reside at our sanctuary facility or will live in a foster home. Our volunteer staff performs basic medical services for our animals two days a week. We document all services in a specialized computer database and provide a journal of care to the adopters.

When they are ready for adoption, the animals will be showcased at our adoption venues where potential adopters can visit and spend quality time with the animals and our adoption counselors. Our volunteer counselors work to match animals with adopters by assessing animal behavior and interviewing prospective adopters.

Adopted animals can be returned to us at any time. In fact, we inform adopters that their contract requires them to return an unwanted animal to us rather than a facility where the animal might be at risk of being euthanized. For this reason, we limit our adoptions to homes located in Western Placer County including Roseville, Lincoln, Rocklin, Penryn, Loomis and Auburn. We also provide resources to encourage adopters to re-home the animal themselves and we ask them to send us contact information on the new adopter.

ADOPTIONS

The adoption center at our sanctuary facility is open to the public from 12 noon to 6 p.m. Wednesday through Sunday. It is closed on Monday and Tuesday and on select holidays. Our web site contains a calendar as well as contact information. Our adoption counselors are also available at PetSmart in Rocklin every Saturday from 12 noon to 6 p.m. We try to have at least 6 to 10 cats at each event and at least 3 to 8 dogs in attendance. Other adoption venues that we use include Petco in Auburn.

The animals are transported to the adoption events by facility volunteers and foster providers. All animals attending the events must be current on their shots and free from any communicable illness. We also require that the animals be able to behave well around strangers.

Not all animals can make it to adoption events so we also feature adoptable animals on our web site and our Facebook page.

Cat Adoptions: In 2015 PPS successfully placed 200 cats into adopted homes. Our goal for this year is to place 240 cats in permanent homes, a 20 percent increase.

Dog Adoptions: In 2015 PPS successfully placed 35 dogs into adopted homes. Our goal for this year is to place at least 50 dogs in forever homes.

FOSTERING

Our network of foster volunteers is the backbone of our organization. Each foster goes through an orientation process where they learn our core values, our programs and services offered, our history and how PPS integrates with other animal organizations in the County.

They also must complete a training program on animal care, animal behavior, common medical issues, documentation and data entry, and tips on how to get their animals adopted. To help our volunteers maintain a quality of service, we provide them with a handbook that details procedures of care and contact information for questions and emergencies. We also offer a refresher course every spring.

PROGRAMS

PPS maintains focused programs to serve the needs of Placer County.

- **SNAP (Spay/Neuter Assistance Program):** A low-cost and no-cost service for pet owners in Roseville and surrounding communities.
- **Mature Cats for Mature People:** A program to place older cats with senior citizens at no cost and with continued support.
- **Adoption Outreach:** Offering animals for adoption at our sanctuary, and at public venues such as PetSmart and Petco.
- **Trap/Neuter/Release:** As a service to the people of Placer County, PPS provides low-cost and no cost spay/neuter services. We lend live traps to help in the capture of stray and feral animals and then take them to a local spay/neuter clinic with which we work. The clinic gives us a deep discount on its services.

Foster and adoption are not our only goals. We also work to encourage pet owners to spay and neuter their companion animals. PPS will continue to develop strategic relationships with local businesses, community groups and individuals who are interested in the welfare of companion animals and willing to help us with our education efforts.

FUNDING

Funding will come from monetary donations, grants, bequests, fundraising events, and adoption fees. PPS keeps its expenses low by maintaining a staff of about 200 dedicated volunteers. All but four positions are unpaid. Therefore, most of our income goes to caring for the animals, community outreach and expanding the organization's operations. Adoption fees are expected to account for about 17 percent of income.

The bulk of our expenses will be for animal care, food, facility leases, veterinary care, trainers, transport, adoption events, outreach, and advertising. We have teamed up with two local veterinarians who give us highly discounted rates. A local spay/neuter clinic provides us services at cost and our local shelter, PCAS performs spay/neuter services at its clinic for any animals that it has agreed to sponsor.

PERSONNEL

In order to keep administration costs to a minimum, PPS has only four paid positions on its staff as follows:

Personnel	Salary
Facility manager	$40,000
Office manager/bookkeeper	$24,000
Animal care (2 part-time)	$24,000
Total administration cost	**$88,000**

MARKETING STRATEGY

PPS has a number of venues through which it reaches the public. Our purpose is to solicit donations, but also to serve as a resource for animal owners and advocates in Placer County.

Web site: Our web site is the primary venue that we use to reach the public. It houses pages that relay our history, purpose, location, contact information, hours of operation, adoption venue locations, pet care and adoption resources, calendar of adoption events, past newsletters, a contact form, donation button, and subscription sign-up button for our newsletter.

Social media: We use our sites on Facebook and Instagram to promote our adoption events, our animals and our fundraisers.

Newsletter: Our quarterly newsletter is mailed to subscribers and includes updates on facility operations, adoption success stories, adoption events, pet care and new adoption tips. Each newsletter also includes a call to action requesting a donation and encouraging supporters to volunteer their time.

We are fortunate to have a staff member who is also an avid photographer. She donates her time to create appealing photos of animals, events and volunteers for our newsletter, web site and other marketing materials.

FUNDRAISERS

Events: Throughout the year we take advantage of public events such as Giving Tuesday, a global day dedicated to giving.

Amazon Smile: We encourage our supporters to participate in the Amazon Smile program where Amazon will donate a portion of eligible purchases to our organization.

Vehicle donations: This year we partnered with DonateCarUSA, a nationwide program where the public can fill in an online form or call an 800 number to donate their car. The car is picked up for free the next day and the donor gets a tax deduction for the fair market value up to $500, whichever is greater. PPS receives a portion of the sale of the vehicle.

Grapes of Love: Placer County is the home for several wineries. Each summer we hold an event where the public can sample and learn about these wines while meeting our animals. Corporate sponsorship has allowed us to include a raffle, food, and live music to complete the experience.

GRANTS

In 2015 we secured a grant from a local group to help cover the costs of food. We recently completed a grant application that would help us purchase more cages for our facility. We are also reaching out to local corporations to ask for donations in funding or in products.

RECORDKEEPING

In addition to using AC+ Rescue Connection online database for keeping medical records, PPS is using QuickBooks Premier desktop software for its financial recordkeeping. The financial statements are being audited each year. This year they will be audited by Tom Powers, CPA.

FUTURE PLANS

In 2017 PPS plans to open a thrift store and café in old-town Roseville. We have found the perfect location in the heart of the shopping district. The area has undergone significant renovation in the past two years including the addition of a two-story parking garage. The area is also home to popular establishments such as the Monks Cellar Microbrewery and Restaurant, Royer Park which hosts several public events during the year, and Sierra College Community Education Campus.

We plan to recruit a staff of volunteers who will stock and staff the store which will include a small enclosed "café" area where patrons can enjoy free coffee and tea while they meet and greet several of our foster animals who are ready for adoption.

A lease has been signed for the location and we move in on February 1, 2017. We have already started holding fundraisers to fuel an operating fund to lease and decorate the store. To get the inventory started we have leased out space in the store to several area artists and crafters who will sell their items on consignment. As part of their lease arrangement, each vendor must agree to staff the store at least four hours per week.

The store will be open Tuesday through Saturday from 10 a.m. to 6 p.m.

Our web site, marketing materials, and newsletter include information about the store along with requests for donations of goods to the store.

FINANCIAL DOCUMENTS

Startup Item	Cost
Building	$16,000
Renovations	$30,000
Furnishings	$ 3,000
Medical equipment	$ 4,500
Supplies	$ 750
Staff training	$ 250
Marketing, fundraising	$ 1,800
Working capital	$ 2,200
Total startup cost	**$58,500**

		2017 Budget (projected)
Revenue		
Donations		$ 85,000
Grants		$ 12,000
Program services		$ 25,000
Adoption fees		$ 45,000
Investments		$ 200
Thrift store sales		$ 42,000
Thrift store vendor lease fees		$ 14,000
Fundraising events	$25,500	
Less: direct expenses fundraising events	$ 3,500	
Net income: fundraising events		$ 22,000
Total revenue		**$245,200**
Expenses		
Lease fees: Facility location	$12,000	
Lease: thrift store	$24,000	
Payroll	$88,000	
Payroll taxes/benefits	$13,200	
Vet care	$26,000	
Medication/vaccines	$ 7,000	
Food	$ 8,000	
Special food	$ 2,000	
Supplies	$ 2,500	
Advertising/promotion	$ 2,200	
Office expense	$ 1,000	
Insurance	$ 5,000	
Legal	$ 1,200	
Auditing	$ 1,000	
Depreciation	$ 6,500	
Utilities/telephone	$ 2,800	
Web hosting/maintenance	$ 1,200	
Printing	$ 1,200	
Postage	$ 2,000	
Training materials/supplies	$ 1,300	
Repairs/maintenance	$ 700	
Cleaning/supplies	$ 750	
Transportation	$ 2,500	
Software fees	$ 3,200	
Bank/PayPal fees	$ 1,100	
Sales tax	$ 1,500	
Total expenses		**$217,850**
Net income		**$ 27,350**

Proforma Balance Sheet (projected)

[December 31, 2017]

Assets		
Current assets		
Cash	$20,000	
Savings	$ 5,000	
Pledges	$ 2,000	
Total current assets		**$27,000**
Property, plant, equipment		
Equipment	$ 7,500	
Building	$16,000	
Improvements	$32,000	
Less: accumulated depreciation	$ (6,500)	$ 49,000
Total assets		**$76,000**
Liabilities		
Current liabilities		
Accounts payable		$ 1,850
Capital		
Paid in capital	$20,000	
Retained earnings	$26,800	
Earnings	$27,350	
Total capital		**$74,150**
Total liabilities and capital		**$76,000**

Private Investigator

FBEyes

210 Huntington St.
Midland, TX 04401

Gerald Rekve

This business plan details the goals and objectives for an independent Private Investigator (PI) firm founded by three former police officers.

This business plan appeared in ***Business Plans Handbook, Volume 11.*** *It has been updated for this volume.*

EXECUTIVE SUMMARY

FBEyes was founded in 2017, by three former police officers. They're friends from the same police force for over 30 years.

In this time the three had gone different paths in the Midland Police force. James Walsh had spent the majority of his career in the fraud section. Colin Day had spent the majority of his time in the narcotics division. Finally Greg Baker had focused his entire career on the administration and management of the police force. While all three partners of the newly formed FBEyes firm had spent their careers in separate divisions of this large police force, they all had one thing in common. They enjoyed the investigation part of their job and had taken all the required steps to educate themselves on all aspects of their respective job functions. These skills had not only made them leaders in their divisions, it also gave them a great amount of access to other police forces in other cities.

All three had decided to take early retirement in order for them to launch their own private investigation firm. While there was a substantial amount of competition from the long-established firms, all three based their decision on solid market statistics that supported the decision to open their own PI firm.

Over a period of twelve months prior to their official retirement, all three members spent their free time gathering and working on the business plan. The also hired a management consulting firm to work with them to build the business plan and look for outside opinions on the business sector.

While most PI firms were a one or two person operation, which focused on the basics of the industry like surveillance and searching for people, etc., FBEyes decided that, while this was a good area, they also wanted to add all their backgrounds and training to the business. Therefore throughout the formulation of the business plan and model these specialized skills were added to the firm's services it would offer to the market.

PRODUCTS & SERVICES

Based on the market, as well the background and training of the three partners within FBEyes, the products and services offered have been determined as follows:

1. Background checks for employers.
2. Fraud investigations for companies when a company reports suspected fraud from an employee. This can also be hired by local police forces, where subjective investigation is required.
3. Competition search for when a company thinks their copyright or products are being copied or sold.
4. Standard surveillance of husbands or wives' promiscuity. This area has a lot of competition; however the partners felt that with their training, they would attract higher paying clients allowing for more of an executive type of client base. Not to mention this area has the highest percentage of income for most PI companies and cannot be overlooked.
5. Bounty hunting. This area is another strong point for FBEyes. With the training as well as work experience, the partners felt they know where to look and the skills required to gain the trust of police forces and clients. The skills of FBEyes would result in quick capture of runners and turn into fast cash flow for the firm. This area would be subcontracted to other officers who still work in the police force, but want to earn money from a part-time job. The present laws in the region allow for police officers to work in similar jobs as long as no information is used from police databases and/or files.
6. Missing persons. This area, while small, still has a lot of potential. Due to the large work load of local police forces, most MPs do not get the proper investigations unless they are deemed to be of a criminal nature. The base fee for this service is high. Part of the reason for this, however, is that we will offer this service free to specific cases, like children or lower income cases. Each case will be reviewed on an individual basis.
7. Stolen Property. This is most likely going to be one of our smaller areas of business services. However due to the large amount of unreported stolen property that takes place each year in the region, we feel with the training and backgrounds that we have in this area we could offer a service and make money at the same time. A large percentage of stolen property is taken by the same criminals or rings. Due to large insurance costs, most businesses don't report items stolen, simply because of the cost of insurance is increased and these costs in most cases, especially when items are less than $5,000 in value, aren't worth reporting to the police force.

COMPETITION

In the present market we have the following competitors:

1. Glassman Investigators—They have been in business for 20 years; they only provide services to the surveillance and missing persons sectors. They are a ten–employee firm that has built a solid foundation in the market. They tend not to target the corporate arena, just the private person market.
2. Hayes Investigations Inc.—This is a large firm that offers services to all the same areas we will be offering. They have been in business for 25 years and a strong affiliation with a national private investor chain. They tend to charge the highest fees and don't seem to have any difficulty getting enough clients to pay these fees. Hayes employs 20 full-time investigators and 10 part-time. Actually, two of the founders of FBEyes had worked for Hayes for 5 years on a part-time basis.

3. Spyware Investigations—This two–person firm only specializes in surveillance area, mostly in marriage/divorce situations. Most of their leads and clients come from lawyers wanting to better their clients' cases with video tape or pictures.
4. There are about four more firms that are run by a single person owner/manager. These firms tend to only get enough revenue to meet the costs of the firm and that is it. There is no growth in this area.
5. The area where we will most likely see the biggest competition will be from outside national chain investigator firms. These firms are hired and basically flown into our market to do their work. Because most of the skills and needs of the clients are such that the company doing the hiring feel, it is required that they hire these firms. With our market research, we have determined that the hiring companies would rather hire a local firm to do the work simply because they feel we would have a better understanding of the market, and therefore would be able to provide quicker and more cost-effective services.

As mentioned in the above competitor breakdown, we have indicated the areas where each competitor focuses all their attention. This in–depth understanding of each competitor's area of expertise will allow us to get a much faster footprint in the market, at a quicker rate.

During the twelve months preceding the launch of our firm, all three partners spent time preparing the company. While each partner when they retire will only be in the age group of 50–54, none of them will require taking a salary from the firm. With their early retirement package they all received a bonus payout of $300,000–$400,000. This, combined with the fact that all partners were wise investors and are debt free, make this possible.

While most start–up companies tend to start with a lot of debt in the first few years, FBEyes will not be in this position. All the required software and training have already been paid for. The only startup expenses are that of advertising and office set-up. It was felt by all partners that an office should be established; while most in this sector tend to be home-based, the clients we were going after, i.e. corporate, would like to have a place they could go to meet, allowing the client to meet in a more confidential manner with our firm. This was really important in cases of fraud and other sensitive topics.

With the start–up it was decided that each partner would focus on their area of expertise and as required would hire contract staff to fill in where they could not.

The key to our strategy will be to make slow inroads into the established markets. This would allow us to grow at our own pace and keep our competitors in the market from noticing our presence. We will take the approach of the turtle in the race, not that of the rabbit.

While we will be bringing specialized skills to the market, we feel there will be times where we will collaborate with other firms, offer advice and/or our services. Over time we feel this will be a key to building strong relationships with our key clients and partners.

MARKETING & SALES

The forms of marketing we will use to market FBEyes:

1. Word-of-mouth—clients telling other clients about our service.
2. Former working relationships we had with others in the police force.
3. Yellow Pages advertising—this will be a small portion of our client acquisitions, yet a required expense.
4. Law firms—we will actively target these firms for business and referrals.

5. Charity work in the community—while this may not seem like a place to find clients, it in our opinion is key to our success. There are a lot of solid relationships made while donating your time.
6. Other police forces around the country, where we will offer specialized forms of services to this sector.
7. We will also offer local newspapers and/or magazines a weekly or monthly editorial column. This will allow us to be known for our services, while getting exposure to our market for free. Nobody in our market does this presently and we have inquired with local newspapers and magazines. Both provided support and said would even pay us for the editorial.
8. We will post a web site that offers free advice to anyone wanting information. Due to legal limitations we cannot go into details in this section. But we will post good, general information about areas of interest to our readers.

Market Analysis

The city of Midland has close to 133,000 people living in the city, with an estimated population of 296,000 in the Midland-Odessa, Texas Combined Statistical Area. This is a new city in the sense of cities. During the 1970s, the population of Midland was around 60,000. However, the oil and energy crises of that decade resulted in an increased demand for petroleum and natural gas from the fields of West Texas. Consequently, Midland grew at an extraordinary pace over the successive decades. This pace of growth has allowed the city to spend billions on infrastructure. While the positives of this growth are evident, the not-so-glamorous area of crime and criminal activities has also flourished.

Based on our Market Analysis we have determined that there is $40,000,000 spent in our sector each year. Our goal is to attain at least 5% of this market in the first two years.

The types of clients and the average per–use charges

1. Typical Surveillance—$700 per day
2. Fraud Investigations—$1500 per day
3. Bounty Hunter—35% of fee paid to courts for bail jumping
4. Background Checks—start at $500 and can go as high as $10,000 based on amount of detail required and position in company of the person being hired.

Note: all the above fees are expense–extra–based.

We have already talked with a few clients and they have signed formal agreements, that when we open, we will be contracted to do work for them. Based on previous three–year average of expenditures, we have determined that this will amount to approximately $300,000 per year in revenue to our firm. Other clients have indicated that, while they could not make a commitment at the time, they would ask us for a quote when they tender certain jobs.

As noted here, all of our revenue contracts we have in place are from companies. Once we advertise that we are in business, we are confident that we will gain a market share of the independent market, and based on the services we will offer, this will come from areas of service we offer that is required in our market, but not yet offered by local firms.

At the present rate of growth, we are very confident that the opening of our firm will position us in the next three years to have hired at least 20 contract investigators.

Over the career of all the partners, they were able to build very strong relationships with other employees in the police force. These relationships allowed the management of the firm to cultivate the ability to add contract staff needed over time. The vast amount of qualified contract staff available to sub–contract for us, will allow us to grow our business at a faster rate of growth than would be normally expected.

Most sub–contractors just want to make a little additional income on a part–time basis. On average these contractors can make $10,000–$20,000 per year from us.

FINANCIAL ANALYSIS

With the start up of FBEyes, each partner invested $10,000 for a total of $30,000; this was to cover the following:

1. Office Rental—$800 per month
2. Telephone Equipment—$1500
3. Incorporation Cost—$700
4. Business License—$220
5. Office Equipment—$2200
6. Computers—$5700
7. Furniture—$2500
8. Supplies—$700
9. Yellow Page Ad (Prepay)—$1600
10. Specialized Equipment—$5600 (already paid)
11. Specialized Software—$8900 (already paid)
12. Lease Company vehicles—$1200 per month
13. Legal Costs—$2000

Some or most of these expenses were paid for by the partners prior to the opening of FBEyes. That being said, the strength of the company is in great start–up shape. No debt and no cash flow pressures on the partners personally or for the company, will allow the partners to grow the company in a stress free situation.

Process Serving Business

Morgan Legal Services

789 E 33rd St.
New York, NY 10153

BizPlanDB.com

Morgan Legal Services will provide serving of legal documents to individuals on behalf of attorneys and the courts in its targeted market. The Company was founded by Robert Morgan.

This business plan appeared in ***Business Plans Handbook, Volume 23.*** *It has been updated for this volume.*

1.0 EXECUTIVE SUMMARY

The purpose of this business plan is to raise $115,000 for the development of a process serving business while showcasing the expected financials and operations over the next three years. Morgan Legal Services ("the Company") is a New York-based corporation that will provide serving of legal documents to individuals on behalf of attorneys and the courts in its targeted market. The Company was founded by Robert Morgan.

1.1 The Services

The primary revenue center will come from serving official court documents to individuals on behalf of courts and attorneys throughout the New York metropolitan area. The business will be appropriately licensed to go onto people's premises to hand official court documents to persons and businesses. At all times, the business will comply with all state and federal laws regarding the serving of official legal documents. At no time will an employee violate these laws especially as they relate to trespassing.

The third section of the business plan will further describe the services offered by the Morgan Legal Services.

1.2 Financing

Mr. Morgan is seeking to raise $115,000 from a bank loan. The interest rate and loan agreement are to be further discussed during negotiation. This business plan assumes that the business will receive a 10-year loan with a 9% fixed interest rate. The financing will be used for the following:

- Development of the office.
- Financing for the first six months of operation.
- Capital to purchase a company vehicle.

Mr. Morgan will contribute $11,500 to the venture.

1.3 Mission Statement

The mission of Morgan Legal Services is to become the recognized leader in its targeted market for processing serving services.

1.4 Management Team

The Company was founded by Robert Morgan. Mr. Morgan has more than 10 years of experience in the paralegal and legal support industry. Through his expertise, he will be able to bring the operations of the business to profitability within its first year of operations.

1.5 Sales Forecasts

Mr. Morgan expects a strong rate of growth at the start of operations. Below are the expected financials over the next three years.

Proforma profit and loss (yearly)

Year	1	2	3
Sales	$468,945	$506,460	$546,977
Operating costs	$339,490	$381,449	$425,694
EBITDA	$ 82,560	$ 74,366	$ 66,585
Taxes, interest, and depreciation	$ 46,144	$ 38,780	$ 35,350
Net profit	$ 36,416	$ 35,586	$ 31,234

Sales, Operating Costs, and Profit Forecast

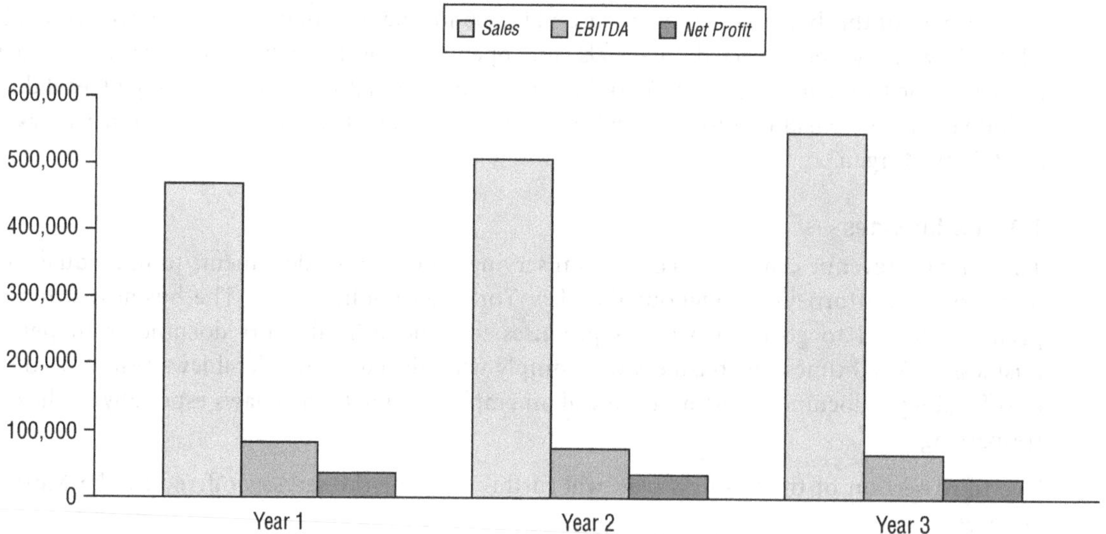

1.6 Expansion Plan

The Founder expects that the business will aggressively expand during the first three years of operation. Mr. Morgan intends to implement marketing campaigns that will effectively target law firms that have process serving needs within the target market.

2.0 COMPANY AND FINANCING SUMMARY

2.1 Registered Name and Corporate Structure

Morgan Legal Services is registered as a corporation in the State of New York.

2.2 Required Funds

At this time, Morgan Legal Services requires $115,000 of debt funds. Below is a breakdown of how these funds will be used:

Projected Startup Costs

Initial lease payments and deposits	$ 11,500
Working capital	$ 40,250
FF&E	$ 26,450
Leasehold improvements	$ 5,750
Security deposits	$ 5,750
Insurance	$ 2,875
Vehicle(s)	$ 19,550
Marketing budget	$ 8,625
Miscellaneous and unforeseen costs	$ 5,750
Total startup costs	**$126,500**

Use of Funds

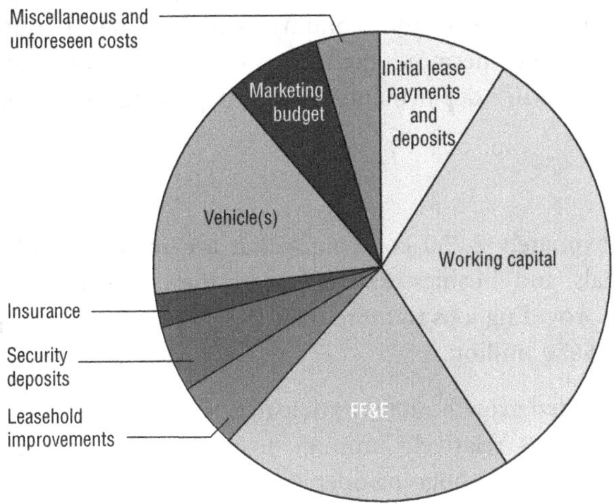

2.3 Investor Equity

Mr. Morgan is not seeking an investment from a third party at this time.

2.4 Management Equity

Robert Morgan owns 100% of the Morgan Legal Services.

2.5 Exit Strategy

If the business is very successful, Mr. Morgan may seek to sell the business to a third party for a significant earnings multiple. Most likely, the Company will hire a qualified business broker to sell the business on behalf of Morgan Legal Services. Based on historical numbers, the business could fetch a sales premium of up to 2 to 4 times the previous year's earnings.

3.0 PRODUCTS AND SERVICES

Below is a description of the services offered by Morgan Legal Services.

3.1 Process Serving

As discussed in the executive summary, Morgan Legal Services (through its employees) will provide legal support services as it relates to serving court papers, official documents, and subpoenas to individuals and businesses throughout the New York metropolitan area. The business is currently in the process of receiving its appropriate licensure to act as a process serving business within the State of New York.

Mr. Morgan is also developing a number of protocols and procedures that ensure that process servers comply with all laws regarding the serving of government-issued and court-issued documents.

4.0 STRATEGIC AND MARKET ANALYSIS

4.1 Economic Outlook

This section of the analysis will detail the economic climate, the process serving industry, the customer profile, and the competition that the business will face as it progresses through its business operations.

Currently, the economic market condition in the United States is moderate. Regardless, Morgan Legal Services is relatively immune from significant changes in the economy as the serving of court-issued documents is required in any economic climate. Furthermore, the rising number of civil lawsuits bodes well for process servers, especially since some sheriff's departments are now beginning to rely on private process servers for timeliness and efficiency.

4.2 Industry Analysis

Within the United States, there are approximately 2,750 companies that are involved with serving official and legal documents to individuals and businesses. Each year, these businesses generate approximately $2.1 billion of revenue while providing jobs to more than 18,000 people. Annual payrolls in each of the last five years have exceeded $650 million.

This is a mature industry, and the future expected growth rate is anticipated to remain on par with that of the general economy. Again, this industry is relatively immune from negative changes in the economy. There is no pending legislation related to the ongoing operation of process serving businesses.

4.3 Customer Profile

Morgan Legal Services's average client will be a law firm or individual attorney practicing in the company's target market. Common traits among clients will include:

- Annual billings exceeding $345,000 per year.
- Operates within 15 miles from the company's location.
- Will spend $230 per serving of documents to an individual or business.

Within the company's targeted market, there are more than 55,000 practicing attorneys within approximately 1/3 of these practitioners operating in a group practice capacity. As such, the business will be able to call on a number of potential clients for their process serving needs.

4.4 Competition

Within the New York metropolitan market, there are approximately 425 companies that are able to provide process serving services on behalf of attorneys, paralegals, and courts. In order to successfully launch business operations, it will be imperative for Morgan Legal Services to provide discounts to new clients. Management will also need to clearly showcase the firm's ability to quickly and properly serve individuals with paperwork.

5.0 MARKETING PLAN

Morgan Legal Services intends to maintain an extensive marketing campaign that will ensure maximum visibility for the business in its targeted market. Below is an overview of the marketing strategies and objectives of Morgan Legal Services.

5.1 Marketing Objectives

- Establish relationships with individually practicing attorneys, law firms, and government agencies within the company's targeted New York market.
- Develop ongoing relationships with other organizations that frequently need process serving and delivery of legal documents.

5.2 Marketing Strategies

Mr. Morgan intends on using a number of marketing strategies that will allow Morgan Legal Services to easily market to the demographics discussed in the fourth section of the business plan within the target market.

The first prong of the company's marketing strategy consists of Mr. Morgan directly contacting attorneys, law firms, law enforcement agencies, and courts in regards to developing ongoing relationships for their process serving needs.

Morgan Legal Services will also use an internet-based strategy. This is very important as many attorneys, paralegals, and law firms frequently begin their searches for finding process servers by searching the internet. The business will have a web development company establish a highly interactive website that showcases the services of the company, costs associated with process serving, the company's licensure to act as a process serving company in the State of New York, and how to contact the business.

Finally, the Company will regularly take out print advertisements within prominent New York-based legal periodicals and within publications that are produced and distributed by the American Bar Association and the New York Bar Association.

5.3 Pricing

For each serving of legal documents, the business will generate $125 to $350 per transaction. Fees will range depending on how difficult it was to serve the party with legal documents.

6.0 ORGANIZATIONAL PLAN AND PERSONNEL SUMMARY

6.1 Corporate Organization

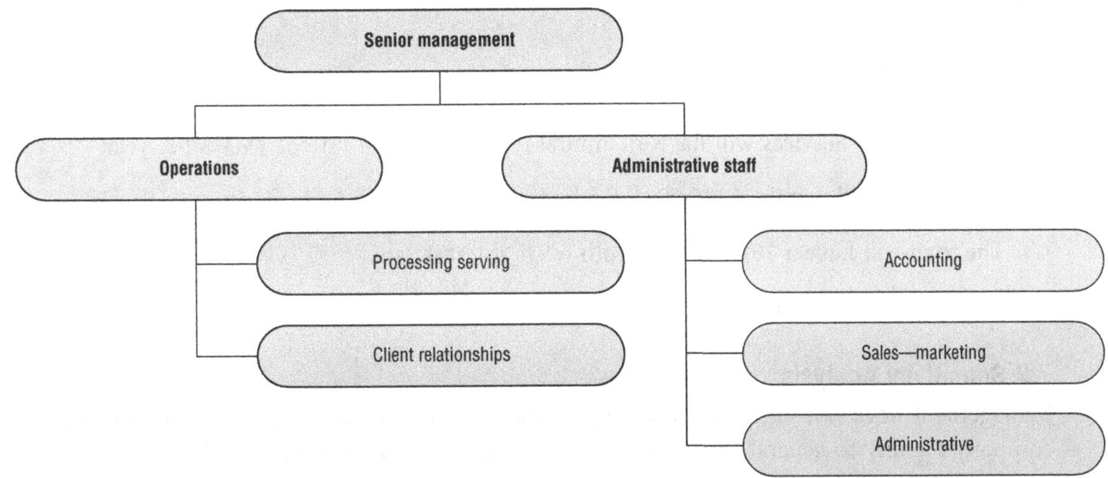

6.2 Organizational Budget

Personnel plan—yearly

Year	1	2	3
Owner	$ 46,000	$ 47,380	$ 48,801
General manager	$ 40,250	$ 41,458	$ 42,702
Owner's assistant	$ 37,375	$ 38,496	$ 39,651
Process servers	$ 75,900	$104,236	$134,204
Administrative	$ 28,750	$ 29,613	$ 30,501
Total	**$228,275**	**$261,183**	**$295,859**
Numbers of personnel			
Owner	1	1	1
General manager	1	1	1
Owner's assistant	1	1	1
Process servers	3	4	5
Administrative	2	2	2
Total	**8**	**9**	**10**

Personnel Expense Breakdown

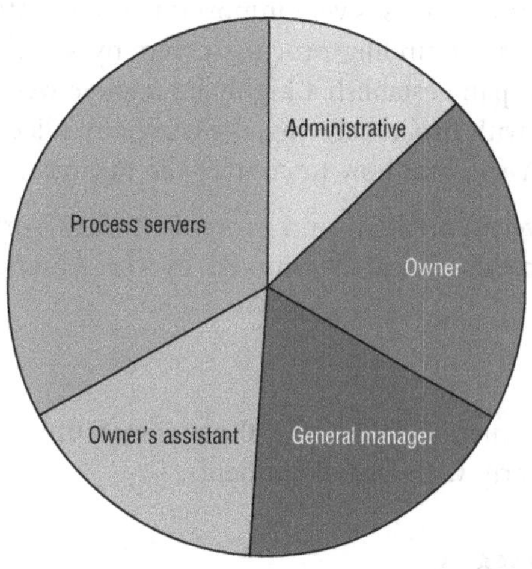

7.0 FINANCIAL PLAN

7.1 Underlying Assumptions

The Company has based its proforma financial statements on the following:

- Morgan Legal Services will have an annual revenue growth rate of 13.3% per year.
- The Owner will acquire $115,000 of debt funds to develop the business.
- The loan will have a 10-year term with a 9% interest rate.
- Management will settle most short-term payables on a monthly basis.

7.2 Sensitivity Analysis

Management does not anticipate that any further negative issues with the economy will hinder the company's ability to generate revenues as courts and law firms will continue to require process serving in any economic climate.

7.3 Source of Funds

Financing

Equity contributions	
Management investment	$ 11,500.00
Total equity financing	**$ 11,500.00**
Banks and lenders	
Banks and lenders	$115,000.00
Total debt financing	**$115,000.00**
Total financing	**$126,500.00**

7.4 General Assumptions

Year	1	2	3
Short term interest rate	9.5%	9.5%	9.5%
Long term interest rate	10.0%	10.0%	10.0%
Federal tax rate	33.0%	33.0%	33.0%
State tax rate	5.0%	5.0%	5.0%
Personnel taxes	15.0%	15.0%	15.0%

7.5 Profit and Loss Statements

Year	1	2	3
Sales	**$468,945**	**$506,460**	**$546,977**
Cost of goods sold	$ 46,895	$ 50,646	$ 54,697
Gross margin	90.00%	90.00%	90.00%
Operating income	**$422,050**	**$455,814**	**$492,279**
Expenses			
Payroll	$228,275	$261,182	$295,858
General and administrative	$ 28,980	$ 30,139	$ 31,344
Marketing expenses	$ 2,345	$ 2,532	$ 2,735
Professional fees and licensure	$ 6,002	$ 6,182	$ 6,368
Insurance costs	$ 2,285	$ 2,399	$ 2,520
Travel and vehicle costs	$ 8,735	$ 9,609	$ 10,570
Rent and utilities	$ 23,000	$ 24,150	$ 25,358
Miscellaneous costs	$ 5,627	$ 6,078	$ 6,564
Payroll taxes	$ 34,241	$ 39,177	$ 44,379
Total operating costs	**$339,490**	**$381,449**	**$425,694**
EBITDA	**$ 82,560**	**$ 74,366**	**$ 66,585**
Federal income tax	$ 27,245	$ 21,454	$ 19,138
State income tax	$ 4,129	$ 3,251	$ 2,900
Interest expense	$ 10,049	$ 9,351	$ 8,588
Depreciation expenses	$ 4,723	$ 4,723	$ 4,723
Net profit	**$ 36,416**	**$ 35,586**	**$ 31,234**
Profit margin	**7.77%**	**7.03%**	**5.71%**

Sales, Operating Costs, and Profit Forecast

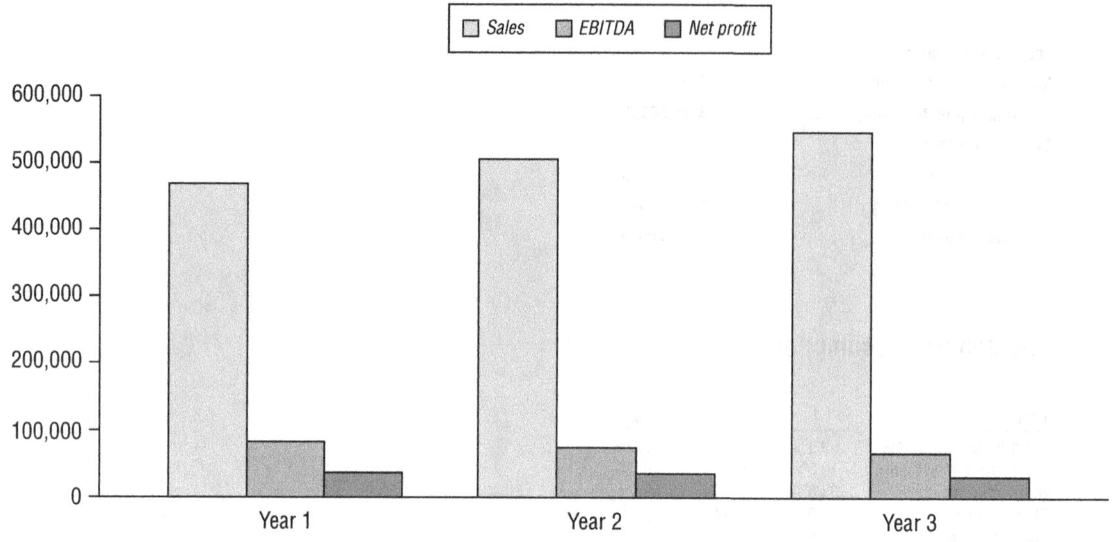

7.6 Cash Flow Analysis

Year	1	2	3
Cash from operations	$ 41,139	$40,309	$35,958
Cash from receivables	$ —	$ —	$ —
Operating cash inflow	**$ 41,139**	**$40,309**	**$35,958**
Other cash inflows			
Equity investment	$ 11,500	$ —	$ —
Increased borrowings	$115,000	$ —	$ —
Sales of business assets	$ —	$ —	$ —
A/P increases	$ 43,587	$50,125	$57,644
Total other cash inflows	**$170,087**	**$50,125**	**$57,644**
Total cash inflow	**$211,226**	**$90,435**	**$93,602**
Cash outflows			
Repayment of principal	$ 7,432	$ 8,131	$ 8,893
A/P decreases	$ 28,632	$34,357	$41,230
A/R increases	$ —	$ —	$ —
Asset purchases	$ 66,125	$ 6,047	$ 5,394
Dividends	$ 32,911	$32,247	$28,766
Total cash outflows	**$135,101**	**$80,782**	**$84,282**
Net cash flow	**$ 76,125**	**$ 9,653**	**$ 9,320**
Cash balance	**$ 76,125**	**$85,779**	**$95,098**

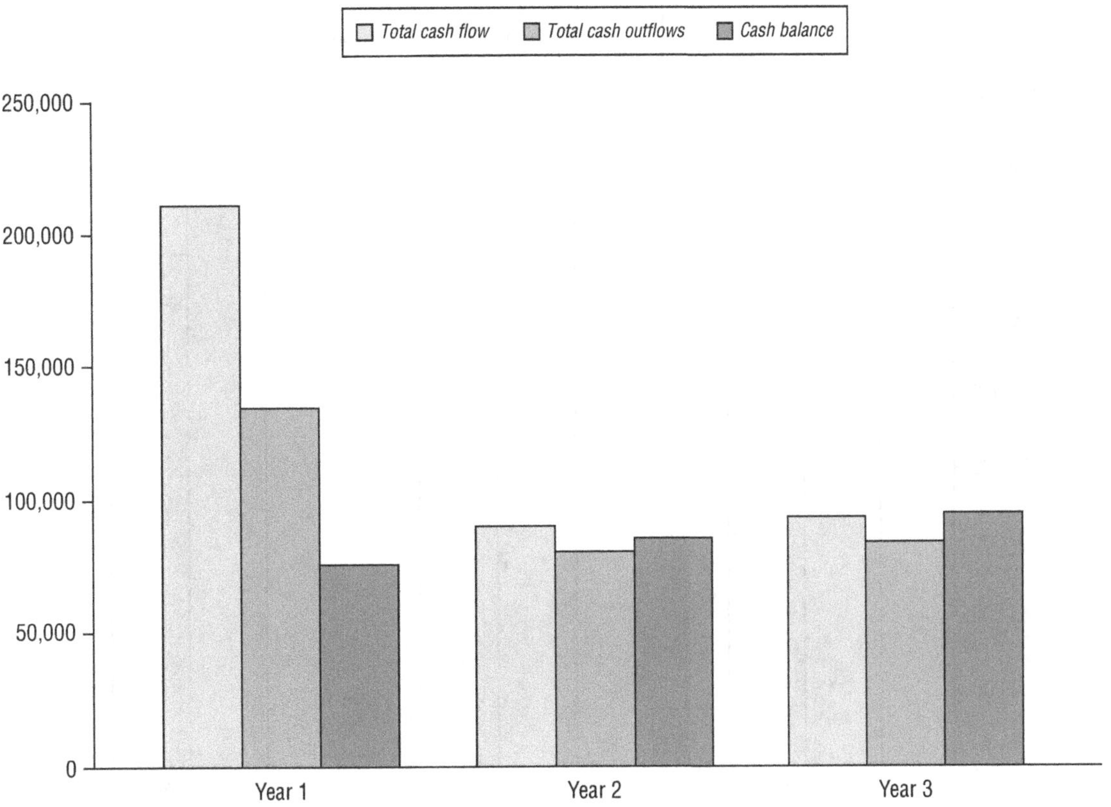

7.7 Balance Sheet

Year	1	2	3
Assets			
Cash	$ 76,125	$ 85,779	$ 95,098
Amortized development/expansion costs	$ 20,125	$ 20,730	$ 21,269
Vehicles	$ 19,550	$ 24,084	$ 28,130
FF&E	$ 26,450	$ 27,357	$ 28,166
Accumulated depreciation	($ 1,273)	($ 9,446)	($ 14,169)
Total assets	**$137,527**	**$148,503**	**$158,494**
Liabilities and equity			
Accounts payable	$ 14,956	$ 30,723	$ 47,139
Long term liabilities	$ 107,568	$ 99,437	$ 91,307
Other liabilities	$ —	$ —	$ —
Total liabilities	**$122,523**	**$130,160**	**$138,445**
Net worth	**$ 15,004**	**$ 18,344**	**$ 20,049**
Total liabilities and equity	**$137,527**	**$148,503**	**$158,494**

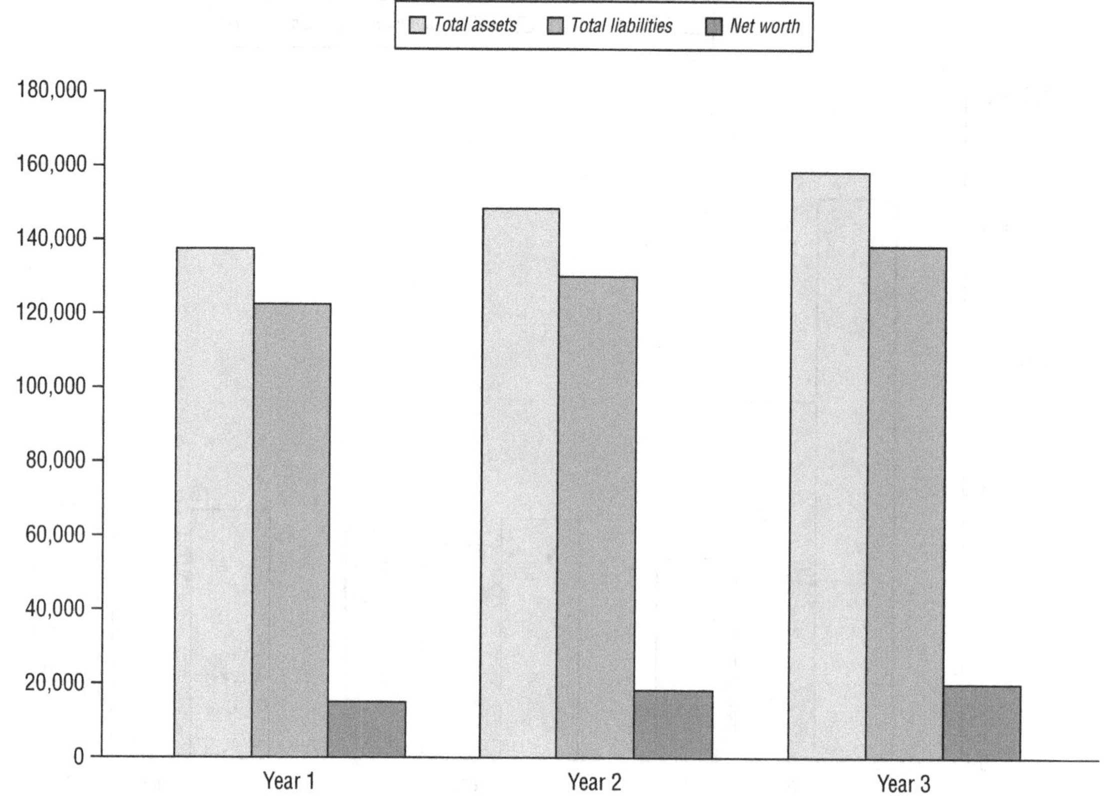

7.8 Breakeven Analysis

Year	1	2	3
Monthly revenue	$ 31,434	$ 35,319	$ 39,416
Yearly revenue	$377,212	$423,833	$472,994

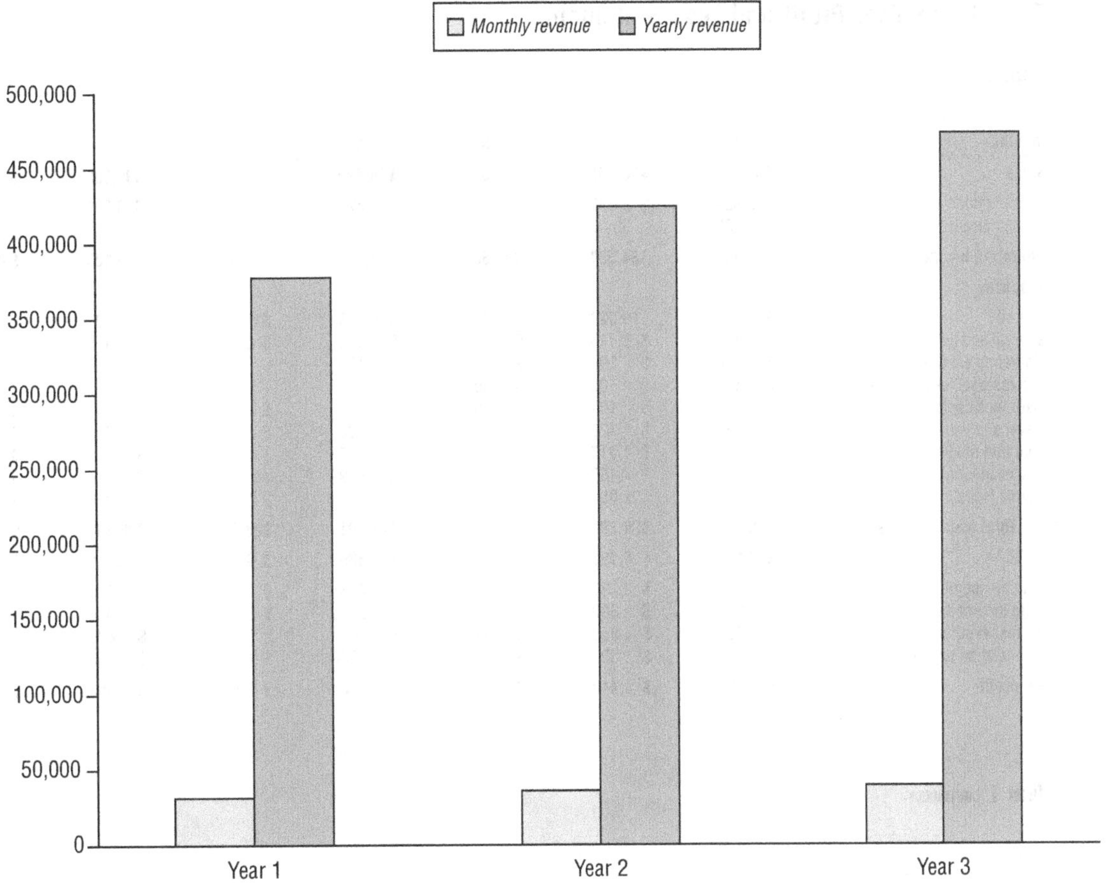

7.9 Business Ratios

Year	1	2	3
Sales			
Sales growth	0.00%	8.0%	8.0%
Gross margin	90.0%	90.0%	90.0%
Financials			
Profit margin	7.77%	7.03%	5.71%
Assets to liabilities	1.12	1.14	1.14
Equity to liabilities	0.12	0.14	0.14
Assets to equity	9.17	8.10	7.91
Liquidity			
Acid test	0.62	0.66	0.69
Cash to assets	0.55	0.58	0.60

7.10 Three Year Profit and Loss Statement

Year 1

Months	1	2	3	4	5	6	7
Sales	**$38,238**	**$38,390**	**$38,543**	**$38,696**	**$38,849**	**$39,002**	**$39,155**
Cost of goods sold	$ 3,824	$ 3,839	$ 3,855	$ 3,870	$ 3,885	$ 3,901	$ 3,916
Gross margin	90.00%	90.00%	90.00%	90.00%	90.00%	90.00%	90.00%
Operating income	**$34,414**	**$34,552**	**$34,689**	**$34,827**	**$34,965**	**$35,103**	**$35,239**
Expenses							
Payroll	$19,023	$19,023	$19,023	$19,023	$19,023	$19,023	$19,023
General and administrative	$ 2,415	$ 2,415	$ 2,415	$ 2,415	$ 2,415	$ 2,415	$ 2,415
Marketing expenses	$ 196	$ 196	$ 196	$ 196	$ 196	$ 196	$ 196
Professional fees and licensure	$ 500	$ 500	$ 500	$ 500	$ 500	$ 500	$ 500
Insurance costs	$ 191	$ 191	$ 191	$ 191	$ 191	$ 191	$ 191
Travel and vehicle costs	$ 728	$ 728	$ 728	$ 728	$ 728	$ 728	$ 728
Rent and utilities	$ 1,917	$ 1,917	$ 1,917	$ 1,917	$ 1,917	$ 1,917	$ 1,917
Miscellaneous costs	$ 469	$ 469	$ 469	$ 469	$ 469	$ 469	$ 469
Payroll taxes	$ 2,853	$ 2,853	$ 2,853	$ 2,853	$ 2,853	$ 2,853	$ 2,853
Total operating costs	**$28,291**	**$28,291**	**$28,291**	**$28,291**	**$28,291**	**$28,291**	**$28,291**
EBITDA	**$ 6,123**	**$ 6,123**	**$ 6,399**	**$ 6,535**	**$ 6,673**	**$ 6,811**	**$ 6,948**
Federal income tax	$ 2,222	$ 2,230	$ 2,239	$ 2,248	$ 2,257	$ 2,266	$ 2,275
State income tax	$ 337	$ 338	$ 339	$ 340	$ 342	$ 344	$ 345
Interest expense	$ 863	$ 858	$ 853	$ 849	$ 844	$ 840	$ 835
Depreciation expenses	$ 393	$ 393	$ 393	$ 393	$ 393	$ 393	$ 393
Net profit	**$ 2,309**	**$ 2,440**	**$ 2,573**	**$ 2,705**	**$ 2,836**	**$ 2,968**	**$ 3,100**

Year 1 [CONTINUED]

Months	8	9	10	11	12	Total
Sales	**$39,308**	**$39,461**	**$39,614**	**$39,767**	**$39,920**	**$468,945**
Cost of goods sold	$ 3,931	$ 3,946	$ 3,962	$ 3,977	$ 3,992	$ 46,895
Gross margin	90.00%	90.00%	90.00%	90.00%	90.00%	90.00%
Operating income	**$35,377**	**$35,515**	**$35,652**	**$35,790**	**$35,928**	**$422,050**
Expenses						
Payroll	$19,023	$19,023	$19,023	$19,023	$19,023	$228,275
General and administrative	$ 2,415	$ 2,415	$ 2,415	$ 2,415	$ 2,415	$ 28,980
Marketing expenses	$ 196	$ 196	$ 196	$ 196	$ 196	$ 2,345
Professional fees and licensure	$ 500	$ 500	$ 500	$ 500	$ 500	$ 6,002
Insurance costs	$ 191	$ 191	$ 191	$ 191	$ 191	$ 2,285
Travel and vehicle costs	$ 728	$ 728	$ 728	$ 728	$ 728	$ 8,735
Rent and utilities	$ 1,917	$ 1,917	$ 1,917	$ 1,917	$ 1,917	$ 23,000
Miscellaneous costs	$ 469	$ 469	$ 469	$ 469	$ 469	$ 5,627
Payroll taxes	$ 2,853	$ 2,853	$ 2,853	$ 2,853	$ 2,853	$ 34,241
Total operating costs	**$28,291**	**$28,291**	**$28,291**	**$28,291**	**$28,291**	**$339,490**
EBITDA	**$ 7,086**	**$ 7,224**	**$ 7,362**	**$ 7,499**	**$ 7,637**	**$ 82,560**
Federal income tax	$ 2,284	$ 2,293	$ 2,301	$ 2,310	$ 2,320	$ 27,245
State income tax	$ 346	$ 347	$ 348	$ 350	$ 352	$ 4,129
Interest expense	$ 830	$ 826	$ 821	$ 817	$ 812	$ 10,049
Depreciation expenses	$ 393	$ 393	$ 393	$ 393	$ 393	$ 4,723
Net profit	**$ 3,233**	**$ 3,365**	**$ 3,497**	**$ 3,629**	**$ 3,762**	**$ 36,416**

Year 2

Quarter	Q1	Q2	Q3	Q4	Total
Sales	**$101,292**	**$126,615**	**$136,744**	**$141,809**	**$506,460**
Cost of goods sold	$ 10,129	$ 12,662	$ 13,675	$ 14,181	$ 50,646
Gross margin	90.00%	90.00%	90.00%	90.00%	90.00%
Operating income	**$ 1,163**	**$113,954**	**$123,070**	**$127,628**	**$455,814**
Expenses					
Payroll	$ 52,029	$ 65,296	$ 70,519	$ 73,131	$261,182
General and administrative	$ 6,028	$ 7,535	$ 8,137	$ 8,439	$ 30,139
Marketing expenses	$ 506	$ 634	$ 684	$ 710	$ 2,532
Professional fees and licensure	$ 1,236	$ 1,546	$ 1,669	$ 1,731	$ 6,182
Insurance costs	$ 480	$ 635	$ 647	$ 672	$ 2,399
Travel and vehicle costs	$ 1,922	$ 2,402	$ 2,594	$ 2,691	$ 9,609
Rent and utilities	$ 4,830	$ 6,038	$ 6,521	$ 6,762	$ 24,150
Miscellaneous costs	$ 1,216	$ 1,519	$ 1,641	$ 1,702	$ 6,078
Payroll taxes	$ 7,835	$ 9,795	$ 10,578	$ 10,970	$ 39,177
Total operating costs	**$ 76,290**	**$ 95,363**	**$102,992**	**$106,805**	**$381,449**
EBITDA	**$ 14,873**	**$ 18,591**	**$ 20,079**	**$ 20,822**	**$ 74,366**
Federal income tax	$ 4,291	$ 5,364	$ 5,793	$ 6,008	$ 21,454
State income tax	$ 650	$ 813	$ 877	$ 910	$ 3,251
Interest expense	$ 2,406	$ 2,361	$ 2,315	$ 2,269	$ 9,351
Depreciation expenses	$ 1,18	$ 1,181	$ 1,181	$ 1,181	$ 4,723
Net profit	**$ 6,346**	**$ 8,873**	**$ 9,912**	**$ 10,455**	**$ 35,586**

Year 3

Quarter	Q1	Q2	Q3	Q4	Total
Sales	**$109,395**	**$136,744**	**$147,684**	**$153,154**	**$546,977**
Cost of goods sold	$ 10,940	$ 13,675	$ 14,768	$15,316	$ 54,697
Gross margin	90.00%	90.00%	90.00%	90.00%	90.00%
Operating income	**$ 98,456**	**$123,070**	**$132,916**	**$137,838**	**$492,279**
Expenses					
Payroll	$ 59,172	$ 73,965	$ 79,881	$ 82,840	$295,858
General and administrative	$ 6,269	$ 7,836	$ 8,463	$ 8,777	$ 31,344
Marketing expenses	$ 547	$ 684	$ 738	$ 766	$ 2,735
Professional fees and licensure	$ 1,273	$ 1,592	$ 1,719	$ 1,783	$ 6,368
Insurance costs	$ 504	$ 630	$ 680	$ 705	$ 2,520
Travel and vehicle costs	$ 2,114	$ 2,643	$ 2,854	$ 2,960	$ 10,570
Rent and utilities	$ 5,072	$ 6,340	$ 6,847	$ 7,100	$ 25,358
Miscellaneous costs	$ 1,313	$ 1,641	$ 1,772	$ 1,838	$ 6,564
Payroll taxes	$ 8,876	$ 11,095	$ 11,982	$ 12,426	$ 44,379
Total operating costs	**$ 85,139**	**$106,423**	**$114,938**	**$119,194**	**$425,694**
EBITDA	**$ 13,317**	**$ 16,646**	**$ 17,978**	**$ 18,644**	**$ 66,585**
Federal income tax	$ 3,827	$ 4,785	$ 5,167	$ 5,359	$ 19,138
State income tax	$ 580	$ 725	$ 783	$ 812	$ 2,900
Interest expense	$ 2,222	$ 2,172	$ 2,123	$ 2,072	$ 8,588
Depreciation expenses	$ 1,181	$ 1,181	$ 1,181	$ 1,181	$ 4,723
Net profit	**$ 5,507**	**$ 7,783**	**$ 8,724**	**$ 9,221**	**$ 31,234**

7.11 Three Year Cash Flow Analysis

Year 1

Months	1	2	4	5	6	7
Cash from operations	$ 2,703	$ 2,834	$ 2,966	$ 3,098	$ 3,230	$ 3,361
Cash from receivables	$ —	$ —	$ —	$ —	$ —	$ —
Operating cash inflow	**$ 2,703**	**$ 2,834**	**$ 2,966**	**$ 3,098**	**$ 3,230**	**$ 3,361**
Other cash inflows						
Equity investment	$ 11,500	$ —	$ —	$ —	$ —	$ —
Increased borrowings	$115,000	$ —	$ —	$ —	$ —	$ —
Sales of business assets	$ —	$ —	$ —	$ —	$ —	$ —
A/P increases	$ 3,633	$ 3,633	$ 3,633	$ 3,633	$ 3,633	$ 3,633
Total other cash inflows	**$130,133**	**$ 3,633**	**$ 3,633**	**$ 3,633**	**$ 3,633**	**$ 3,633**
Total cash inflow	**$132,834**	**$ 6,466**	**$ 6,599**	**$ 6,730**	**$ 6,862**	**$ 6,994**
Cash outflows						
Repayment of principal	$ 595	$ 599	$ 604	$ 607	$ 612	$ 616
A/P decreases	$ 2,386	$ 2,386	$ 2,386	$ 2,386	$ 2,386	$ 2,386
A/R increases	$ —	$ —	$ —	$ —	$ —	$ —
Asset purchases	$ 66,125	$ —	$ —	$ —	$ —	$ —
Dividends	$ —	$ —	$ —	$ —	$ —	$ —
Total cash outflows	**$ 69,106**	**$ 2,984**	**$ 2,989**	**$ 2,993**	**$ 2,998**	**$ 3,003**
Net cash flow	**$ 63,730**	**$ 3,482**	**$ 3,609**	**$ 3,736**	**$ 3,864**	**$ 3,992**
Cash balance	**$ 63,730**	**$67,211**	**$70,820**	**$74,557**	**$78,421**	**$82,412**

Year 1 [continued]

Months	8	9	10	11	12	Total
Cash from operations	$ 3,626	$ 3,758	$ 3,890	$ 4,023	$ 4,155	$ 41,139
Cash from receivables	$ —	$ —	$ —	$ —	$ —	$ —
Operating cash inflow	**$ 3,626**	**$ 3,758**	**$ 3,890**	**$ 4,023**	**$ 4,155**	**$ 41,139**
Other cash inflows						
Equity investment	$ —	$ —	$ —	$ —	$ —	$ 11,500
Increased borrowings	$ —	$ —	$ —	$ —	$ —	$115,000
Sales of business assets	$ —	$ —	$ —	$ —	$ —	$ —
A/P increases	$ 3,633	$ 3,633	$ 3,633	$ 3,633	$ 3,633	$ 43,587
Total other cash inflows	**$ 3,633**	**$ 3,633**	**$ 3,633**	**$ 3,633**	**$ 3,633**	**$170,087**
Total cash inflow	**$ 7,259**	**$ 7,391**	**$ 7,522**	**$ 7,654**	**$ 7,787**	**$211,226**
Cash outflows						
Repayment of principal	$ 627	$ 631	$ 636	$ 641	$ 645	$ 7,432
A/P decreases	$ 2,386	$ 2,386	$ 2,386	$ 2,386	$ 2,386	$ 28,632
A/R increases	$ —	$ —	$ —	$ —	$ —	$ —
Asset purchases	$ —	$ —	$ —	$ —	$ —	$ 66,125
Dividends	$ —	$ —	$ —	$ —	$32,911	$ 32,911
Total cash outflows	**$ 3,012**	**$ 3,016**	**$ 3,021**	**$ 3,027**	**$35,942**	**$135,101**
Net cash flow	**$ 4,246**	**$ 4,373**	**$ 4,501**	**$ 4,629**	**($28,154)**	**$ 76,125**
Cash balance	**$90,778**	**$95,151**	**$99,652**	**$104,281**	**$76,125**	**$ 76,125**

Year 2

Quarter	Q1	Q2	Q3	Q4	Total
Cash from operations	$ 8,062	$10,077	$10,884	$11,286	$40,309
Cash from receivables	$ —	$ —	$ —	$ —	$ —
Operating cash inflow	**$ 8,062**	**$10,077**	**$10,884**	**$11,286**	**$40,309**
Other cash inflows					
Equity investment	$ —	$ —	$ —	$ —	$ —
Increased borrowings	$ —	$ —	$ —	$ —	$ —
Sales of business assets	$ —	$ —	$ —	$ —	$ —
A/P increases	$10,025	$12,532	$13,534	$14,035	$50,125
Total other cash inflows	**$10,025**	**$12,532**	**$13,534**	**$14,035**	**$50,125**
Total cash inflow	**$18,087**	**$22,609**	**$24,417**	**$25,322**	**$90,435**
Cash outflows					
Repayment of principal	$ 1,964	$ 2,009	$ 2,055	$ 2,101	$ 8,131
A/P decreases	$ 6,871	$ 8,589	$ 9,277	$ 9,620	$34,357
A/R increases	$ —	$ —	$ —	$ —	$ —
Asset purchases	$ 1,210	$ 1,511	$ 1,633	$ 1,693	$ 6,047
Dividends	$ 6,449	$ 8,062	$ 8,707	$ 9,029	$32,247
Total cash outflows	**$16,494**	**$20,172**	**$21,671**	**$22,443**	**$80,782**
Net cash flow	**$ 1,592**	**$ 2,437**	**$ 2,746**	**$ 2,877**	**$ 9,653**
Cash balance	**$77,717**	**$80,154**	**$82,900**	**$85,779**	**$85,779**

Year 3

Quarter	Q1	Q2	Q3	Q4	Total
Cash from operations	$ 7,192	$ 8,990	$ 9,708	$10,068	$35,958
Cash from receivables	$ —	$ —	$ —	$ —	$ —
Operating cash inflow	**$ 7,192**	**$ 8,990**	**$ 9,708**	**$10,068**	**$35,958**
Other cash inflows					
Equity investment	$ —	$ —	$ —	$ —	$ —
Increased borrowings	$ —	$ —	$ —	$ —	$ —
Sales of business assets	$ —	$ —	$ —	$ —	$ —
A/P increases	$11,529	$14,411	$15,564	$16,140	$57,644
Total other cash inflows	**$11,529**	**$14,411**	**$15,564**	**$16,140**	**$57,644**
Total cash inflow	**$18,721**	**$23,400**	**$25,272**	**$26,209**	**$93,602**
Cash outflows					
Repayment of principal	$ 2,149	$ 2,198	$ 2,247	$ 2,299	$ 8,893
A/P decreases	$ 8,246	$10,307	$11,132	$11,544	$41,230
A/R increases	$ —	$ —	$ —	$ —	$ —
Asset purchases	$ 1,079	$ 1,349	$ 1,456	$ 1,510	$ 5,394
Dividends	$ 5,753	$ 7,192	$ 7,767	$ 8,055	$28,766
Total cash outflows	**$17,227**	**$21,045**	**$22,602**	**$23,407**	**$84,282**
Net cash flow	**$ 1,494**	**$ 2,355**	**$ 2,670**	**$ 2,801**	**$ 9,320**
Cash balance	**$87,272**	**$89,628**	**$92,297**	**$95,098**	**$95,098**

Publicist

Vitelli & Smith Inc.

28 California Ave., Ste. 600
Columbus, IN 46000

Paul Greenland

Vitelli & Smith Inc. is an independent publicity firm specializing in the healthcare sector.

EXECUTIVE SUMMARY

Publicists generate visibility and exposure for their customers, who may be authors, athletes, executives, musicians, organizations, or professionals like doctors. Often times, publicists specialize in serving a particular type of client or work within an industry where they have extensive experience. In addition, some publicists also limit their work to a specific geographic area. Regardless of their focus, successful publicists usually have extensive contacts in their chosen specialty.

Vitelli & Smith Inc. is an independent publicity firm specializing in the healthcare sector. Established by experienced healthcare publicity professionals Peter Vitelli and Karen Smith, the firm specializes in working with healthcare providers such as physicians, physical therapists, mental health professionals, chiropractors, and dentists. The following business plan outlines how Vitelli & Smith will grow their new firm into a successful enterprise.

INDUSTRY ANALYSIS

Depending on their area of specialization, publicists can benefit from membership in a number of different professional and trade associations. One organization that is useful to all publicists is the Public Relations Society of America (https://www.prsa.org). With roots dating back to 1947, more public relations professionals belong to PRSA than any other organization in the world. In 2016 the organization had approximately 22,000 professional members and another 10,000 student members. According to PRSA, it "provides professional development, sets standards of excellence and upholds principles of ethics for its members." PRSA members benefit from access to a wide range of webinars, publications, and conferences. The organization also provides members with opportunities to become certified in the public relations profession, giving them added credibility in the marketplace.

In addition to PRSA, Vitelli and Smith also are members of organizations specific to the healthcare industry, including the Society for Healthcare Strategy & Market Development (http://www.shsmd.org). Part of the American Hospital Association, SHSMD is "the largest and most prominent voice and resource for healthcare strategists, planners, marketers, and communications and public relations professionals nationwide." Among the organization's 4,000 members are marketing and public relations professionals from physician groups, hospitals, healthcare systems, public relations agencies, and consulting firms. Members have access to a variety of resources that help them advance within the profession, including an annual conference that attracts professionals from throughout the country.

In addition to national organizations, publicists also have opportunities to belong to organizations at the local, state, and regional level. For example, Vitelli and Smith are both members of the Indiana Healthcare Marketing and Public Relations Society (http://ihmprs.org). Affiliated with the Indiana Hospital Association, IHMPRS "strives to connect Indiana marketing communication professionals while providing the latest industry and integrated marketing communication news and ideas."

MARKET ANALYSIS

Target Markets

The healthcare industry was expanding rapidly toward the end of 2016. At that time, faster-than-average job growth was projected for many of the professionals who provide healthcare services. One key driver of this growth is the aging population, which will result in increased demand for a wide range of medical services.

According to the U.S. Department of Labor, national employment of professionals within Vitelli & Smith's target market categories broke down as follows in 2014:

- Dentists & Orthodontists: 151,500
- Chiropractors: 45,200
- Physicians & Surgeons: 708,300
- Physical Therapists: 210,900
- Speech-Language Pathologists: 135,400
- Occupational Therapists: 114,600

Using a database at their local library, the owners conducted an analysis of the Indianapolis market and discovered that more than 8,000 establishments operate within the local health services industry. Collectively, these businesses employ more than 42,000 people.

Publicity Outlets

Based on their experience in and familiarity with the local market, the owners have identified the following media outlets as potential publicity sources for their clients:

Magazines & Newspapers:

- *Indianapolis Business Journal*
- *Indianapolis Monthly*
- *Indianapolis Recorder*
- *Indianapolis Star*
- *NUVO*

TV Stations:

- WFYI (Public Television)
- WISH TV (CBS)
- WRTV (ABC)

- WTHR (NBC)
- WXIB (FOX)

FM Radio Stations:
- WFBQ 94.7 FM
- WFMS 95.5 FM
- WFYI 90.1 FM
- WHHH 96.3 FM
- WJJK 104.5 FM
- WKLU 101.9FM
- WLHK 97.1 FM
- WNOU 100.9 FM
- WNTR 107.9 FM
- WRZX 103.3 FM
- WTTS 92.3 FM
- WYXB 105.7 FM
- WZPL 99.5 FM

AM Radio Stations:
- WBRI 1500 AM
- WFNI 1070 AM
- WNDE 1260 AM
- WTLC 1310 AM

In addition, local blogs and Web sites offer additional opportunities for publicity.

Competition

A number of noteworthy firms already offer publicity/public relations services in the Indianapolis market, including:

- Borshoff
- Bose Public Affairs Group
- Coles Marketing
- Dittoe Public Relations
- Hirons & Company
- Hostetler Public Relations
- IronStrike
- Kyle Communications
- Mass Ave Public Relations
- McFarland PR and Public Affairs, Inc.
- Miller Brooks
- Pivot Marketing

- Radius
- Raidious
- Sease Gerig & Associates
- Shank Public Relations Counselors, Inc.
- SSPR Indianapolis
- The MEK Group
- TrendyMinds
- Westcomm

Many of these firms serve customers from a wide variety of geographies and industries. Vitelli & Smith's healthcare specialty and local focus will provide the firm with a strong differential. In addition, because the firm is small in size, Vitelli & Smith will emphasize personalized service in its marketing approach.

SERVICES

At Central Indianapolis Hospital, Peter Vitelli and Karen Smith single-handedly secured more media coverage for their organization's programs and providers than any other local healthcare organization. The key to their success was being both responsive to incoming media requests for interviews *and* proactively developing story ideas and pitching them to the same media outlets. By following this approach, Vitelli and Smith became an indispensable source of content for local media outlets. This allowed them to develop strong relationships with local reporters, anchors, and news directors. The owners will take this very same approach while running their own firm, working hard to develop stories that put their clients front and center.

Services offered by Vitelli & Smith include:

- Content Marketing
- Corporate Communications
- Crisis Communications
- Employee Engagement
- Media Relations
- Media Training
- Product/Service Introductions
- Publicity Campaigns
- Reputation Management
- Social Media Promotion

Process

The owners will offer prospective customers a free one-hour consultation to identify their goals and objectives and learn how Vitelli & Smith can help accomplish them. Based on this information, they will develop a detailed time and cost estimate for their services. In some cases, the owners will contract with customers via a retainer arrangement for a dedicated number of hours every month. However, in other situations (e.g., specific campaigns, product/service introductions, media training sessions, etc.), services will be provided on an hourly or per project basis.

Results

Vitelli & Smith understand that their services are a significant investment for clients, and that concrete results are important. With this in mind, the firm will provide clients with regular reporting (frequency based on customer need), providing objective publicity-related insight. This will be accomplished using media monitoring software tools and services that track things like sentiment (a metric based on the positive or negative nature of media coverage), media mentions/placements, and news coverage pertaining to competitors. One popular service utilized by Vitelli & Smith makes it convenient for the agency to save actual clips from news publications for their customers and generate a wide range of reports summarizing coverage during specific time frames. Another tool, focused specifically on television coverage, allows the firm to capture and archive video clips from various TV news outlets.

Fees

Vitelli & Smith typically will base their services on an hourly rate of $135, although this is subject to variability based on the nature of a given project or arrangement. Based on conversations with other publicists, the owners anticipate that, on average, they will charge clients monthly retainers of approximately $1,500.

OPERATIONS

Facility & Location

Vitelli & Smith has leased office space at Guilford Crossing, a former mansion that local developers converted into office space. Situated in an easily accessible location, with convenient proximity to downtown, tenants in the office building include attorneys, advertising agencies, accountants, and consultants. Vitelli & Smith's office includes a small reception area, four individual offices, and a conference room. Tenants have access to a shared kitchenette and restroom facilities.

Business Structure

Vitelli & Smith is organized as an S Corporation in the state of Indiana, which provides the owners with certain tax and liability advantages. A local business attorney helped to establish the corporation.

Tools & Equipment

The owners will need to purchase the following equipment to operate their business, at a cost of approximately $11,500:

- 2 credenzas: $600
- Reception desk: $800
- 2 L-shaped desks: $1,300
- Four-drawer lateral filing cabinet: $240
- 3 office chairs: $375
- 48-inch metal storage cabinet: $75
- 8-foot conference table: $800
- 8 conference room chairs: $600
- 3 Desktop PCs: $1,500
- 2 Tablet computers: $2,000
- 1 Storage cabinet: $200

- 3 Filing cabinets: $500
- 2 credenzas: $1,000
- Wireless router: $200
- Coffee pot: $50
- IP telephone system: $750
- Office décor: $500

PERSONNEL

Vitelli & Smith is led by experienced public relations professionals Peter Vitelli and Karen Smith. Prior to establishing their own firm, Peter and Karen formed the media relations team for Central Indianapolis Hospital, a leading 525-bed acute care hospital with approximately 17,500 annual admissions. The hospital includes a regional trauma center, a large network of primary care and specialty clinics with more than 350,000 visits annually, a regional cancer center, and a network of community health services. Due to their efforts, Central Indianapolis Hospital, its programs, and its providers consistently outclassed competing hospitals in gaining local and regional media coverage.

Peter Vitelli, President

When Central Indianapolis Hospital was acquired by a larger, multi-state healthcare organization, Peter Vitelli's position as director of public relations was terminated, providing him with an opportunity to establish his own business. Vitelli is a graduate of Indiana University, where he earned both undergraduate and graduate business degrees. Prior to working for Central Indianapolis Hospital for 15 years, Vitelli spent five years working for a local public relations firm.

Karen Smith, Vice President

Seeking greater financial reward for her hard work, as well as a more flexible schedule, Smith was inspired to join Vitelli in establishing Vitelli & Smith. Smith is a graduate of Mountain View College, where she earned an undergraduate liberal arts degree, followed by a graduate corporate communications degree from West Virginia University. She has 11 years of experience in healthcare public relations, as well as three years of corporate communications experience at the non-profit level.

Personnel Plan

Vitelli & Smith will begin operations with the owners and one administrative assistant. One publicity associate will be hired during the second year of operation, followed by a second publicity associate during the third year. Following is an overview of the firm's projected personnel plan:

Title	2017	2018	2019
President	$ 85,000	$100,000	$115,000
Vice president	$ 75,000	$ 90,000	$105,000
Administrative assistant	$ 35,000	$ 36,750	$ 38,588
Publicity specialist	$ 0	$ 45,000	$ 47,250
Publicity specialist	$ 0	$ 0	$ 45,000
Total	**$195,000**	**$271,750**	**$350,838**

Professional & Advisory Support

Vitelli & Smith has established a business banking account with the Bank of Indianapolis, including a merchant account for accepting credit card payments. Tax advisement is provided by

Branson & Associates. Andrew McMahon, a local business attorney, will provide legal counsel when needed, and has provided the owners with basic agreements they can use with their customers. Finally, Vitelli & Smith has secured adequate liability insurance in partnership with a local insurance agency.

GROWTH STRATEGY

Year One: Secure seven clients on retainer and bill 1,440 additional (non-retainer) service hours. Generate net income of $55,000 on gross sales of $320,400.

Year Two: Secure an additional two clients on retainer (total of nine) and bill 1,920 additional service hours. Generate net income of $61,037 on gross sales of $421,200.

Year Three: Secure an additional six clients on retainer (total of 15) and bill 1,920 additional service hours. Generate net income of $64,386 on gross sales of $522,000.

MARKETING & SALES

Vitelli & Smith will market its publicity services using the following tactics:

1. Four-color folder that contains inserts describing the firm's key services and providing information about the owners.
2. A Web site with profiles of the owners and descriptions of services offered.
3. A blog for local healthcare providers that contains information about publicity strategies, tips, and trends, as well as case study examples (success stories) featuring Vitelli & Smith's clients.
4. Regular sales calls to the leading prospects in the local market.
5. A social media strategy that includes a presence on LinkedIn, Facebook, and Twitter.
6. Quarterly direct mailings to healthcare providers in the local market. The owners have developed a series of marketing collateral to be used for campaigns, including a sales letter, trifold brochure, and four-color glossy postcard. A mailing list broker has provided a list that can be used multiple times throughout the year, with a 97 percent deliverability rate.
7. Membership in the Indy Chamber, the city's local chamber of commerce.
8. Regular advertisements in Indy Chamber publications, such as *Catalyst* magazine and *Monday Morning Memo,* and on www.indychamber.com.
9. Regular advertisements on the Indianapolis Medical Society's Web site.

FINANCIAL ANALYSIS

Peter Vitelli and Karen Smith will invest $50,000 to establish their firm. Peter will contribute $35,000 from his personal savings, and Karen will contribute the remaining $15,000. This will cover the aforementioned $11,500 in startup costs, as well as capital for ongoing operations. The owners expect to recoup their investment toward the end of the first year.

Following is a breakdown of projected revenue, expenses, and net income for Vitelli & Smith's first three years of operations. Additional financial projections are available upon request.

Revenue	2016	2017	2018
Retainers	$126,000	$162,000	$198,000
Hourly fees (non-retainer)	$194,400	$259,200	$324,000
Total revenue	**$320,400**	**$421,200**	**$522,000**
Expenses			
Salary	$195,000	$271,750	$350,838
Payroll tax	$ 29,250	$ 40,763	$ 52,626
Insurance	$ 600	$ 650	$ 700
Accounting & legal	$ 1,500	$ 1,750	$ 2,000
Office supplies	$ 650	$ 700	$ 750
Software licenses	$ 6,500	$ 7,000	$ 7,500
Equipment leasing	$ 1,500	$ 1,500	$ 1,500
Marketing & advertising	$ 15,000	$ 20,000	$ 25,000
Office lease	$ 10,800	$ 10,800	$ 10,800
Telecommunications & Internet	$ 1,800	$ 1,800	$ 1,800
Professional development	$ 700	$ 900	$ 1,100
Donations & contributions	$ 500	$ 600	$ 700
Subscriptions & dues	$ 1,100	$ 1,450	$ 1,800
Miscellaneous	$ 500	$ 500	$ 500
Total expenses	**$265,400**	**$360,163**	**$457,614**
Net income	**$ 55,000**	**$ 61,037**	**$ 64,386**

Quilt Making Business

Canary Quilts

1715 8th Ave.
Fenton Village, IA 55623

Paul Greenland

Canary Quilts is a custom quilt-making business located in the Cherry Creek region of Iowa, which includes many popular tourist destinations.

EXECUTIVE SUMMARY

Samantha Kassel had no idea that quilt-making would be her chosen profession. However, several years ago her grandmother encouraged her to learn the craft that she had enjoyed for so many years. Samantha soon discovered a newfound passion for making quilts, as well as a knack for making quilts that were incredibly unique thanks to her skill as an artist. After enjoying quilt-making as a hobby, Samantha soon began making custom quilts for neighbors, friends, and family members. Strong word-of-mouth recommendations produced a steady stream of requests, prompting Samantha to establish her own business. She adopted the quirky name, Canary Quilts, in honor of her two pet canaries, which reside in her quilting space.

INDUSTRY ANALYSIS

Hobbyist and commercial quilters alike have access to an organization that includes members with similar interests. The non-profit National Quilting Association Inc. (http://www.nqaquilts.org) is considered to be the oldest quilting industry organization, with roots dating back nearly 50 years. According to the NQA, it is "a professional quilting organization which operates exclusively for the continuance of its charitable mission, strong programming, and the promotion of the art of quilting." In addition to a newsletter, NQA operates local chapters and publishes *The Quilting Quarterly* magazine.

Another leading industry organization is The American Quilter's Society (http://www.americanquilter.com), whose objective is "to provide a forum for quilters of all skill levels to expand their horizons in quilt making, design, self-expression, and quilt collecting." Members benefit from resources such as magazines, books, workshops, and quilt shows.

In addition to these organizations, industry participants have access to local quilting circles and groups, along with online videos, DVDs, books, and other resources that help them to advance in their craft.

MARKET ANALYSIS

Overview

Canary Quilts will serve customers from throughout the United States and Canada. However, the owner estimates that the vast majority of her customers will reside in the Midwestern United States. Canary Quilts is a custom quilt-making business located in the Cherry Creek region of Iowa, which includes many popular tourist destinations. The business is situated in the village of Fenton, which features a quaint Main Street with a variety of storefronts that are populated by art galleries, cafes, gift shops, and more. Tourists are drawn to the town by its 19th century architecture, broad selection of hand-crafted goods, independent retailers, and nearby bed-and-breakfast inns, golf courses, wineries, and breweries. Fenton is home to some 225 establishments, including 64 retailers. Of these, only a few sell handmade quilts or promote local quilters, providing an opportunity for Canary Quilts.

Growth Projections

According to a study conducted by the Village of Fenton and the Cherry Creek Economic Development Agency, retail sales within the Cherry Creek region reached $19 million in 2015. This reflects a five-year annual growth rate of 7.5 percent. According to the study, growth of 6.9 percent is projected through 2020.

Competition

Canary Quilts operates in a market where there are a limited number of other quilt-makers, providing excellent opportunities for growth. In addition, the business's strongest competitors focus mainly on traditional quilts, as opposed to the more contemporary designs that owner Samantha Kassel specializes in, giving her a strong differential in the regional market.

SERVICES

Overview

As opposed to traditional quilts, which feature patchworks of geometric patterns (e.g., triangles, hexagons, rectangles, etc.), Canary Quilts' designs are more contemporary in nature. Unlike some quilters, Samantha has a background in traditional art and design. She will use these skills to produce unique shapes, pictures, and designs to feature on her customers' quilts, sometimes incorporating special fabrics that have sentimental or personal meaning. For example, she recently created a quilt featuring fabric pieces from T-shirts, jerseys, and sweatshirts to commemorate a young man's college athletic career. The fabric pieces were interwoven with squares featuring unique patterns that she developed per her customer's input.

Process

Samantha Kassel typically takes the following approach when working with customers:

1. **Consultation.** Canary Quilts will begin all projects with a customer consultation, during which Samantha will learn more about her client and the quilt that they would like her to make.

2. **Planning & Design.** Next, Samantha will determine the size of the quilt. In some cases, she will produce a drawing of the proposed quilt, showing the block pattern to scale on a sheet of graph paper. In other cases, quilt design software may be used. The planning and design phase may look differently based upon the unique requirements of each customer. Customers may desire one of several different types of designs, including outline, pattern, or allover.

3. **Supplies.** After determining the size and design, Samantha will perform calculations to determine the supplies she will need to produce the quilt (e.g., fabric, filling, backing, and binding). As in the aforementioned example, some of the material needed for the quilt maker may come directly from the customer.
4. **Production.** Finally, Samantha will produce the actual quilt. Generally, this process involves producing square or rectangular blocks, which are then combined to produce the top of the quilt (a process known as setting). The production process may happen differently depending upon whether the quilt is produced by hand or machine. Finally, an edge finish will be applied.

Rates

Although some quilting businesses charge customers by the hour, others charge by the size of the quilt (typically by the square inch or square yard). Many customers find the latter arrangement to be more agreeable, since the price is known up front. For this reason, Canary Quilts will charge a flat fee for every quilting project, with slightly higher fees for customers who want their quilts sewn by hand, as opposed to being sewn by machine. Although some quilts will be more complex/time-consuming than others, over time a flat fee approach tends to even out, sales wise, according to other quilters that Samantha has spoken to.

Quilt Sizes

Following are typical sizes for the most common types of quilts produced by Canary Quilts:

- Baby Crib (30 in. x 46 in.)
- California King (114 in. x 117 in.)
- Full (70 in. x 88 in.)
- King (94 in. x 108 in.)
- Lap Quilt (52 in. x 16 in.)
- Queen (88 in. x 99 in.)
- Toddler (46 in. x 70 in.)
- Twin (64 in. x 72 in.)

Turnaround time for quilts typically will range between three and nine weeks, depending on the size of the quilt and whether the customer wishes it to be handmade or machine made.

To calculate the cost of her quilts, Samantha multiplies the size of the quilt in square inches by her rate (.05/square inch), arriving at her labor cost. She then adds an additional 33 percent for supplies, materials, shipping, and a reasonable profit. Labor charges for handmade quilts typically are 25 percent greater than charges for machine-made quilts.

The Queen-sized quilt (machine-made) listed above (8,712 square inches), would result in a labor charge of $436, coupled with an additional $144 in costs, for a total cost of $580. Samantha estimates that she can make a Queen quilt in nine hours, resulting in an hourly labor rate of nearly $50.

OPERATIONS

Location

Samantha already has a designated space for quilt-making in her home. Although it has been sufficient for her as a hobbyist, more adequate surroundings will be needed for commercial operation. Based on her own experience, Samantha knows that adequate lighting and a comfortable table are key considerations for every quilting business owner to avoid or minimize eyestrain, back discomfort, and other potential ergonomic injuries. Having enough square footage also is important. For these reasons, she will relocate her supplies and equipment from a small bedroom to a larger space in her basement, which is exposed and has a separate entry door prospective customers can use to enter and exit without walking through the rest of her home.

Business Structure

Canary Quilts will begin operations as a sole proprietorship.

Hours of Operation

As a home-based business, Canary Quilts will see customers by appointment. Samantha will be flexible to meet the needs of her customers, who may wish to meet in the evening or on weekends.

Communications

Samantha has obtained a dedicated business phone line for Canary Quilts. In addition, she has purchased a dedicated domain name for the business, providing her with an e-mail address that includes her business name.

Bookkeeping & Billing

Canary Quilts will use a popular cloud-based accounting and invoicing service that allows business owners to track their time and expenses, and generate invoices for customers with a credit card payment option. Customers will be required to pay 50 percent of the fee for their quilt in advance, with the remainder due upon completion.

Shipping & Receiving

Canary Quilts will receive material from customers for their quilts in person, or via a leading carrier service that allows package tracking and provides the customer with the option of insuring their shipment. Samantha will take a time/date-stamped photograph of all materials as soon as they are received, and perform a thorough assessment to ensure that she is familiar with the condition of fabric, etc. This will provide her with a degree of liability protection in the event that a customer claims that she stained or damaged fabric that was provided for a specific quilt. Even though they likely will have received their own shipping confirmation, Samantha will personally call all customers to let them know she has received their package. In addition, she will describe any imperfections or blemishes on quilting materials so that the customer is aware of these prior to her beginning any work. Quilts that have been completed will be shipped to customers using FedEx or UPS. Customers will be responsible for paying shipping and handling charges.

Supplies

Canary Quilts will require an inventory of the following supplies on a regular basis:

- Fabric
- Thread
- Batting
- Bias strips

Although Samantha already has a limited inventory of supplies, she will need to invest an additional $800 to have enough materials for business operations. In order to keep costs low, Samantha will purchase supplies in bulk at wholesale (e.g., buying batting by the roll, etc.). She has identified several national suppliers who can meet her needs.

Equipment

In addition, the business will require the following equipment for operations. Although the owner already owns most of these items, she will need to purchase a long-arm quilting machine. These can be quite expensive when purchased new, costing anywhere from $10,000 to $20,000. However, many individuals purchase used machines that last for many years. Samantha will purchase a high quality used machine at a cost of $3,500 for her business.

- Bias bars/Celtic bars
- Cutting mat
- Iron
- Long-arm quilting machine
- Marking tools
- Mechanical pencils
- Needles
- Pens
- Quilt design software
- Rotary cutter
- Rulers (transparent)
- Safety pens
- Scissors/shears
- Sewing machine
- Tablet computer
- Templates
- Trembles
- White chalk pencil

PERSONNEL

Samantha Kassel had no idea that quilt-making would be her chosen profession. However, several years ago her grandmother encouraged her to learn the craft that she had enjoyed for so many years. Samantha soon discovered a newfound passion for making quilts, as well as a knack for making quilts that were incredibly unique. After enjoying quilt-making as a hobby, Samantha soon began making custom quilts for neighbors, friends, and family members. Strong word-of-mouth recommendations produced a steady stream of requests, prompting Samantha to establish her own business.

In addition to performing the actual work (quilt-making), Samantha realizes that she will need to have fundamental small business management skills. For this reason, she has taken a course in small business management at her local community college and read several related books. Samantha also hired a local accountant to assist her with bookkeeping and tax preparation. Finally, she opened a business checking account at her local bank. Although there is a small fee involved, she has gained the ability to accept credit card payments through her cloud-based accounting software.

BUSINESS STRATEGY

Canary Quilts will concentrate on growing organically and keeping overhead low during its first three years of operations. During this time period, Samantha will build her customer base through strong word-of-mouth referrals. As volume increases, and she begins to establish a name throughout the region, Samantha will consider establishing a dedicated retail presence for Canary Quilts in downtown Fenton, which enjoys robust tourism-related business from late spring through late fall. Samantha's husband, a local architect, is planning to establish his own independent practice in the near future, which may provide an opportunity for husband and wife to lease a building that would meet both of their needs.

MARKETING & SALES

Samantha has determined that strong word-of-mouth promotion is critical to the growth and success of her quilting business. For this reason, she will employ a variety of free or low-cost approaches to generate buzz about Canary Quilts, including:

1. The use of social media channels such as Pinterest and Facebook to showcase her work and build engagement with current and prospective customers.
2. Networking through local social, church, and business groups.
3. Hosting exclusive, invitation-only special events (in her home or at an alternate location) for existing customers, who will be allowed to bring one guest. These events, held only two or three times per year, will give customers the chance to see Samantha's latest designs, win prizes, and make purchases at a slight discount.
4. Membership in local and regional craft circles.
5. Membership in the Fenton Chamber of Commerce.
6. Participation in select local, regional, and national craft shows.
7. Development of a professional portfolio (photo book) showcasing the different types of quilts that Samantha has made, along with a selection of quilt samples that can be displayed at craft shows and other exhibitions.
8. A Web site for Canary Quilts, with information about Samantha and how she works, links to her social media pages, and a gallery of her work.
9. Establishing a local quilting club for teenagers and young adults, providing additional networking opportunities.
10. Volunteering to teach quilting to local Girl Scout troops, including coordination with the troop leader to procure simple quilting kits for the participants.
11. Exhibition at the annual Fenton Village Fall Arts Festival, which attracts more than 25,000 visitors.
12. Renting a small display space at Cherry Creek Gallery, which features artwork and handcrafted goods from local artisans.
13. An advertisement in the *Cherry Creek Visitors Guide*, which is updated quarterly and distributed to thousands of tourists visiting the Cherry Creek region.
14. A quilting blog, where Samantha will share her knowledge and expertise with fellow quilters and prospective customers.

FINANCIAL ANALYSIS

The owner of a quilting business must consider not only the cost of materials, but especially the amount of time required to create custom goods. With a firm understanding of material and labor costs, the owner can then determine an appropriate price, which will allow for a reasonable profit.

After considering all of the aforementioned factors, Samantha is projecting gross revenue of $39,300 for her first year of operations. She is confident that sales will increase at a compound annual rate of 15 percent during the second and third years, resulting in gross revenue of $45,195 and $51,974, respectively. The owner estimates that, after factoring in the cost of materials, labor, utilities, liability insurance, marketing, and other incidental expenses, her profit margin will be approximately 18 percent, resulting in a net profit of $7,074 during year one, $8,135 during year two, and $9,355 during year three.

SWOT ANALYSIS

- ***Strengths:*** Canary Quilts' competition focuses mainly on traditional quilts, as opposed to the more contemporary designs that Samantha specializes in, giving her a strong differential in the regional market.
- ***Weaknesses:*** In addition to being the only source of production, Samantha also must devote valuable time to administrative/business tasks, which may impact her availability/capacity if she is not efficient.
- ***Opportunities:*** Canary Quilts operates in a market where there are a limited number of other quilters, providing excellent opportunities for growth.
- ***Threats:*** During difficult economic times, the business will be at risk because its products are discretionary in nature. In addition, Samantha is the only source of production, which may put the business at financial risk in the event of a lengthy illness or injury.

Safety Consultant

Safety Solutions, LLC

12534 Side Winder Blvd.
Austin, TX 78714

Fran Fletcher

Safety Solutions is a consulting company based in Austin, Texas offering OSHA-approved safety consulting services. Safety Solutions is owned and operated by Alex Jones.

BUSINESS OVERVIEW

Safety Solutions is a consulting company based in Austin, Texas offering OSHA-approved safety consulting services. Safety Solutions is owned and operated by Alex Jones.

Mr. Jones started Safety Solutions after ten years in manufacturing. He worked in many capacities during his career, where he found he has a passion for workplace safety. He worked in his former employer's safety department for seven years and gained valuable experience and training during that time that he can use when assisting the customers of Safety Solutions. Mr. Jones understands that complying with and maintaining safety plans can be quite labor intensive for employees who are unfamiliar with regulations or who are completing the task in addition to other responsibilities. Mr. Jones will work from his home office and will travel to the client and evaluate their sites for safety issues. Safety Solutions wants to make safety compliance effortless by putting tried and true plans into place. He will mainly work with small companies who cannot afford to hire a full-time employee specifically for this task, but will also serve as a consultant for larger companies.

Safety Solutions will offer the following services:

- Safety plans
- Safety manuals
- Safety training
- Safety consulting
- Audit preparedness

There are currently two other businesses in the region that exclusively provide onsite safety consulting. There is an increasing need for this service due to the expansion of safety requirements from regulatory agencies. Mr. Jones will set himself apart from the competition by offering services and prices to fit any budget.

The company's marketing plan includes offering on-site or off-site safety training as well as online training modules. Advertising will include placing ads in multiple industry journals. Mr. Jones will also call and send brochures to industries in the Austin area that will benefit from his services.

Mr. Jones hopes to quickly build clientele and make a name for himself as an expert in safety consulting. In the short term, he has plans to expand his services to the entire state of Texas. Long-term goals include expanding his online training modules to include a larger variety of industries.

Mr. Jones does not need to seek outside financing at this time. He received a severance package when his employer closed its doors. Using conservative estimates, Safety Solutions should be able to pay back Mr. Jones's savings account in approximately eighteen months.

COMPANY DESCRIPTION

Location

Safety Solutions is headquartered in Austin, Texas. Mr. Jones will operate his business from his home office.

Hours of Operation

Monday—Friday, 8 to 5

Extended hours offered by appointment

Personnel

Alex Jones (owner/consultant)
Mr. Jones received a certificate in industrial maintenance from Tumbleweed Technical Institute. He is also a licensed electrician. He has worked in various manufacturing facilities during his career, and has served in various positions, including Safety Manager.

Products and Services

Safety Solutions will initially offer the following services:

- Safety plans
- Safety manuals
- Safety training
- Safety consulting
- Audit preparedness

Safety Training will consist of 2-day onsite or offsite training sessions. The subject matter of the seminars will be tailored to meet the client's needs.

Online Safety Training Modules will also be available to purchase. New modules will be added as they are created. Current safety modules include:

- Slips, Trips, and Falls
- Personal Protective Equipment
- Back Safety—Proper Lifting
- General Safety
- Chemical Exposure

- Emergency Preparedness
- Laboratory Safety
- Electrical Safety
- Confined Spaces
- Asbestos

MARKET ANALYSIS

Industry Overview

The food industry is constantly being bombarded with new quality requirements from government regulatory agencies. With an increase of quality policies in the industrial setting, there is an exponential increase in the amount of paperwork that must be completed by personnel. Companies are always looking for ways to increase profits and decrease overhead. Contracting the work instead of hiring an employee is one way of accomplishing this.

Target Market

The target market for Safety Solutions is manufacturing facilities in Southeast Texas. Over time, the target market will expand to include the entire state of Texas.

Mr. Jones also plans to reach a large customer base with his online safety training modules.

Competition

Mr. Jones is aware of two other businesses in the southeast region that currently provide safety consulting. There are also other companies that offer online safety training. He plans to set himself apart by offering custom safety plans and videos that are informative and keep the audience's attention.

GROWTH STRATEGY

The overall growth strategy of Safety Solutions is to obtain online customers in addition to obtaining substantial safety consulting work in the southeast region of Texas.

Referrals are imperative in obtaining clients. Mr. Jones's primary focus will be tailoring his services to the specific needs of each individual customer so that they will contact him for future endeavors and refer him to their colleagues.

Sales and Marketing

Mr. Jones has identified key tactics to support the company's growth strategy.

Advertising/marketing will include:

- Providing safety seminars
- Pens, notepads, etc. with company logo
- Advertising in industry and trade journals
- Mailing business brochures to applicable industries

FINANCIAL ANALYSIS

Start-up Costs

The majority of start-up related costs will be used for video production. It is estimated that Safety Solutions will need approximately $5,000 to produce professional safety video modules. Additionally, Safety Solutions will purchase items and brochures to give away to prospective customers.

Start-up Costs

Business license	$ 250
Business cards	$ 150
Brochures	$ 500
Video production	$5,000
Total	**$5,900**

Estimated Monthly Expenses

Mr. Jones will not pay himself a set salary. He will use his personal vehicle for work.

Monthly Expenses

Loan payment	$ 300
Phone/Internet	$ 150
Advertising	$ 150
Travel expenses	$1,000
Total	**$1,600**

Estimated Monthly Income

The number of clients will determine estimated income. Mr. Jones estimates that it will take six months to get his videos produced.

Price Schedule

Service	Price
Safety plan	$ 3,000
Safety manual	$ 5,000
Safety training onsite 2-day course	$ 10,000
Safety training offsite 2-day course	$ 12,000
Safety consulting	$1,000–$5,000
Audit preparedness	$ 5,000
Online training module	$50/module

Profit/Loss

Mr. Jones is using a conservative estimate to determine monthly profit/loss. He is estimating that he will have one client per month that will require a safety plan. He also estimates that he will conduct one 2-day training course each quarter. He estimates that his online safety courses will be ready for purchase after six months and that at that time, he will average selling forty training modules per month.

Quarterly Profit/Loss

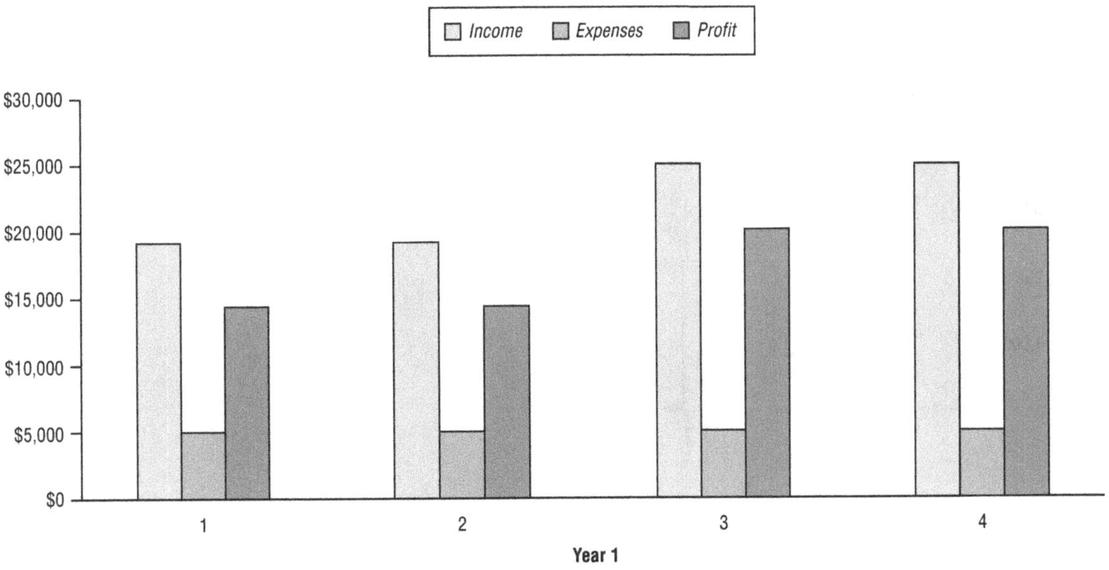

Profit projections assume that Safety Solutions will continue to grow. During the second year of operations, the owner expects expenses to remain constant. Mr. Jones projects that he will have two clients per month that will require safety plans. He expects to conduct one training session per quarter, and additionally he expects to sell 50 training modules per month.

Quarterly Profit Projection

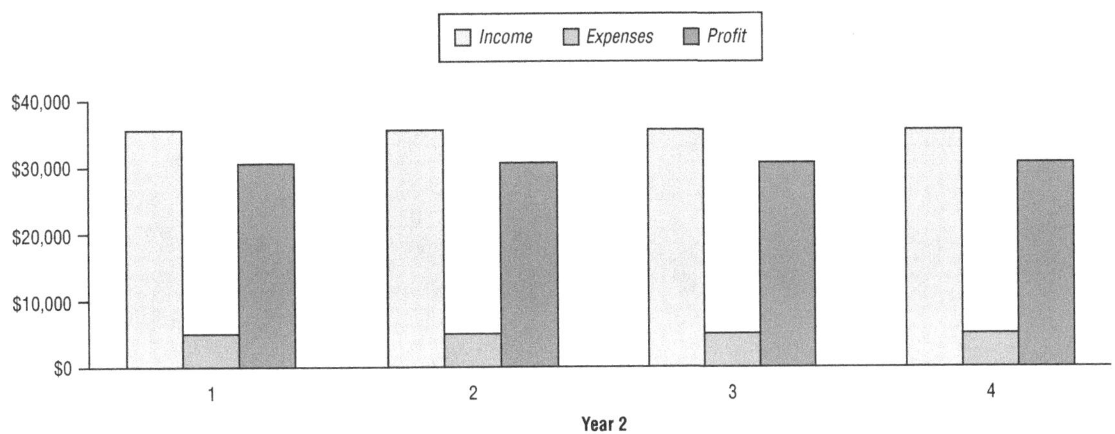

Financing

Mr. Jones is personally financing Safety Solutions. He will take $5,900 from his savings account to start the business.

Loan Repayment Plan

Mr. Jones estimates that Safety Solutions should be able to pay back his savings account easily within two years.

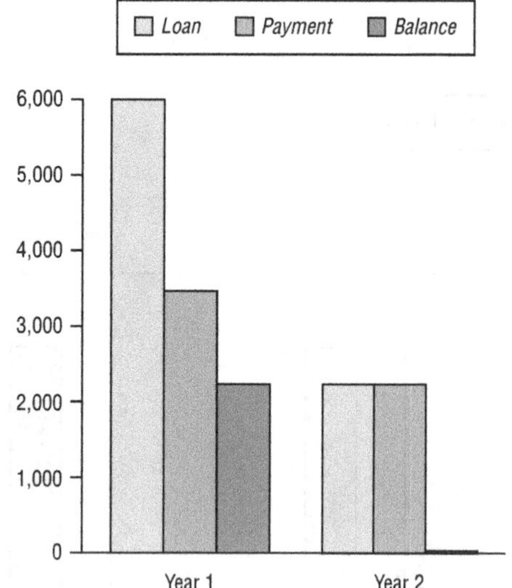
Loan
Payment
Balance
6,000
5,000
4,000
3,000
2,000
1,000
0
Year 1
Year 2

Sealcoating Business

A1 Sealcoating LLC

28 Oak Ave. SW
Langley, GA 30009

Paul Greenland

A1 Sealcoating is a newly established sealcoating business in Langley, Georgia.

EXECUTIVE SUMMARY

Although some driveways and parking lots are made of concrete, many more have an asphalt surface. In order to protect asphalt services from substances such as oil, antifreeze, and gas, as well as damage from the elements, it is necessary to periodically apply a layer of coal tar emulsion through a process known as sealcoating. A1 Sealcoating is a newly established sealcoating business in Langley, Georgia. The business will begin operations on a part-time basis, with services provided directly by owner Mark Lumley and his son, Rick. The following business plan details the Lumleys' strategy for steadily transforming A1 Sealcoating into a full-time operation with strong profit potential.

INDUSTRY ANALYSIS

The sealcoating industry is highly fragmented. In addition to a large number of small businesses like A1 Sealcoating, the industry also includes larger contractors who perform the biggest commercial jobs. The financial performance of these large contractors is one measure of industry growth. According to the publication, *Pavement Maintenance & Reconstruction* (http://www.forconstructionpros.com), the industry's 75 largest contractors generated sealcoating-specific sales of $249 million in 2015, an increase of 60 percent from 2014 levels of $150 million. In addition, the publication reports that the largest industry players are diversified operations that do more than just sealcoating, including:

- Sweeping (17%)
- Pavement repair (76%)
- Paving (84%)
- Striping (85%)

Pavement Maintenance & Reconstruction, which is published eight times per year, is targeted specifically toward contractors involved in all of the aforementioned categories. In addition to providing useful information that industry participants can use to grow their businesses, the publication also offers the tradeshow, National Pavement Expo, along with other helpful resources.

MARKET ANALYSIS

A1 Sealcoating is based in Langley, Georgia, and will begin operations with a focus on property owners in the Edgewood subdivision, which included approximately 550 homes in 2016. The business subsequently will expand the scope of its operations to include nearby subdivisions, including Webster Ridge (350 homes), Timberline (425 homes), and Homewood (260 homes), providing ample growth opportunities during the first several years of operations.

In 2016 Langley's population included about 189,000 people. At that time, 63 percent of the community's housing units were single-family homes, 35 percent were structures with two or more units (e.g., apartments and/or condominiums), and 2 percent were trailers or mobile homes. Because property owners, including landlords, are in need of property maintenance services, there is ample opportunity within this market segment.

Competition

A1 Sealcoating's main competition will come from the following businesses:

- B & J Sealcoating
- Manning Pavement Co.
- Langley Professional Services Inc.
- Tremblay Asphalt & Property Management Services LLC

A1 Sealcoating will differentiate itself from these existing competitors by emphasizing the fact that the owners are trusted neighbors, with a proud commitment of caring for area properties just their his own. Some of the company's largest competitors are based more than 60 miles away and visit the Langley market once per week, resulting in unresponsive customer service when residents are unhappy with the service they received. In this regard, A1 Sealcoating's status as a local provider will work to the business's advantage.

SERVICES

By its third year of operation, A1 Sealcoating will provide sealcoating services for a variety of asphalt surfaces, including:

- Driveways
- Pathways
- Walkways
- Private roadways
- Small parking lots

In addition, the business also will provide pavement striping/marking.

Pricing

A1 Sealcoating will charge 15-25 cents per square foot for most sealcoating jobs, based on the condition of the surface. Additional charges will apply for services such as additional coats, crack filling, line striping, etc. Finally, volume discounts are offered to customers in need of larger jobs.

Process

Generally speaking, the business will employ the following steps when performing sealcoating work:

1. *Evaluation:* The owners will personally assess the size and condition of the surface area.

2. *Estimation:* A firm time and cost estimate will be provided to the property owner, based on the evaluation and any special options (e.g., double coats, striping, etc.).
3. *Filling:* All cracks and holes in the surface will be filled prior to sealcoating.
4. *Edging:* Using a string trimmer, grass along the edges of driveways and parking lots will be trimmed thoroughly.
5. *Surface Preparation:* Because sealcoating requires a clean surface for proper adhesion, all debris and dirt will be removed from the surface using a power blower.
6. *Application:* Thin coats of sealant will be applied to the surface, using the appropriate tools. A double coat will be applied if necessary.
7. *Flagging:* Following completion of the sealcoating process, surfaces must be given proper time (generally 48 hours) to dry. Stakes and yellow caution tape (or orange cones in the case of parking lots) will be used to mark off areas so that vehicles and pedestrians do not walk or drive on recently sealcoated surfaces.

OPERATIONS

Business Structure

A1 Sealcoating is organized as a limited liability company in the state of Georgia. This will allow the owners to benefit from a certain level of liability protection with a business structure that is simpler than that of a corporation. A popular online legal document service was used to establish the Lumleys' LLC as cost-effectively as possible.

Location

The Lumleys will operate A1 Sealcoating as a home-based business for its first two years of operations. The owners already have a pickup truck that can be used for the business, and a shed for tool and equipment storage. The Lumleys will communicate with prospective and existing customers through voice, text, or e-mail via their smart phones, allowing them to respond in a timely manner from any location.

Equipment

After researching a number of reputable suppliers, the owners have determined that they will need to purchase $5,000 in equipment to begin their sealcoating business operation, including:

- Brush coaters
- Brush tank
- Caution tape
- Crack cleaning tools
- Crack fill melting kettle
- Pavement blowers
- Replacement squeegee blades
- Shovels
- Squeegees (edge, curved, slanted, etc.)
- Tampers
- Wire wheels
- Wooden stakes

When expanding to full-time operation in year two, the Lumleys will make additional purchases required for a larger-scale service, including:

- Asphalt roller ($3,500)
- Hot box trailer ($10,000)
- Hydraulic asphalt sealcoating machine ($8,000)

Insurance

The Lumleys have secured an appropriate level of liability insurance for their business, after consulting with their insurance agent.

PERSONNEL

A1 Sealcoating is being established by Mark Lumley and his son, Rick, who worked part-time for a sealcoating business as a high school student. Seeing the profit potential first-hand, Rick convinced his father, a long-time road construction worker who is seeking a less physically demanding job, to start a business they can build together. Mark's other son, Trent Lumley, also will be able to join the family business in several years, when he is of working age.

Professional & Advisory Support

A1 Sealcoating has established a business banking account with Midland Bank, including a merchant account for accepting credit card payments. The owners will use the service, Square, to easily accept credit card payments using their mobile devices. Tax advisement is provided by Peach Grove Accounting.

GROWTH STRATEGY

Year One: Establish A1 Sealcoating as a part-time, home-based business in the Langley market. Focus initial marketing efforts on the Lumley's immediate subdivision, emphasizing their status as "trusted neighbors." Limit service to driveways.

Year Two: Transition A1 Sealcoating to full-time operations, with all services provided directly by Mark and Rick Lumley. Expand service to include small parking lots. Begin performing asphalt crack repair in addition to sealcoating.

Year Three: Concentrate on continued organic growth. Begin formulating an expansion plan that can be executed in year four.

Year Four: Expand service offerings to include parking lot line striping. Begin leasing a dedicated location for the business, including a small office area and room for trucks and other equipment. Hire two employees and purchase additional equipment, allowing A1 Sealcoating to double service capacity by offering two crews.

Year Five: Consider the addition of a third crew, based on business volume.

Following is the projected breakdown of the business's volume for its first three years of operations:

Service	2017	2018	2019
Driveways	300	400	750
Parking lots	0	25	50

MARKETING & SALES

The owners of A1 Sealcoating have identified several marketing tactics for promoting and growing their business:

1. A color flyer promoting the business, with a space for writing in an estimate for a specific residence. This flyer can be distributed door to door, throughout the neighborhoods in Langley that are serviced by the business.
2. A customer loyalty program that provides a 15 percent discount to those referring a friend or family member.
3. A simple Web site with details about A1 Sealcoating and the Lumleys, including a contact form where customers can request a fast (two business days or less) estimate.
4. Membership in the Langley Georgia Chamber of Commerce, including a listing in the chamber's online and print business directories.
5. Registration with the Better Business Bureau to strengthen credibility.
6. The use of social media outlets such as Facebook (to reach consumers) and LinkedIn (to reach business owners).
7. Highly targeted quarterly mailings to residents in the neighborhoods served by A1 Sealcoating. The Lumleys have partnered with a mailing list broker, obtaining block data allowing them to target specific homeowners/businesses in their community.
8. Magnetic vehicle signage on the Lumleys vehicles, providing a cost-effective form of mobile marketing.

FINANCIAL ANALYSIS

A1 Sealcoating will generate relatively modest profits during its first two years of operations, as operations transition from part-time to full-time and the scope of services increases. The first two years also will require substantial capital investments. Mark Lumley will provide $20,000 in capital for equipment purchases and cash flow, which he will recoup by the end of year three, by which time the business will have generated nearly $110,000 in profits that can be used for potential expansion in years four and five.

Prior to establishing A1 Sealcoating, the Lumleys conducted research to arrive at a reasonable pricing structure for the business. In addition to material costs, the owners calculated their labor costs, based on approximately how much time it will take to sealcoat the average driveway. Based on this information, and conversations with other sealcoating providers in the region, the owners determined that an 80 percent profit margin will be possible for most jobs (sometimes 85 percent). The following financial projections are based on a conservative rate of 15 cents per square foot.

	2017	2018	2019
Driveways	$27,000	$ 36,000	$ 67,500
Parking lots	$ 0	$ 93,750	$187,500
Crack repair	$ 9,450	$ 45,413	$ 89,250
Total	**$36,450**	**$175,163**	**$344,250**
Expenses			
Salary	$ 6,000	$ 80,000	$125,000
Payroll taxes	$ 900	$ 12,000	$ 18,750
Supplies	$ 7,290	$ 35,033	$ 68,850
Insurance	$ 750	$ 950	$ 1,150
Accounting & legal	$ 1,200	$ 900	$ 900
Office supplies	$ 500	$ 600	$ 700
Equipment	$ 5,000	$ 21,500	$ 3,500
Marketing & advertising	$ 5,500	$ 10,000	$ 15,000
Telecommunications & Internet	$ 1,200	$ 1,200	$ 1,200
Maintenance & repair	$ 1,000	$ 2,000	$ 3,000
Vehicles	$ 0	$ 0	$ 12,500
Miscellaneous	$ 500	$ 600	$ 700
Total expenses	**$29,840**	**$164,783**	**$251,250**
Net income	**$ 6,610**	**$ 10,380**	**$ 93,000**

Temporary Employment Agency

College Co-op Temp Agency

2484 College Park Blvd., Ste. 109
Jacksonville, FL 32237

Fran Fletcher

College Co-op Temp Agency (CCTA) is a Jacksonville-based temporary employment agency that places college students in jobs with local businesses to enable them to gain experience in their field while attending college.

BUSINESS OVERVIEW

College Co-op Temp Agency (CCTA) is a Jacksonville-based temporary employment agency that places college students in jobs with local businesses to enable them to gain experience in their field while attending college.

The owners of CCTA are Jerry Douglas and Warren Broxton. These former college roommates saw a need for this service in Jacksonville while they were in school. As college students, they found that it could be extremely difficult to find a job related to one's field of study while also trying to earn a degree. They also witnessed that their friends who were engineering students or nursing students were able to gain experience while in school. However, it proved more difficult for other areas of study, and a large percentage of their classmates were left not knowing where to apply or not receiving job positions due to lack of experience. This still holds true several years later. So the owners wish to help local college students obtain experience in their field of studies, in order to offset the price of college and assist them in finding employment after graduation.

The business will serve the needs of both college students looking for work opportunities and local businesses and industries that are looking to invest in the future of these students while filling staffing needs.

CCTA will refer students of colleges located in the Jacksonville metro area. There are currently four major colleges/universities in Jacksonville and several smaller institutions that CCTA will work with. The owners expect to place one hundred students at nine different businesses within 6 months.

There are currently no competitors in the area specializing in providing job opportunities exclusively for college students. CCTA has contacted local college and university professors to determine needs and has approached local industries about hiring these students to fill vacancies. The Jacksonville Chamber of Commerce is a supporter of this business venture and many Chamber members have pledged support prior to business start-up.

CCTA will eliminate job hunting for students by referring them to jobs related to their college major. CCTA's income will be made by collecting a fee from the temp agency employees.

CCTA expects to steadily add clients and employees over time. CCTA hopes to expand its services after the third year of operation, but could do this sooner if demand increases for their services.

The owners currently have an opportunity to rent a 2,000 sq. ft. office space in Jacksonville. The space is centrally located and is ready to occupy. CCTA is currently seeking $31,200 in financing for this venture to cover start-up costs and expenses for the first two months. CCTA expects to repay the loan in 48 months or less.

COMPANY DESCRIPTION

Location

CCTA will lease a 2,000 sq. ft. office space in Jacksonville, Florida from which it will conduct business.

Hours of Operation

Office Hours are Monday through Friday, from 8 AM—5 PM.

Services

CCTA refers college students for employment opportunities with area businesses and industries.

CCTA will work with the following colleges and universities:

- University of North Florida
- Florida State College at Jacksonville
- Edward Waters College
- Jacksonville University
- Florida Coastal School of Law
- Florida Technical College of Jacksonville
- Jones College
- Webster University

CCTA will work with the following industries to place student workers:

- Airport
- Insurance
- Banking
- Robotics
- Healthcare
- Manufacturing

Personnel

Jerry Douglas (owner)
Mr. Douglas holds an MBA from Jacksonville University and has seven years of experience working in the manufacturing industry. His primary focus will be obtaining contracts with area industries to participate in the program.

Warren Broxton (owner)
Mr. Broxton holds a B.S. degree in business administration from Florida State University at Jacksonville. He has five years of experience in the insurance industry. His primary focus will be the day- to-

day operations of the business and making sure there is a steady stream of potential employees for industry participants.

MARKET ANALYSIS

Industry Overview

According to the Bureau of Labor Statistics, the job placement industry is expected to increase by 9% over the next decade.

There are four major colleges/universities and four smaller colleges/tech schools in Jacksonville with numerous areas of study. This provides a large pool of applicants to work and gain valuable experience within the numerous different industries in the Jacksonville area.

Target Market

CCTA will focus on two target markets: students at local colleges and universities and the industries who will hire them.

1. The owners need to first target businesses in the Jacksonville metro area that will provide employment for the college students.
2. The owners need to target college students by offering a variety of job opportunities for a variety of majors.

According to demographic information, Jacksonville had a population of 800,000 in 2015. There are 4 major colleges/universities and 4 smaller colleges/tech schools located in Jacksonville.

The owners plan to possibly expand their referral service to other cities in Florida as the demand for its services grows. The target market will expand to include these areas as needed.

Competition

There are no other local agencies that specialize in job placement for college students.

GROWTH STRATEGY

The overall strategy of CCTA is to quickly gain the reputation for being able to successfully place bright and hardworking students with industries for which they are suited. They plan to get this reputation by referring the best employee to each job situation. CCTA hopes to eventually expand their services to other areas of Florida.

Once the business has shown growth and success for a year or two, CCTA expects the colleges to use their job placement services as a selling point for potential students who are deciding where to attend college.

Sales and Marketing

The sales and marketing is two-fold. First, the owners must attract businesses and area industries to participate and hire these college students. Second, the owners must market their organization to college students in the area in order to provide a steady stream of students to fill the positions.

Advertising/marketing to attract employees will include:

- Advertising in Jacksonville area newspapers

- Advertising in campus newspapers
- Sending notices to applicable college departments

Advertising/marketing to attract businesses will include:

- Contacting Chamber of Commerce members

FINANCIAL ANALYSIS

Start-up Costs

The cost to start CCTA will consist of leasing an office space, general legal and accounting fees, and advertising expenses.

Start-up Costs

Legal fees	$3,000
Accounting fees	$1,000
Business license	$ 500
Advertising	$2,000
Office furniture	$3,000
Total cost	**$9,500**

Estimated Monthly Expenses

Generally, the cost of monthly expenses is fixed. Monthly rent is $800 and includes electricity and water. The owners will sign a three-year lease, which ensures that rent will not increase during this period. The company will use an accounting firm for payroll services. Salaries for the owners will increase as the number of clients increase.

Monthly expenses	Month 1	Months 2–6	Months 7–12
Rent	$ 800	$ 800	$ 800
Business loan	$ 300	$ 300	$ 300
CPA	$1,000	$ 1,000	$ 1,000
Phone/Internet	$ 150	$ 150	$ 150
Advertising	$ 100	$ 100	$ 100
Insurance	$ 100	$ 100	$ 100
Payroll	$6,800	$10,000	$10,000
Total	**$9,250**	**$12,450**	**$12,450**

Estimated Monthly Income

Monthly income will largely depend on the demand for CCTA's services. Income is projected to steadily increase during the first year of operation and expenses are expected to stay constant.

Price Schedule

Prices for services

Employee/weekly	$40
Employer/weekly	Payroll/social security

The following companies have already agreed to become clients of CCTA:

Company	Number of positions	Best majors for the job
Fancy Beer Company	15	Biology, chemistry, general science, engineering
Jacksonville Insurance	5	Business
First Downtown Bank	5	Business, finance
River Robotics	2	Engineering, graphic design, art
Big Pharma Inc.	15	Biology, chemistry, engineering
Chloe's Clothing Company	20	Business, art
Water Bottling of Florida	15	Biology, chemistry
Florida Hotels and Suites	8	Business, hotel management
North Florida Rehab	2	Allied health

There are a total of 87 jobs available at business start-up. Job opportunities range from 4 weeks to one year.

Profit/Loss

Conservative estimates predict that they will place 43 students into jobs during the first month. The goal is to have 87 clients by the second month and remain steady through the sixth month. Then, it is predicted that 100 jobs will be filled during months 7 through 12. Profits are expected to gradually increase as job placements increase. The owners do not expect to raise prices for services but will use increased profits to give themselves a bonus at the end of each year.

Monthly Profit/Loss

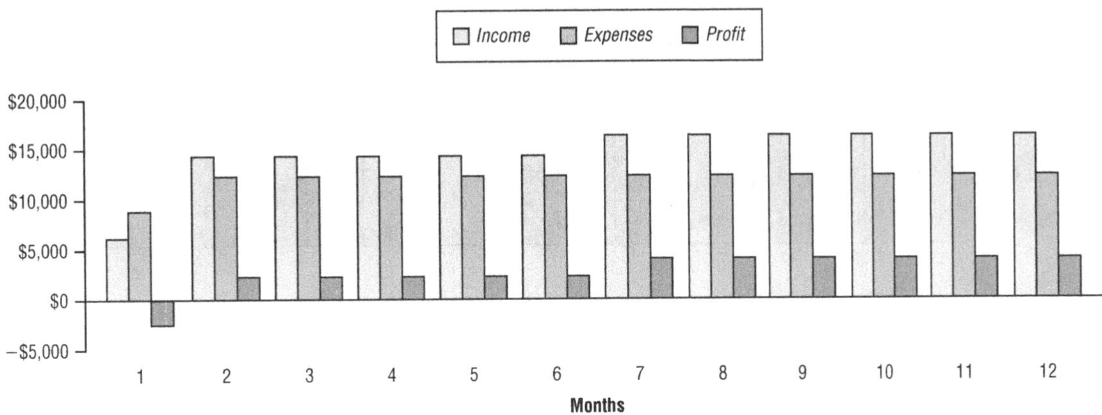

3-Year Profit Projections

Financing

The owners of CCTA wish to obtain financing in the form of a business line of credit for the amount needed to cover the start up costs and operating expenses for the first two months. This loan would be in the amount of $31,200.

Repayment Plan

Loan payments are set at $300 per month. An additional payment will be made at the end of each year using 20% of the company's annual profit. This would be approximately $5,200 per year according to profit projections. According to the estimated expenses vs. income, CCTA will pay back the loan in 48 months.

Loan Repayment Plan

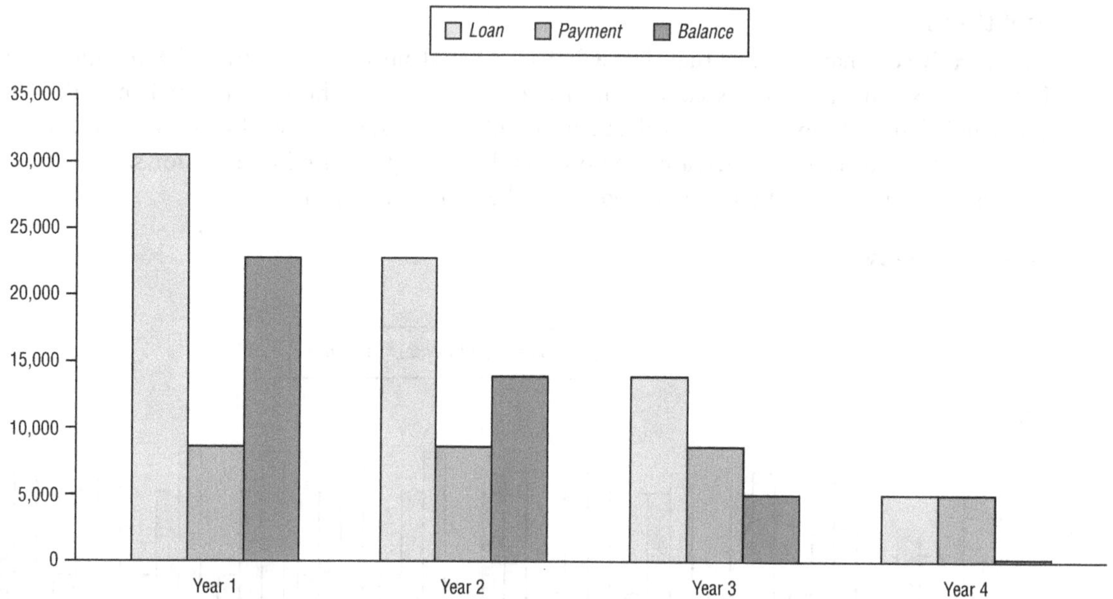

Yoga Studio

Barefoot Yoga

2585 Northgate Ln.
Dothan, AL 36304

Fran Fletcher

Barefoot Yoga is a private yoga studio located in Dothan, Alabama. Barefoot Yoga's goal is to help clients gain balance, core strength, self-confidence, and noticeable results through yoga. Barefoot Yoga will offer multiple levels of instruction to help combat feelings of intimidation for beginning students or for heavier students. Private yoga instruction will be offered for individualized training. Additionally, Barefoot Yoga will offer a variety of yoga accessories that may be purchased at the studio.

BUSINESS SUMMARY

Barefoot Yoga is a private yoga studio located in Dothan, Alabama. Pari Singh is the owner and the instructor. Even though Ms. Singh has a full-time job as a teacher at Dogwood Elementary School, she wishes to boost her earnings by teaching yoga. She started practicing yoga while in college and gained her yoga instructor certification this past summer. Ms. Singh wants to share her experience, knowledge, and love for yoga with yogis (people who enjoy yoga) of all ages and abilities in the Dothan area.

Ms. Singh plans to make modifications to her home's existing sunroom and use it as a yoga studio. Classes will be offered 7 days per week according to a published schedule. Ms. Singh will offer group and private instruction. For convenience, Ms. Singh will also provide yoga instruction two afternoons per week at Dogwood Elementary and two evenings per week at Southeast Alabama Medical Center.

Women between the ages of 18 and 60 are Barefoot Yoga's target market. Sixty-eight percent of Dothan's female population falls into this category and provides a large potential customer base for the business.

Barefoot Yoga's goal is to help clients gain balance, core strength, self-confidence, and noticeable results through yoga. Barefoot Yoga will offer multiple levels of instruction to help combat feelings of intimidation for beginning students or for heavier students. Private yoga instruction will be offered for individualized training. Additionally, Barefoot Yoga will offer a variety of yoga accessories that may be purchased at the studio.

According to the Bureau of Labor Statistics, the job outlook for fitness trainers/instructors is expected to increase by 8% over the next decade. That is not a large increase and is why Ms. Singh will be using the business to supplement her existing income. There are several other businesses offering yoga classes in the area, but Ms. Singh is confident that both individualized instruction and summer camps will set Barefoot Yoga apart from its competitors.

Barefoot Yoga's business strategy is to fill classes to maximum capacity, to obtain new clients, and to retain these clients throughout the year. The business will advertise its class schedule at Dogwood Elementary, Southeast Alabama Medical Center, local chiropractor offices, and on social media. These advertising avenues should help the business reach its intended target market.

Barefoot Yoga is currently seeking financing in the amount of $9,250 to cover start-up costs. Ms. Singh plans to repay the financing in approximately two years.

COMPANY DESCRIPTION

Location

Barefoot Yoga will be located at Ms. Singh's home in Dothan, Alabama. She has a 20 x 20 sunroom that will be used as a yoga studio. The studio is conveniently located to Dogwood Elementary and the hospital, where she will offer group instruction.

Hours of Operation

Barefoot Yoga will offer classes 7 days a week at times determined by a published schedule.

Personnel

Pari Singh (owner/ instructor)
Ms. Singh is a yoga instructor certified through the International Yoga Association. Ms. Singh has been practicing yoga for six years. Last summer, she gained her instructor certification by attending an 8-week training program in Los Angeles, California. Ms. Singh is a third-grade teacher at Dogwood Elementary School.

Products and Services

Products

- Yoga mats
- Yoga straps with buckles
- Yoga straps without buckles
- Yoga bolsters
- Yoga blanket
- Yoga blocks
- Water bottles
- Yoga apparel
- Yoga starter kit

Services

- Private instruction
- Group instruction
- Summer yoga camp

Class Schedule (August- May)

	Dogwood Elementary	Southeast AL Medical Center	Studio Group Instruction	Studio Private Instruction
Monday		All levels 6:00 p.m.	Intermediate/Advanced 5:00 a.m. Curvy Class 7:30 p.m.	4:00 p.m. 8:30 p.m.
Tuesday	All levels 4:00 p.m.		Advanced 5:00 a.m.	5:30 p.m. 6:30 p.m. 7:30 p.m.
Wednesday		All levels 6:00 p.m.	Intermediate/Advanced 5:00 a.m. Beginners 7:30 p.m.	
Thursday	All levels 4:00 p.m.		Advanced 5:00 a.m. All levels 6:00 p.m.	7:30 p.m.
Friday			Intermediate/Advanced 5:00 a.m. All levels 5:30 p.m.	4:00 p.m. 7:00 p.m.
Saturday			7:00 a.m. Intermediate/Advanced 8:30 a.m. Beginners 10:00 a.m. Mommy/Mommy to Be 11:00 a.m. Curvy Class	
Sunday				2:00 p.m. 3:00 p.m.

Class Schedule (June and July)

	Camp	Southeast AL Medical Center	Studio Group Instruction	Studio Private Instruction
Monday	June—Week 2 Ages 5–8	All levels 6:00 p.m.	Intermediate/Advanced 5:00 a.m. Curvy Class 7:30 p.m.	4:00 p.m. 8:30 p.m.
Tuesday	June—Week 3 Ages 9–12		Advanced 5:00 a.m. All levels 6:00 p.m.	5:30 p.m. 6:30 p.m. 7:30 p.m.
Wednesday	June—Week 4 Ages 13–18	All levels 6:00 p.m.	Intermediate/Advanced 5:00 a.m. Beginners 7:30 p.m.	
Thursday	All camps are Monday through Friday		Advanced 5:00 a.m. All levels 6:00 p.m.	7:30 p.m.
Friday	8:00 a.m.–5:00 p.m.		Intermediate/Advanced 5:00 a.m. All levels 5:30 p.m.	4:00 p.m. 7:00 p.m.
Saturday			7:00 a.m. Intermediate/Advanced 8:30 a.m. Beginners 10:00 a.m. Mommy/Mommy to Be 11:00 a.m. Curvy Class	
Sunday				2:00 p.m. 3:00 p.m.

MARKETING ANALYSIS

Industry Overview

According to the Bureau of Labor Statistics, the job outlook for fitness trainers/instructors is expected to increase by 8% over the next decade.

Competition

There are currently two gyms that offer yoga classes within twenty miles of Barefoot Yoga. Barefoot Yoga plans to set itself apart by offering private instruction and summer camps for kids.

1. JJ's Gym
2. All Time Fitness

Target Market

Women between the ages of 18 and 60 who want to improve their balance, coordination, and overall well-being will be the target market of Barefoot Yoga.

The latest demographics reveal that Dothan's female population was approximately 58,000 and consisted of the following age groups:

Target Market by Age

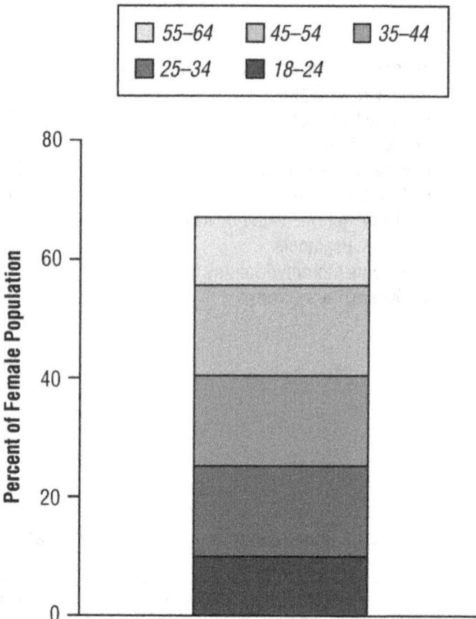

Approximately 39,000 females in Dothan meet the criteria for Barefoot Yoga's target market. Barefoot Yoga will strive to tap into this market with its marketing strategies.

GROWTH STRATEGY

The overall growth strategy of Barefoot Yoga is to offer a serene environment where women can practice yoga and achieve their personal goals for flexibility and balance. Clients who practice two or three times and quit are the toughest obstacles currently facing yoga professionals. Ms. Singh is determined to keep clients motivated and coming back. She is offering a variety of class times to fit the busy schedules of clients. She will also offer private instruction for beginners so that they can learn various yoga poses before attending a group class. Ms. Singh knows that if clients enjoy their time and start seeing results and improvement, they will be less inclined to skip classes or quit. This will ensure that the studio continues growing.

The business strategy is to fill classes to maximum capacity, to obtain new clients, and to retain these clients throughout the year. Ms. Singh will change her strategy after 6 months if classes are not filled to capacity. The strategy would include offering classes at another nearby school, rearranging class times at the studio, adding specialized classes (women with prior back injuries, new moms), or adding additional weeks of summer camp.

Sales and Marketing

The company has identified key tactics to support the company's growth strategy.

Advertising will include:

- Advertising at Dogwood Elementary
- Advertising at Southeast Alabama Medical Center

- Advertising at local chiropractic clinics
- Advertising on social media

Ongoing marketing strategies:

- Using social media
- Holding yoga camps for kids

FINANCIAL ANALYSIS

Start-up Costs

Ms. Singh will use her sunroom as her yoga studio. It has an exterior door and a bathroom. She also has plenty of parking for clients.

A few additions are needed to make the sunroom more inviting as a yoga studio. Ms. Singh wants to add shelving for yoga equipment, bins where clients can place their personal belongings, a relaxing water feature, a sound system, and some softer lighting.

Estimated Monthly Expenses

Estimated Start-up Costs

Water feature	$2,000
Shelving/bins	$1,000
Legal fees	$2,500
Office furniture	$1,500
Business license	$ 250
Initial advertising	$ 500
Inventory of yoga supplies	$1,500
Total	**$9,250**

Expenses are expected to remain constant each month.

Monthly Expenses

Phone/Internet	$100.00
Advertising	$ 20.00
Insurance	$100.00
Inventory	$250.00
Loan repayment	$400.00
Total	**$870.00**

Estimated Monthly Income

Monthly income will be determined by the number of clients, but is expected to steadily increase every three months. One month during the summer is expected to see increased income due to the three yoga camps.

Prices for Services

Service	Price
Group instruction at school	$ 10
Group instruction at hospital	$ 10
Group instruction at studio	$ 15
Individual instruction at studio	$ 20
Camp	$150

Most classes are scheduled for one hour. Class sizes are not limited at the school or hospital; however, class size at the studio is limited to 8. Spaces will be assigned and clients must pay to keep their space in the class, whether they attend or not. A waiting list will be maintained for each class. Individual instruction is limited to 10 time slots per week and will be filled by appointment only. Two of the 10 individual time slots will be held for new students who need instruction on yoga poses. Summer yoga camps are limited to 15 kids for each week of camp.

Profit/Loss

According to estimated expenses and conservative income data, Barefoot Yoga will start making income from the start. The profit estimate for the first three months is based on 5 clients attending each of the school and hospital classes, and 42 clients meeting for the various class times offered at the studio. The profit estimate for the next 6 months is based on an increase to 8 clients attending school and hospital classes, and 68 clients meeting for the various studio class times. Barefoot Yoga will offer three weeks of yoga camp during the summer in addition to offering classes at the hospital and studio.

The company estimates that income will increase 5% during the second year of operation and that expenses will remain the same.

Monthly Profit/Loss

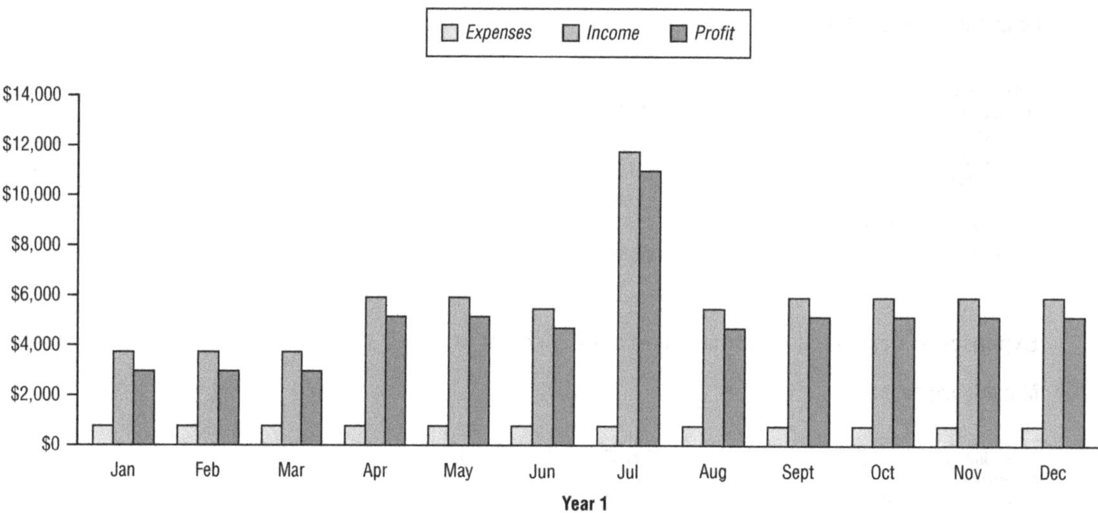

Annual Profit/Loss

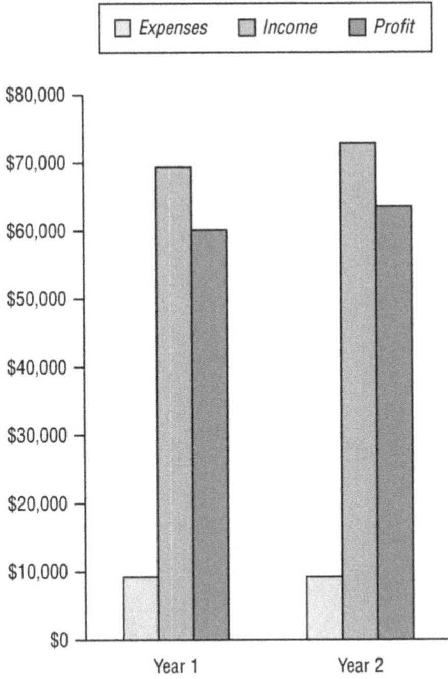

Financing

Barefoot Yoga is currently seeking financing in the amount of $9,250. This would cover start-up expenses incurred while adding the water feature to the studio and purchasing items to sell. Ms. Singh is confident that she will be able to repay this loan in approximately two years as illustrated in the "Repayment Plan" chart.

Repayment Plan

BUSINESS PLAN HANDBOOK

USING THIS TEMPLATE

A business plan carefully spells out a company's projected course of action over a period of time, usually the first two to three years after the start-up. In addition, banks, lenders, and other investors examine the information and financial documentation before deciding whether or not to finance a new business venture. Therefore, a business plan is an essential tool in obtaining financing and should describe the business itself in detail as well as all important factors influencing the company, including the market, industry, competition, operations and management policies, problem solving strategies, financial resources and needs, and other vital information. The plan enables the business owner to anticipate costs, plan for difficulties, and take advantage of opportunities, as well as design and implement strategies that keep the company running as smoothly as possible.

This template has been provided as a model to help you construct your own business plan. Please keep in mind that there is no single acceptable format for a business plan, and that this template is in no way comprehensive, but serves as an example.

The business plans provided in this section are fictional and have been used by small business agencies as models for clients to use in compiling their own business plans.

GENERIC BUSINESS PLAN

Main headings included below are topics that should be covered in a comprehensive business plan. They include:

Business Summary

Purpose
Provides a brief overview of your business, succinctly highlighting the main ideas of your plan.

Includes

- Topic Headings and Subheadings
- Page Number References

Table of Contents

Purpose
Organized in an Outline Format, the Table of Contents illustrates the selection and arrangement of information contained in your plan.

Includes

- Name and Type of Business
- Description of Product/Service
- Business History and Development
- Location
- Market
- Competition
- Management
- Financial Information
- Business Strengths and Weaknesses
- Business Growth

Business History and Industry Outlook

Purpose

Examines the conception and subsequent development of your business within an industry specific context.

Includes

- Start-up Information
- Owner/Key Personnel Experience
- Location
- Development Problems and Solutions
- Investment/Funding Information
- Future Plans and Goals
- Market Trends and Statistics
- Major Competitors
- Product/Service Advantages
- National, Regional, and Local Economic Impact

Product/Service

Purpose

Introduces, defines, and details the product and/or service that inspired the information of your business.

Includes

- Unique Features
- Niche Served
- Market Comparison
- Stage of Product/Service Development
- Production
- Facilities, Equipment, and Labor
- Financial Requirements
- Product/Service Life Cycle
- Future Growth

Market Examination

Purpose

Assessment of product/service applications in relation to consumer buying cycles.

Includes

- Target Market
- Consumer Buying Habits
- Product/Service Applications
- Consumer Reactions
- Market Factors and Trends
- Penetration of the Market
- Market Share
- Research and Studies
- Cost
- Sales Volume and Goals

Competition

Purpose

Analysis of Competitors in the Marketplace.

Includes

- Competitor Information
- Product/Service Comparison
- Market Niche
- Product/Service Strengths and Weaknesses
- Future Product/Service Development

Marketing

Purpose
Identifies promotion and sales strategies for your product/service.

Includes

- Product/Service Sales Appeal
- Special and Unique Features
- Identification of Customers
- Sales and Marketing Staff
- Sales Cycles
- Type of Advertising/ Promotion
- Pricing
- Competition
- Customer Services

Operations

Purpose
Traces product/service development from production/inception to the market environment.

Includes

- Cost Effective Production Methods
- Facility
- Location
- Equipment
- Labor
- Future Expansion

Administration and Management

Purpose
Offers a statement of your management philosophy with an in-depth focus on processes and procedures.

Includes

- Management Philosophy
- Structure of Organization
- Reporting System
- Methods of Communication
- Employee Skills and Training
- Employee Needs and Compensation
- Work Environment
- Management Policies and Procedures
- Roles and Responsibilities

Key Personnel

Purpose
Describes the unique backgrounds of principle employees involved in business.

Includes

- Owner(s)/Employee Education and Experience
- Positions and Roles
- Benefits and Salary
- Duties and Responsibilities
- Objectives and Goals

Potential Problems and Solutions

Purpose
Discussion of problem solving strategies that change issues into opportunities.

Includes

- Risks
- Litigation
- Future Competition
- Economic Impact
- Problem Solving Skills

Financial Information

Purpose

Secures needed funding and assistance through worksheets and projections detailing financial plans, methods of repayment, and future growth opportunities.

Includes

- Financial Statements
- Bank Loans
- Methods of Repayment
- Tax Returns
- Start-up Costs
- Projected Income (3 years)
- Projected Cash Flow (3 Years)
- Projected Balance Statements (3 years)

Appendices

Purpose

Supporting documents used to enhance your business proposal.

Includes

- Photographs of product, equipment, facilities, etc.
- Copyright/Trademark Documents
- Legal Agreements
- Marketing Materials
- Research and or Studies
- Operation Schedules
- Organizational Charts
- Job Descriptions
- Resumes
- Additional Financial Documentation

Fictional Food Distributor

Commercial Foods, Inc.

3003 Avondale Ave.
Knoxville, TN 37920

This plan demonstrates how a partnership can have a positive impact on a new business. It demonstrates how two individuals can carve a niche in the specialty foods market by offering gourmet foods to upscale restaurants and fine hotels. This plan is fictional and has not been used to gain funding from a bank or other lending institution.

STATEMENT OF PURPOSE

Commercial Foods, Inc. seeks a loan of $75,000 to establish a new business. This sum, together with $5,000 equity investment by the principals, will be used as follows:

- Merchandise inventory $25,000
- Office fixture/equipment $12,000
- Warehouse equipment $14,000
- One delivery truck $10,000
- Working capital $39,000
- Total $100,000

DESCRIPTION OF THE BUSINESS

Commercial Foods, Inc. will be a distributor of specialty food service products to hotels and upscale restaurants in the geographical area of a 50 mile radius of Knoxville. Richard Roberts will direct the sales effort and John Williams will manage the warehouse operation and the office. One delivery truck will be used initially with a second truck added in the third year. We expect to begin operation of the business within 30 days after securing the requested financing.

MANAGEMENT

A. Richard Roberts is a native of Memphis, Tennessee. He is a graduate of Memphis State University with a Bachelor's degree from the School of Business. After graduation, he worked for a major manufacturer of specialty food service products as a detail sales person for five years, and, for the past three years, he has served as a product sales manager for this firm.

B. John Williams is a native of Nashville, Tennessee. He holds a B.S. Degree in Food Technology from the University of Tennessee. His career includes five years as a product development chemist in gourmet food products and five years as operations manager for a food service distributor.

Both men are healthy and energetic. Their backgrounds complement each other, which will ensure the success of Commercial Foods, Inc. They will set policies together and personnel decisions will be made jointly. Initial salaries for the owners will be $1,000 per month for the first few years. The spouses of both principals are successful in the business world and earn enough to support the families.

They have engaged the services of Foster Jones, CPA, and William Hale, Attorney, to assist them in an advisory capacity.

PERSONNEL

The firm will employ one delivery truck driver at a wage of $8.00 per hour. One office worker will be employed at $7.50 per hour. One part-time employee will be used in the office at $5.00 per hour. The driver will load and unload his own trucks. Mr. Williams will assist in the warehouse operation as needed to assist one stock person at $7.00 per hour. An additional delivery truck and driver will be added the third year.

LOCATION

The firm will lease a 20,000 square foot building at 3003 Avondale Ave., in Knoxville, which contains warehouse and office areas equipped with two-door truck docks. The annual rental is $9,000. The building was previously used as a food service warehouse and very little modification to the building will be required.

PRODUCTS AND SERVICES

The firm will offer specialty food service products such as soup bases, dessert mixes, sauce bases, pastry mixes, spices, and flavors, normally used by upscale restaurants and nice hotels. We are going after a niche in the market with high quality gourmet products. There is much less competition in this market than in standard run of the mill food service products. Through their work experiences, the principals have contacts with supply sources and with local chefs.

THE MARKET

We know from our market survey that there are over 200 hotels and upscale restaurants in the area we plan to serve. Customers will be attracted by a direct sales approach. We will offer samples of our products and product application data on use of our products in the finished prepared foods. We will cultivate the chefs in these establishments. The technical background of John Williams will be especially useful here.

COMPETITION

We find that we will be only distributor in the area offering a full line of gourmet food service products. Other foodservice distributors offer only a few such items in conjunction with their standard product

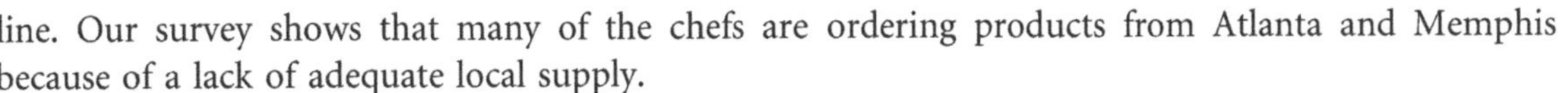

line. Our survey shows that many of the chefs are ordering products from Atlanta and Memphis because of a lack of adequate local supply.

SUMMARY

Commercial Foods, Inc. will be established as a foodservice distributor of specialty food in Knoxville. The principals, with excellent experience in the industry, are seeking a $75,000 loan to establish the business. The principals are investing $25,000 as equity capital.

The business will be set up as an S Corporation with each principal owning 50% of the common stock in the corporation.

Fictional Hardware Store

Oshkosh Hardware, Inc.

123 Main St.
Oshkosh, WI 54901

The following plan outlines how a small hardware store can survive competition from large discount chains by offering products and providing expert advice in the use of any product it sells. This plan is fictional and has not been used to gain funding from a bank or other lending institution.

EXECUTIVE SUMMARY

Oshkosh Hardware, Inc. is a new corporation that is going to establish a retail hardware store in a strip mall in Oshkosh, Wisconsin. The store will sell hardware of all kinds, quality tools, paint, and housewares. The business will make revenue and a profit by servicing its customers not only with needed hardware but also with expert advice in the use of any product it sells.

Oshkosh Hardware, Inc. will be operated by its sole shareholder, James Smith. The company will have a total of four employees. It will sell its products in the local market. Customers will buy our products because we will provide free advice on the use of all of our products and will also furnish a full refund warranty.

Oshkosh Hardware, Inc. will sell its products in the Oshkosh store staffed by three sales representatives. No additional employees will be needed to achieve its short and long range goals. The primary short range goal is to open the store by October 1, 1994. In order to achieve this goal a lease must be signed by July 1, 1994 and the complete inventory ordered by August 1, 1994.

Mr. James Smith will invest $30,000 in the business. In addition, the company will have to borrow $150,000 during the first year to cover the investment in inventory, accounts receivable, and furniture and equipment. The company will be profitable after six months of operation and should be able to start repayment of the loan in the second year.

THE BUSINESS

The business will sell hardware of all kinds, quality tools, paint, and housewares. We will purchase our products from three large wholesale buying groups.

In general our customers are homeowners who do their own repair and maintenance, hobbyists, and housewives. Our business is unique in that we will have a complete line of all hardware items and will be able to get special orders by overnight delivery. The business makes revenue and profits by servicing our customers not only with needed hardware but also with expert advice in the use of any product we sell. Our major costs for bringing our products to market are cost of merchandise of 36%, salaries of $45,000, and occupancy costs of $60,000.

Oshkosh Hardware, Inc.'s retail outlet will be located at 1524 Frontage Road, which is in a newly developed retail center of Oshkosh. Our location helps facilitate accessibility from all parts of town and reduces our delivery costs. The store will occupy 7500 square feet of space. The major equipment involved in our business is counters and shelving, a computer, a paint mixing machine, and a truck.

THE MARKET

Oshkosh Hardware, Inc. will operate in the local market. There are 15,000 potential customers in this market area. We have three competitors who control approximately 98% of the market at present. We feel we can capture 25% of the market within the next four years. Our major reason for believing this is that our staff is technically competent to advise our customers in the correct use of all products we sell.

After a careful market analysis, we have determined that approximately 60% of our customers are men and 40% are women. The percentage of customers that fall into the following age categories are:

Under 16: 0%

17-21: 5%

22-30: 30%

31-40: 30%

41-50: 20%

51-60: 10%

61-70: 5%

Over 70: 0%

The reasons our customers prefer our products is our complete knowledge of their use and our full refund warranty.

We get our information about what products our customers want by talking to existing customers. There seems to be an increasing demand for our product. The demand for our product is increasing in size based on the change in population characteristics.

SALES

At Oshkosh Hardware, Inc. we will employ three sales people and will not need any additional personnel to achieve our sales goals. These salespeople will need several years experience in home repair and power tool usage. We expect to attract 30% of our customers from newspaper ads, 5% of our customers from local directories, 5% of our customers from the yellow pages, 10% of our customers from family and friends, and 50% of our customers from current customers. The most cost effect source will be current customers. In general our industry is growing.

MANAGEMENT

We would evaluate the quality of our management staff as being excellent. Our manager is experienced and very motivated to achieve the various sales and quality assurance objectives we have set. We will use a management information system that produces key inventory, quality assurance, and sales data on a weekly basis. All data is compared to previously established goals for that week, and deviations are the primary focus of the management staff.

GOALS IMPLEMENTATION

The short term goals of our business are:

1. Open the store by October 1, 1994
2. Reach our breakeven point in two months
3. Have sales of $100,000 in the first six months

In order to achieve our first short term goal we must:

1. Sign the lease by July 1, 1994
2. Order a complete inventory by August 1, 1994

In order to achieve our second short term goal we must:

1. Advertise extensively in Sept. and Oct.
2. Keep expenses to a minimum

In order to achieve our third short term goal we must:

1. Promote power tool sales for the Christmas season
2. Keep good customer traffic in Jan. and Feb.

The long term goals for our business are:

1. Obtain sales volume of $600,000 in three years
2. Become the largest hardware dealer in the city
3. Open a second store in Fond du Lac

The most important thing we must do in order to achieve the long term goals for our business is to develop a highly profitable business with excellent cash flow.

FINANCE

Oshkosh Hardware, Inc. Faces some potential threats or risks to our business. They are discount house competition. We believe we can avoid or compensate for this by providing quality products complimented by quality advice on the use of every product we sell. The financial projections we have prepared are located at the end of this document.

JOB DESCRIPTION-GENERAL MANAGER

The General Manager of the business of the corporation will be the president of the corporation. He will be responsible for the complete operation of the retail hardware store which is owned by the corporation. A detailed description of his duties and responsibilities is as follows.

Sales

Train and supervise the three sales people. Develop programs to motivate and compensate these employees. Coordinate advertising and sales promotion effects to achieve sales totals as outlined in budget. Oversee purchasing function and inventory control procedures to insure adequate merchandise at all times at a reasonable cost.

Finance

Prepare monthly and annual budgets. Secure adequate line of credit from local banks. Supervise office personnel to insure timely preparation of records, statements, all government reports, control of receivables and payables, and monthly financial statements.

Administration

Perform duties as required in the areas of personnel, building leasing and maintenance, licenses and permits, and public relations.

Organizations, Agencies, & Consultants

A listing of Associations and Consultants of interest to entrepreneurs, followed by the Small Business Administration Regional Offices, Small Business Development Centers, Service Corps of Retired Executives offices, and Venture Capital and Finance Companies.

Associations

This section contains a listing of associations and other agencies of interest to the small business owner. Entries are listed alphabetically by organization name.

American Business Women's Association
9820 Metcalf Ave., Ste. 110
Overland Park, MO 66212
(800)228-0007
Fax: (913)660-0101
E-mail: webmail@abwa.org
Website: http://www.abwa.org
Rene Street, Exec. Dir.

American Franchisee Association
53 W Jackson Blvd., Ste. 1256
Chicago, IL 60604
(312)431-0545
Fax: (312)431-1469
E-mail: spkezios@franchisee.org
Website: http://www.franchisee.org
Susan P. Kezios, Pres.

American Independent Business Alliance
222 S Black Ave.
Bozeman, MT 59715
(406)582-1255
Website: http://www.amiba.net
Jennifer Rockne, Co-Dir.
Jeff Milchen, Co-Dir.

American Small Business Coalition
PO Box 2786
Columbia, MD 21045
(410)381-7378
Website: https://www.theasbc.org
Margaret H. Timberlake, Pres.

American Small Business League
3910 Cypress Dr., Ste. B
Petaluma, CA 94954
(707)789-9575
Fax: (707)789-9580
E-mail: jspatola@asbl.com
Website: http://www.asbl.com
Lloyd Chapman, Founder

American Small Business Travelers Alliance
3112 Bent Oak Cir.
Flower Mound, TX 75022
(972)836-8064
E-mail: info@asbta.com
Website: http://www.asbta.com/
Chuck Sharp, Pres./CEO

America's Small Business Development Center
8990 Burke Lake Rd., 2nd Fl.
Burke, VA 22015
(703)764-9850
Fax: (703)764-1234
E-mail: info@americassbdc.org
Website: http://americassbdc.org
Charles Rowe, Pres./CEO

Association for Enterprise Opportunity
1310 L St NW, Ste. 830
Washington, DC 22209
(202)650-5580
E-mail: cevans@aeoworks.org
Website: http://www.aeoworks.org
Connie Evans, Pres./CEO

Association of Printing and Data Solutions Professionals
PO Box 2249
Oak Park, IL 60303
(708)218-7755
E-mail: ed.avis@irga.com
Website: http://www.apdsp.org
Ed Avis, Mng. Dir.

Association of Publishers for Special Sales
PO Box 9725
Colorado Springs, CO 80932-0725
(719)924-5534
Fax: (719)213-2602
E-mail: BrianJud@bookapss.org
Website: http://community.bookapss.org
Brian Jud, Exec. Dir.

BEST Association
17701 Mitchell N
Irvine, CA 92614-6028
866-706-2225
Website: http://www.beassoc.org

Business Planning Institute, LLC
580 Village Blvd., Ste. 150
West Palm Beach, FL 33409
(561)236-5533
Fax: (561)689-5546
E-mail: info@bpiplans.com
Website: http://www.bpiplans.com

Coalition for Government Procurement
1990 M St. NW, Ste. 450
Washington, DC 20036
(202)331-0975
Fax: (202)521-3533
E-mail: rwaldron@thecgp.org
Website: http://thecgp.org
Roger Waldron, Pres.

Ewing Marion Kauffman Foundation
4801 Rockhill Rd.
Kansas City, MO 64110
(816)932-1000
Website: http://www.kauffman.org
Wendy Guillies, Pres./CEO

Family Business Coalition
PO Box 722
Washington, DC 20044
(202)393-8959
E-mail: info@familybusinesscoalition.org
Website: http://familybusinesscoalition.org
Palmer Schoening, Chm.

Family Firm Institute, Inc.
200 Lincoln St., Ste. 201
Boston, MA 02111
(617)482-3045
Fax: (617)482-3049
E-mail: ffi@ffi.org
Website: http://www.ffi.org
Judy Green, Pres.

Film Independent
9911 W Pico Blvd., 11th Fl.
Los Angeles, CA 90035
(310)432-1200
Fax: (310)432-1203
E-mail: jwelsh@filmindependent.org
Website: http://www.filmindependent.org
Josh Welsh, Pres.

HR People and Strategy
1800 Duke St.
Alexandria, VA 223142
(703)535-6056
Fax: (703)535-6490
E-mail: info@hrps.org
Website: http://www.hrps.org
Lisa Connell, Exec. Dir.

Independent Visually Impaired Entrepreneurs
2121 Scott Rd., No. 105
Burbank, CA 91504-1228
(818)238-9321
E-mail: abazyn@bazyncommunications.com
Website: http://www.ivie-acb.org
Ardis Bazyn, Pres.

International Council for Small Business
Funger Hall, Ste. 315
2201 G St. NW
Washington, DC 20052
(202)994-0704
Fax: (202)994-4930
E-mail: icsb@gwu.edu
Website: http://www.icsb.org
Dr. Ayman El Tarabishy, Exec. Dir.

LearnServe International
PO Box 6203
Washington, DC 20015
(202)370-1865
Fax: (202)355-0993
E-mail: info@learn-serve.org
Website: http://learn-serve.org
Scott Rechler, Dir./CEO

National Association for the Self-Employed
PO Box 241
Annapolis Junction, MD 20701-0241
800-232-6273
800-649-6273 (Alaska and Hawaii only)
E-mail: media@nase.org
Website: http://www.nase.org
Keith R. Hall, CPA, Pres./CEO

National Association of Business Owners
1509 Green Mountain Dr.
Little Rock, AR 72211
(501)227-8423
Website: http://nabo.org

National Association of Small Business Contractors
700 12th St. NW, Ste. 700
Washington, DC 20005
Free: 888-861-9290
Website: http://www.nasbc.org
Cris Young, Pres.

National Business Association
15305 Dallas Pkwy., Ste. 300
Addison, TX 75001
800-456-0440
Fax: (972)960-9149
E-mail: database@nationalbusiness.org
Website: http://www.nationalbusiness.org

National Federation of Independent Business
1201 F St. NW
Washington, DC 20004
(615)872-5800
800-NFIBNOW
Fax: (615)872-5353
Website: http://www.nfib.org
Juanita Duggan, Pres./CEO

National Small Business Association
1156 15th St. NW, Ste. 502
Washington, DC 20005
800-345-6728
E-mail: info@nsba.biz
Website: http://www.nsba.biz
Todd McCracken, Pres.

Professional Association of Small Business Accountants
6405 Metcalf Ave., Ste. 503
Shawnee Mission, KS 66202
866-296-0001
E-mail: director@pasba.org
Website: http://community.pasba.org/home
Jordan Bennett, Exec. Dir.

Rainbow PUSH Wall Street Project
1441 Broadway, Ste. 5051
New York, NY 10018
(646)569-5889
(212)425-7874
E-mail: info@rainbowpush.org
Website: http://www.rainbowpush.org
Chee Chee Williams, Exec. Dir.

Root Cause
11 Avenue de Lafayette
Boston, MA 02111
(617)492-2300
E-mail: info@rootcause.org
Website: http://www.rootcause.org
Andrew Wolk, Founder/CEO

Sales Professionals USA
1400 W 122nd Ave., No. 101
Westminster, CO 80234
(303)578-2020
E-mail: support@dmdude.com
Website: http://www.salesprofessionals-usa.com
Peter Brissette, Pres.

Score Association
1175 Herndon Pkwy., Ste. 900
Herndon, VA 20170
(202)205-6762
800-634-0245
E-mail: help@score.org
Website: http://www.score.org
W. Kenneth Yancey, Jr., CEO

Seedco
22 Cortlandt St., 33rd Fl.
New York, NY 10007
(212)473-0255
E-mail: info@seedco.org
Website: http://www.seedco.org
Barbara Dwyer Gunn, Pres./CEO

Small Business and Entrepreneurship Council
301 Maple Ave. W, Ste. 690
Vienna, VA 22180
(703)242-5840
Website: http://www.sbecouncil.org
Karen Kerrigan, Pres./CEO

Small Business Council of America
Brandywine East
1523 Concord Pike, Ste. 300
Wilmington, DE 19803
(302)691-SBCA
E-mail: lredstone@shanlaw.com
Website: http://sbca.net
Leanne Redstone, Exec. Dir.

Small Business Exporters Association of the United States
1156 15th St. NW, Ste. 502
Washington, DC 20005
(202)552-2903
800-345-6728
E-mail: info@sbea.org
Website: http://www.sbea.org
Jody Milanese, VP, Government Affairs

Small Business Investor Alliance
1100 H St. NW, Ste. 1200
Washington, DC 20005
(202)628-5055
E-mail: info@sbia.org
Website: http://www.sbia.org
Brett Palmer, Pres.

Small Business Legislative Council
4800 Hampden Ln., 6th Fl.
Bethesda, MD 20814
(301)652-8302
Website: http://www.sblc.org
Paula Calimafde, Pres.

Small Business Service Bureau, Inc.
554 Main St.
PO Box 15014
Worcester, MA 01615-0014
800-343-0939
E-mail: info@sbsb.com
Website: http://www.sbsb.com
Lisa M. Carroll, MS, MPH, RN, Pres.

Support Services Alliance
165 Main St.
Oneida, NY 13421
(315)363-65842
Website: http://www.oneidachamb
erny.org/supportservices.html
Michele Hummel, Contact

United States Association for Small Business and Entrepreneurship
University of Wisconsin
Whitewater College of Business and Economics
Hyland Hall
809 W Starin Rd.
Whitewater, WI 53190
(262)472-1449
E-mail: psnyder@usasbe.org
Website: http://www.usasbe.org
Patrick Snyder, Exec. Dir.

Consultants

This section contains a listing of consultants specializing in small business development. It is arranged alphabetically by country, then by state or province, then by city, then by firm name.

Canada

Alberta

Dark Horse Strategies
20 Coachway Rd. SW, Ste. 262
Calgary, AB, Canada T3H 1E6
(403)605-3881
E-mail: info@darkhorsestrategies.com
Website: http://www.darkhorse
strategies.com

Kenway Mack Slusarchuk Stewart L.L.P.
333 11th Ave. SW, Ste. 1500
Calgary, AB, Canada T2R 1L9
(403)233-7750
Fax: (403)266-5267
E-mail: info@kmss.ca
Website: http://www.kmss.ca

Kenway Mack Slusarchuk Stewart L.L.P.
714 10 St., Ste. 3
Canmore , AB, Canada T1W 2A6
(403)675-1010
Fax: (403)675-6789
Website: http://kmss.ca/about-us/
canmore-office/

Tenato Strategy Inc.
1229A 9th Ave. SE
Calgary, AB, Canada T2G 0S9
(403)242-1127
E-mail: info@tenato.com
Website: http://www.tenato.com

Nichols Applied Management Inc.
10104 103rd Ave. NW, Ste. 2401
Edmonton, AB, Canada T5J 0H8
(780)424-0091
Fax: (780)428-7644
E-mail: info@nicholsappliedmanagement
.com
Website: http://nicholsconsulting.com/WP

Abonar Business Consultants Ltd.
240-222 Baseline Rd., Ste. 212
Sherwood Park, AB, Canada T8H 1S8
(780)862-0282
Fax: (866)405-4510
E-mail: info@abonarconsultants.com
Website: http://www.abonarconsultants.
com/index.html

AJL Consulting
52312 Range Rd. 225, Ste. 145
Sherwood Park, AB, Canada T8C 1E1
(780)467-6040
Fax: (780)449-2993
Website: http://www.ajlconsulting.ca

Taylor Warwick Consulting Ltd.
121 Courtenay Terr.
Sherwood Park, AB, Canada T8A 5S6
(780)669-1605
E-mail: info@taylorwarwick.ca
Website: http://www.taylorwarwick.ca

British Columbia

Stevenson Community Consultants
138 Pritchard Rd.
Comox, BC, Canada V9M 2T2
(250)890-0297
Fax: (250)890-0296
E-mail: dagit@island.net

Andrew R. De Boda Consulting
1523 Milford Ave.
Coquitlam, BC, Canada V3J 2V9
(604)936-4527
Fax: (604)936-4527
E-mail: deboda@intergate.bc.ca

Reality Marketing Associates
3049 Sienna Ct.
Coquitlam, BC, Canada V3E 3N7
(604)944-8603
Fax: (604)944-4708
E-mail: info@realityassociates.com
Website: http://www.realityassociates.com

Landmark Sq. II, 1708 Dolphin Ave., Ste. 806
Kelowna, BC, Canada V1Y 9S4
(250)763-4716
Fax: (877)353-8608
Free: 877-763-4022
E-mail: steve@burnsinnovation.com
Website: http://www.burnsinnovation.com

Kuber Business Consultants Ltd.
3003 Saint John's St., Ste. 202
Port Moody, BC, Canada V3H 2C4
(604)568-3055
Fax: (604)608-2903
E-mail: info@kuberbiz.ca
Website: http://www.kuberbiz.ca

Seajay Consulting Ltd.
800-15355 24th Ave., Ste. 527
Surrey, BC, Canada V4A 2H9
(604)541-0148
E-mail: chris@seajayconsulting.ca
Website: http://www.seajayconsulting.ca

Einblau and Associates Ltd.
999 W Broadway, Ste. 720
Vancouver, BC, Canada V5Z 1K5
(604)684–7164
Fax: (604)873–8256
E-mail: office@einblau.com
Website: http://www.einblau.com

Pinpoint Tactics Business Consulting
5525 West Blvd., Ste. 330
Vancouver, BC, Canada V6M 3W6
(604)263-4698
Fax: (604)909-4916

E-mail: info@pinpointtactics.com
Website: http://www.pinpointtactics.com

Synergy Complete Management Consulting
1489 Marine Dr., Ste. 317
West Vancouver, BC, Canada V7T 1B8
(604)260-5477
Free: 866-866-8755
E-mail: info@synergy-cmc.com
Website: http://www.synergy-cmc.com

Nova Scotia

The Marketing Clinic
1384 Bedford Hwy.
Bedford, NS, Canada B4A 1E2
(902)835-4122
Fax: (902)832-9389
Free: 877-401-9398
E-mail: office@themarketingclinic.ca
Website: http://www.themarketing clinic.ca

Thyagrissen Consulting Ltd.
35 Talon Ct.
Bible Hill, NS, Canada B2N 7B4
(902)895-1414
Fax: (902)895-5188
E-mail: yvonne@thyagrissenconsulting.ca
Website: http://www.thyagrissen consulting.ca

Coburg Consultants Ltd.
6100 University Ave.
Halifax, NS, Canada B3H 3J5
E-mail: info@coburgconsultants.ca
Website: http://www.coburgconsultants.ca

MacDonnell Group Consulting Ltd.
1505 Barrington St., Ste. 1100
Halifax, NS, Canada B3J 3K5
(902)425-3980
Fax: (902)423-7593
Website: http://www.macdonnell.com

Ontario

The Cynton Co.
17 Massey St.
Brampton, ON, Canada L6S 2V6
(905)792-7769
Fax: (905)792-8116
E-mail: cynton@cynton.com
Website: http://www.cynton.com

Fresh Insights Consulting
901 Guelph Line
Burlington, ON, Canada L7R 3N8
(905)634-6500
E-mail: info@freshinsightsconsulting.ca
Website: http://freshinsightsconsulting.ca

Globe Consult Corp.
34 Willow Shore Way
Carleton Place, ON, Canada K7C 0B1
(613)257-8265
Fax: (613)253-2436
E-mail: infoid@globeconsult.ca
Website: http://www.globeconsult.ca

KLynn Inc.
4421 Hwy. 45
Cobourg, ON K9A 4J9
(905)373-4909
Free: 888-717-2220
E-mail: info@klynnbusinessconsulting .com
Website: www.klynnbusiness consulting.com

Heaslip Associates
50 West St., Unit 2
Collingwood, ON, Canada L9Y 3T1
(613)537-8900
E-mail: info@heaslipassociates.com
Website: http://www.heaslip associates.com

JThomson & Co. CPA
645 Upper James St. S
Hamilton, ON, Canada L9C 2Y9
(905)388-7229
Fax: (905)388-3134
Website: http://www.jthomsonco.com

Queen's Business Consulting
Queen's University
Stephen J.R. Smith School of Business
Goodes Hall, Rm. LL201
Kingston, ON, Canada K7L 3N6
(613)533-2309
Fax: (613)533-2744
E-mail: qbc@business.queensu.ca
Website: http://smith.queensu.ca/ centres/business-consulting/index.php

Fronchak Corporate Development Inc.
23-500 Fairway Rd. S, Ste. 209
Kitchener, ON, Canada N2C 1X3
(519)896-9950
E-mail: mike@fronchak.com
Website: http://www.fronchak.com

Eigenmacht Crackower
345 Renfrew Dr., Ste. 202
Markham, ON, Canada L3R 9S9
(905)305-9722
(905)607-6468
Fax: (905)305-9502
E-mail: jack@eigenmachtcrackower.com
Website: http://www.eigenmacht crackower.com

JPL Consulting
236 Millard Ave.
Newmarket, ON, Canada L3Y 1Z2
(416)606-9124
E-mail: jplbiz1984@gmail.com
Website: http://www.jplbiz.ca

Roger Hay & Associates Ltd.
1272 Elgin Cres.
Oakville, ON, Canada L6H 2J7
(416)848-0997
E-mail: info@rogerhay.ca
Website: http://www.rogerhay.ca

Comgate Engineering Ltd.
236 1st Ave.
Ottawa, ON, Canada K1S 2G6
(613)235-4778
Fax: (613)248-4644
E-mail: info_eng@comgate.com
Website: http://www.comgate.com

PMC Training
858 Bank St., Ste. 109
Ottawa, ON, Canada K1S 3W3
(613)234-2020
Fax: (613)569-1333
E-mail: info@pmctraining.com
Website: http://pmctraining.com/

Arbex Forest Resource Consultants Ltd.
1555 Scotch Line Rd. E
Oxford Mills, ON, Canada K0G 1S0
(613)798-3099
Website: http://www.arbex.ca

G.R. Eagleson Consulting Inc.
69436 Mollard Line
RR3
Parkhill, ON, Canada N0M 2K0
(519)238-2676
Fax: (519)238-1224
E-mail: eagleson@hay.net
Website: http://www.eagleson.com/ consulting

Mark H. Goldberg & Associates Inc.
91 Forest Lane Dr.
Thornhill, ON, Canada L4J 3P2
(905)882-0417
Fax: (905)882-2219
E-mail: info@mhgoldberg.com
Website: http://www.mhgoldberg.com

Petersen Consulting
136 Cedar St. S
Timmons, ON, Canada P4N 2G8
(705)264-5323
E-mail: pcmanage@nt.net
Website: http://www.petersenconsulting.ca

Care Concepts & Communications
21 Spruce Hill Rd.
Toronto, ON, Canada M4E 3G2
(416)420-8840
E-mail: info@cccbizconsultants.com
Website: http://www.cccbizconsultants.com

FHG International Inc.
99 Crown's Ln., 1st Fl.
Toronto, ON, Canada M5R 3P4
(416)402-8000
E-mail: info@fhgi.com
Website: http://www.fhgi.com

KLynn Inc.
6 Bartlett Ave., Ste. 8
Toronto, ON M6H 3E6
Free: 888-717-2220
E-mail: info@klynnbusinessconsulting.com
Website: www.klynnbusinessconsulting.com

PWR Health Consultants, Inc.
720 Spadina Ave., Ste. 303
Toronto, ON, Canada M5S 2T9
(416)467-1844
Fax: (416)467-5600
Fax: (416)323-3166
E-mail: ldoupe@pwr.ca
Website: http://www.pwr.ca

Ryerson Consulting Group
575 Bay St., Ste. 2-005
Toronto, ON, Canada M5G 2C5
(416)979-5059
E-mail: info@rcginsight.com
Website: http://www.rcginsight.com

David Trahair CPA, CA
15 Coldwater Rd., Ste. 101
Toronto, ON, Canada M3B 1Y8
(416)420-8840
Fax: (416)385-3813
Website: http://www.trahair.com

Quebec

PGP Consulting
17 Linton
Dollard-des-Ormeaux, QC, Canada H9B 1P2
(514)796-7613
(514)862-5837
Fax: (866)750-0947
E-mail: pierre@pgpconsulting.com
Website: http://www.pgpconsulting.com

Conseil Saint-Paul
400 Blvd. Saint-Martin Ouest, Bureau 121
Laval, QC, Canada H7M 3Y8
(450)664-4442
Fax: (450)664-3631
E-mail: info@spaul.ca
Website: http://spaul.ca

KLynn Inc.
2025 Rue de la Visitation
Montreal, QC H2L 3C8
Free: 888-717-2220
E-mail: info@klynnbusinessconsulting.com
Website: www.klynnbusinessconsulting.com

Komand Consulting Inc.
1250 Rene Levesque Blvd. W, Ste. 2200
Montreal, QC, Canada H3B 4W8
(514)934-9281
E-mail: info@komand.ca
Website: http://www.komand.ca

Lemay-Yates Associates Inc.
2015 Peel St., Ste. 425
Montreal, QC, Canada H3A 1T8
(514)288-6555
E-mail: lya@lya.com
Website: http://www.lya.com

Groupe Dancause Inc.
3175 Chemin des Quatre-Bourgeois, Ste. 375
Quebec, QC, Canada G1W 2K7
(418)681-0268
E-mail: groupe@dancause.net
Website: http://www.dancause.net

Saskatchewan

Abonar Business Consultants Ltd.
3110 8th St. E, Ste. 8B-376
Saskatoon, SK, Canada S7H 0W2
Fax: (866)405-4510
Free: 866-405-4510
E-mail: info@abonarconsultants.com
Website: http://www.abonarconsultants.com/index.html

Banda Marketing Group
3-1124 8th St. E
Saskatoon, SK, Canada S7H 0S4
(306)343-6100
E-mail: brent.banda@bandagroup.com
Website: http://www.bandagroup.com

Hoggard International
435 McKercher Dr.
Saskatoon, SK, Canada S7H 4G3
(306)374-6747
Fax: (306)653-7252
E-mail: bhoggard@shaw.ca
Website: http://hoggardinternational.com

United States

Alabama

Accounting & Business Consultants Inc.
1711 9th Ave. N
Bessemer, AL 35020
E-mail: tclay@abcconsultants.com
Website:http://www.abcconsultants.com

Accounting & Business Consultants Inc.
4120 2nd Ave. S
Birmingham, AL 35222
(205)425-9000
E-mail: tclay@abcconsultants.com
Website: http://www.abcconsultants.com

MILBO, LLC
2214 3rd Ave. N, Ste. 204
Birmingham, AL 35203
(205)543-0645
Website: http://www.milbollc.com

Jackson Thorton Dothan Office
304 Jamestown Blvd.
Dothan, AL 36301
(334)793-7001
Fax: (334)793-7004
Website: http://www.jacksonthornton.com

Mason, Bearden & Diehl, Inc.
4100 Bob Wallace Ave.
Huntsville, AL 35805
(256)533-0806
Fax: (256)533-7742 fax
E-mail: mbd@mbdaccounting.com
Website: http://www.mbdaccounting.com

SEL & Associates
103 Cabot Circ., Ste. 201
Madison, AL 35758
(256)325-9809
Fax: (256)325-9809
E-mail: steven@stevenlevyassociates.com
Website: http://www.stevenlevyassociates.com

Jackson Thorton Montgomery Office
200 Commerce St.
Montgomery, AL 36104
(334)834-7660
Fax: (334)956-5090
Website: http://www.jacksonthornton.com

Jackson Thorton Auburn/Opelka Office
100 N 9th St.
Opelika, AL 36801
(334)749-8191
Fax: (334)749-9358
Website: http://www.jacksonthornton.com

Jackson Thorton Prattville Office
310 S Washington St.
Prattville, AL 36067
(334)365-1445
Fax: (334)956-5066
Website: http://www.jacksonthornton.com

Jackson Thorton Wetumpka Office
194 Fort Toulouse
Wetumpka, AL 36092
(334)567-3400
Fax: (334)956-5005
Website: http://www.jacksonthornton.com

Alaska

Agnew::Beck Consulting
441 W 5th Ave., Ste. 202
Anchorage, AK 99501
(907)222-5424
Fax: (907)222-5426
E-mail: admin@agnewbeck.com
Website: http://agnewbeck.com

McDowell Group
1400 W Benson Blvd., Ste. 510
Anchorage, AK 99503
(907)274-3200
Fax: (907)274-3201
E-mail: info@mcdowellgroup.net
Website: http://www.mcdowellgroup.net

The Foraker Group
161 Klevin St., Ste. 101
Anchorage AK 99508
(907)743-1200
Fax: (907)276-5014
Free: 877-834-5003
Website: http://www.forakergroup.org

Consulting Professionals of Alaska
17137 Park Place St.
Eagle River, AK, 99577
(907)694-0105
Fax: (907)694-0107
Website: http://www.cpalaska.com

McDowell Group
9360 Glacier Hwy., Ste. 201
Juneau, AK 99801
(907)586-6126
Fax: (907)586-2673
E-mail: info@mcdowellgroup.net
Website: http://www.mcdowellgroup.net

Sheinberg Associates
1107 W 8th St., Ste. 4
Juneau, AK 99801
(907)586-3141
Fax: (907)586-2331
Website: http://www.sheinberg
associates.com

Arizona

Comgate Telemanagement Ltd.
428 E Thunderbird Rd., Ste. 133
Phoenix, AZ 85022
(602)485-5708
Fax: (602)485-5709
E-mail: info_telemgmt@comgate.com
Website: http://www.comgate.com

Kalil & Associates, LLC
245 S Plumer Ave., Ste. 16
Tucson, AZ 85719
(520)628-4264
Fax: (520)903-0347
E-mail: info@kalilassociates.com
Website: https://www.kalilassociates.com

California

Cayenne Consulting, LLC
155 N Riverview Dr.
Anaheim Hills, CA 92808
Website: https://www.caycon.com

Fessel International, Inc.
20 E Foothill Blvd., Ste. 128
Arcadia, CA 91006
(626)566-3500
Fax: (626)566-3875
Free: 877-432-8380
Website: http://www.fessel.com/default.asp

Streamline Planning Consultants
1062 G St. Suite I
Arcata, CA 95521
(707)822-5785
Fax: (707)822-5786
Website: http://streamlineplanning.net

The One Page Business Plan Co.
1798 Fifth St.
Berkeley, CA 94710
(510)705-8400
Fax: (510)705-8403
E-mail: info@onepagebusinessplan.com
Website: http://www.onepagebusiness
plan.com

Business Consulting Group
30 Landing Cir. 300
Chico, CA 95973
(530)864-5980
E-mail: info@bcgca.com
Website: http://www.bcgca.com

Go Jade Solutions
9808 Valgrande Way
Elk Grove, CA 95757
(916)538-7561
E-mail: info@gojadesolutions.com
Website: http://gojadesolutions.com

La Piana Consulting
5858 Horton St., Ste. 272
Emeryville, CA 94608-2007
(510)601-9056
Fax: (510)420-0478
E-mail: info@lapiana.org
Website: http://lapiana.org

Norris Bernstein, CMC
9309 Marina Pacifica Dr. N
Long Beach, CA 90803
(562)493-5458
Fax: (562)493-5459
E-mail: norris@norrisbernstein.com
Website: http://www.norrisbernstein.com

Blue Garnet Associates L.L.C.
8055 W Manchester Ave., Ste. 430
Los Angeles, CA 90293
(310)439-1930
E-mail: hello@bluegarnet.net
Website: http://www.bluegarnet.net

Edeska LLC (dba Go Business Plans)
Bldg. D, Fl. 3
12777 W Jefferson Blvd., Ste. 3119
Los Angeles, CA 90066
Free: 855-546-0037
Website: http://edeska.com

Growthink Inc.
12655 W Jefferson Blvd.
Los Angeles, CA 90045
Free: 800-647-6983
E-mail: services@growthink.com
Website: http://www.growthink.com

Paul Yelder Consulting
3964 Hubert Ave.
Los Angeles, CA 90008-2620
(323)295-7652
E-mail: email: consulting@yelder.com
Website: http://www.yelder.com

BizplanSource
1048 Irvine Ave., Ste. 621
Newport Beach, CA 92660
Free: 888-253-0974
Fax: (800)859-8254
E-mail: info@bizplansource.com
Website: http://www.bizplansource.com

MakeGreenGo!
240 3rd St., Ste. 2A
Oakland, CA 94607
(510)250-9890
Website: http://makegreengo.com

Accessible Business, LLC
18325 Keswick St.
Reseda, CA 91335
(818)264-7830

Free: 800-490-8362
Fax: (818)264-7833
E-mail: info@accessiblebusiness.com
Website: https://www.accessiblebusiness.com

International Business Partners
8045 Darby Pl.
Reseda, CA 91335
(714)875-3604
E-mail: admin@IBPconsultants.com
Website: http://www.ibpconsultants.com/home.html

Jackson Law Firm, P.C.
979 Golf Course Dr., Ste. 300
Rohnert Park, CA 94928
(707)584-4529
(707)584-9033
E-mail: shawnjackson@businessdevelopmentattorney.com
Website: http://jacksonlawfirm.net/

Business Performance Consultants
9777 Caminito Joven
San Diego, CA 92131
(858)583-4159
E-mail: larrymiller@businessperformanceconsultants.com
Website: http://businessperformanceconsultants.com/

The Startup Garage
San Diego, CA 92109
(858)876-4597
E-mail: info@thestartupgarage.com
Website: https://thestartupgarage.com

Venture Builder, Inc.
1286 University Ave., Ste. 315
San Diego, CA 92103
(619)563-1841
Website: http://www.venturebuilderinc.com

Growthink Inc.
55 2nd St., Ste. 570
San Francisco, CA 94105
Free: 800-647-6983
E-mail: services@growthink.com
Website: http://www.growthink.com

San Francisco Management Group
1048 Union St., Ste. 7
San Francisco, CA 94133
(415)775-3405
E-mail: info@sfmanagementgroup.com
Website: http://www.sfmanagementgroup.com/

The Wright Consultants
835 Market St.
San Francisco, CA 94105
(415)928-2071
Website: http://www.thewrightconsultants.com

Business Group
369-B 3rd St., Ste. 387
San Rafael, CA 94901
(415)491-1896
Fax: (415)459-6472
E-mail: mvh@businessgroup.biz
Website: http://www.businessownerstoolbox.com

Manex Inc.
2010 Crow Canyon Pl., Ste. 320
San Ramon, CA 94583
(925)807-5100
Free: 877-336-2639
Website: http://www.manexconsulting.com

Bargain Business Plan, Inc.
12400 Ventura Blvd., Ste. 658
Studio City, CA 91604
Free: 800-866-9971
Fax: (800)866-9971
E-mail: info@bargainbusinessplan.com
Website: http://www.bargainbusinessplan.com

Out of Your Mind...and Into the Marketplace
13381 White Sands Dr.
Tustin, CA 92780-4565
(714)544-0248
Fax: (714)730-1414
Free: 800-419-1513
E-mail: lpinson@aol.com
Website: http://www.business-plan.com

Colorado

Comer & Associates, LLC
5255 Holmes Pl.
Boulder, CO 80303
(303)786-7986
E-mail: info@comerassociates.com
Website: http://www.comerassociates.com

McCord Consulting Group
2525 Arapahoe Ave., Ste. 515
Boulder, CO 80302
(720)443-0894
E-mail: nikki@mcconsultgroup.com
Website: http://mcconsultgroup.com/

The Startup Expert
661 Eldorado Blvd. Ste. 623
Broomfield, CO 80021
(303)534-1019
Website: http://thestartupexpert.com/

Ameriwest Business Consultants, Inc.
PO Box 26266
Colorado Springs, CO 80936
(719)380-7096
Fax: (719)380-7096
E-mail: email@abchelp.com
Website: http://www.abchelp.com

GVNW Consulting Inc.
2270 La Montana Way, Ste. 200
Colorado Springs, CO 80918
(719)594-5800
E-mail: jushio@gvnw.com
Website: http://www.gvnw.com

Wilson Hughes Consulting LLC
2100 Humboldt St., Ste. 302
Denver, CO 80205
(303)680-7889
E-mail: bhughescnm@gmail.com
Website: http://wilsonhughesconsulting.com/

Extelligent Inc.
8400 E Crescent Pky., Ste. 600
Greenwood Village, CO 80111
(720)201-5672
E-mail: clientrelations@extelligent.com
Website: http://www.extelligent.com

The Schallert Group, Inc.
321 Main St.
Longmont, CO 80501
(303)774-6522
Website: http://jonschallert.com/

Vaughn CPA
210 E 29th St.
Loveland, CO 80538
(970)667-2123
E-mail: vaughn@vaughncpa.com
Website: http://vaughncpa.com/loveland-cpa-firm

Connecticut

Alltis Corp.
PO Box 1292
Farmington, CT 06034-1292
(860)255-7610
Fax: (860)674-8168
E-mail: info@alltis.com
Website: http://www.alltis.com

Christiansen Consulting
56 Scarborough St.
Hartford, CT 06105
(860)586-8265
Fax: (860)233-3420
E-mail: Francine@ChristiansenConsulting.com
Website: http://www.christiansenconsulting.com/

Musevue360
555 Millbrook Rd.
Middletown, CT 06457

(860)463-7722
Fax: (860)346-3013
E-mail: jennifer.eifrig@musevue360.com
Website: http://www.musevue360.com

Kalba International Inc.
116 McKinley Ave.
New Haven, CT 06515
(203)397-2199
Fax: (781)240-2657
E-mail: kas.kalba@kalbainternational.com
Website: http://www.kalbainternational.com

Delaware

Doherty & Associates
Stoney Batter Office Bldg.
5301 Limestone Rd., Ste. 100
Wilmington, DE 19808
(302)239-3500
Fax: (302)239-3600
E-mail: info@dohertyandassociates.com
Website: http://www.dohertyand associates.com

Gunnip & Co. LLP
Little Falls Centre 2
2751 Centerville Rd., Ste. 300
Wilmington, DE 19808-1627
(302)225-5000
Fax: (302)225-5100
E-mail: info@gunnip.com
Website: http://www.gunnip.com

Master, Sidlow & Associates, P.A.
2002 W 14th St.
Wilmington, DE 19806
(302)652-3480
Fax: (302)656-8778
E-mail: imail@mastersidlow.com
Website: http://www.mastersidlow.com

Florida

BackBone, Inc.
20404 Hacienda Ct.
Boca Raton, FL 33498
(561)470-0965
Fax: (561)908-4038
E-mail: che@backboneinc.com
Website: http://www.backboneinc.com

Dr. Eric H. Shaw & Associates
500 S Ocean Blvd., Ste. 2105
Boca Raton, FL 33432
(561)338-5151
E-mail: ericshaw@bellsouth.net
Website: http://www.ericshaw.com

Professional Planning Associates, Inc.
1440 NE 35th St.
Oakland Park, FL 33334
(954)829-2523
Fax:(954)537-7945
E-mail: mgoldstein@proplana.com
Website: http://proplana.com

Alfred Endeio LLC
8700 Maitland Summit Blvd., Ste. 214
Orlando, FL 32810
Website: http://www.alfredeconsulting.com

Hughes Consulting Services LLC
522 Alternate 19
Palm Harbor, FL 34683
(727)631-2536
Fax: (727)474-9818
Website: http://consultinghughes.com

Strategic Business Planning Co.
PO Box 821006
South Florida, FL 33082
(954)704-9100
Fax: (888)704-3290
Free: 888-704-9100
E-mail: info@SBPlan.com
Website: http://www.ipplan.com

Cohen & Grieb, P.A.
500 N Westshore Blvd., Ste. 700
Tampa, FL 33609
(813)739-7200
Fax: (813)282-7225
E-mail: info@cohengrieb.com
Website: http://www.cohengrieb.com/ contact

Dufresne Consulting Group, Inc.
13014 N Dale Mabry, Ste. 175
Tampa, FL 33618-2808
(813)264-4775
E-mail: info@dcgconsult.com
Website: http://www.dcgconsult.com

Reliance Consulting, LLC
13940 N Dale Mabry Hwy.
Tampa, FL, 33618
(813)931-7258
Fax: (813)931-5555
Website: http://www.reliancecpa.com

Tunstall Consulting LLC
13153 N Dale Mabry Hwy., Ste. 200
Tampa, FL 33618
(813)968-4461
Fax: (813)961-2315
E-mail: info@tunstallconsulting.com
Website: http://www.tunstallconsulting .com

The Business Planning Institute, LLC.
580 Village Blvd., Ste. 150
West Palm Beach, FL 33409
(561)236-5533
Fax: (561)689-5546
E-mail: info@bpiplans.com
Website: http://www.bpiplans.com

Georgia

CHScottEnterprises
227 Sandy Springs Pl. NE, Ste. 720702
Atlanta, GA 30358-9032
(770)356-4808
E-mail: info@chscottenterprises.com
Website: http://www.chscottenterprises .com

Fountainhead Consulting Group, Inc.
3970 Old Milton Pkwy, Ste. 210
Atlanta, GA 30005
(770)642-4220
Website: http://www.fountainhead consultinggroup.com

PSMJ Resources Inc.
2746 Rangewood Dr.
Atlanta, GA 30345
(770)723-9651
Fax: (815)461-7478
Free: 800-537-7765
Website: http://www.psmj.com

Scullyworks, LLC
PO Box 8641
Atlanta, GA 31106-0641
(404)310-9499
Website: http://www.scullyworks.com

Theisen Consulting LLC
865 Waddington Ct.
Atlanta, GA 30350
(770)396-7344
Fax: (404)393-3527
E-mail: terri@theisenconsulting.com
Website: http://www.theisenconsulting.com

Sterling Rose Consulting Corp.
722 Collins Hill Rd., Ste. H-307
Lawrenceville, GA 30046
(678)892-8528
E-mail: info@sterlingroseconsultingcorp .com
Website: http://www.sterlingrose consultingcorp.com

Lemongrass Consulting, Inc.
951 Gettysburg Way
Locust Grove, GA 30248
(678)235-5901
E-mail: chamilton@lemongrass planning.com
Website: http://lemongrassplanning.com

Samet Consulting
4672 Oxford Cir.
Macon, GA 31210

(478)757-1070
Fax:(478)757-1984
Website: http://sametconsulting.com/

Hawaii

Maui Venture Consulting LLC
PO Box 81515
Haiku, HI 96708
(808)269-1031
E-mail: df@mauiventure.net
Website: http://www.mauiventure.net

Business Plans Hawaii
3059 Maigret St.
Honolulu, HI 96816
(808)735-5597
E-mail: valerie@ businessplanshawaii .com
Website: http://www.businessplans hawaii.com

John V. McCoy Communications Consultant
425 Ena Rd., Apt. 1204-B
Honolulu, HI 96815
(510)219-2276
E-mail: mccoy.jv@gmail.com
Website: http://www.busplan.com

Idaho

Agnew::Beck Consulting
802 W Bannock St., Ste. 803
Boise, ID 83702
(208)342-3976
E-mail: admin@agnewbeck.com
Website: http://agnewbeck.com

Kairosys
16645 Plum Rd.
Caldwell, ID 83607
(208)454-0086
E-mail: support@kairosys.net
Website: http://kairosys.net

Illinois

Midwest Business Consulting, LLC
Midway Corporate Ctr.
6640 S Cicero Ave., Ste. 204
Bedford Park, IL 60638
(708)571-3401
Fax: (708)571-3409
E-mail: inquiries@mbconsultingco.com
Website: https://www.mbconsultingco.com

Anchor Advisors, Ltd.
5366 N Elston Ave., Ste. 203
Chicago, IL 60630
(773)282-7677
Website: http://anchoradvisors.com

Brighton Windsor Group, LLC
Chicago, IL 60602
Free: 888-781-1304
E-mail: hello@brightonwindsor.com
Website: http://brightonwindsor.com

Ground Floor Partners, Inc.
150 N Michigan Ave., Ste. 2800
Chicago, IL 60601
(312)726-1981
Website: http://groundfloorpartners.com

Midwest Business Consulting, LLC
Chicago Temple Bldg.
77 W Washington, Ste. 718
Chicago, IL 60602
(312)415-0340
Fax: (312)994-8554
E-mail: inquiries@mbconsultingco.com
Website: https://www.mbconsultingco .com

Gold Consulting, Inc.
18 Exmoor Ct.
Highwood, IL 60040
(847)433-8141
Fax: (847)433-2446
E-mail: ron@goldconsultinginc.com
Website: http://goldconsultinginc.com

Francorp
20200 Governors Dr.
Olympia Fields, IL 60461
(708)481-2900
Free: 800-372-6244
E-mail: francorp@aol.com
Website: http://www.francorp.com

MD Consultants of America, Inc.
6738 N Frostwood Pkwy.
Peoria, IL 61615
Free: 877-272-1631
Fax: (309)414-0298
E-mail: info@mdconsultantus.com
Website: http://www.mdconsultantus.com

Quiet Storm Enterprises Ltd.
3701 Trilling Ave., Ste. 201
Rockford IL 61103-2157
(815)315-0146
Free: 877-958-0160
E-mail: info@qsenterprisesltd.net
Website: http://www.qsenterprisesltd.net

Public Sector Consulting
5718 Barlow Rd.
Sherman, IL 62684
(217)629-9869
Fax: (217)629-9732
E-mail: mail@gotopsc.com
Website: http://www.gotopsc.com

GVNW Illinois
3220 Pleasant Run, Ste. A
Springfield, IL 62711
(217)698-2700
E-mail: jushio@gvnw.com
Website: http://www.gvnw.com

Indiana

Compass CPA Group
435 Ann St.
Fort Wayne, IN 46774
(260)749-2200
Free: 866-788-9789
E-mail: information@compasscpagroup .com
Website: http://www.compasscpagroup. com

Cox and Co.
3930 Mezzanine Dr. Ste A
Lafayette, IN, 47905
(765)449-4495
Fax: (765)449-1218
E-mail: stan@coxpa.com
Website: http://coxcpa.com

Kimmel Consulting LLC
136 S 9th St Ste 320
Noblesville, IN 46060
(317)773-3810
Fax: (317)770-8787
E-mail: info@kimmelconsultingllc.com
Website: http://www.kimmel consultingllc.com

Iowa

TD&T CPAs and Advisors, P.C. Burlington Office
323 Jefferson St.
Burlington, IA 52601
(319)753-9877
Fax: (319)753-1156
E-mail: briani@tdtpc.com
Website: http://www.tdtpc.com/ index.php

TD&T CPAs and Advisors, P.C. Cedar Rapids Office
1700 42nd St. NE
Cedar Rapids, IA 52402
(319)393-2374
Fax: (319)393-2375
E-mail: amandal@tdtpc.com
Website: http://www.tdtpc.com/ index.php

Terry, Lockridge and Dunn
210 2nd St. SE
Cedar Rapids, IA 52407
(319)364-2945

Fax: (319)362-4487
E-mail: info@tld-inc.com
Website: http://www.tld-inc.com

TD&T CPAs and Advisors, P.C. Centerville Office
101 W Van Buren St.
Centerville, IA 52544
(641)437-4296
Fax: (641)437-1574
E-mail: markl@tdtpc.com
Website: http://www.tdtpc.com/index.php

TD&T CPAs and Advisors, P.C. Fairfield Office
2109 W Jefferson Ave.
Fairfield, IA 52556
(641)472-6171
Fax: (641)472-6632
E-mail: jodik@tdtpc.com
Website: http://www.tdtpc.com/index.php

Steve Meyer Consulting LLC
304 E Maple
Garrison, IA 52229
(319)477-5041
E-mail: gfdchief@netins.net
Website: http://www.stevemeyerconsulting.com/

Terry, Lockridge and Dunn
2225 Mormon Trek Blvd.
Iowa City, IA 52246
(319)339-4884
Fax: (319)358-9113
E-mail: info@tld-inc.com
Website: http://www.tld-inc.com

TD&T CPAs and Advisors, P.C. Mount Pleasant Office
204 N Main
Mount Pleasant, IA 52641
(319)385-9718
Fax: (319)385-2612
E-mail: tomh@tdtpc.com
Website: http://www.tdtpc.com/index.php

TD&T CPAs and Advisors, P.C. Muscatine Office
500 Cedar St.
Muscatine, IA 52761
(563)264-2727
Fax: (563)263-7777
E-mail: vickib@tdtpc.com; dennyt@tdtpc.com
Website: http://www.tdtpc.com/index.php

TD&T CPAs and Advisors, P.C. Oskaloosa Office
317 High Ave. E
Oskaloosa, IA 52577
(641)672-2523
Fax: (641)673-7453
E-mail: joshb@tdtpc.com
Website: http://www.tdtpc.com/index.php

TD&T CPAs and Advisors, P.C. Ottumwa Office
117 S Court
Ottumwa, IA 52501
(641)683-1823
Fax: (641)683-1868
E-mail: dougm@tdtpc.com
Website: http://www.tdtpc.com/index.php

TD&T CPAs and Advisors, P.C. Pella Office
1108 Washington St.
Pella, IA 50219
(641)628-9411
Fax: (641)628-1321
E-mail: justinp@tdtpc.com
Website: http://www.tdtpc.com/index.php

Murk-n-T, Inc.
209 Rose Ave. SW
Swisher, IA 52338
(319)857-4638
Fax: (319)857-4648
E-mail: info@murknt.com
Website: http://www.murknt.com/index.php

TD&T CPAs and Advisors, P.C. West Des Moines Office
1240 Office Plaza Dr.
West Des Moines, IA 50266
(515)657-5800
Fax: (515)657-5801
E-mail: davef@tdtpc.com
Website: http://www.tdtpc.com/index.php

Kansas

Nail CPA Firm, LLC
4901 W 136th St.
Leawood, KS 66224
(913)663-2500
E-mail: info@nailcpafirm.com
Website: http://www.nailcpafirm.com

Shockey Consulting Services, LLC
12351 W 96th Ter., Ste. 107
Lenexa, KS 66215
(913)248-9585
E-mail: solutions@shockeyconsulting.com
Website: http://www.shockeyconsulting.com/

Aspire Business Development
10955 Lowell Ave., Ste. 400
Overland Park, KS 66210
(913)660-9400
Free: 888-548-1504
Website: http://www.aspirekc.com

Wichita Technology Corp.
7829 E Rockhill Rd., Ste. 307
Wichita, KS 67206
(316)651-5900
Free: 866-810-6671
E-mail: wtc@wichitatechnology.com
Website: http://www.wichitatechnology.com

Kentucky

BizFixes
277 E High St.
Lexington, KY 40507
(859)552-5151
Website: http://bizfixes.com

Louisiana

Cathy Denison, PhD & Associates Professional Services, Inc.
9655 Perkins Rd., Ste. C-123
Baton Rouge, LA 70810
(337)502-1911
E-mail: cdenison@denisonassociates.com
Website: http://www.denisonassociates.com

Rabalais Business Consulting
209 Rue Louis XIV, Ste. B
Lafayette, LA 70508
(337)981-2577
Fax: (337)981-2579
Website: http://rabbiz.com

Terk Consulting Business Plans
3819A Magazine St.
New Orleans, LA 70115
(504)237-0480
E-mail: info@terkconsulting.com
Website: https://terkconsulting.com

Maine

PFBF CPAs Bath Office
259 Front St.
Bath, ME 04530
(207)371-8002
Fax: (207)877-7407
E-mail: mail@pfbf.com
Website: http://www.pfbf.com

John Rust Consulting
PO Box 459
Hampden, ME 04444
(207)337-5858
E-mail: john@johnrustconsulting.com
Website: http://www.johnrustconsulting.com

PFBF CPAs Oakland Office
46 First Park Dr.
Oakland, ME 04963
(207)873-1603
Fax: (207)877-7407
E-mail: mail@pfbf.com
Website: http://www.pfbf.com

Maryland

Maryland Capital Enterprises, Inc. Baltimore Area Office
333 N Charles St.
Baltimore, MD 21201
(410)546-1900
Fax: (410)546-9718
E-mail: info@marylandcapital.org
Website: http://www.marylandcapital.org

Burdeshaw Associates Ltd.
4701 Sangamore Rd.
Bethesda, MD 20816
(301)229-5800
E-mail: jstacy@burdeshaw.com
Website: http://www.burdeshaw.com

Jacoby
2304 Frederick Rd.
Catonsville, MD 21228
(410)744-3900
Fax: (410)747-7850
Free: 877-799-GROW
E-mail: info@artjacoby.com

Black Rock Accounting & Consulting
13424 Burnt Woods Pl.
Germantown, MD 20874
(301)928-7600
Fax: (301)515-1840
E-mail: mike@blackrockaccounting.com
Website: http://www.blackrockaccounting.com

L&H Business Consulting
1212 York Rd., Ste. C-300
Lutherville, MD 21093
(410)828-4177
Fax: (410)321-1588
E-mail: info@lhbusinessconsulting.com
Website: http://www.lhbusinessconsulting.com

Maryland Capital Enterprises, Inc. Eastern Shore Office
144 E Main St.
Salisbury, MD 21801
(410)546-1900
Fax: (410)546-9718
E-mail: info@marylandcapital.org
Website: http://www.marylandcapital.org

Massachusetts

The Carrot Project
89 South St.
Boston, MA 02111
(617)674-2371
E-mail: info@thecarrotproject.org
Website: http://www.thecarrotproject.org/home

Julia Shanks Food Consulting
37 Tremont St.
Cambridge, MA 02139
(617)945-8718
E-mail: info@juliashanks.com
Website: http://www.juliashanks.com

CYTO Consulting
363 N Emerson Rd.
Lexington, MA 02420
(339)707-0767
E-mail: info@cytoconsulting.com
Website: http://www.cytoconsulting.com

Foxboro Consulting Group Inc.
36 Lancashire Dr.
Mansfield, MA 02048
(774)719-2236
E-mail: moreinfo@foxboro-consulting.com
Website: http://www.foxboro-consulting.com

Dahn Consulting Group
Newburyport, MA 01950
(978)314-1722
E-mail: info@dahnconsulting.com
Website: http://www.dahnconsulting.com

PSMJ Resources Inc.
10 Midland Ave.
Newton, MA 02458
(617)965-0055
Fax: (617)965-5152
Free: 800-537-7765
Website: http://www.psmj.com

Spark Business Consulting
167 Washington St.
Norwell, MA 02061
(781)871-1003
Website: http://sparkbusinessconsulting.com

Bruno P.C.
57 Obery St., Ste. 4
Plymouth, MA 02360
(508)830-0800
Fax: (508)830-0801
E-mail: info@BrunoAccountants.com
Website: https://www.brunoaccountants.com

Non Profit Capital Management
41 Main St.
Sterling, MA 01564
(781)933-6726
Fax: (978)563-1007
E-mail: info@npcm.com
Website: http://www.npcm.com/

Michigan

Aimattech Consulting LLC
568 Woodway Ct., Ste. 1
Bloomfield Hills, MI 48302-1572
(248)540-3758
Fax: (775)305-4755
E-mail: dweaver@aimattech.com
Website: http://www.aimattech.com

BBC Entrepreneurial Training & Consulting LLC
12671 E Old U.S. 12
Chelsea, MI 48118
(734)930-9741
Fax: (734)930-6629
E-mail: info@bbcetc.com
Website: http://www.bioconsultants.com

LifeLine Business Consulting
1400 Woodbridge St., 4th Fl.
Detroit, MI 48207
(313)965-3155
E-mail: hello@thelifelinenetwork.com
Website: https://thelifelinenetwork.com

TL Cramer Associates LLC
1788 Broadstone Rd.
Grosse Pointe Woods, MI 48236
(313)332-0182
E-mail: info@tlcramerassociates.com
Website: http://www.tlcramerassociates.com

Jackson Small Business Support Center
950 W Monroe St., Ste. G-100
Jackson, MI 49202
(517)796-8151
Website: http://www.smallbusinesssupportcenter.com

Tedder Whitlock Consulting
17199 N Laurel Park Dr.
Livonia, MI 48152
(734)542-4200

Fax: (734)542-4201
E-mail: info@tedderwhitlock.com
Website: http://www.tedderwhitlock.com

MarketingHelp Inc.
6647 Riverwoods Ct. NE
Rockford, MI 49341
(616)856-0148
Website: http://www.mktghelp.com

Lucid Business Strategies
8187 Rhode Dr., Ste. D
Shelby Township, MI 48317
(586)254-0095
E-mail: results@lucidbusiness.com
Website: http://www.lucidbusiness.com

QT Business Solution
24901 Northwestern Hwy., Ste. 305
Southfield, MI 48075
(248)416-1755
Free: 877-859-6768
E-mail: info@qtbizsolutions.com
Website: http://qtbizsolutions.com
Waterford, MI 48328
(248)683-1130
E-mail: info@cool-associates.com
Website: http://www.cool-associates.com

Griffioen Consulting Group, Inc.
6689 Orchard Lake Rd., Ste. 295
West Bloomfield, MI 48322
Free: 888-262-5850
Fax: (248)855-4084
Website: http://www.griffioenconsulting.com

NooJoom Immigration Services & Business Plan
35253 Warren Rd.
Westland, MI 48185
(734)728-5755
E-mail: wadak@noojoom.org
Website: http://www.noojoomimmigrationservices.com

Minnesota

Devoted Business Development
2434 E 117th St., Ste. 100
Burnsville, Minnesota
(952) 582-4669
E-mail: info@devoted-business.com
Website: http://devoted-business.com

Community & Economic Development Associates (CEDA)
1500 S Hwy. 52
Chatfield, MN 55923
(507)867-3164
E-mail: ron.zeigler@cedausa.com
Website: https://www.cedausa.com

Metropolitan Consortium of Community Developers (MCCD)
Open to Business Program
3137 Chicago Ave.
Minneapolis, MN 55407
(612)789-7337
Fax: (612)822-1489
E-mail: info@opentobusinessmn.org
Website: http://www.opentobusinessmn.org

Metropolitan Economic Development Association (MEDA)
250 2nd Ave. S, Ste. 106
Minneapolis, MN 55401
(612)332-6332
E-mail: info@meda.net
Website: http://meda.net

WomenVenture
2021 E Hennepin Ave., Ste. 200
Minneapolis, MN 55413
(612)224-9540
Fax: (612)200-8369
E-mail: info@womenventure.org
Website: https://www.womenventure.org/index.html

Mississippi

The IRON Network, LLC
1636 Popps Ferry Rd., Ste. 201
Biloxi, MS 39532
(412)336-8807
E-mail: sales@theironcom.com
Website: http://theironcom.com/services/business-consulting

Richardson's Writing Service
3285 Squirrel Lake Rd.
Sledge, MS 38670
(662)326-3996
Website: http://www.richws.com

Missouri

Taylor Management Group, LLC (TMG)
PO Box 50155
Clayton, MO 63015
(314)488-1566
Website: http://taymg.com

Stuff
316 W 63rd St.
Kansas City, MO 64113
(816)361-8222
E-mail: sloaneandcasey@pursuegoodstuff.com
Website: http://www.pursuegoodstuff.com

Westphal-Kelpe Consulting Inc.
4050 Broadway, Ste. 201
Kansas City, MO 64111
(816)931-7141
Fax: (816)931-7180
E-mail: info@wkcrestaurants.com
Website: http://www.westphal-kelpe.com

Shockey Consulting Services, LLC
441 Alice Ave.
Kirkwood, MO 66122
(314)497-3126
E-mail: solutions@shockeyconsulting.com
Website: http://www.shockeyconsulting.com/

Sanford, Lea & Associates
1655 S Enterprise Ave., Ste. B-4
Springfield, MO 65804
(417)886-2220
Fax: (417)886-3979
E-mail: david@adifferentcpa.com
Website: https://www.adifferentcpa.com

EMD Consulting
11111 Conway Rd.
Saint Louis, MO 63131
(314)692-7551
E-mail: info@emdconsulting.com
Website: http://www.emdconsulting.com

M.A. Birsinger & Company, LLC
2464 Taylor Rd., Ste. 106
Wildwood, MO 63040
(314)249-7076
E-mail: brook@mabirsinger.com
Website: http://www.mabirsinger.com

Nebraska

McDermott & Miller, P.C.
2722 S Locust St.
Grand Island, NE 68802
(308)382-7850
Fax: (308)382-7240
E-mail: nsaale@mmcpas.com
Website: http://www.mmcpas.com

McDermott & Miller, P.C.
747 N Burlington Ave., Ste. 401
Hastings, NE 68902
(402)462-4154
Fax: (402)462-5057
E-mail: nsaale@mmcpas.com
Website: http://www.mmcpas.com

McDermott & Miller, P.C.
404 E 25th St.
Kearney, NE 68848
(308)234-5565
Fax: (308)234-2990

E-mail: nsaale@mmcpas.com
Website: http://www.mmcpas.com

Lincoln Partnership for Economic Development (LPED)
3 Landmark Centre
1128 Lincoln Mall, Ste. 100
Lincoln, NE 68508
(402)436-2350
E-mail: info@selectlincoln.org
Website: http://www.selectlincoln.org

Farm Credit Services of America
5015 S 118th St.
Omaha, NE 68137
Free: 800-884-FARM
Website: https://www.fcsamerica.com

McDermott & Miller, P.C.
11602 W Center Rd., Ste. 125
Omaha, NE 68144
(402)391-1207
Fax: (402)391-3424
E-mail: nsaale@mmcpas.com
Website: http://www.mmcpas.com

Nebraska Credit Union League (NCUL)
4885 S 118th St., Ste. 150
Omaha, NE 68137
(402)333-9331
Fax: (402)333-9431
Free: 800-950-4455
E-mail: ssullivan@nebrcul.org
Website: http://www.nebrcul.org

Steier & Prchal, Ltd.
1015 N 98th St., Ste. 100
Omaha, NE 68114
(402)390-9090
Fax: (402)505-5044
E-mail: info@steiertax.com
Website: http://www.steiertax.com/bizplan.php

Nevada

Anderson Business Advisors, PLLC
3225 McLeod Dr., Ste. 100
Las Vegas, NV 89121
Free: 800-706-4741
Fax: (702)664-0545
E-mail: info@andersonadvisors.com
Website: https://andersonadvisors.com

Stone Law Offices, Ltd.
3295 N Fort Apache Rd., Ste. 150
Las Vegas, NV 89129
Free: 877-800-3424
Fax: (702)998-0443
Website: http://nvestateplan.com

Wise Business Plans
7251 W Lake Mead Blvd., Ste. 300
Las Vegas, NV 89128
Free: 800-496-1056 (United States)
Free: 702-562-4247 (International)
E-mail: info@wisebusinessplans.com
Website: https://wisebusinessplans.com

Drew Aguilar, CPA
1663 Hwy. 395, Ste. 201
Minden, NV 89423
(775)782-7874
Fax: (775)782-8374
E-mail: drew@carsonvalleyaccounting.com
Website: http://www.carsonvalleyaccounting.com

Thunder Vick & Co.
1325 Airmotive Way, Ste. 125
Reno, NV 89502
(775)323-4440
Fax: (775)323-8977
E-mail: admin@thunderrandcpa.com
Website: http://www.thundervickcpa.com

New Hampshire

HJ Marshall Associates
136 Sewalls Falls Rd.
Concord, NH 03301
(603)224-7073
E-mail: franmarshall@comcast.net
Website: http://www.hjmarshallassociates.com

Rodger O. Howells, LLC
6 Loudon Rd., Ste. 205
Concord, New Hampshire 03301
(603)224-3224
Free: 877-224-3224
E-mail: info@rhowellsconsulting.com
Website: http://www.rhowellsconsulting.com

Nathan Wechsler & Co.
70 Commercial St., 4th Fl.
Concord, NH 03301
(603)224-5357
Fax: (603)224-3792
Website: http://www.nathanwechsler.com

Kieschnick Consulting Services
9 Woodland Rd.
Dover, NH 03820
(603)749-2922
E-mail: peggy@kieschnickconsulting.com
Website: http://www.kieschnickconsulting.com

Trojan Consulting Group LLC
PO Box 27
Dover, NH 03821
(603)343-1707
E-mail: MNT@TrojanConsultingGroup.com
Website: http://trojanconsultinggroup.com

Executive Service Corps (ESC)
80 Locke Rd.
Hampton, NH 03842
(603)926-0752
Website: http://www.nonprofit-consultants.org

Hannah Grimes Center for Entrepreneurship
25 Roxbury St.
Keene, NH 03431
(603)352-5063
Fax: (603)352-5538
E-mail: info@hannahgrimes.com
Website: https://www.hannahgrimes.com/

Nathan Wechsler & Co.
59 Emerald St.
Keene, NH 03431
(603)357-7665
Fax: (603)358-6800
Website: http://www.nathanwechsler.com

Nathan Wechsler & Co.
44 School St.
Lebanon, NH 03766
(603)448-2650
Fax: (603)448-2476
Website: http://www.nathanwechsler.com

Blue Ribbon Consulting, LDO, LLC
PO Box 435
New Ipswich, NH 03071
(603)878-1694
E-mail: lisa@blueribbonconsulting.com
Website: www.blueribbonconsulting.com

Dare Mighty Things, LLC
1 New Hampshire Ave., Ste. 125
Portsmouth, NH 03801
(603)431-4331
Fax: (603)431-4332
E-mail: info@daremightythings.com
Website: http://www.daremightythings.com

New Jersey

Huffman & Huffman LLC
Changebridge Plaza
2 Changebridge Rd., Ste. 204
Montville, NJ 07045
(973)334-2600
Fax: (973)334-2627
E-mail: jhuffman@huffmancompany.com

Website: http://www.huffman company.com

New Venture Design
Sperro Corporate Ctr.
2 Skyline Dr.
Montville, NJ 07045
(973)331-0022
Fax: (973)335-2656
Free: 866-639-3527
E-mail: info@newventuredesign.com
Website: http://www.newventuredesign.com

Patterson & Associates LLC
Glendale Executive Campus
1000 White Horse Rd., Ste. 304
Voorhees, NJ 08043-4409
(856)435-2700
Fax: (856)435-1190
E-mail: info@pattersonassociatesllc.com
Website: http://www.patterson associatesllc.com

New Mexico

Hinkle + Landers, P.C.
2500 9th St. NW
Albuquerque, NM 87102
(505)883-8788
Fax: (505)883-8797
E-mail: info@HL-cpas.com
Website: http://www.hl-cpas.com

Vaughn CPA
6605 Uptown Blvd., Ste. 370
Albuquerque, NM 87110
(505)828-0900
E-mail: vaughn@vaughncpa.com
Website: http://vaughncpa.com

WESST
WESST Enterprise Center
609 Broadway Blvd. NE
Albuquerque, NM 87102
(505)246-6900
Fax: (505)243-3035
Free: 800-GO-WESST
Website: https://www.wesst.org

WESST Farmington
San Juan College Quality Center for Business
5101 College Blvd., Ste. 5060
Farmington, NM 87402
(505)566-3715
Fax: (505)566-3698
Website: https://www.wesst.org/farmington

WESST Las Cruces
221 N Main St., #104a
Las Cruces, NM 88001
(575)541-1583
Website: https://www.wesst.org/las-cruces

WESST Rio Rancho
New Mexico Bank & Trust Bldg.
4001 Southern Blvd. SE, Ste. B
Rio Rancho, NM 87124-2069
(505)892-1238
Fax: (505)892-6157
Website: https://www.wesst.org/rio-rancho

WESST Roswell
Bank of America Bldg.
500 N Main St., Ste. 700
Roswell, NM 88201
Fax: (575)624-9850
Free: 575-624-9845
Website: https://www.wesst.org/roswell

Hinkle + Landers, P.C.
404 Brunn School Rd., Bldg. B
Santa Fe, NM 87505
(505)883-8788
Fax: (505)883-8797
E-mail: info@HL-cpas.com
Website: http://www.hl-cpas.com

WESST Santa Fe
Santa Fe Business Incubator
3900 Paseo del Sol, Ste. 351
Santa Fe, NM 87507
(505)474-6556
Fax: (505)474-6687
Website: https://www.wesst.org/santa-fe

New York

Key Accounting of New York
2488 Grand Concourse, Ste. 320B
Bronx, NY 10458
(718)584-8097
Fax: (866)496-5624
E-mail: info@keyaccnewyork.com
Website: http://keyaccnewyork.com

Soundview Business Consulting
53 Prospect Park W, Ste. 4A
Brooklyn, NY 11215
(718)499-0809
Fax: (718)499-0829
E-mail: brendan@soundviewfirm.com
Website: http://www.soundviewfirm.com

Addenda Solutions
5297 Parkside Dr., Ste. 412
Canandaigua, NY 14424
(585)394-4950
Free: 888-851-0414
Website: http://addendasolutions.com

Aspire Consulting, Ltd.
1 Horseshoe Dr.
Hyde Park, NY 12538
(845)803-0438
Fax: (845)229-8262
E-mail: info@AspireAdvantage.com
Website: http://www.aspireadvantage.com/index.html

Capacity Business Consulting
3 Wallkill Ave.
Montgomery, NY 12549
(845)764-9484
E-mail: info@capacityconsultinginc.com
Website: http://www.capacitybusiness consulting.com

Growthink Inc.
27 Radio Circle Dr., Ste. 202
Mount Kisco, NY 10549
Free: 800-647-6983
E-mail: services@growthink.com
Website: http://www.growthink.com

Gershon Consulting
833 Broadway, 2nd Fl.
New York, NY 10003
Free: 800-701-0176
E-mail: info@gershonconsulting.com
Website: http://www.gershonconsulting.com

New York Business Consultants LLC
Chrysler Bldg.
405 Lexington Ave.
New York, NY 10174
(315)572-1938
Fax: (888)201-9524
Free: 800-481-2707
E-mail: info@newyorkbusiness consultants.com
Website: http://www.newyorkbusiness consultants.com/index.html

The Wright Consultants
394 Broadway
New York, NY 10013
(415)928-2071
Website: http://www.thewrightconsultants.com

Addenda Solutions
1100 University Ave., Ste. 122
Rochester, NY 14607
(585)461-2654
Free: 888-851-0414
Website: http://addendasolutions.com

Addenda Solutions
126 Kiwassa Rd.
Saranac Lake, NY 12983
(518)891-1681
Free: 888-851-0414
Website: http://addendasolutions.com

North Carolina

Birds Eye Business Planning & Adventures
153 S Lexington Ave.
Asheville, NC 28801
(828)367-7248
E-mail: info@birdseye.info
Website: http://www.birdseye.info

Mountain BizWorks
153 S Lexington Ave.
Asheville, NC 28801
(828)253-2834
Free: 855-296-0048
E-mail: info@mountainbizworks.org
Website: https://www.mountain bizworks.org

Allied Tax & Accounting Consultants, LLC
5550 77 Center Dr., Ste. 245
Charlotte, NC 28217
(704)676-1882
Fax: (704)676-1884
Free: 888-849-5119
E-mail: help@alliedtaxaccounting.com
Website: http://www.alliedtaxaccounting.com/services/business-consulting

Brewery Business Plan
9205 Cub Run Dr.
Concord, NC 28027
(704)960-4032
Website: https://brewerybusiness plan.com

EMD Consulting
140 Foothills Dr.
Hendersonville, NC 28792
E-mail: info@emdconsulting.com
Website: http://www.emdconsulting .com

Anagard Business Consulting, LLC
9360 Falls of Neuse Rd., Ste. 205
Raleigh, NC 27615
(919)876-1314
E-mail: info@ANAGARD.com
Website: http://www.anagard.com/index.html

Davis Group, PA, CPAs
640 Statesville Blvd., Ste. 1
Salisbury, NC 28145-1307
(704)636-1040
Fax: (704)637-3084
E-mail: gary@dgcpa.com
Website: https://www.dgcpa.com/business-advisory

North Dakota

Center for Innovation
Ina Mae Rude Entrepreneur Ctr.
4200 James Ray Dr.
Grand Forks, ND 58203
(701)777-3132
Fax: (701)777-2339
E-mail: info@innovators.net
Website: http://www.innovators.net

Ohio

Brown Consulting Group LLC
7965 North High St., Ste. 130
Columbus, OH 43235
(614)205-5323
E-mail: keith@browngroupcpa.com
Website: http://browngroupcpa.com

Oklahoma

Wymer Brownlee
3650 SE Camelot Dr.
Bartlesville, OK 74006
(918)333-7291
Fax: (918)333-7295
E-mail: info@wymerbrownlee.com
Website: http://www.wymerbrownlee.com

Wymer Brownlee
201 N Grand, Ste. 100
Enid, OK 73701
(580)237-0060
Fax: (580)237-0092
E-mail: info@wymerbrownlee.com
Website: http://www.wymerbrownlee.com

Wymer Brownlee
126 S Main
Fairview, OK 73737
(580)227-4709
Fax: (580)227-2166
E-mail: info@wymerbrownlee.com
Website: http://www.wymerbrownlee.com

Entrepot
5711 E 72nd Ct.
Tulsa, Oklahoma 74136
(918)497-1748
Website: http://www.entrepotusa.com

Wymer Brownlee
7645 E 63rd St., Ste. 120
Tulsa, OK 74133
(918)392-8600
Fax: (918)392-8601
E-mail: info@wymerbrownlee.com
Website: http://www.wymerbrownlee.com

Wymer Brownlee
10936 NW Expressway
Yukon, OK 73099
(405)283-0100
Fax: (405)283-0200
E-mail: info@wymerbrownlee.com
Website: http://www.wymerbrownlee.com

Oregon

Timothy J. Berry
44 W Broadway Ste. 500
Eugene, OR, 97401
(541)683-6162
Website: http://timberry.com/business-plan-expert

Advanced Trainers & Consultants, LLC (ATAC)
116 SE Hood
Gresham, OR 97080
(503)661-4013
Fax: (503)665-0775
E-mail: info@advancedtrainers.com
Website: http://www.advancedtrainers.com

Alten Sakai & Company LLP
10260 SW Greenburg Rd., Ste. 300
Portland, OR 97223
(503)297-1072
Fax: (503)297-6634
E-mail: info@altensakai.com
Website: http://www.altensakai.com

Pointman Consulting, LLC
1130 SW Morrison
Portland, OR 97205
(503)804-2074
E-mail: noah@pointmanconsulting.com
Website: http://www.pointman consulting.com/index.htm

GVNW Oregon
8050 SW Warm Springs St.
Tualatin, OR 97062
(503)612-4400
E-mail: jrennard@gvnw.com
Website: http://www.gvnw.com

Pennsylvania

Main Line Rail Management, Inc.
116 N Bellevue Ave., Ste. 206
Langhorne, PA 19047
(215)741-6007
Fax: (215)741-6009
E-mail: dsg@voicenet.com
Website: http://www.mlrail.com

Fairmount Ventures, Inc.
2 Penn Ctr.
1500 JFK Blvd., Ste. 1150
Philadelphia, PA 19102
(215)717-2299

E-mail: info@fairmountinc.com
Website: http://fairmountinc.com

RINK Consulting
1420 Locust St., Ste. 31N
Philadelphia, PA 19102
(215)546-5863
Website: http://www.lindarink.com

FlagShip Business Plans and Consulting
2 Gateway Ctr.
?603 Stanwix St., Ste. 1626
Pittsburgh, PA 15222
(412)219-8157
E-mail: info@flagshipbusinessplans.com
Website: http://www.flagshipbusiness plans.com/page.html

Puerto Rico

Manuel L. Porrata & Associates
898 Muñoz Rivera Ave., Ste. 300
San Juan, PR 00927
(787)765-2140
Fax: (787)754-3285
E-mail: mporrata@manuelporrata.com
Website: http://www.manuelporrata .com/home.html

Rhode Island

Ledoux, Petruska & Co., Inc.
1006 Charles St.
North Providence, RI 02904
(401)727-8100
Fax: (401)727-8181
E-mail: beancounter@lpcpari.com
Website: http://www.lpcpari.com/services/ business-consulting-and-solutions

South Carolina

Fluent Decisions, LLC
701 Gervais St., Ste. 150-157
Columbia, SC 29201
(803)748-2933
Website: https://www.fluentdecisions.com

South Dakota

South Dakota Enterprise Institute
Research Park at South Dakota State University
2301 Research Park Way, Ste. 114
Brookings, SD 57006
(605)697-5015
E-mail: info@sdei.org
Website: http://www.sdei.org

Tennessee

Jackson Thorton Nashville Office
333 Commerce St., Ste. 1050
Nashville, TN 37201
(615)869-2050
Website: http://www.jacksonthornton.com

Texas

Zaetric Business Solutions LLC
27350 Blueberry Hill, Ste. 14
Conroe, TX 77385
(281)298-1878
Fax: (713)621-4885
E-mail: inquiries@zaetric.com
Website: http://www.zaetric.com

Optimus Business Plans
13355 Noel Rd., Ste. 1100
Dallas, TX 75240
(844)760-0903
Website: http://optimusbusinessplans.com

GVNW Texas
1001 Water St., Ste. A-100
Kerrville, TX 78028
(830)896-5200
E-mail: sgatto@gvnw.com
Website: http://www.gvnw.com

Butler Consultants
555 Republic Dr., Ste. 200
Plano, TX 75074
(214)491-4001
E-mail: Info@Financial-Projections.com
Website: http://contact.financial-projections.com

Central Texas Business Consultants (CTBC)
PO Box 2213
Wimberley, TX 78676
(512)626-2938
Fax: (512)847-5541
E-mail: info@centraltexasbusiness consulting.com
Website: http://www.centraltexasbusiness consulting.com

Utah

Vector Resources
7651 S Main St., Ste. 106
Midvale, UT 84047-7158
(801)352-8500
Fax: (801)352-8506
E-mail: info@vectorresources.com
Website: http://www.vectorresources.com

Ron Woodbury Consulting, Inc.
2899 E 3240 South St.
Saint George, UT 84790
(435)275-2978
E-mail: ron@ronwoodburyconsulting.com
Website: http://ronwoodburyconsulting .com

Vermont

CDS Consulting Co-op
659 Old Codding Rd.
Putney, VT 05346
(802)387-6013
Website: http://www.cdsconsulting.coop

Virginia

The Profit Partner, LLC
3900 Jermantown Rd., Ste. 300
Fairfax, VA 22030
(703)934-4630
Website: http://www.theprofitpartner.com

Dare Mighty Things, LLC
805 Park Ave.
Herndon, VA 20170
(703)424-3119
Fax: (603)431-4332
E-mail: info@daremightythings.com
Website: http://www.daremightythings.com

Washington

ECG Management Consultants Inc.
1111 3rd Ave., Ste. 2700
Seattle, WA 98101-3201
(206)689-2200
Fax: (206)689-2209
E-mail: ecg@ecgmc.com
Website: http://www.ecgmc.com

West Virginia

Cava & Banko, PLLC
117 E Main St.
Bridgeport, WV 26330
(304)842-4499
Fax: (304)842-4585
Website: http://cavabankocpa.com

Wisconsin

Virtual Management Solutions
959 Primrose Center Rd.
Belleville, WI 53508-9376
(608)832-8003
E-mail: davelind@chorus.net
Website: http://www.virtualmanagement solutions.com

Wyoming

CPA Consulting Group, LLP
300 Country Club Rd., Ste. 302
Casper, WY 82609
(307)577-4040
E-mail: taxes@cpawyo.com
Website: http://www.cpacasper.com

CA Boner Business Plans
3218 Rock Springs St.
Cheyenne, WY 82001
(307)214-2043
Website: http://caboner.biz

CPA Group of Laramie, LLC
1273 N 15th St., Ste. 121
Laramie, WY 82072
(307)745-7241
Fax: (307)745-7292
Website: http://www.cpalaramie.com/index.php

Small business administration regional offices

This section contains a listing of Small Business Administration offices arranged numerically by region. Service areas are provided. Contact the appropriate office for a referral to the nearest field office, or visit the Small Business Administration online at www.sba.gov.

Region I

U.S. Small Business Administration New England Office
10 Causeway St., Ste. 265A
Boston, MA 02222
Phone: (617)565-8416
Fax: (617)565-8420
Website: http://www.sba.gov/offices/regional/i
Serves Connecticut, Maine, Massachusetts, New Hampshire, Rhode Island, and Vermont.

Region II

U.S. Small Business Administration Atlantic Office
26 Federal Plaza, Ste. 3108
New York, NY 10278
Phone: (212)264-1450
Website: http://www.sba.gov/offices/regional/ii
Serves New Jersey, New York, Puerto Rico, and the U.S. Virgin Islands.

Region III

U.S. Small Business Administration Mid-Atlantic Office
1150 1st Ave., Ste. 1001
King of Prussia, PA 19406
(610)382-3092
Website: http://www.sba.gov/offices/regional/iii
Serves Delaware, Maryland, Pennsylvania, Virginia, Washington, DC, and West Virginia.

Region IV

U.S. Small Business Administration Southeast Office
233 Peachtree St. NE, Ste. 1800
Atlanta, GA 30303
Phone: (404)331-4999
Fax: (404)331-2354
Website: http://www.sba.gov/offices/regional/iv
Serves Alabama, Florida, Georgia, Kentucky, Mississippi, North Carolina, South Carolina, and Tennessee.

Region V

U.S. Small Business Administration Great Lakes Office
500 W Madison St., Ste. 1150
Chicago, IL 60661
Phone: (312)353-0357
Fax: (312)353-3426
Website: http://www.sba.gov/offices/regional/v
Serves Illinois, Indiana, Michigan, Minnesota, Ohio, and Wisconsin.

Region VI

U.S. Small Business Administration South Central Office
4300 Amon Carter Blvd., Ste. 108
Fort Worth, TX 76155
Phone: (817)684-5581
Fax: (817)684-5588
TTY/TDD: (817)684-5552
Website: http://www.sba.gov/offices/regional/vi
Serves Arkansas, Louisiana, New Mexico, Oklahoma, and Texas.

Region VII

U.S. Small Business Administration Great Plains Office
1000 Walnut, Ste. 530
Kansas City, MO 64106
Phone: (816)426-4840
Fax: (816)426-4848
Website: http://www.sba.gov/offices/regional/vii
Serves Iowa, Kansas, Missouri, and Nebraska.

Region VIII

U.S. Small Business Administration Rocky Mountains Office
721 19th St., Ste. 400
Denver, CO 80202
Fax: (303)844-0506
Website: http://www.sba.gov/offices/regional/viii
Serves Colorado, Montana, North Dakota, South Dakota, Utah, and Wyoming.

Region IX

U.S. Small Business Administration Pacific Office
330 N Brand Blvd., Ste. 1200
Glendale, CA 91203
Phone: (818)552-3437
Fax: (202)481-0344
Website: http://www.sba.gov/offices/regional/ix
Serves Arizona, California, Guam, Hawaii, and Nevada.

Region X

U.S. Small Business Administration Pacific Northwest Office
2401 4th Ave., Ste. 400
Seattle, WA 98121
Phone: (206)553-5676
Fax: (206)553-4155
Website: http://www.sba.gov/offices/regional/x
Serves Alaska, Idaho, Oregon, and Washington.

Small business development centers

This section contains a listing of all Small Business Development Centers, organized alphabetically by state/U.S. territory, then by city, then by agency name.

Alabama

Alabama SBDC

UNIVERSITY OF ALABAMA
2800 Milan Court Suite 124
Birmingham, AL 35211-6908
Phone: 205-943-6750
Fax: 205-943-6752
E-Mail: wcampbell@provost.uab.edu
Website: http://www.asbdc.org
Mr. William Campbell Jr, State Director

Alaska

Alaska SBDC

UNIVERSITY OF ALASKA - ANCHORAGE
430 West Seventh Avenue, Suite 110
Anchorage, AK 99501

Phone: 907-274 -7232
Fax: 907-272-0565
E-Mail: Isaac.Vanderburg@aksbdc.org
Website: http://www.aksbdc.org
Isaac Vanderburg, State Director

American Samoa

American Samoa SBDC

AMERICAN SAMOA COMMUNITY COLLEGE
P.O. Box 2609
Pago Pago, American Samoa 96799
Phone: 011-684-699-4830
Fax: 011-684-699-6132
E-Mail: hthweatt.sbdc@hotmail.com
Website: www.as-sbdc.org
Mr. Herbert Thweatt, Director

Arizona

Arizona SBDC

MARICOPA COUNTY COMMUNITY COLLEGE
2411 West 14th Street, Suite 114
Tempe, AZ 85281
Phone: (480)731-8720
Fax: (480)731-8729
E-Mail: janice.washington@domail.maricopa.edu
Website: http://www.azsbdc.net
Janice Washington, State Director

Arkansas

Arkansas SBDC

UNIVERSITY OF ARKANSAS
2801 South University Avenue
Little Rock, AR 72204
Phone: 501-683-7700
Fax: 501-683-7720
E-Mail: jmroderick@ualr.edu
Website: http://asbtdc.org
Ms. Janet M. Roderick, State Director

California

California - Northern California Regional SBDC

Northern California SBDC

HUMBOLDT STATE UNIVERSITY
1 Harpst Street 2006A, 209 Siemens Hall
Arcata, CA, 95521
Phone: 707-826-3920
Fax: 707-826-3912
E-Mail: Kristin.Johnson@humboldt.edu
Website: https://www.norcalsbdc.org
Kristin Johnson, Regional Director

California - Northern California SBDC

CALIFORNIA STATE UNIVERSITY - CHICO
35 Main St., Rm 203rr
Chico, CA 95929-0765
Phone: 530-898-5443
Fax: 530-898-4734
E-Mail: dripke@csuchico.edu
Website: https://www.necsbdc.org
Mr. Dan Ripke, Interim Regional Director

California - San Diego and Imperial SBDC

SOUTHWESTERN COMMUNITY COLLEGE
880 National City Boulevard, Suite 103
National City, CA 91950
Phone: 619-216-6721
Fax: 619-216-6692
E-Mail: awilson@swccd.edu
Website: http://www.SBDCRegionalNetwork.org
Aleta Wilson, Regional Director

California - UC Merced SBDC

UC Merced Lead Center

UNIVERSITY OF CALIFORNIA - MERCED
550 East Shaw, Suite 105A
Fresno, CA 93710
Phone: 559-241-6590
Fax: 559-241-7422
E-Mail: dhowerton@ucmerced.edu
Website: http://sbdc.ucmerced.edu
Diane Howerton, State Director

California - Orange County/Inland Empire SBDC

Tri-County Lead SBDC

CALIFORNIA STATE UNIVERSITY - FULLERTON
800 North State College Boulevard, SGMH 5313
Fullerton, CA 92834
Phone: 714-278-5168
Fax: 714-278-7101
E-Mail: kmpayne@fullerton.edu
Website: http://www.leadsbdc.org
Katrina Payne Smith, Lead Center Director

California - Los Angeles Region SBDC

LONG BEACH CITY COLLEGE
4900 E Conant Street, Building 2
Long Beach, CA 90808
Phone: 562-938-5006
Fax: 562-938-5030
E-Mail: jtorres@lbcc.edu
Website: http://www.smallbizla.org
Jesse Torres, Lead Center Director

Colorado

Colorado SBDC

COLORADO SBDC
1625 Broadway, Suite 2700
Denver, CO 80202
Phone: 303-892-3864
Fax: 303-892-3848
E-Mail: Kelly.Manning@state.co.us
Website: http://www.www.coloradosbdc.org
Ms. Kelly Manning, State Director

Connecticut

Connecticut SBDC

UNIVERSITY OF CONNECTICUT
2100 Hillside Road, Unit 1044
Storrs, CT 06269
Phone: 855-428-7232
E-Mail: ecarter@uconn.edu
Website: www.ctsbdc.com
Emily Carter, State Director

Delaware

Delaware SBDC

DELAWARE TECHNOLOGY PARK
1 Innovation Way, Suite 301
Newark, DE 19711
Phone: 302-831-4283
Fax: 302-831-1423
E-Mail: jmbowman@udel.edu
Website: http://www.delawaresbdc.org
Mike Bowman, State Director

District of Columbia

District of Columbia SBDC

HOWARD UNIVERSITY
2600 6th Street, NW Room 128
Washington, DC 20059
Phone: 202-806-1550
Fax: 202-806-1777
E-Mail: darrell.brown@howard.edu
Website: http://www.dcsbdc.com
Darrell Brown, Executive Director

Florida

Florida SBDC

UNIVERSITY OF WEST FLORIDA
11000 University Parkway, Building 38
Pensacola, FL 32514
Phone: 850-473-7800

Fax: 850-473-7813
E-Mail: mmyhre@uwf.edu
Website: http://www.floridasbdc.com
Michael Myhre, State Director

Georgia

Georgia SBDC

UNIVERSITY OF GEORGIA
1180 East Broad Street
Athens, GA 30602
Phone: 706-542-6762
Fax: 706-542-7935
E-mail: aadams@georgiasbdc.org
Website: http://www.georgiasbdc.org
Mr. Allan Adams, State Director

Guam

Guam Small Business Development Center

UNIVERSITY OF GUAM
Pacific Islands SBDC
P.O. Box 5014 - U.O.G. Station
Mangilao, GU 96923
Phone: 671-735-2590
Fax: 671-734-2002
E-mail: casey@pacificsbdc.com
Website: http://www.uog.edu/sbdc
Mr. Casey Jeszenka, Director

Hawaii

Hawaii SBDC

UNIVERSITY OF HAWAII - HILO
200 W Kawili Street, Suite 107
Hilo, HI 96720
Phone: 808-974-7515
Fax: 808-974-7683
E-Mail: cathy.wiltse@hisbdc.org
Website: http://www.hisbdc.org
Cathy Wiltse, State Director

Idaho

Idaho SBDC

BOISE STATE UNIVERSITY
1910 University Drive
Boise, ID 83725
Phone: 208-426-3838
Fax: 208-426-3877
E-mail: ksewell@boisestate.edu
Website: http://www.idahosbdc.org
Katie Sewell, State Director

Illinois

Illinois SBDC

DEPARTMENT OF COMMERCE AND ECONOMIC OPPORTUNITY
500 E Monroe
Springfield, IL 62701
Phone: 217-524-5700
Fax: 217-524-0171
E-mail: mark.petrilli@illinois.gov
Website: http://www.ilsbdc.biz
Mr. Mark Petrilli, State Director

Indiana

Indiana SBDC

INDIANA ECONOMIC DEVELOPMENT CORPORATION
One North Capitol, Suite 700
Indianapolis, IN 46204
Phone: 317-232-8805
Fax: 317-232-8872
E-mail: JSchpok@iedc.in.gov
Website: http://www.isbdc.org
Jacob Schpok, State Director

Iowa

Iowa SBDC

IOWA STATE UNIVERSITY
2321 North Loop Drive, Suite 202
Ames, IA 50010
Phone: 515-294-2030
Fax: 515-294-6522
E-mail: lshimkat@iastate.edu
Website: http://www.iowasbdc.org
Lisa Shimkat, State Director

Kansas

Kansas SBDC

FORT HAYS STATE UNIVERSITY
214 SW Sixth Street, Suite 301
Topeka, KS 66603
Phone: 785-296-6514
Fax: 785-291-3261
E-mail: panichello@ksbdc.net
Website: http://www.fhsu.edu/ksbdc
Greg Panichello, State Director

Kentucky

Kentucky SBDC

UNIVERSITY OF KENTUCKY
One Quality Street
Lexington, KY 40507
Phone: 859-257-7668
Fax: 859-323-1907
E-mail: lrnaug0@uky.edu
Website: http://www.ksbdc.org
Becky Naugle, State Director

Louisiana

Louisiana SBDC

UNIVERSITY OF LOUISIANA - MONROE

College of Business Administration
700 University Avenue
Monroe, LA 71209
Phone: 318-342-5507
Fax: 318-342-5510
E-mail: rkessler@lsbdc.org
Website: http://www.lsbdc.org
Rande Kessler, State Director

Maine

Maine SBDC

UNIVERSITY OF SOUTHERN MAINE
96 Falmouth Street P.O. Box 9300
Portland, ME 04104
Phone: 207-780-4420
Fax: 207-780-4810
E-mail: mark.delisle@maine.edu
Website: http://www.mainesbdc.org
Mark Delisle, State Director

Maryland

Maryland SBDC

UNIVERSITY OF MARYLAND
7100 Baltimore Avenue, Suite 401
College Park, MD 20742
Phone: 301-403-8300
Fax: 301-403-8303
E-mail: rsprow@mdsbdc.umd.edu
Website: http://www.mdsbdc.umd.edu
Renee Sprow, State Director

Massachusetts

Massachusetts SBDC

UNIVERSITY OF MASSACHUSETTS
23 Tillson Farm Road
Amherst, MA 01003
Phone: 413-545-6301
Fax: 413-545-1273
E-mail: gparkin@msbdc.umass.edu
Website: http://www.www.msbdc.org
Georgianna Parkin, State Director

Michigan

Michigan SBTDC

GRAND VALLEY STATE UNIVERSITY
510 West Fulton Avenue
Grand Rapids, MI 49504

Phone: 616-331-7480
Fax: 616-331-7485
E-mail: boesen@gvsu.edu
Website: http://www.misbtdc.org
Nancy Boese, State Director

Minnesota

Minnesota SBDC

MINNESOTA SMALL BUSINESS DEVELOPMENT CENTER
1st National Bank Building
332 Minnesota Street, Suite E200
Saint Paul, MN 55101-1349
Phone: 651-259-7420
Fax: 651-296-5287
E-mail: Bruce.Strong@state.mn.us
Website: http://www.mnsbdc.com
Bruce H. Strong, State Director

Mississippi

Mississippi SBDC

UNIVERSITY OF MISSISSIPPI
122 Jeanette Phillips Drive
P.O. Box 1848
University, MS 38677
Phone: 662-915-5001
Fax: 662-915-5650
E-mail: wgurley@olemiss.edu
Website: http://www.mssbdc.org
Doug Gurley, Jr., State Director

Missouri

Missouri SBDC

UNIVERSITY OF MISSOURI
410 South 6th Street, ?200 Engineering North
Columbia, MO 65211
Phone: 573-882-9206
Fax: 573-884-4297
E-mail: bouchardc@missouri.edu
Website: http://www.missouribusiness.net
Chris Bouchard, State Director

Montana

Montana SBDC

DEPARTMENT OF COMMERCE
301 S Park Avenue, Room 114
Helena, MT 59601
Phone: 406-841-2746
Fax: 406-841-2728
E-mail: adesch@mt.gov
Website: http://www.sbdc.mt.gov
Ms. Ann Desch, State Director

Nebraska

Nebraska SBDC

UNIVERSITY OF NEBRASKA - OMAHA
200 Mammel Hall, 67th & Pine Streets
Omaha, NE 68182
Phone: 402-554-2521
Fax: 402-554-3473
E-mail: rbernier@unomaha.edu
Website: http://nbdc.unomaha.edu
Robert Bernier, State Director

Nevada

Nevada SBDC

UNIVERSITY OF NEVADA - RENO
Reno College of Business, Room 411
Reno, NV 89557-0100
Phone: 775-784-1717
Fax: 775-784-4337
E-mail: males@unr.edu
Website: http://www.nsbdc.org
Sam Males, State Director

New Hampshire

New Hampshire SBDC

UNIVERSITY OF NEW HAMPSHIRE
10 Garrison Avenue
Durham, NH 03824-3593
Phone: 603-862-2200
Fax: 603-862-4876
E-mail: Mary.Collins@unh.edu
Website: http://www.nhsbdc.org
Mary Collins, State Director

New Jersey

New Jersey SBDC

RUTGERS UNIVERSITY
1 Washington Park, 3rd Floor
Newark, NJ 07102
Phone: 973-353-1927
Fax: 973-353-1110
E-mail: bhopper@njsbdc.com
Website: http://www.njsbdc.com
Brenda Hopper, State Director

New Mexico

New Mexico SBDC

SANTA FE COMMUNITY COLLEGE
6401 Richards Avenue
Santa Fe, NM 87508
Phone: 505-428-1362
Fax: 505-428-1469
E-mail: russell.wyrick@sfcc.edu
Website: http://www.nmsbdc.org
Russell Wyrick, State Director

New York

New York SBDC

STATE UNIVERSITY OF NEW YORK
22 Corporate Woods, 3rd Floor
Albany, NY 12246
Phone: 518-443-5398
Fax: 518-443-5275
E-mail: j.king@nyssbdc.org
Website: http://www.nyssbdc.org
Jim King, State Director

North Carolina

North Carolina SBDTC

UNIVERSITY OF NORTH CAROLINA
5 West Hargett Street, Suite 600
Raleigh, NC 27601
Phone: 919-715-7272
Fax: 919-715-7777
E-mail: sdaugherty@sbtdc.org
Website: http://www.sbtdc.org
Scott Daugherty, State Director

North Dakota

North Dakota SBDC

UNIVERSITY OF NORTH DAKOTA
1200 Memorial Highway, PO Box 5509
Bismarck, ND 58506
Phone: 701-328-5375
Fax: 701-250-4304
E-mail: dkmartin@ndsbdc.org
Website: http://www.ndsbdc.org
David Martin, State Director

Ohio

Ohio SBDC

OHIO DEPARTMENT OF DEVELOPMENT
77 South High Street, 28th Floor
Columbus, OH 43216
Phone: 614-466-2711
Fax: 614-466-1789
E-mail: ezra.escudero@development.ohio.gov
Website: http://www.ohiosbdc.org
Ezra Escudero, State Director

Oklahoma

Oklahoma SBDC

SOUTHEAST OKLAHOMA STATE UNIVERSITY
1405 N. 4th Avenue, PMB 2584
Durant, OK 74701

Phone: 580-745-2955
Fax: 580-745-7471
E-mail: wcarter@se.edu
Website: http://www.osbdc.org
Grady Pennington, State Director

Oregon

Oregon SBDC

LANE COMMUNITY COLLEGE
1445 Willamette Street, Suite 5
Eugene, OR 97401
Phone: 541-463-5250
Fax: 541-345-6006
E-mail: gregorym@lanecc.edu
Website: http://www.bizcenter.org
Mark Gregory, State Director

Pennsylvania

Pennsylvania SBDC

UNIVERSITY OF PENNSYLVANIA

The Wharton School
3819-33 Chestnut Street, Suite 325
Philadelphia, PA 19104
Phone: 215-898-1219
Fax: 215-573-2135
E-mail: cconroy@wharton.upenn.edu
Website: http://pasbdc.org
Christian Conroy, State Director

Puerto Rico

Puerto Rico SBDC

INTER-AMERICAN UNIVERSITY OF PUERTO RICO
416 Ponce de Leon Avenue, Union Plaza, Tenth Floor
Hato Rey, PR 00918
Phone: 787-763-6811
Fax: 787-763-6875
E-mail: cmarti@prsbdc.org
Website: http://www.prsbdc.org
Carmen Marti, Executive Director

Rhode Island

Rhode Island SBDC

UNIVERSITY OF RHODE ISLAND
75 Lower College Road, 2nd Floor
Kingston, RI 02881
Phone: 401-874-4576
E-mail: gsonnenfeld@uri.edu
Website: http://www.risbdc.org
Gerald Sonnenfeld, State Director

South Carolina

South Carolina SBDC

UNIVERSITY OF SOUTH CAROLINA

Moore School of Business
1014 Greene Street
Columbia, SC 29208
Phone: 803-777-0749
Fax: 803-777-6876
E-mail: michele.abraham@moore.sc.edu
Website: http://www.scsbdc.com
Michele Abraham, State Director

South Dakota

South Dakota SBDC

UNIVERSITY OF SOUTH DAKOTA
414 East Clark Street, Patterson Hall
Vermillion, SD 57069
Phone: 605-677-5103
Fax: 605-677-5427
E-mail: jeff.eckhoff@usd.edu
Website: http://www.usd.edu/sbdc
Jeff Eckhoff, State Director

Tennessee

Tennessee SBDC

MIDDLE TENNESSEE STATE UNIVERSITY
3050 Medical Center Parkway, Ste. 200
Nashville, TN 37129
Phone: 615-849-9999
Fax: 615-893-7089
E-mail: pgeho@tsbdc.org
Website: http://www.tsbdc.org
Patrick Geho, State Director

Texas

Texas-North SBDC

DALLAS COUNTY COMMUNITY COLLEGE
1402 Corinth Street
Dallas, TX 75215
Phone: 214-860-5832
Fax: 214-860-5813
E-mail: m.langford@dcccd.edu
Website: http://www.ntsbdc.org
Mark Langford, Region Director

Texas Gulf Coast SBDC

UNIVERSITY OF HOUSTON
2302 Fannin, Suite 200
Houston, TX 77002
Phone: 713-752-8444
Fax: 713-756-1500
E-mail: fyoung@uh.edu
Website: http://sbdcnetwork.uh.edu
Mike Young, Executive Director

Texas-NW SBDC

TEXAS TECH UNIVERSITY
2579 South Loop 289, Suite 114
Lubbock, TX 79423
Phone: 806-745-3973
Fax: 806-745-6207
E-mail: c.bean@nwtsbdc.org
Website: http://www.nwtsbdc.org
Craig Bean, Executive Director

Texas-South-West Texas Border Region SBDC

UNIVERSITY OF TEXAS - SAN ANTONIO
501 West Durango Boulevard
San Antonio, TX 78207-4415
Phone: 210-458-2480
Fax: 210-458-2425
E-mail: albert.salgado@utsa.edu
Website: https://www.txsbdc.org
Alberto Salgado, Region Director

Utah

Utah SBDC

SALT LAKE COMMUNITY COLLEGE
9750 South 300 West
Salt Lake City, UT 84070
Phone: 801-957-5384
Fax: 801-985-5300
E-mail: Sherm.Wilkinson@slcc.edu
Website: http://www.utahsbdc.org
Sherm Wilkinson, State Director

Vermont

Vermont SBDC

VERMONT TECHNICAL COLLEGE
PO Box 188, 1 Main Street
Randolph Center, VT 05061-0188
Phone: 802-728-9101
Fax: 802-728-3026
E-mail: lrossi@vtsbdc.org
Website: http://www.vtsbdc.org
Linda Rossi, State Director

Virgin Islands

Virgin Islands SBDC

UNIVERSITY OF THE VIRGIN ISLANDS
8000 Nisky Center, Suite 720
Saint Thomas, VI 00802
Phone: 340-776-3206
Fax: 340-775-3756
E-mail: ldottin@uvi.edu
Website: http://www.sbdcvi.org
Leonor Dottin, State Director

Virginia

Virginia SBDC

GEORGE MASON UNIVERSITY
4031 University Drive, Suite100
Fairfax, VA 22030
Phone: 703-277-7727
Fax: 703-352-8518
E-mail: jkeenan@gmu.edu
Website: http://www.virginiasbdc.org
Jody Keenan, Director

Washington

Washington SBDC

WASHINGTON STATE UNIVERSITY
1235 N. Post Street, Suite 201
Spokane, WA 99201
Phone: 509-358-7765
Fax: 509-358-7764
E-mail: duane.fladland@wsbdc.org
Website: http://www.wsbdc.org
Duane Fladland, State Director

West Virginia

West Virginia SBDC

WEST VIRGINIA DEVELOPMENT OFFICE
Capital Complex, Building 6, Room 652
1900 Kanawha Boulevard
Charleston, WV 25305
Phone: 304-957-2087
Fax: 304-558-0127
E-mail: Kristina.J.Oliver@wv.gov
Website: http://www.wvsbdc.org
Mr. Conley Salyor, State Director

Wisconsin

Wisconsin SBDC

UNIVERSITY OF WISCONSIN
432 North Lake Street, Room 423
Madison, WI 53706
Phone: 608-263-7794
Fax: 608-263-7830
E-mail: bon.wikenheiser@uwex.edu
Website: http://www.uwex.edu/sbdc
Bon Wikenheiser, State Director

Wyoming

Wyoming SBDC

UNIVERSITY OF WYOMING
1000 E University Ave., Dept. 3922
Laramie, WY 82071-3922
Phone: (307)766-3405
Fax: (307)766-3406
E-mail: jkline@uwyo.edu
Website: http://www.wyomingentrepreneur.biz
Jill Kline, Acting State Director

Service corps of retired executives (score) offices

This section contains a listing of all SCORE offices organized alphabetically by state/U.S. territory, then by city, then by agency name.

Alabama

SCORE Office (Northeast Alabama)
1400 Commerce Blvd., Northeast
Anniston, AL 36207
(256)241-6111

SCORE Office (North Alabama)
1731 1st Ave. North, Ste. 200
Birmingham, AL 35203
(205)264-8425
Fax: (205)934-0538

SCORE Office (Baldwin County)
327 Fairhope Avenue
Fairhope, AL 36532
(251)928-6387

SCORE Office (Mobile)
451 Government Street
Mobile, AL 36652
(251)431-8614
Fax: (251)431-8646

SCORE Office (Alabama Capitol City)
600 S Court St.
Montgomery, AL 36104
(334)240-6868
Fax: (334)240-6869

SCORE Office (Tuscaloosa)
2200 University Blvd.
Tuscaloosa, AL 35402
(205)758-7588

Alaska

SCORE Office (Anchorage)
420 L St., Ste. 300
Anchorage, AK 99501
(907)271-4022
Fax: (907)271-4545

Arizona

SCORE Office (Greater Phoenix)
2828 N. Central Ave., Ste. 800
Phoenix, AZ 85004
(602)745-7250
Fax: (602)745-7210
E-mail: e-mail@SCORE-phoenix.org
Website: http://www.greaterphoenix.score.org

SCORE Office (Northern Arizona)
1228 Willow Creek Rd., Ste. 2
Prescott, AZ 86301
(928)778-7438
Fax: (928)778-0812
Website: http://www.northernarizona.score.org

SCORE Office (Southern Arizona)
1400 W Speedway Blvd.
Tucson, AZ 85745
(520)505-3636
Fax: (520)670-5011
Website: http://www.southernarizona.score.org

Arkansas

SCORE Office (South Central)
201 N. Jackson Ave.
El Dorado, AR 71730-5803
(870)863-6113
Fax: (870)863-6115

SCORE Office (Northwest Arkansas)
614 E Emma St., Room M412
Springdale, AR 72764
(479)725-1809
Website: http://www.northwestarkansas.score.org

SCORE Office (Little Rock)
2120 Riverfront Dr., Ste. 250
Little Rock, AR 72202-1747
(501)324-7379
Fax: (501)324-5199
Website: http://www.littlerock.score.org

SCORE Office (Southeast Arkansas)
P.O. Box 5069
Pine Bluff, AR 71611-5069
(870)535-0110
Fax: (870)535-1643

California

SCORE Office (Bakersfield)
P.O. Box 2426
Bakersfield, CA 93303
(661)861-9249
Fax: (661)395-4134
Website: http://www.bakersfield.score.org

SCORE Office (Santa Cruz County)
716 G Capitola Ave.
Capitola, CA 95010
(831)621-3735
Fax: (831)475-6530
Website: http://santacruzcounty.score.org

SCORE Office (Greater Chico Area)
1324 Mangrove St., Ste. 114
Chico, CA 95926

(530)342-8932
Fax: (530)342-8932
Website: http://www.greaterchicoarea.score.org

SCORE Office (El Centro)
1850 W Main St, Ste. C
El Centro, CA 92243
(760)337-2692
Website: http://www.sandiego.score.org

SCORE Office (Central Valley)
801 R St., Ste. 201
Fresno, CA 93721
(559)487-5605
Fax: (559)487-5636
Website: http://www.centralvalley.score.org

SCORE Office (Los Angeles)
330 N. Brand Blvd., Ste. 190
Glendale, CA 91203-2304
(818)552-3206
Fax: (818)552-3323
Website: http://www.greaterlosangeles.score.org

SCORE Office (Modesto Merced)
1880 W Wardrobe Ave.
Merced, CA 95340
(209)725-2033
Fax: (209)577-2673
Website: http://www.modestomerced.score.org

SCORE Office (Monterey Bay)
Monterey Chamber of Commerce
30 Ragsdale Dr.
Monterey, CA 93940
(831)648-5360
Website: http://www.montereybay.score.org

SCORE Office (East Bay)
492 9th St., Ste. 350
Oakland, CA 94607
(510)273-6611
Fax: (510)273-6015
E-mail: webmaster@eastbayscore.org
Website: http://www.eastbay.score.org

SCORE Office (Ventura County)
400 E Esplanade Dr., Ste. 301
Oxnard, CA 93036
(805)204-6022
Fax: (805)650-1414
Website: http://www.ventura.score.org

SCORE Office (Coachella)
43100 Cook St., Ste. 104
Palm Desert, CA 92211
(760)773-6507
Fax: (760)773-6514
Website: http://www.coachellavalley.score.org

SCORE Office (Antelope Valley)
1212 E Avenue, S Ste. A3
Palmdale, CA 93550
(661)947-7679
Website: http://www.antelopevalley.score.org

SCORE Office (Inland Empire)
11801 Pierce St., 2nd Fl.
Riverside, CA 92505
(951)-652-4390
Fax: (951)929-8543
Website: http://www.inlandempire.score.org

SCORE Office (Sacramento)
4990 Stockton Blvd.
Sacramento, CA 95820
(916)635-9085
Fax: (916)635-9089
Website: http://www.sacramento.score.org

SCORE Office (San Diego)
550 West C. St., Ste. 550
San Diego, CA 92101-3540
(619)557-7272
Website: http://www.sandiego.score.org

SCORE Office (San Francisco)
455 Market St., 6th Fl.
San Francisco, CA 94105
(415)744-6827
Fax: (415)744-6750
E-mail: sfscore@sfscore.
Website: http://www.sanfrancisco.score.org

SCORE Office (Silicon Valley)
234 E Gish Rd., Ste. 100
San Jose, CA 95112
(408)453-6237
Fax: (408)494-0214
E-mail: info@svscore.org
Website: http://www.siliconvalley.score.org

SCORE Office (San Luis Obispo)
711 Tank Farm Rd., Ste. 210
San Luis Obispo, CA 93401
(805)547-0779
Website: http://www.sanluisobispo.score.org

SCORE Office (Orange County)
200 W Santa Anna Blvd., Ste. 700
Santa Ana, CA 92701
(714)550-7369
Fax: (714)550-0191
Website: http://www.orangecounty.score.org

SCORE Office (Santa Barbara)
924 Anacapa St.
Santa Barbara, CA 93101
(805)563-0084
Website: http://www.santabarbara.score.org

SCORE Office (North Coast)
777 Sonoma Ave., Rm. 115E
Santa Rosa, CA 95404
(707)571-8342
Fax: (707)541-0331
Website: http://www.northcoast.score.org

SCORE Office (Tuolumne County)
222 S Shepherd St.
Sonora, CA 95370
(209)532-4316
Fax: (209)588-0673
Website: http://www.tuolumnecounty.score.org

Colorado

SCORE Office (Colorado Springs)
3595 E Fountain Blvd., Ste. E-1
Colorado Springs, CO 80910
(719)636-3074
Fax: (719)635-1571
Website: http://www.coloradosprings.score.org

SCORE Office (Denver)
US Custom's House, 4th Fl.
721 19th St.
Denver, CO 80202
(303)844-3985
Fax: (303)844-6490
Website: http://www.denver.score.org

SCORE Office (Tri-River)
1102 Grand Ave.
Glenwood Springs, CO 81601
(970)945-6589

SCORE Office (Grand Junction)
2591 B & 3/4 Rd.
Grand Junction, CO 81503
(970)243-5242

SCORE Office (Gunnison)
608 N. 11th
Gunnison, CO 81230
(303)641-4422

SCORE Office (Montrose)
1214 Peppertree Dr.
Montrose, CO 81401
(970)249-6080

SCORE Office (Pagosa Springs)
PO Box 4381
Pagosa Springs, CO 81157
(970)731-4890

SCORE Office (Rifle)
0854 W Battlement Pky., Apt. C106
Parachute, CO 81635
(970)285-9390

SCORE Office (Pueblo)
302 N. Santa Fe
Pueblo, CO 81003
(719)542-1704
Fax: (719)542-1624
Website: http://www.pueblo.score.org

SCORE Office (Ridgway)
143 Poplar Pl.
Ridgway, CO 81432

SCORE Office (Silverton)
PO Box 480
Silverton, CO 81433
(303)387-5430

SCORE Office (Minturn)
PO Box 2066
Vail, CO 81658
(970)476-1224

Connecticut

SCORE Office (Greater Bridgeport)
230 Park Ave.
Bridgeport, CT 06604
(203)450-9484
Fax: (203)576-4388

SCORE Office (Western Connecticut)
155 Deer Hill Ave.
Danbury, CT 06010
(203)794-1404
Website: http://www.westernconnecticut.score.org

SCORE Office (Greater Hartford County)
330 Main St., 2nd Fl.
Hartford, CT 06106
(860)240-4700
Fax: (860)240-4659
Website: http://www.greaterhartford.score.org

SCORE Office (Manchester)
20 Hartford Rd.
Manchester, CT 06040
(203)646-2223
Fax: (203)646-5871

SCORE Office (New Britain)
185 Main St., Ste. 431
New Britain, CT 06051
(203)827-4492
Fax: (203)827-4480

SCORE Office (New Haven)
60 Sargent Dr.
New Haven, CT 06511
(203)865-7645
Website: http://www.newhaven.score.org

SCORE Office (Fairfield County)
111 East Ave.
Norwalk, CT 06851
(203)847-7348
Fax: (203)849-9308
Website: http://www.fairfieldcounty.score.org

SCORE Office (Southeastern Connecticut)
665 Boston Post Rd.
Old Saybrook, CT 06475
(860)388-9508
Website: http://www.southeasternconnecticut.score.org

SCORE Office (Northwest Connecticut)
333 Kennedy Dr.
Torrington, CT 06790
(560)482-6586
Website: http://www.northwestconnecticut.score.org

Delaware

SCORE Office (Dover)
Treadway Towers
PO Box 576
Dover, DE 19903
(302)678-0892
Fax: (302)678-0189

SCORE Office (Lewes)
PO Box 1
Lewes, DE 19958
(302)645-8073
Fax: (302)645-8412

SCORE Office (Milford)
204 NE Front St.
Milford, DE 19963
(302)422-3301

SCORE Office (Wilmington)
824 Market St., Ste. 610
Wilmington, DE 19801
(302)573-6652
Fax: (302)573-6092
Website: http://www.scoredelaware.com

District of Columbia

SCORE Office (George Mason University)
409 3rd St. SW, 4th Fl.
Washington, DC 20024
800-634-0245

SCORE Office (Washington DC)
1110 Vermont Ave. NW, 9th Fl.
Washington, DC 20043
(202)606-4000
Fax: (202)606-4225
E-mail: dcscore@hotmail.com
Website: http://www.scoredc.org

Florida

SCORE Office (Desota County Chamber of Commerce)
16 South Velucia Ave.
Arcadia, FL 34266
(941)494-4033

SCORE Office (Suncoast/Pinellas)
Airport Business Ctr.
4707 - 140th Ave. N, No. 311
Clearwater, FL 33755
(813)532-6800
Fax: (813)532-6800

SCORE Office (DeLand)
336 N. Woodland Blvd.
DeLand, FL 32720
(904)734-4331
Fax: (904)734-4333

SCORE Office (South Palm Beach)
1050 S Federal Hwy., Ste. 132
Delray Beach, FL 33483
(561)278-7752
Fax: (561)278-0288

SCORE Office (Fort Lauderdale)
Federal Bldg., Ste. 123
299 E Broward Blvd.
Fort Lauderdale, FL 33301
(954)356-7263
Fax: (954)356-7145

SCORE Office (Southwest Florida)
The Renaissance
8695 College Pky., Ste. 345 & 346
Fort Myers, FL 33919
(941)489-2935
Fax: (941)489-1170

SCORE Office (Treasure Coast)
Professional Center, Ste. 2
3220 S US, No. 1
Fort Pierce, FL 34982
(561)489-0548

SCORE Office (Gainesville)
101 SE 2nd Pl., Ste. 104
Gainesville, FL 32601
(904)375-8278

SCORE Office (Hialeah Dade Chamber)
59 W 5th St.
Hialeah, FL 33010

(305)887-1515
Fax: (305)887-2453

SCORE Office (Daytona Beach)
921 Nova Rd., Ste. A
Holly Hills, FL 32117
(904)255-6889
Fax: (904)255-0229
E-mail: score87@dbeach.com

SCORE Office (South Broward)
3475 Sheridian St., Ste. 203
Hollywood, FL 33021
(305)966-8415

SCORE Office (Citrus County)
5 Poplar Ct.
Homosassa, FL 34446
(352)382-1037

SCORE Office (Jacksonville)
7825 Baymeadows Way, Ste. 100-B
Jacksonville, FL 32256
(904)443-1911
Fax: (904)443-1980
E-mail: scorejax@juno.com
Website: http://www.scorejax.org

SCORE Office (Jacksonville Satellite)
3 Independent Dr.
Jacksonville, FL 32256
(904)366-6600
Fax: (904)632-0617

SCORE Office (Central Florida)
5410 S Florida Ave., No. 3
Lakeland, FL 33801
(941)687-5783
Fax: (941)687-6225

SCORE Office (Lakeland)
100 Lake Morton Dr.
Lakeland, FL 33801
(941)686-2168

SCORE Office (Saint Petersburg)
800 W Bay Dr., Ste. 505
Largo, FL 33712
(813)585-4571

SCORE Office (Leesburg)
9501 US Hwy. 441
Leesburg, FL 34788-8751
(352)365-3556
Fax: (352)365-3501

SCORE Office (Cocoa)
1600 Farno Rd., Unit 205
Melbourne, FL 32935
(407)254-2288

SCORE Office (Melbourne)
Melbourne Professional Complex
1600 Sarno, Ste. 205
Melbourne, FL 32935
(407)254-2288
Fax: (407)245-2288

SCORE Office (Merritt Island)
1600 Sarno Rd., Ste. 205
Melbourne, FL 32935
(407)254-2288
Fax: (407)254-2288

SCORE Office (Space Coast)
Melbourn Professional Complex
1600 Sarno, Ste. 205
Melbourne, FL 32935
(407)254-2288
Fax: (407)254-2288

SCORE Office (Dade)
49 NW 5th St.
Miami, FL 33128
(305)371-6889
Fax: (305)374-1882
E-mail: score@netrox.net
Website: http://www.netrox.net/~score

SCORE Office (Naples of Collier)
International College
2654 Tamiami Trl. E
Naples, FL 34112
(941)417-1280
Fax: (941)417-1281
E-mail: score@naples.net
Website: http://www.naples.net/clubs/score/index.htm

SCORE Office (Pasco County)
6014 US Hwy. 19, Ste. 302
New Port Richey, FL 34652
(813)842-4638

SCORE Office (Southeast Volusia)
115 Canal St.
New Smyrna Beach, FL 32168
(904)428-2449
Fax: (904)423-3512

SCORE Office (Ocala)
110 E Silver Springs Blvd.
Ocala, FL 34470
(352)629-5959

Clay County SCORE Office
Clay County Chamber of Commerce
1734 Kingsdey Ave.
PO Box 1441
Orange Park, FL 32073
(904)264-2651
Fax: (904)269-0363

SCORE Office (Orlando)
80 N. Hughey Ave.
Rm. 445 Federal Bldg.
Orlando, FL 32801
(407)648-6476
Fax: (407)648-6425

SCORE Office (Emerald Coast)
19 W Garden St., No. 325
Pensacola, FL 32501
(904)444-2060
Fax: (904)444-2070

SCORE Office (Charlotte County)
201 W Marion Ave., Ste. 211
Punta Gorda, FL 33950
(941)575-1818
E-mail: score@gls3c.com
Website: http://www.charlotte-florida.com/business/scorepg01.htm

SCORE Office (Saint Augustine)
1 Riberia St.
Saint Augustine, FL 32084
(904)829-5681
Fax: (904)829-6477

SCORE Office (Bradenton)
2801 Fruitville, Ste. 280
Sarasota, FL 34237
(813)955-1029

SCORE Office (Manasota)
2801 Fruitville Rd., Ste. 280
Sarasota, FL 34237
(941)955-1029
Fax: (941)955-5581
E-mail: score116@gte.net
Website: http://www.score-suncoast.org

SCORE Office (Tallahassee)
200 W Park Ave.
Tallahassee, FL 32302
(850)487-2665

SCORE Office (Hillsborough)
4732 Dale Mabry Hwy. N, Ste. 400
Tampa, FL 33614-6509
(813)870-0125

SCORE Office (Lake Sumter)
122 E Main St.
Tavares, FL 32778-3810
(352)365-3556

SCORE Office (Titusville)
2000 S Washington Ave.
Titusville, FL 32780
(407)267-3036
Fax: (407)264-0127

SCORE Office (Venice)
257 N. Tamiami Trl.
Venice, FL 34285
(941)488-2236
Fax: (941)484-5903

SCORE Office (Palm Beach)
500 Australian Ave. S, Ste. 100
West Palm Beach, FL 33401
(561)833-1672
Fax: (561)833-1712

SCORE Office (Wildwood)
103 N. Webster St.
Wildwood, FL 34785

Georgia

SCORE Office (Atlanta)
Harris Tower, Suite 1900
233 Peachtree Rd., NE
Atlanta, GA 30309
(404)347-2442
Fax: (404)347-1227

SCORE Office (Augusta)
3126 Oxford Rd.
Augusta, GA 30909
(706)869-9100

SCORE Office (Columbus)
School Bldg.
PO Box 40
Columbus, GA 31901
(706)327-3654

SCORE Office (Dalton-Whitfield)
305 S Thorton Ave.
Dalton, GA 30720
(706)279-3383

SCORE Office (Gainesville)
PO Box 374
Gainesville, GA 30503
(770)532-6206
Fax: (770)535-8419

SCORE Office (Macon)
711 Grand Bldg.
Macon, GA 31201
(912)751-6160

SCORE Office (Brunswick)
4 Glen Ave.
Saint Simons Island, GA 31520
(912)265-0620
Fax: (912)265-0629

SCORE Office (Savannah)
111 E Liberty St., Ste. 103
Savannah, GA 31401
(912)652-4335
Fax: (912)652-4184
E-mail: info@scoresav.org
Website: http://www.coastalempire.com/score/index.htm

Guam

SCORE Office (Guam)
Pacific News Bldg., Rm. 103
238 Archbishop Flores St.
Agana, GU 96910-5100
(671)472-7308

Hawaii

SCORE Office (Hawaii, Inc.)
1111 Bishop St., Ste. 204
PO Box 50207
Honolulu, HI 96813
(808)522-8132
Fax: (808)522-8135
E-mail: hnlscore@juno.com

SCORE Office (Kahului)
250 Alamaha, Unit N16A
Kahului, HI 96732
(808)871-7711

SCORE Office (Maui, Inc.)
590 E Lipoa Pkwy., Ste. 227
Kihei, HI 96753
(808)875-2380

Idaho

SCORE Office (Treasure Valley)
1020 Main St., No. 290
Boise, ID 83702
(208)334-1696
Fax: (208)334-9353

SCORE Office (Eastern Idaho)
2300 N. Yellowstone, Ste. 119
Idaho Falls, ID 83401
(208)523-1022
Fax: (208)528-7127

Illinois

SCORE Office (Fox Valley)
40 W Downer Pl.
PO Box 277
Aurora, IL 60506
(630)897-9214
Fax: (630)897-7002

SCORE Office (Greater Belvidere)
419 S State St.
Belvidere, IL 61008
(815)544-4357
Fax: (815)547-7654

SCORE Office (Bensenville)
1050 Busse Hwy. Suite 100
Bensenville, IL 60106
(708)350-2944
Fax: (708)350-2979

SCORE Office (Central Illinois)
402 N. Hershey Rd.
Bloomington, IL 61704
(309)644-0549
Fax: (309)663-8270
E-mail: webmaster@central-illinois-score.org
Website: http://www.central-illinois-score.org

SCORE Office (Southern Illinois)
150 E Pleasant Hill Rd.
Box 1
Carbondale, IL 62901
(618)453-6654
Fax: (618)453-5040

SCORE Chicago
500 W Madison St., Ste. 1150
Chicago, IL 60661
(312)353-7724
Fax: (312)886-4879
E-mail: info@scorechicago.org
Website: http://scorechicago.org

SCORE Office (Danville)
28 W N. Street
Danville, IL 61832
(217)442-7232
Fax: (217)442-6228

SCORE Office (Decatur)
Milliken University
1184 W Main St.
Decatur, IL 62522
(217)424-6297
Fax: (217)424-3993
E-mail: charding@mail.millikin.edu
Website: http://www.millikin.edu/academics/Tabor/score.html

SCORE Office (Downers Grove)
925 Curtis
Downers Grove, IL 60515
(708)968-4050
Fax: (708)968-8368

SCORE Office (Elgin)
24 E Chicago, 3rd Fl.
PO Box 648
Elgin, IL 60120
(847)741-5660
Fax: (847)741-5677

SCORE Office (Freeport Area)
26 S Galena Ave.
Freeport, IL 61032
(815)233-1350
Fax: (815)235-4038

SCORE Office (Galesburg)
292 E Simmons St.
PO Box 749

Galesburg, IL 61401
(309)343-1194
Fax: (309)343-1195

SCORE Office (Glen Ellyn)
500 Pennsylvania
Glen Ellyn, IL 60137
(708)469-0907
Fax: (708)469-0426

SCORE Office (Greater Alton)
Alden Hall
5800 Godfrey Rd.
Godfrey, IL 62035-2466
(618)467-2280
Fax: (618)466-8289
Website: http://www.altonweb.com/score

SCORE Office (Grayslake)
19351 W Washington St.
Grayslake, IL 60030
(708)223-3633
Fax: (708)223-9371

SCORE Office (Harrisburg)
303 S Commercial
Harrisburg, IL 62946-1528
(618)252-8528
Fax: (618)252-0210

SCORE Office (Joliet)
100 N. Chicago
Joliet, IL 60432
(815)727-5371
Fax: (815)727-5374

SCORE Office (Kankakee)
101 S Schuyler Ave.
Kankakee, IL 60901
(815)933-0376
Fax: (815)933-0380

SCORE Office (Macomb)
216 Seal Hall, Rm. 214
Macomb, IL 61455
(309)298-1128
Fax: (309)298-2520

SCORE Office (Matteson)
210 Lincoln Mall
Matteson, IL 60443
(708)709-3750
Fax: (708)503-9322

SCORE Office (Mattoon)
1701 Wabash Ave.
Mattoon, IL 61938
(217)235-5661
Fax: (217)234-6544

SCORE Office (Quad Cities)
622 19th St.
Moline, IL 61265
(309)797-0082
Fax: (309)757-5435
E-mail: score@qconline.com
Website: http://www.qconline.com/business/score

SCORE Office (Naperville)
131 W Jefferson Ave.
Naperville, IL 60540
(708)355-4141
Fax: (708)355-8355

SCORE Office (Northbrook)
2002 Walters Ave.
Northbrook, IL 60062
(847)498-5555
Fax: (847)498-5510

SCORE Office (Palos Hills)
10900 S 88th Ave.
Palos Hills, IL 60465
(847)974-5468
Fax: (847)974-0078

SCORE Office (Peoria)
124 SW Adams, Ste. 300
Peoria, IL 61602
(309)676-0755
Fax: (309)676-7534

SCORE Office (Prospect Heights)
1375 Wolf Rd.
Prospect Heights, IL 60070
(847)537-8660
Fax: (847)537-7138

SCORE Office (Quincy Tri-State)
300 Civic Center Plz., Ste. 245
Quincy, IL 62301
(217)222-8093
Fax: (217)222-3033

SCORE Office (River Grove)
2000 5th Ave.
River Grove, IL 60171
(708)456-0300
Fax: (708)583-3121

SCORE Office (Northern Illinois)
515 N. Court St.
Rockford, IL 61103
(815)962-0122
Fax: (815)962-0122

SCORE Office (Saint Charles)
103 N. 1st Ave.
Saint Charles, IL 60174-1982
(847)584-8384
Fax: (847)584-6065

SCORE Office (Springfield)
511 W Capitol Ave., Ste. 302
Springfield, IL 62704
(217)492-4416
Fax: (217)492-4867

SCORE Office (Sycamore)
112 Somunak St.
Sycamore, IL 60178
(815)895-3456
Fax: (815)895-0125

SCORE Office (University)
Hwy. 50 & Stuenkel Rd. Ste. C3305
University Park, IL 60466
(708)534-5000
Fax: (708)534-8457

Indiana

SCORE Office (Anderson)
205 W 11th St.
Anderson, IN 46015
(317)642-0264

SCORE Office (Bloomington)
Star Center
216 W Allen
Bloomington, IN 47403
(812)335-7334
E-mail: wtfische@indiana.edu
Website: http://www.brainfreezemedia.com/score527

SCORE Office (South East Indiana)
500 Franklin St.
Box 29
Columbus, IN 47201
(812)379-4457

SCORE Office (Corydon)
310 N. Elm St.
Corydon, IN 47112
(812)738-2137
Fax: (812)738-6438

SCORE Office (Crown Point)
Old Courthouse Sq. Ste. 206
PO Box 43
Crown Point, IN 46307
(219)663-1800

SCORE Office (Elkhart)
418 S Main St.
Elkhart, IN 46515
(219)293-1531
Fax: (219)294-1859

SCORE Office (Evansville)
1100 W Lloyd Expy., Ste. 105
Evansville, IN 47708
(812)426-6144

SCORE Office (Fort Wayne)
1300 S Harrison St.
Fort Wayne, IN 46802

(219)422-2601
Fax: (219)422-2601

SCORE Office (Gary)
973 W 6th Ave., Rm. 326
Gary, IN 46402
(219)882-3918

SCORE Office (Hammond)
7034 Indianapolis Blvd.
Hammond, IN 46324
(219)931-1000
Fax: (219)845-9548

SCORE Office (Indianapolis)
429 N. Pennsylvania St., Ste. 100
Indianapolis, IN 46204-1873
(317)226-7264
Fax: (317)226-7259
E-mail: inscore@indy.net
Website: http://www.score-indianapolis.org

SCORE Office (Jasper)
PO Box 307
Jasper, IN 47547-0307
(812)482-6866

SCORE Office (Kokomo/Howard Counties)
106 N. Washington St.
Kokomo, IN 46901
(765)457-5301
Fax: (765)452-4564

SCORE Office (Logansport)
300 E Broadway, Ste. 103
Logansport, IN 46947
(219)753-6388

SCORE Office (Madison)
301 E Main St.
Madison, IN 47250
(812)265-3135
Fax: (812)265-2923

SCORE Office (Marengo)
Rt. 1 Box 224D
Marengo, IN 47140
Fax: (812)365-2793

SCORE Office (Marion/Grant Counties)
215 S Adams
Marion, IN 46952
(765)664-5107

SCORE Office (Merrillville)
255 W 80th Pl.
Merrillville, IN 46410
(219)769-8180
Fax: (219)736-6223

SCORE Office (Michigan City)
200 E Michigan Blvd.
Michigan City, IN 46360
(219)874-6221
Fax: (219)873-1204

SCORE Office (South Central Indiana)
4100 Charleston Rd.
New Albany, IN 47150-9538
(812)945-0066

SCORE Office (Rensselaer)
104 W Washington
Rensselaer, IN 47978

SCORE Office (Salem)
210 N. Main St.
Salem, IN 47167
(812)883-4303
Fax: (812)883-1467

SCORE Office (South Bend)
300 N. Michigan St.
South Bend, IN 46601
(219)282-4350
E-mail: chair@southbend-score.org
Website: http://www.southbend-score.org

SCORE Office (Valparaiso)
150 Lincolnway
Valparaiso, IN 46383
(219)462-1105
Fax: (219)469-5710

SCORE Office (Vincennes)
27 N. 3rd
PO Box 553
Vincennes, IN 47591
(812)882-6440
Fax: (812)882-6441

SCORE Office (Wabash)
PO Box 371
Wabash, IN 46992
(219)563-1168
Fax: (219)563-6920

Iowa

SCORE Office (Burlington)
Federal Bldg.
300 N. Main St.
Burlington, IA 52601
(319)752-2967

SCORE Office (Cedar Rapids)
2750 1st Ave. NE, Ste 350
Cedar Rapids, IA 52401-1806
(319)362-6405
Fax: (319)362-7861
E:mail: score@scorecr.org
Website: http://www.scorecr.org

SCORE Office (Illowa)
333 4th Ave. S
Clinton, IA 52732
(319)242-5702

SCORE Office (Council Bluffs)
7 N. 6th St.
Council Bluffs, IA 51502
(712)325-1000

SCORE Office (Northeast Iowa)
3404 285th St.
Cresco, IA 52136
(319)547-3377

SCORE Office (Des Moines)
Federal Bldg., Rm. 749
210 Walnut St.
Des Moines, IA 50309-2186
(515)284-4760

SCORE Office (Fort Dodge)
Federal Bldg., Rm. 436
205 S 8th St.
Fort Dodge, IA 50501
(515)955-2622

SCORE Office (Independence)
110 1st. St. E
Independence, IA 50644
(319)334-7178
Fax: (319)334-7179

SCORE Office (Iowa City)
210 Federal Bldg.
PO Box 1853
Iowa City, IA 52240-1853
(319)338-1662

SCORE Office (Keokuk)
401 Main St.
Pierce Bldg., No. 1
Keokuk, IA 52632
(319)524-5055

SCORE Office (Central Iowa)
Fisher Community College
709 S Center
Marshalltown, IA 50158
(515)753-6645

SCORE Office (River City)
15 West State St.
Mason City, IA 50401
(515)423-5724

SCORE Office (South Central)
SBDC, Indian Hills Community College
525 Grandview Ave.
Ottumwa, IA 52501
(515)683-5127
Fax: (515)683-5263

SCORE Office (Dubuque)
10250 Sundown Rd.
Peosta, IA 52068
(319)556-5110

SCORE Office (Southwest Iowa)
614 W Sheridan
Shenandoah, IA 51601
(712)246-3260

SCORE Office (Sioux City)
Federal Bldg.
320 6th St.
Sioux City, IA 51101
(712)277-2324
Fax: (712)277-2325

SCORE Office (Iowa Lakes)
122 W 5th St.
Spencer, IA 51301
(712)262-3059

SCORE Office (Vista)
119 W 6th St.
Storm Lake, IA 50588
(712)732-3780

SCORE Office (Waterloo)
215 E 4th
Waterloo, IA 50703
(319)233-8431

Kansas

SCORE Office (Southwest Kansas)
501 W Spruce
Dodge City, KS 67801
(316)227-3119

SCORE Office (Emporia)
811 Homewood
Emporia, KS 66801
(316)342-1600

SCORE Office (Golden Belt)
1307 Williams
Great Bend, KS 67530
(316)792-2401

SCORE Office (Hays)
PO Box 400
Hays, KS 67601
(913)625-6595

SCORE Office (Hutchinson)
1 E 9th St.
Hutchinson, KS 67501
(316)665-8468
Fax: (316)665-7619

SCORE Office (Southeast Kansas)
404 Westminster Pl.
PO Box 886
Independence, KS 67301
(316)331-4741

SCORE Office (McPherson)
306 N. Main
PO Box 616
McPherson, KS 67460
(316)241-3303

SCORE Office (Salina)
120 Ash St.
Salina, KS 67401
(785)243-4290
Fax: (785)243-1833

SCORE Office (Topeka)
1700 College
Topeka, KS 66621
(785)231-1010

SCORE Office (Wichita)
100 E English, Ste. 510
Wichita, KS 67202
(316)269-6273
Fax: (316)269-6499

SCORE Office (Ark Valley)
205 E 9th St.
Winfield, KS 67156
(316)221-1617

Kentucky

SCORE Office (Ashland)
PO Box 830
Ashland, KY 41105
(606)329-8011
Fax: (606)325-4607

SCORE Office (Bowling Green)
812 State St.
PO Box 51
Bowling Green, KY 42101
(502)781-3200
Fax: (502)843-0458

SCORE Office (Tri-Lakes)
508 Barbee Way
Danville, KY 40422-1548
(606)231-9902

SCORE Office (Glasgow)
301 W Main St.
Glasgow, KY 42141
(502)651-3161
Fax: (502)651-3122

SCORE Office (Hazard)
B & I Technical Center
100 Airport Gardens Rd.
Hazard, KY 41701
(606)439-5856
Fax: (606)439-1808

SCORE Office (Lexington)
410 W Vine St., Ste. 290, Civic C
Lexington, KY 40507
(606)231-9902
Fax: (606)253-3190
E-mail: scorelex@uky.campus.mci.net

SCORE Office (Louisville)
188 Federal Office Bldg.
600 Dr. Martin L. King Jr. Pl.
Louisville, KY 40202
(502)582-5976

SCORE Office (Madisonville)
257 N. Main
Madisonville, KY 42431
(502)825-1399
Fax: (502)825-1396

SCORE Office (Paducah)
Federal Office Bldg.
501 Broadway, Rm. B-36
Paducah, KY 42001
(502)442-5685

Louisiana

SCORE Office (Central Louisiana)
802 3rd St.
Alexandria, LA 71309
(318)442-6671

SCORE Office (Baton Rouge)
564 Laurel St.
PO Box 3217
Baton Rouge, LA 70801
(504)381-7130
Fax: (504)336-4306

SCORE Office (North Shore)
2 W Thomas
Hammond, LA 70401
(504)345-4457
Fax: (504)345-4749

SCORE Office (Lafayette)
804 St. Mary Blvd.
Lafayette, LA 70505-1307
(318)233-2705
Fax: (318)234-8671
E-mail: score302@aol.com

SCORE Office (Lake Charles)
120 W Pujo St.
Lake Charles, LA 70601
(318)433-3632

SCORE Office (New Orleans)
365 Canal St., Ste. 3100
New Orleans, LA 70130
(504)589-2356
Fax: (504)589-2339

SCORE Office (Shreveport)
400 Edwards St.
Shreveport, LA 71101
(318)677-2536
Fax: (318)677-2541

Maine

SCORE Office (Augusta)
40 Western Ave.
Augusta, ME 04330
(207)622-8509

SCORE Office (Bangor)
Peabody Hall, Rm. 229
One College Cir.
Bangor, ME 04401
(207)941-9707

SCORE Office (Central & Northern Arroostock)
111 High St.
Caribou, ME 04736
(207)492-8010
Fax: (207)492-8010

SCORE Office (Penquis)
South St.
Dover Foxcroft, ME 04426
(207)564-7021

SCORE Office (Maine Coastal)
Mill Mall
Box 1105
Ellsworth, ME 04605-1105
(207)667-5800
E-mail: score@arcadia.net

SCORE Office (Lewiston-Auburn)
BIC of Maine-Bates Mill Complex
35 Canal St.
Lewiston, ME 04240-7764
(207)782-3708
Fax: (207)783-7745

SCORE Office (Portland)
66 Pearl St., Rm. 210
Portland, ME 04101
(207)772-1147
Fax: (207)772-5581
E-mail: Score53@score.maine.org
Website: http://www.score.maine.org/chapter53

SCORE Office (Western Mountains)
255 River St.
PO Box 252
Rumford, ME 04257-0252
(207)369-9976

SCORE Office (Oxford Hills)
166 Main St.
South Paris, ME 04281
(207)743-0499

Maryland

SCORE Office (Southern Maryland)
2525 Riva Rd., Ste. 110
Annapolis, MD 21401
(410)266-9553
Fax: (410)573-0981
E-mail: score390@aol.com
Website: http://members.aol.com/score390/index.htm

SCORE Office (Baltimore)
The City Crescent Bldg., 6th Fl.
10 S Howard St.
Baltimore, MD 21201
(410)962-2233
Fax: (410)962-1805

SCORE Office (Bel Air)
108 S Bond St.
Bel Air, MD 21014
(410)838-2020
Fax: (410)893-4715

SCORE Office (Bethesda)
7910 Woodmont Ave., Ste. 1204
Bethesda, MD 20814
(301)652-4900
Fax: (301)657-1973

SCORE Office (Bowie)
6670 Race Track Rd.
Bowie, MD 20715
(301)262-0920
Fax: (301)262-0921

SCORE Office (Dorchester County)
203 Sunburst Hwy.
Cambridge, MD 21613
(410)228-3575

SCORE Office (Upper Shore)
210 Marlboro Ave.
Easton, MD 21601
(410)822-4606
Fax: (410)822-7922

SCORE Office (Frederick County)
43A S Market St.
Frederick, MD 21701
(301)662-8723
Fax: (301)846-4427

SCORE Office (Gaithersburg)
9 Park Ave.
Gaithersburg, MD 20877
(301)840-1400
Fax: (301)963-3918

SCORE Office (Glen Burnie)
103 Crain Hwy. SE
Glen Burnie, MD 21061
(410)766-8282
Fax: (410)766-9722

SCORE Office (Hagerstown)
111 W Washington St.
Hagerstown, MD 21740
(301)739-2015
Fax: (301)739-1278

SCORE Office (Laurel)
7901 Sandy Spring Rd. Ste. 501
Laurel, MD 20707
(301)725-4000
Fax: (301)725-0776

SCORE Office (Salisbury)
300 E Main St.
Salisbury, MD 21801
(410)749-0185
Fax: (410)860-9925

Massachusetts

SCORE Office (NE Massachusetts)
100 Cummings Ctr., Ste. 101 K
Beverly, MA 01923
(978)922-9441
Website: http://www1.shore.net/~score

SCORE Office (Boston)
10 Causeway St., Rm. 265
Boston, MA 02222-1093
(617)565-5591
Fax: (617)565-5598
E-mail: boston-score-20@worldnet.att.net
Website: http://www.scoreboston.org

SCORE office (Bristol/Plymouth County)
53 N. 6th St., Federal Bldg.
Bristol, MA 02740
(508)994-5093

SCORE Office (SE Massachusetts)
60 School St.
Brockton, MA 02401
(508)587-2673
Fax: (508)587-1340
Website: http://www.metrosouthchamber.com/score.html

SCORE Office (North Adams)
820 N. State Rd.
Cheshire, MA 01225
(413)743-5100

SCORE Office (Clinton Satellite)
1 Green St.
Clinton, MA 01510
Fax: (508)368-7689

SCORE Office (Greenfield)
PO Box 898
Greenfield, MA 01302
(413)773-5463
Fax: (413)773-7008

SCORE Office (Haverhill)
87 Winter St.
Haverhill, MA 01830
(508)373-5663
Fax: (508)373-8060

SCORE Office (Hudson Satellite)
PO Box 578
Hudson, MA 01749
(508)568-0360
Fax: (508)568-0360

SCORE Office (Cape Cod)
Independence Pk., Ste. 5B
270 Communications Way
Hyannis, MA 02601
(508)775-4884
Fax: (508)790-2540

SCORE Office (Lawrence)
264 Essex St.
Lawrence, MA 01840
(508)686-0900
Fax: (508)794-9953

SCORE Office (Leominster Satellite)
110 Erdman Way
Leominster, MA 01453
(508)840-4300
Fax: (508)840-4896

SCORE Office (Bristol/Plymouth Counties)
53 N. 6th St., Federal Bldg.
New Bedford, MA 02740
(508)994-5093

SCORE Office (Newburyport)
29 State St.
Newburyport, MA 01950
(617)462-6680

SCORE Office (Pittsfield)
66 West St.
Pittsfield, MA 01201
(413)499-2485

SCORE Office (Haverhill-Salem)
32 Derby Sq.
Salem, MA 01970
(508)745-0330
Fax: (508)745-3855

SCORE Office (Springfield)
1350 Main St.
Federal Bldg.
Springfield, MA 01103
(413)785-0314

SCORE Office (Carver)
12 Taunton Green, Ste. 201
Taunton, MA 02780
(508)824-4068
Fax: (508)824-4069

SCORE Office (Worcester)
33 Waldo St.
Worcester, MA 01608
(508)753-2929
Fax: (508)754-8560

Michigan

SCORE Office (Allegan)
PO Box 338
Allegan, MI 49010
(616)673-2479

SCORE Office (Ann Arbor)
425 S Main St., Ste. 103
Ann Arbor, MI 48104
(313)665-4433

SCORE Office (Battle Creek)
34 W Jackson Ste. 4A
Battle Creek, MI 49017-3505
(616)962-4076
Fax: (616)962-6309

SCORE Office (Cadillac)
222 Lake St.
Cadillac, MI 49601
(616)775-9776
Fax: (616)768-4255

SCORE Office (Detroit)
477 Michigan Ave., Rm. 515
Detroit, MI 48226
(313)226-7947
Fax: (313)226-3448

SCORE Office (Flint)
708 Root Rd., Rm. 308
Flint, MI 48503
(810)233-6846

SCORE Office (Grand Rapids)
111 Pearl St. NW
Grand Rapids, MI 49503-2831
(616)771-0305
Fax: (616)771-0328
E-mail: scoreone@iserv.net
Website: http://www.iserv.net/~scoreone

SCORE Office (Holland)
480 State St.
Holland, MI 49423
(616)396-9472

SCORE Office (Jackson)
209 East Washington
PO Box 80
Jackson, MI 49204
(517)782-8221
Fax: (517)782-0061

SCORE Office (Kalamazoo)
345 W Michigan Ave.
Kalamazoo, MI 49007
(616)381-5382
Fax: (616)384-0096
E-mail: score@nucleus.net

SCORE Office (Lansing)
117 E Allegan
PO Box 14030
Lansing, MI 48901
(517)487-6340
Fax: (517)484-6910

SCORE Office (Livonia)
15401 Farmington Rd.
Livonia, MI 48154
(313)427-2122
Fax: (313)427-6055

SCORE Office (Madison Heights)
26345 John R
Madison Heights, MI 48071
(810)542-5010
Fax: (810)542-6821

SCORE Office (Monroe)
111 E 1st
Monroe, MI 48161
(313)242-3366
Fax: (313)242-7253

SCORE Office (Mount Clemens)
58 S/B Gratiot
Mount Clemens, MI 48043
(810)463-1528
Fax: (810)463-6541

SCORE Office (Muskegon)
PO Box 1087
230 Terrace Plz.
Muskegon, MI 49443
(616)722-3751
Fax: (616)728-7251

SCORE Office (Petoskey)
401 E Mitchell St.
Petoskey, MI 49770
(616)347-4150

SCORE Office (Pontiac)
Executive Office Bldg.
1200 N. Telegraph Rd.
Pontiac, MI 48341
(810)975-9555

SCORE Office (Pontiac)
PO Box 430025
Pontiac, MI 48343
(810)335-9600

SCORE Office (Port Huron)
920 Pinegrove Ave.
Port Huron, MI 48060
(810)985-7101

SCORE Office (Rochester)
71 Walnut Ste. 110
Rochester, MI 48307
(810)651-6700
Fax: (810)651-5270

SCORE Office (Saginaw)
901 S Washington Ave.
Saginaw, MI 48601
(517)752-7161
Fax: (517)752-9055

SCORE Office (Upper Peninsula)
2581 I-75 Business Spur
Sault Ste. Marie, MI 49783
(906)632-3301

SCORE Office (Southfield)
21000 W 10 Mile Rd.
Southfield, MI 48075
(810)204-3050
Fax: (810)204-3099

SCORE Office (Traverse City)
202 E Grandview Pkwy.
PO Box 387
Traverse City, MI 49685
(616)947-5075
Fax: (616)946-2565

SCORE Office (Warren)
30500 Van Dyke, Ste. 118
Warren, MI 48093
(810)751-3939

Minnesota

SCORE Office (Aitkin)
Aitkin, MN 56431
(218)741-3906

SCORE Office (Albert Lea)
202 N. Broadway Ave.
Albert Lea, MN 56007
(507)373-7487

SCORE Office (Austin)
PO Box 864
Austin, MN 55912
(507)437-4561
Fax: (507)437-4869

SCORE Office (South Metro)
Ames Business Ctr.
2500 W County Rd., No. 42
Burnsville, MN 55337
(612)898-5645
Fax: (612)435-6972
E-mail: southmetro@scoreminn.org
Website: http://www.scoreminn.org/southmetro

SCORE Office (Duluth)
1717 Minnesota Ave.
Duluth, MN 55802
(218)727-8286
Fax: (218)727-3113
E-mail: duluth@scoreminn.org
Website: http://www.scoreminn.org

SCORE Office (Fairmont)
PO Box 826
Fairmont, MN 56031
(507)235-5547
Fax: (507)235-8411

SCORE Office (Southwest Minnesota)
112 Riverfront St.
Box 999
Mankato, MN 56001
(507)345-4519
Fax: (507)345-4451
Website: http://www.scoreminn.org

SCORE Office (Minneapolis)
North Plaza Bldg., Ste. 51
5217 Wayzata Blvd.
Minneapolis, MN 55416
(612)591-0539
Fax: (612)544-0436
Website: http://www.scoreminn.org

SCORE Office (Owatonna)
PO Box 331
Owatonna, MN 55060
(507)451-7970
Fax: (507)451-7972

SCORE Office (Red Wing)
2000 W Main St., Ste. 324
Red Wing, MN 55066
(612)388-4079

SCORE Office (Southeastern Minnesota)
220 S Broadway, Ste. 100
Rochester, MN 55901
(507)288-1122
Fax: (507)282-8960
Website: http://www.scoreminn.org

SCORE Office (Brainerd)
Saint Cloud, MN 56301

SCORE Office (Central Area)
1527 Northway Dr.
Saint Cloud, MN 56301
(320)240-1332
Fax: (320)255-9050
Website: http://www.scoreminn.org

SCORE Office (Saint Paul)
350 St. Peter St., No. 295
Lowry Professional Bldg.
Saint Paul, MN 55102
(651)223-5010
Fax: (651)223-5048
Website: http://www.scoreminn.org

SCORE Office (Winona)
Box 870
Winona, MN 55987
(507)452-2272
Fax: (507)454-8814

SCORE Office (Worthington)
1121 3rd Ave.
Worthington, MN 56187
(507)372-2919
Fax: (507)372-2827

Mississippi

SCORE Office (Delta)
915 Washington Ave.
PO Box 933
Greenville, MS 38701
(601)378-3141

SCORE Office (Gulfcoast)
1 Government Plaza
2909 13th St., Ste. 203
Gulfport, MS 39501
(228)863-0054

SCORE Office (Jackson)
1st Jackson Center, Ste. 400
101 W Capitol St.
Jackson, MS 39201
(601)965-5533

SCORE Office (Meridian)
5220 16th Ave.
Meridian, MS 39305
(601)482-4412

Missouri

SCORE Office (Lake of the Ozark)
University Extension
113 Kansas St.
PO Box 1405
Camdenton, MO 65020
(573)346-2644
Fax: (573)346-2694
E-mail: score@cdoc.net
Website: http://sites.cdoc.net/score

Chamber of Commerce (Cape Girardeau)
PO Box 98
Cape Girardeau, MO 63702-0098
(314)335-3312

SCORE Office (Mid-Missouri)
1705 Halstead Ct.
Columbia, MO 65203
(573)874-1132

SCORE Office (Ozark-Gateway)
1486 Glassy Rd.
Cuba, MO 65453-1640
(573)885-4954

SCORE Office (Kansas City)
323 W 8th St., Ste. 104
Kansas City, MO 64105
(816)374-6675
Fax: (816)374-6692
E-mail: SCOREBIC@AOL.COM
Website: http://www.crn.org/score

SCORE Office (Sedalia)
Lucas Place
323 W 8th St., Ste.104
Kansas City, MO 64105
(816)374-6675

SCORE office (Tri-Lakes)
PO Box 1148
Kimberling, MO 65686
(417)739-3041

SCORE Office (Tri-Lakes)
HCRI Box 85
Lampe, MO 65681
(417)858-6798

SCORE Office (Mexico)
111 N. Washington St.
Mexico, MO 65265
(314)581-2765

SCORE Office (Southeast Missouri)
Rte. 1, Box 280
Neelyville, MO 63954
(573)989-3577

SCORE office (Poplar Bluff Area)
806 Emma St.
Poplar Bluff, MO 63901
(573)686-8892

SCORE Office (Saint Joseph)
3003 Frederick Ave.
Saint Joseph, MO 64506
(816)232-4461

SCORE Office (Saint Louis)
815 Olive St., Rm. 242
Saint Louis, MO 63101-1569
(314)539-6970
Fax: (314)539-3785
E-mail: info@stlscore.org
Website: http://www.stlscore.org

SCORE Office (Lewis & Clark)
425 Spencer Rd.
Saint Peters, MO 63376
(314)928-2900
Fax: (314)928-2900
E-mail: score01@mail.win.org

SCORE Office (Springfield)
620 S Glenstone, Ste. 110
Springfield, MO 65802-3200
(417)864-7670
Fax: (417)864-4108

SCORE office (Southeast Kansas)
1206 W First St.
Webb City, MO 64870
(417)673-3984

Montana

SCORE Office (Billings)
815 S 27th St.
Billings, MT 59101
(406)245-4111

SCORE Office (Bozeman)
1205 E Main St.
Bozeman, MT 59715
(406)586-5421

SCORE Office (Butte)
1000 George St.
Butte, MT 59701
(406)723-3177

SCORE Office (Great Falls)
710 First Ave. N
Great Falls, MT 59401
(406)761-4434
E-mail: scoregtf@in.tch.com

SCORE Office (Havre, Montana)
518 First St.
Havre, MT 59501
(406)265-4383

SCORE Office (Helena)
Federal Bldg.
301 S Park
Helena, MT 59626-0054
(406)441-1081

SCORE Office (Kalispell)
2 Main St.
Kalispell, MT 59901
(406)756-5271
Fax: (406)752-6665

SCORE Office (Missoula)
723 Ronan
Missoula, MT 59806
(406)327-8806
E-mail: score@safeshop.com
Website: http://missoula.bigsky.net/score

Nebraska

SCORE Office (Columbus)
Columbus, NE 68601
(402)564-2769

SCORE Office (Fremont)
92 W 5th St.
Fremont, NE 68025
(402)721-2641

SCORE Office (Hastings)
Hastings, NE 68901
(402)463-3447

SCORE Office (Lincoln)
8800 O St.
Lincoln, NE 68520
(402)437-2409

SCORE Office (Panhandle)
150549 CR 30
Minatare, NE 69356
(308)632-2133
Website: http://www.tandt.com/SCORE

SCORE Office (Norfolk)
3209 S 48th Ave.
Norfolk, NE 68106
(402)564-2769

SCORE Office (North Platte)
3301 W 2nd St.
North Platte, NE 69101
(308)532-4466

SCORE Office (Omaha)
11145 Mill Valley Rd.
Omaha, NE 68154
(402)221-3606
Fax: (402)221-3680
E-mail: infoctr@ne.uswest.net
Website: http://www.tandt.com/score

Nevada

SCORE Office (Incline Village)
969 Tahoe Blvd.
Incline Village, NV 89451
(702)831-7327
Fax: (702)832-1605

SCORE Office (Carson City)
301 E Stewart
PO Box 7527
Las Vegas, NV 89125
(702)388-6104

SCORE Office (Las Vegas)
300 Las Vegas Blvd. S, Ste. 1100
Las Vegas, NV 89101
(702)388-6104

SCORE Office (Northern Nevada)
SBDC, College of Business Administration
Univ. of Nevada
Reno, NV 89557-0100
(702)784-4436
Fax: (702)784-4337

New Hampshire

SCORE Office (North Country)
PO Box 34
Berlin, NH 03570
(603)752-1090

SCORE Office (Concord)
143 N. Main St., Rm. 202A
PO Box 1258
Concord, NH 03301
(603)225-1400
Fax: (603)225-1409

SCORE Office (Dover)
299 Central Ave.
Dover, NH 03820
(603)742-2218
Fax: (603)749-6317

SCORE Office (Monadnock)
34 Mechanic St.
Keene, NH 03431-3421
(603)352-0320

SCORE Office (Lakes Region)
67 Water St., Ste. 105
Laconia, NH 03246
(603)524-9168

SCORE Office (Upper Valley)
Citizens Bank Bldg., Rm. 310
20 W Park St.
Lebanon, NH 03766
(603)448-3491
Fax: (603)448-1908
E-mail: billt@valley.net
Website: http://www.valley.net/~score

SCORE Office (Merrimack Valley)
275 Chestnut St., Rm. 618
Manchester, NH 03103
(603)666-7561
Fax: (603)666-7925

SCORE Office (Mount Washington Valley)
PO Box 1066
North Conway, NH 03818
(603)383-0800

SCORE Office (Seacoast)
195 Commerce Way, Unit-A
Portsmouth, NH 03801-3251
(603)433-0575

New Jersey

SCORE Office (Somerset)
Paritan Valley Community College, Rte. 28
Branchburg, NJ 08807
(908)218-8874
E-mail: nj-score@grizbiz.com.
Website: http://www.nj-score.org

SCORE Office (Chester)
5 Old Mill Rd.
Chester, NJ 07930
(908)879-7080

SCORE Office (Greater Princeton)
4 A George Washington Dr.
Cranbury, NJ 08512
(609)520-1776

SCORE Office (Freehold)
36 W Main St.
Freehold, NJ 07728
(908)462-3030
Fax: (908)462-2123

SCORE Office (North West)
Picantinny Innovation Ctr.
3159 Schrader Rd.
Hamburg, NJ 07419
(973)209-8525
Fax: (973)209-7252
E-mail: nj-score@grizbiz.com
Website: http://www.nj-score.org

SCORE Office (Monmouth)
765 Newman Springs Rd.
Lincroft, NJ 07738
(908)224-2573
E-mail: nj-score@grizbiz.com
Website: http://www.nj-score.org

SCORE Office (Manalapan)
125 Symmes Dr.
Manalapan, NJ 07726
(908)431-7220

SCORE Office (Jersey City)
2 Gateway Ctr., 4th Fl.
Newark, NJ 07102
(973)645-3982
Fax: (973)645-2375

SCORE Office (Newark)
2 Gateway Center, 15th Fl.
Newark, NJ 07102-5553
(973)645-3982
Fax: (973)645-2375
E-mail: nj-score@grizbiz.com
Website: http://www.nj-score.org

SCORE Office (Bergen County)
327 E Ridgewood Ave.
Paramus, NJ 07652
(201)599-6090
E-mail: nj-score@grizbiz.com
Website: http://www.nj-score.org

SCORE Office (Pennsauken)
4900 Rte. 70
Pennsauken, NJ 08109
(609)486-3421

SCORE Office (Southern New Jersey)
4900 Rte. 70
Pennsauken, NJ 08109
(609)486-3421
E-mail: nj-score@grizbiz.com
Website: http://www.nj-score.org

SCORE Office (Greater Princeton)
216 Rockingham Row
Princeton Forrestal Village
Princeton, NJ 08540
(609)520-1776
Fax: (609)520-9107
E-mail: nj-score@grizbiz.com
Website: http://www.nj-score.org

SCORE Office (Shrewsbury)
Hwy. 35
Shrewsbury, NJ 07702
(908)842-5995
Fax: (908)219-6140

SCORE Office (Ocean County)
33 Washington St.
Toms River, NJ 08754
(732)505-6033
E-mail: nj-score@grizbiz.com
Website: http://www.nj-score.org

SCORE Office (Wall)
2700 Allaire Rd.
Wall, NJ 07719
(908)449-8877

SCORE Office (Wayne)
2055 Hamburg Tpke.
Wayne, NJ 07470
(201)831-7788
Fax: (201)831-9112

New Mexico

SCORE Office (Albuquerque)
525 Buena Vista, SE
Albuquerque, NM 87106
(505)272-7999
Fax: (505)272-7963

SCORE Office (Las Cruces)
Loretto Towne Center
505 S Main St., Ste. 125
Las Cruces, NM 88001
(505)523-5627
Fax: (505)524-2101
E-mail: score.397@zianet.com

SCORE Office (Roswell)
Federal Bldg., Rm. 237
Roswell, NM 88201
(505)625-2112
Fax: (505)623-2545

SCORE Office (Santa Fe)
Montoya Federal Bldg.
120 Federal Place, Rm. 307
Santa Fe, NM 87501
(505)988-6302
Fax: (505)988-6300

New York

SCORE Office (Northeast)
1 Computer Dr. S
Albany, NY 12205
(518)446-1118
Fax: (518)446-1228

SCORE Office (Auburn)
30 South St.
PO Box 675
Auburn, NY 13021
(315)252-7291

SCORE Office (South Tier Binghamton)
Metro Center, 2nd Fl.
49 Court St.
PO Box 995
Binghamton, NY 13902
(607)772-8860

SCORE Office (Queens County City)
12055 Queens Blvd., Rm. 333
Borough Hall, NY 11424
(718)263-8961

SCORE Office (Buffalo)
Federal Bldg., Rm. 1311
111 W Huron St.
Buffalo, NY 14202
(716)551-4301
Website: http://www2.pcom.net/score/buf45.html

SCORE Office (Canandaigua)
Chamber of Commerce Bldg.
113 S Main St.
Canandaigua, NY 14424
(716)394-4400
Fax: (716)394-4546

SCORE Office (Chemung)
333 E Water St., 4th Fl.
Elmira, NY 14901
(607)734-3358

SCORE Office (Geneva)
Chamber of Commerce Bldg.
PO Box 587
Geneva, NY 14456
(315)789-1776
Fax: (315)789-3993

SCORE Office (Glens Falls)
84 Broad St.
Glens Falls, NY 12801
(518)798-8463
Fax: (518)745-1433

SCORE Office (Orange County)
40 Matthews St.
Goshen, NY 10924
(914)294-8080
Fax: (914)294-6121

SCORE Office (Huntington Area)
151 W Carver St.
Huntington, NY 11743
(516)423-6100

SCORE Office (Tompkins County)
904 E Shore Dr.
Ithaca, NY 14850
(607)273-7080

SCORE Office (Long Island City)
120-55 Queens Blvd.
Jamaica, NY 11424
(718)263-8961
Fax: (718)263-9032

SCORE Office (Chatauqua)
101 W 5th St.
Jamestown, NY 14701
(716)484-1103

SCORE Office (Westchester)
2 Caradon Ln.
Katonah, NY 10536
(914)948-3907
Fax: (914)948-4645
E-mail: score@w-w-w.com
Website: http://w-w-w.com/score

SCORE Office (Queens County)
Queens Borough Hall
120-55 Queens Blvd. Rm. 333
Kew Gardens, NY 11424
(718)263-8961
Fax: (718)263-9032

SCORE Office (Brookhaven)
3233 Rte. 112
Medford, NY 11763
(516)451-6563
Fax: (516)451-6925

SCORE Office (Melville)
35 Pinelawn Rd., Rm. 207-W
Melville, NY 11747
(516)454-0771

SCORE Office (Nassau County)
400 County Seat Dr., No. 140
Mineola, NY 11501
(516)571-3303
E-mail: Counse1998@aol.com
Website: http://members.aol.com/Counse1998/Default.htm

SCORE Office (Mount Vernon)
4 N. 7th Ave.
Mount Vernon, NY 10550
(914)667-7500

SCORE Office (New York)
26 Federal Plz., Rm. 3100
New York, NY 10278
(212)264-4507
Fax: (212)264-4963
E-mail: score1000@erols.com
Website: http://users.erols.com/score-nyc

SCORE Office (Newburgh)
47 Grand St.
Newburgh, NY 12550
(914)562-5100

SCORE Office (Owego)
188 Front St.
Owego, NY 13827
(607)687-2020

SCORE Office (Peekskill)
1 S Division St.
Peekskill, NY 10566
(914)737-3600
Fax: (914)737-0541

SCORE Office (Penn Yan)
2375 Rte. 14A
Penn Yan, NY 14527
(315)536-3111

SCORE Office (Dutchess)
110 Main St.
Poughkeepsie, NY 12601
(914)454-1700

SCORE Office (Rochester)
601 Keating Federal Bldg., Rm. 410
100 State St.
Rochester, NY 14614
(716)263-6473
Fax: (716)263-3146
Website: http://www.ggw.org/score

SCORE Office (Saranac Lake)
30 Main St.
Saranac Lake, NY 12983
(315)448-0415

SCORE Office (Suffolk)
286 Main St.
Setauket, NY 11733
(516)751-3886

SCORE Office (Staten Island)
130 Bay St.
Staten Island, NY 10301
(718)727-1221

SCORE Office (Ulster)
Clinton Bldg., Rm. 107
Stone Ridge, NY 12484
(914)687-5035
Fax: (914)687-5015
Website: http://www.scoreulster.org

SCORE Office (Syracuse)
401 S Salina, 5th Fl.
Syracuse, NY 13202
(315)471-9393

SCORE Office (Utica)
SUNY Institute of Technology, Route 12
Utica, NY 13504-3050
(315)792-7553

SCORE Office (Watertown)
518 Davidson St.
Watertown, NY 13601
(315)788-1200
Fax: (315)788-8251

North Carolina

SCORE office (Asheboro)
317 E Dixie Dr.
Asheboro, NC 27203
(336)626-2626
Fax: (336)626-7077

SCORE Office (Asheville)
Federal Bldg., Rm. 259
151 Patton
Asheville, NC 28801-5770
(828)271-4786
Fax: (828)271-4009

SCORE Office (Chapel Hill)
104 S Estes Dr.
PO Box 2897
Chapel Hill, NC 27514
(919)967-7075

SCORE Office (Coastal Plains)
PO Box 2897
Chapel Hill, NC 27515
(919)967-7075
Fax: (919)968-6874

SCORE Office (Charlotte)
200 N. College St., Ste. A-2015
Charlotte, NC 28202
(704)344-6576
Fax: (704)344-6769
E-mail: CharlotteSCORE47@AOL.com
Website: http://www.charweb.org/business/score

SCORE Office (Durham)
411 W Chapel Hill St.
Durham, NC 27707
(919)541-2171

SCORE Office (Gastonia)
PO Box 2168
Gastonia, NC 28053
(704)864-2621
Fax: (704)854-8723

SCORE Office (Greensboro)
400 W Market St., Ste. 103
Greensboro, NC 27401-2241
(910)333-5399

SCORE Office (Henderson)
PO Box 917
Henderson, NC 27536
(919)492-2061
Fax: (919)430-0460

SCORE Office (Hendersonville)
Federal Bldg., Rm. 108
W 4th Ave. & Church St.
Hendersonville, NC 28792
(828)693-8702
E-mail: score@circle.net
Website: http://www.wncguide.com/score/Welcome.html

SCORE Office (Unifour)
PO Box 1828
Hickory, NC 28603
(704)328-6111

SCORE Office (High Point)
1101 N. Main St.
High Point, NC 27262
(336)882-8625
Fax: (336)889-9499

SCORE Office (Outer Banks)
Collington Rd. and Mustain
Kill Devil Hills, NC 27948
(252)441-8144

SCORE Office (Down East)
312 S Front St., Ste. 6
New Bern, NC 28560
(252)633-6688
Fax: (252)633-9608

SCORE Office (Kinston)
PO Box 95
New Bern, NC 28561
(919)633-6688

SCORE Office (Raleigh)
Century Post Office Bldg., Ste. 306
300 Federal St. Mall
Raleigh, NC 27601
(919)856-4739
E-mail: jendres@ibm.net
Website: http://www.intrex.net/score96/score96.htm

SCORE Office (Sanford)
1801 Nash St.
Sanford, NC 27330
(919)774-6442
Fax: (919)776-8739

SCORE Office (Sandhills Area)
1480 Hwy. 15-501
PO Box 458
Southern Pines, NC 28387
(910)692-3926

SCORE Office (Wilmington)
Corps of Engineers Bldg.
96 Darlington Ave., Ste. 207
Wilmington, NC 28403
(910)815-4576
Fax: (910)815-4658

North Dakota

SCORE Office (Bismarck-Mandan)
700 E Main Ave., 2nd Fl.
PO Box 5509
Bismarck, ND 58506-5509
(701)250-4303

SCORE Office (Fargo)
657 2nd Ave., Rm. 225
Fargo, ND 58108-3083
(701)239-5677

SCORE Office (Upper Red River)
4275 Technology Dr., Rm. 156
Grand Forks, ND 58202-8372
(701)777-3051

SCORE Office (Minot)
100 1st St. SW
Minot, ND 58701-3846
(701)852-6883
Fax: (701)852-6905

Ohio

SCORE Office (Akron)
1 Cascade Plz., 7th Fl.
Akron, OH 44308
(330)379-3163
Fax: (330)379-3164

SCORE Office (Ashland)
Gill Center
47 W Main St.
Ashland, OH 44805
(419)281-4584

SCORE Office (Canton)
116 Cleveland Ave. NW, Ste. 601
Canton, OH 44702-1720
(330)453-6047

SCORE Office (Chillicothe)
165 S Paint St.
Chillicothe, OH 45601
(614)772-4530

SCORE Office (Cincinnati)
Ameritrust Bldg., Rm. 850
525 Vine St.
Cincinnati, OH 45202
(513)684-2812
Fax: (513)684-3251
Website: http://www.score.chapter34.org

SCORE Office (Cleveland)
Eaton Center, Ste. 620
1100 Superior Ave.
Cleveland, OH 44114-2507
(216)522-4194
Fax: (216)522-4844

SCORE Office (Columbus)
2 Nationwide Plz., Ste. 1400
Columbus, OH 43215-2542
(614)469-2357
Fax: (614)469-2391
E-mail: info@scorecolumbus.org
Website: http://www.scorecolumbus.org

SCORE Office (Dayton)
Dayton Federal Bldg., Rm. 505
200 W Second St.
Dayton, OH 45402-1430
(513)225-2887
Fax: (513)225-7667

SCORE Office (Defiance)
615 W 3rd St.
PO Box 130
Defiance, OH 43512
(419)782-7946

SCORE Office (Findlay)
123 E Main Cross St.
PO Box 923
Findlay, OH 45840
(419)422-3314

SCORE Office (Lima)
147 N. Main St.
Lima, OH 45801
(419)222-6045
Fax: (419)229-0266

SCORE Office (Mansfield)
55 N. Mulberry St.
Mansfield, OH 44902
(419)522-3211

SCORE Office (Marietta)
Thomas Hall
Marietta, OH 45750
(614)373-0268

SCORE Office (Medina)
County Administrative Bldg.
144 N. Broadway
Medina, OH 44256
(216)764-8650

SCORE Office
(Licking County)
50 W Locust St.
Newark, OH 43055
(614)345-7458

SCORE Office (Salem)
2491 State Rte. 45 S
Salem, OH 44460
(216)332-0361

SCORE Office (Tiffin)
62 S Washington St.
Tiffin, OH 44883
(419)447-4141
Fax: (419)447-5141

SCORE Office (Toledo)
608 Madison Ave, Ste. 910
Toledo, OH 43624
(419)259-7598
Fax: (419)259-6460

SCORE Office (Heart of Ohio)
377 W Liberty St.
Wooster, OH 44691
(330)262-5735
Fax: (330)262-5745

SCORE Office (Youngstown)
306 Williamson Hall
Youngstown, OH 44555
(330)746-2687

Oklahoma

SCORE Office (Anadarko)
PO Box 366
Anadarko, OK 73005
(405)247-6651

SCORE Office (Ardmore)
410 W Main
Ardmore, OK 73401
(580)226-2620

SCORE Office
(Northeast Oklahoma)
210 S Main
Grove, OK 74344
(918)787-2796
Fax: (918)787-2796
E-mail: Score595@greencis.net

SCORE Office (Lawton)
4500 W Lee Blvd., Bldg. 100, Ste. 107
Lawton, OK 73505
(580)353-8727
Fax: (580)250-5677

SCORE Office (Oklahoma City)
210 Park Ave., No. 1300
Oklahoma City, OK 73102
(405)231-5163
Fax: (405)231-4876
E-mail: score212@usa.net

SCORE Office (Stillwater)
439 S Main
Stillwater, OK 74074
(405)372-5573
Fax: (405)372-4316

SCORE Office (Tulsa)
616 S Boston, Ste. 406
Tulsa, OK 74119
(918)581-7462
Fax: (918)581-6908
Website: http://www.ionet.net/~tulscore

Oregon

SCORE Office (Bend)
63085 N. Hwy. 97
Bend, OR 97701
(541)923-2849
Fax: (541)330-6900

SCORE Office (Willamette)
1401 Willamette St.
PO Box 1107
Eugene, OR 97401-4003
(541)465-6600
Fax: (541)484-4942

SCORE Office (Florence)
3149 Oak St.
Florence, OR 97439
(503)997-8444
Fax: (503)997-8448

SCORE Office (Southern Oregon)
33 N. Central Ave., Ste. 216
Medford, OR 97501
(541)776-4220
E-mail: pgr134f@prodigy.com

SCORE Office (Portland)
1515 SW 5th Ave., Ste. 1050
Portland, OR 97201
(503)326-3441
Fax: (503)326-2808
E-mail: gr134@prodigy.com

SCORE Office (Salem)
416 State St. (corner of Liberty)
Salem, OR 97301
(503)370-2896

Pennsylvania

SCORE Office (Altoona-Blair)
1212 12th Ave.
Altoona, PA 16601-3493
(814)943-8151

SCORE Office (Lehigh Valley)
Rauch Bldg. 37
Lehigh University
621 Taylor St.
Bethlehem, PA 18015
(610)758-4496
Fax: (610)758-5205

SCORE Office (Butler County)
100 N. Main St.
PO Box 1082
Butler, PA 16003
(412)283-2222
Fax: (412)283-0224

SCORE Office (Harrisburg)
4211 Trindle Rd.
Camp Hill, PA 17011
(717)761-4304
Fax: (717)761-4315

SCORE Office (Cumberland Valley)
75 S 2nd St.
Chambersburg, PA 17201
(717)264-2935

SCORE Office (Monroe County-Stroudsburg)
556 Main St.
East Stroudsburg, PA 18301
(717)421-4433

SCORE Office (Erie)
120 W 9th St.
Erie, PA 16501
(814)871-5650
Fax: (814)871-7530

SCORE Office (Bucks County)
409 Hood Blvd.
Fairless Hills, PA 19030
(215)943-8850
Fax: (215)943-7404

SCORE Office (Hanover)
146 Broadway
Hanover, PA 17331
(717)637-6130
Fax: (717)637-9127

SCORE Office (Harrisburg)
100 Chestnut, Ste. 309
Harrisburg, PA 17101
(717)782-3874

SCORE Office (East Montgomery County)
Baederwood Shopping Center
1653 The Fairways, Ste. 204
Jenkintown, PA 19046
(215)885-3027

SCORE Office (Kittanning)
2 Butler Rd.
Kittanning, PA 16201
(412)543-1305
Fax: (412)543-6206

SCORE Office (Lancaster)
118 W Chestnut St.
Lancaster, PA 17603
(717)397-3092

SCORE Office (Westmoreland County)
300 Fraser Purchase Rd.
Latrobe, PA 15650-2690
(412)539-7505
Fax: (412)539-1850

SCORE Office (Lebanon)
252 N. 8th St.
PO Box 899
Lebanon, PA 17042-0899
(717)273-3727
Fax: (717)273-7940

SCORE Office (Lewistown)
3 W Monument Sq., Ste. 204
Lewistown, PA 17044
(717)248-6713
Fax: (717)248-6714

SCORE Office (Delaware County)
602 E Baltimore Pike
Media, PA 19063
(610)565-3677
Fax: (610)565-1606

SCORE Office (Milton Area)
112 S Front St.
Milton, PA 17847
(717)742-7341
Fax: (717)792-2008

SCORE Office (Mon-Valley)
435 Donner Ave.
Monessen, PA 15062
(412)684-4277
Fax: (412)684-7688

SCORE Office (Monroeville)
William Penn Plaza
2790 Mosside Blvd., Ste. 295
Monroeville, PA 15146
(412)856-0622
Fax: (412)856-1030

SCORE Office (Airport Area)
986 Brodhead Rd.
Moon Township, PA 15108-2398
(412)264-6270
Fax: (412)264-1575

SCORE Office (Northeast)
8601 E Roosevelt Blvd.
Philadelphia, PA 19152
(215)332-3400
Fax: (215)332-6050

SCORE Office (Philadelphia)
1315 Walnut St., Ste. 500
Philadelphia, PA 19107
(215)790-5050
Fax: (215)790-5057
E-mail: score46@bellatlantic.net
Website: http://www.pgweb.net/score46

SCORE Office (Pittsburgh)
1000 Liberty Ave., Rm. 1122
Pittsburgh, PA 15222
(412)395-6560
Fax: (412)395-6562

SCORE Office (Tri-County)
801 N. Charlotte St.
Pottstown, PA 19464
(610)327-2673

SCORE Office (Reading)
601 Penn St.
Reading, PA 19601
(610)376-3497

SCORE Office (Scranton)
Oppenheim Bldg.
116 N. Washington Ave., Ste. 650
Scranton, PA 18503
(717)347-4611
Fax: (717)347-4611

SCORE Office (Central Pennsylvania)
200 Innovation Blvd., Ste. 242-B
State College, PA 16803
(814)234-9415
Fax: (814)238-9686
Website: http://countrystore.org/business/score.htm

SCORE Office (Monroe-Stroudsburg)
556 Main St.
Stroudsburg, PA 18360
(717)421-4433

SCORE Office (Uniontown)
Federal Bldg.
Pittsburg St.
PO Box 2065 DTS
Uniontown, PA 15401
(412)437-4222
E-mail: uniontownscore@lcsys.net

SCORE Office (Warren County)
315 2nd Ave.
Warren, PA 16365
(814)723-9017

SCORE Office (Waynesboro)
323 E Main St.
Waynesboro, PA 17268
(717)762-7123
Fax: (717)962-7124

SCORE Office (Chester County)
Government Service Center, Ste. 281
601 Westtown Rd.
West Chester, PA 19382-4538
(610)344-6910
Fax: (610)344-6919
E-mail: score@locke.ccil.org

SCORE Office (Wilkes-Barre)
7 N. Wilkes-Barre Blvd.
Wilkes Barre, PA 18702-5241
(717)826-6502
Fax: (717)826-6287

SCORE Office (North Central Pennsylvania)
240 W 3rd St., Rm. 227
PO Box 725
Williamsport, PA 17703
(717)322-3720
Fax: (717)322-1607
E-mail: score234@mail.csrlink.net
Website: http://www.lycoming.org/score

SCORE Office (York)
Cyber Center
2101 Pennsylvania Ave.
York, PA 17404
(717)845-8830
Fax: (717)854-9333

Puerto Rico

SCORE Office (Puerto Rico & Virgin Islands)
PO Box 12383-96
San Juan, PR 00914-0383
(787)726-8040
Fax: (787)726-8135

Rhode Island

SCORE Office (Barrington)
281 County Rd.
Barrington, RI 02806
(401)247-1920
Fax: (401)247-3763

SCORE Office (Woonsocket)
640 Washington Hwy.
Lincoln, RI 02865
(401)334-1000
Fax: (401)334-1009

SCORE Office (Wickford)
8045 Post Rd.
North Kingstown, RI 02852
(401)295-5566
Fax: (401)295-8987

SCORE Office (J.G.E. Knight)
380 Westminster St.
Providence, RI 02903
(401)528-4571
Fax: (401)528-4539
Website: http://www.riscore.org

SCORE Office (Warwick)
3288 Post Rd.
Warwick, RI 02886
(401)732-1100
Fax: (401)732-1101

SCORE Office (Westerly)
74 Post Rd.
Westerly, RI 02891
(401)596-7761
800-732-7636
Fax: (401)596-2190

South Carolina

SCORE Office (Aiken)
PO Box 892
Aiken, SC 29802
(803)641-1111
800-542-4536
Fax: (803)641-4174

SCORE Office (Anderson)
Anderson Mall
3130 N. Main St.
Anderson, SC 29621
(864)224-0453

SCORE Office (Coastal)
284 King St.
Charleston, SC 29401
(803)727-4778
Fax: (803)853-2529

SCORE Office (Midlands)
Strom Thurmond Bldg., Rm. 358
1835 Assembly St., Rm 358
Columbia, SC 29201
(803)765-5131
Fax: (803)765-5962
Website: http://www.scoremidlands.org

SCORE Office (Piedmont)
Federal Bldg., Rm. B-02
300 E Washington St.
Greenville, SC 29601
(864)271-3638

SCORE Office (Greenwood)
PO Drawer 1467
Greenwood, SC 29648
(864)223-8357

SCORE Office (Hilton Head Island)
52 Savannah Trail
Hilton Head, SC 29926
(803)785-7107
Fax: (803)785-7110

SCORE Office (Grand Strand)
937 Broadway
Myrtle Beach, SC 29577
(803)918-1079
Fax: (803)918-1083
E-mail: score381@aol.com

SCORE Office (Spartanburg)
PO Box 1636
Spartanburg, SC 29304
(864)594-5000
Fax: (864)594-5055

South Dakota

SCORE Office (West River)
Rushmore Plz. Civic Ctr.
444 Mount Rushmore Rd., No. 209
Rapid City, SD 57701
(605)394-5311
E-mail: score@gwtc.net

SCORE Office (Sioux Falls)
First Financial Center
110 S Phillips Ave., Ste. 200
Sioux Falls, SD 57104-6727
(605)330-4231
Fax: (605)330-4231

Tennessee

SCORE Office (Chattanooga)
Federal Bldg., Rm. 26
900 Georgia Ave.
Chattanooga, TN 37402
(423)752-5190
Fax: (423)752-5335

SCORE Office (Cleveland)
PO Box 2275
Cleveland, TN 37320
(423)472-6587
Fax: (423)472-2019

SCORE Office (Upper Cumberland Center)
1225 S Willow Ave.
Cookeville, TN 38501
(615)432-4111
Fax: (615)432-6010

SCORE Office (Unicoi County)
PO Box 713
Erwin, TN 37650
(423)743-3000
Fax: (423)743-0942

SCORE Office (Greeneville)
115 Academy St.
Greeneville, TN 37743
(423)638-4111
Fax: (423)638-5345

SCORE Office (Jackson)
194 Auditorium St.
Jackson, TN 38301
(901)423-2200

SCORE Office (Northeast Tennessee)
1st Tennessee Bank Bldg.
2710 S Roan St., Ste. 584
Johnson City, TN 37601
(423)929-7686
Fax: (423)461-8052

SCORE Office (Kingsport)
151 E Main St.
Kingsport, TN 37662
(423)392-8805

SCORE Office (Greater Knoxville)
Farragot Bldg., Ste. 224
530 S Gay St.
Knoxville, TN 37902
(423)545-4203
E-mail: scoreknox@ntown.com
Website: http://www.scoreknox.org

SCORE Office (Maryville)
201 S Washington St.
Maryville, TN 37804-5728
(423)983-2241
800-525-6834
Fax: (423)984-1386

SCORE Office (Memphis)
Federal Bldg., Ste. 390
167 N. Main St.
Memphis, TN 38103
(901)544-3588

SCORE Office (Nashville)
50 Vantage Way, Ste. 201
Nashville, TN 37228-1500
(615)736-7621

Texas

SCORE Office (Abilene)
2106 Federal Post Office and Court Bldg.
Abilene, TX 79601
(915)677-1857

SCORE Office (Austin)
2501 S Congress
Austin, TX 78701
(512)442-7235
Fax: (512)442-7528

SCORE Office (Golden Triangle)
450 Boyd St.
Beaumont, TX 77704
(409)838-6581
Fax: (409)833-6718

SCORE Office (Brownsville)
3505 Boca Chica Blvd., Ste. 305
Brownsville, TX 78521
(210)541-4508

SCORE Office (Brazos Valley)
3000 Briarcrest, Ste. 302
Bryan, TX 77802
(409)776-8876
E-mail: 102633.2612@compuserve.com

SCORE Office (Cleburne)
Watergarden Pl., 9th Fl., Ste. 400
Cleburne, TX 76031
(817)871-6002

SCORE Office (Corpus Christi)
651 Upper North Broadway, Ste. 654
Corpus Christi, TX 78477
(512)888-4322
Fax: (512)888-3418

SCORE Office (Dallas)
6260 E Mockingbird
Dallas, TX 75214-2619
(214)828-2471
Fax: (214)821-8033

SCORE Office (El Paso)
10 Civic Center Plaza
El Paso, TX 79901
(915)534-0541
Fax: (915)534-0513

SCORE Office (Bedford)
100 E 15th St., Ste. 400
Fort Worth, TX 76102
(817)871-6002

SCORE Office (Fort Worth)
100 E 15th St., No. 24
Fort Worth, TX 76102
(817)871-6002
Fax: (817)871-6031
E-mail: fwbac@onramp.net

SCORE Office (Garland)
2734 W Kingsley Rd.
Garland, TX 75041
(214)271-9224

SCORE Office (Granbury Chamber of Commerce)
416 S Morgan
Granbury, TX 76048
(817)573-1622
Fax: (817)573-0805

SCORE Office (Lower Rio Grande Valley)
222 E Van Buren, Ste. 500
Harlingen, TX 78550
(956)427-8533
Fax: (956)427-8537

SCORE Office (Houston)
9301 Southwest Fwy., Ste. 550
Houston, TX 77074
(713)773-6565
Fax: (713)773-6550

SCORE Office (Irving)
3333 N. MacArthur Blvd., Ste. 100
Irving, TX 75062
(214)252-8484
Fax: (214)252-6710

SCORE Office (Lubbock)
1205 Texas Ave., Rm. 411D
Lubbock, TX 79401
(806)472-7462
Fax: (806)472-7487

SCORE Office (Midland)
Post Office Annex
200 E Wall St., Rm. P121
Midland, TX 79701
(915)687-2649

SCORE Office (Orange)
1012 Green Ave.
Orange, TX 77630-5620
(409)883-3536
800-528-4906
Fax: (409)886-3247

SCORE Office (Plano)
1200 E 15th St.
PO Drawer 940287
Plano, TX 75094-0287
(214)424-7547
Fax: (214)422-5182

SCORE Office (Port Arthur)
4749 Twin City Hwy., Ste. 300
Port Arthur, TX 77642
(409)963-1107
Fax: (409)963-3322

SCORE Office (Richardson)
411 Belle Grove
Richardson, TX 75080
(214)234-4141
800-777-8001
Fax: (214)680-9103

SCORE Office (San Antonio)
Federal Bldg., Rm. A527
727 E Durango
San Antonio, TX 78206
(210)472-5931
Fax: (210)472-5935

SCORE Office (Texarkana State College)
819 State Line Ave.
Texarkana, TX 75501
(903)792-7191
Fax: (903)793-4304

SCORE Office (East Texas)
RTDC
1530 SSW Loop 323, Ste. 100
Tyler, TX 75701
(903)510-2975
Fax: (903)510-2978

SCORE Office (Waco)
401 Franklin Ave.
Waco, TX 76701
(817)754-8898
Fax: (817)756-0776
Website: http://www.brc-waco.com

SCORE Office (Wichita Falls)
Hamilton Bldg.
900 8th St.
Wichita Falls, TX 76307
(940)723-2741
Fax: (940)723-8773

Utah

SCORE Office (Northern Utah)
160 N. Main
Logan, UT 84321
(435)746-2269

SCORE Office (Ogden)
1701 E Windsor Dr.
Ogden, UT 84604
(801)629-8613
E-mail: score158@netscape.net

SCORE Office (Central Utah)
1071 E Windsor Dr.
Provo, UT 84604
(801)373-8660

SCORE Office (Southern Utah)
225 South 700 East
Saint George, UT 84770
(435)652-7751

SCORE Office (Salt Lake)
310 S Main St.
Salt Lake City, UT 84101
(801)746-2269
Fax: (801)746-2273

Vermont

SCORE Office (Champlain Valley)
Winston Prouty Federal Bldg.
11 Lincoln St., Rm. 106
Essex Junction, VT 05452
(802)951-6762

SCORE Office (Montpelier)
87 State St., Rm. 205
PO Box 605
Montpelier, VT 05601
(802)828-4422
Fax: (802)828-4485

SCORE Office (Marble Valley)
256 N. Main St.
Rutland, VT 05701-2413
(802)773-9147

SCORE Office (Northeast Kingdom)
20 Main St.
PO Box 904
Saint Johnsbury, VT 05819
(802)748-5101

Virgin Islands

SCORE Office (Saint Croix)
United Plaza Shopping Center
PO Box 4010, Christiansted
Saint Croix, VI 00822
(809)778-5380

SCORE Office (Saint Thomas-Saint John)
Federal Bldg., Rm. 21
Veterans Dr.
Saint Thomas, VI 00801
(809)774-8530

Virginia

SCORE Office (Arlington)
2009 N. 14th St., Ste. 111
Arlington, VA 22201
(703)525-2400

SCORE Office (Blacksburg)
141 Jackson St.
Blacksburg, VA 24060
(540)552-4061

SCORE Office (Bristol)
20 Volunteer Pkwy.
Bristol, VA 24203
(540)989-4850

SCORE Office (Central Virginia)
1001 E Market St., Ste. 101
Charlottesville, VA 22902
(804)295-6712
Fax: (804)295-7066

SCORE Office (Alleghany Satellite)
241 W Main St.
Covington, VA 24426
(540)962-2178
Fax: (540)962-2179

SCORE Office (Central Fairfax)
3975 University Dr., Ste. 350
Fairfax, VA 22030
(703)591-2450

SCORE Office (Falls Church)
PO Box 491
Falls Church, VA 22040
(703)532-1050
Fax: (703)237-7904

SCORE Office (Glenns)
Glenns Campus
Box 287
Glenns, VA 23149
(804)693-9650

SCORE Office (Peninsula)
6 Manhattan Sq.
PO Box 7269
Hampton, VA 23666
(757)766-2000
Fax: (757)865-0339
E-mail: score100@seva.net

SCORE Office (Tri-Cities)
108 N. Main St.
Hopewell, VA 23860
(804)458-5536

SCORE Office (Lynchburg)
Federal Bldg.
1100 Main St.
Lynchburg, VA 24504-1714
(804)846-3235

SCORE Office (Greater Prince William)
8963 Center St
Manassas, VA 20110
(703)368-4813
Fax: (703)368-4733

SCORE Office (Martinsvile)
115 Broad St.
Martinsville, VA 24112-0709
(540)632-6401
Fax: (540)632-5059

SCORE Office (Hampton Roads)
Federal Bldg., Rm. 737
200 Grandby St.
Norfolk, VA 23510
(757)441-3733
Fax: (757)441-3733
E-mail: scorehr60@juno.com

SCORE Office (Norfolk)
Federal Bldg., Rm. 737
200 Granby St.
Norfolk, VA 23510
(757)441-3733
Fax: (757)441-3733

SCORE Office (Virginia Beach)
Chamber of Commerce
200 Grandby St., Rm 737
Norfolk, VA 23510
(804)441-3733

SCORE Office (Radford)
1126 Norwood St.
Radford, VA 24141
(540)639-2202

SCORE Office (Richmond)
Federal Bldg.
400 N. 8th St., Ste. 1150
PO Box 10126
Richmond, VA 23240-0126
(804)771-2400
Fax: (804)771-8018
E-mail: scorechapter12@yahoo.com
Website: http://www.cvco.org/score

SCORE Office (Roanoke)
Federal Bldg., Rm. 716
250 Franklin Rd.
Roanoke, VA 24011
(540)857-2834
Fax: (540)857-2043
E-mail: scorerva@juno.com
Website: http://hometown.aol.com/scorerv/Index.html

SCORE Office (Fairfax)
8391 Old Courthouse Rd., Ste. 300
Vienna, VA 22182
(703)749-0400

SCORE Office (Greater Vienna)
513 Maple Ave. West
Vienna, VA 22180
(703)281-1333
Fax: (703)242-1482

SCORE Office (Shenandoah Valley)
301 W Main St.
Waynesboro, VA 22980
(540)949-8203
Fax: (540)949-7740
E-mail: score427@intelos.net

SCORE Office (Williamsburg)
201 Penniman Rd.
Williamsburg, VA 23185
(757)229-6511
E-mail: wacc@williamsburgcc.com

SCORE Office (Northern Virginia)
1360 S Pleasant Valley Rd.
Winchester, VA 22601
(540)662-4118

Washington

SCORE Office (Gray's Harbor)
506 Duffy St.
Aberdeen, WA 98520
(360)532-1924
Fax: (360)533-7945

SCORE Office (Bellingham)
101 E Holly St.
Bellingham, WA 98225
(360)676-3307

SCORE Office (Everett)
2702 Hoyt Ave.
Everett, WA 98201-3556
(206)259-8000

SCORE Office (Gig Harbor)
3125 Judson St.
Gig Harbor, WA 98335
(206)851-6865

SCORE Office (Kennewick)
PO Box 6986
Kennewick, WA 99336
(509)736-0510

SCORE Office (Puyallup)
322 2nd St. SW
PO Box 1298
Puyallup, WA 98371
(206)845-6755
Fax: (206)848-6164

SCORE Office (Seattle)
1200 6th Ave., Ste. 1700
Seattle, WA 98101
(206)553-7320
Fax: (206)553-7044
E-mail: score55@aol.com
Website: http://www.scn.org/civic/score-online/index55.html

SCORE Office (Spokane)
801 W Riverside Ave., No. 240
Spokane, WA 99201
(509)353-2820
Fax: (509)353-2600
E-mail: score@dmi.net
Website: http://www.dmi.net/score

SCORE Office (Clover Park)
PO Box 1933
Tacoma, WA 98401-1933
(206)627-2175

SCORE Office (Tacoma)
1101 Pacific Ave.
Tacoma, WA 98402
(253)274-1288
Fax: (253)274-1289

SCORE Office (Fort Vancouver)
1701 Broadway, S-1
Vancouver, WA 98663
(360)699-1079

SCORE Office (Walla Walla)
500 Tausick Way
Walla Walla, WA 99362
(509)527-4681

SCORE Office (Mid-Columbia)
1113 S 14th Ave.
Yakima, WA 98907
(509)574-4944
Fax: (509)574-2943
Website: http://www.ellensburg.com/~score

West Virginia

SCORE Office (Charleston)
1116 Smith St.
Charleston, WV 25301
(304)347-5463
E-mail: score256@juno.com

SCORE Office (Virginia Street)
1116 Smith St., Ste. 302
Charleston, WV 25301
(304)347-5463

SCORE Office (Marion County)
PO Box 208
Fairmont, WV 26555-0208
(304)363-0486

SCORE Office (Upper Monongahela Valley)
1000 Technology Dr., Ste. 1111
Fairmont, WV 26555
(304)363-0486
E-mail: score537@hotmail.com

SCORE Office (Huntington)
1101 6th Ave., Ste. 220
Huntington, WV 25701-2309
(304)523-4092

SCORE Office (Wheeling)
1310 Market St.
Wheeling, WV 26003
(304)233-2575
Fax: (304)233-1320

Wisconsin

SCORE Office (Fox Cities)
227 S Walnut St.
Appleton, WI 54913

(920)734-7101
Fax: (920)734-7161

SCORE Office (Beloit)
136 W Grand Ave., Ste. 100
PO Box 717
Beloit, WI 53511
(608)365-8835
Fax: (608)365-9170

SCORE Office (Eau Claire)
Federal Bldg., Rm. B11
510 S Barstow St.
Eau Claire, WI 54701
(715)834-1573
E-mail: score@ecol.net
Website: http://www.ecol.net/~score

SCORE Office (Fond du Lac)
207 N. Main St.
Fond du Lac, WI 54935
(414)921-9500
Fax: (414)921-9559

SCORE Office (Green Bay)
835 Potts Ave.
Green Bay, WI 54304
(414)496-8930
Fax: (414)496-6009

SCORE Office (Janesville)
20 S Main St., Ste. 11
PO Box 8008
Janesville, WI 53547
(608)757-3160
Fax: (608)757-3170

SCORE Office (La Crosse)
712 Main St.
La Crosse, WI 54602-0219
(608)784-4880

SCORE Office (Madison)
505 S Rosa Rd.
Madison, WI 53719
(608)441-2820

SCORE Office (Manitowoc)
1515 Memorial Dr.
PO Box 903
Manitowoc, WI 54221-0903
(414)684-5575
Fax: (414)684-1915

SCORE Office (Milwaukee)
310 W Wisconsin Ave., Ste. 425
Milwaukee, WI 53203
(414)297-3942
Fax: (414)297-1377

SCORE Office (Central Wisconsin)
1224 Lindbergh Ave.
Stevens Point, WI 54481
(715)344-7729

SCORE Office (Superior)
Superior Business Center Inc.
1423 N. 8th St.
Superior, WI 54880
(715)394-7388
Fax: (715)393-7414

SCORE Office (Waukesha)
223 Wisconsin Ave.
Waukesha, WI 53186-4926
(414)542-4249

SCORE Office (Wausau)
300 3rd St., Ste. 200
Wausau, WI 54402-6190
(715)845-6231

SCORE Office (Wisconsin Rapids)
2240 Kingston Rd.
Wisconsin Rapids, WI 54494
(715)423-1830

Wyoming

SCORE Office (Casper)
Federal Bldg., No. 2215
100 East B St.
Casper, WY 82602
(307)261-6529
Fax: (307)261-6530

Venture capital & financing companies

This section contains a listing of financing and loan companies in the United States and Canada. These listing are arranged alphabetically by country, then by state or province, then by city, then by organization name.

Canada

Alberta

Launchworks Inc.
1902J 11th St., SE
Calgary, AB, Canada T2G 3G2
(403)269-1119
Fax: (403)269-1141
Website: http://www.launchworks.com

Native Venture Capital Company, Inc.
21 Artist View Point, Box 7
Site 25, RR 12
Calgary, AB, Canada T3E 6W3
(903)208-5380

Miralta Capital Inc.
4445 Calgary Trail South
888 Terrace Plaza Alberta
Edmonton, AB, Canada T6H 5R7
(780)438-3535
Fax: (780)438-3129

Vencap Equities Alberta Ltd.
10180-101st St., Ste. 1980
Edmonton, AB, Canada T5J 3S4
(403)420-1171
Fax: (403)429-2541

British Columbia

Discovery Capital
5th Fl., 1199 West Hastings
Vancouver, BC, Canada V6E 3T5
(604)683-3000
Fax: (604)662-3457
E-mail: info@discoverycapital.com
Website: http://www.discoverycapital.com

Greenstone Venture Partners
1177 West Hastings St.
Ste. 400
Vancouver, BC, Canada V6E 2K3
(604)717-1977
Fax: (604)717-1976
Website: http://www.greenstonevc.com

Growthworks Capital
2600-1055 West Georgia St.
Box 11170 Royal Centre
Vancouver, BC, Canada V6E 3R5
(604)895-7259
Fax: (604)669-7605
Website: http://www.wofund.com

MDS Discovery Venture Management, Inc.
555 W Eighth Ave., Ste. 305
Vancouver, BC, Canada V5Z 1C6
(604)872-8464
Fax: (604)872-2977
E-mail: info@mds-ventures.com

Ventures West Management Inc.
1285 W Pender St., Ste. 280
Vancouver, BC, Canada V6E 4B1
(604)688-9495
Fax: (604)687-2145
Website: http://www.ventureswest.com

Nova Scotia

ACF Equity Atlantic Inc.
Purdy's Wharf Tower II
Ste. 2106
Halifax, NS, Canada B3J 3R7
(902)421-1965
Fax: (902)421-1808

Montgomerie, Huck & Co.
146 Bluenose Dr.
PO Box 538

Lunenburg, NS, Canada B0J 2C0
(902)634-7125
Fax: (902)634-7130

Ontario

IPS Industrial Promotion Services Ltd.
60 Columbia Way, Ste. 720
Markham, ON, Canada L3R 0C9
(905)475-9400
Fax: (905)475-5003

Betwin Investments Inc.
Box 23110
Sault Ste. Marie, ON, Canada P6A 6W6
(705)253-0744
Fax: (705)253-0744

Bailey & Company, Inc.
594 Spadina Ave.
Toronto, ON, Canada M5S 2H4
(416)921-6930
Fax: (416)925-4670

BCE Capital
200 Bay St.
South Tower, Ste. 3120
Toronto, ON, Canada M5J 2J2
(416)815-0078
Fax: (416)941-1073
Website: http://www.bcecapital.com

Castlehill Ventures
55 University Ave., Ste. 500
Toronto, ON, Canada M5J 2H7
(416)862-8574
Fax: (416)862-8875

CCFL Mezzanine Partners of Canada
70 University Ave.
Ste. 1450
Toronto, ON, Canada M5J 2M4
(416)977-1450
Fax: (416)977-6764
E-mail: info@ccfl.com
Website: http://www.ccfl.com

Celtic House International
100 Simcoe St., Ste. 100
Toronto, ON, Canada M5H 3G2
(416)542-2436
Fax: (416)542-2435
Website: http://www.celtic-house.com

Clairvest Group Inc.
22 St. Clair Ave. East
Ste. 1700
Toronto, ON, Canada M4T 2S3
(416)925-9270
Fax: (416)925-5753

Crosbie & Co., Inc.
One First Canadian Place
9th Fl.
PO Box 116
Toronto, ON, Canada M5X 1A4
(416)362-7726
Fax: (416)362-3447
E-mail: info@crosbieco.com
Website: http://www.crosbieco.com

Drug Royalty Corp.
Eight King St. East
Ste. 202
Toronto, ON, Canada M5C 1B5
(416)863-1865
Fax: (416)863-5161

Grieve, Horner, Brown & Asculai
8 King St. E, Ste. 1704
Toronto, ON, Canada M5C 1B5
(416)362-7668
Fax: (416)362-7660

Jefferson Partners
77 King St. West
Ste. 4010
PO Box 136
Toronto, ON, Canada M5K 1H1
(416)367-1533
Fax: (416)367-5827
Website: http://www.jefferson.com

J.L. Albright Venture Partners
Canada Trust Tower, 161 Bay St.
Ste. 4440
PO Box 215
Toronto, ON, Canada M5J 2S1
(416)367-2440
Fax: (416)367-4604
Website: http://www.jlaventures.com

McLean Watson Capital Inc.
One First Canadian Place
Ste. 1410
PO Box 129
Toronto, ON, Canada M5X 1A4
(416)363-2000
Fax: (416)363-2010
Website: http://www.mcleanwatson.com

Middlefield Capital Fund
One First Canadian Place
85th Fl.
PO Box 192
Toronto, ON, Canada M5X 1A6
(416)362-0714
Fax: (416)362-7925
Website: http://www.middlefield.com

Mosaic Venture Partners
24 Duncan St.
Ste. 300
Toronto, ON, Canada M5V 3M6
(416)597-8889
Fax: (416)597-2345

Onex Corp.
161 Bay St.
PO Box 700
Toronto, ON, Canada M5J 2S1
(416)362-7711
Fax: (416)362-5765

Penfund Partners Inc.
145 King St. West
Ste. 1920
Toronto, ON, Canada M5H 1J8
(416)865-0300
Fax: (416)364-6912
Website: http://www.penfund.com

Primaxis Technology Ventures Inc.
1 Richmond St. West, 8th Fl.
Toronto, ON, Canada M5H 3W4
(416)313-5210
Fax: (416)313-5218
Website: http://www.primaxis.com

Priveq Capital Funds
240 Duncan Mill Rd., Ste. 602
Toronto, ON, Canada M3B 3P1
(416)447-3330
Fax: (416)447-3331
E-mail: priveq@sympatico.ca

Roynat Ventures
40 King St. West, 26th Fl.
Toronto, ON, Canada M5H 1H1
(416)933-2667
Fax: (416)933-2783
Website: http://www.roynatcapital.com

Tera Capital Corp.
366 Adelaide St. East, Ste. 337
Toronto, ON, Canada M5A 3X9
(416)368-1024
Fax: (416)368-1427

Working Ventures Canadian Fund Inc.
250 Bloor St. East, Ste. 1600
Toronto, ON, Canada M4W 1E6
(416)934-7718
Fax: (416)929-0901
Website: http://www.workingventures.ca

Quebec

Altamira Capital Corp.
202 University
Niveau de Maisoneuve, Bur. 201
Montreal, QC, Canada H3A 2A5
(514)499-1656
Fax: (514)499-9570

Federal Business Development Bank
Venture Capital Division
Five Place Ville Marie, Ste. 600
Montreal, QC, Canada H3B 5E7
(514)283-1896
Fax: (514)283-5455

Hydro-Quebec Capitech Inc.
75 Boul, Rene Levesque Quest
Montreal, QC, Canada H2Z 1A4
(514)289-4783
Fax: (514)289-5420
Website: http://www.hqcapitech.com

Investissement Desjardins
2 complexe Desjardins
C.P. 760
Montreal, QC, Canada H5B 1B8
(514)281-7131
Fax: (514)281-7808
Website: http://www.desjardins.com/id

Marleau Lemire Inc.
One Place Ville-Marie, Ste. 3601
Montreal, QC, Canada H3B 3P2
(514)877-3800
Fax: (514)875-6415

Speirs Consultants Inc.
365 Stanstead
Montreal, QC, Canada H3R 1X5
(514)342-3858
Fax: (514)342-1977

Tecnocap Inc.
4028 Marlowe
Montreal, QC, Canada H4A 3M2
(514)483-6009
Fax: (514)483-6045
Website: http://www.technocap.com

Telsoft Ventures
1000, Rue de la Gauchetiere
Quest, 25eme Etage
Montreal, QC, Canada H3B 4W5
(514)397-8450
Fax: (514)397-8451

Saskatchewan

Saskatchewan Government Growth Fund
1801 Hamilton St., Ste. 1210
Canada Trust Tower
Regina, SK, Canada S4P 4B4
(306)787-2994
Fax: (306)787-2086

United States

Alabama

FHL Capital Corp.
600 20th Street North
Suite 350
Birmingham, AL 35203
(205)328-3098
Fax: (205)323-0001

Harbert Management Corp.
One Riverchase Pkwy. South
Birmingham, AL 35244
(205)987-5500
Fax: (205)987-5707
Website: http://www.harbert.net

Jefferson Capital Fund
PO Box 13129
Birmingham, AL 35213
(205)324-7709

Private Capital Corp.
100 Brookwood Pl., 4th Fl.
Birmingham, AL 35209
(205)879-2722
Fax: (205)879-5121

21st Century Health Ventures
One Health South Pkwy.
Birmingham, AL 35243
(256)268-6250
Fax: (256)970-8928

FJC Growth Capital Corp.
200 Westside Sq., Ste. 340
Huntsville, AL 35801
(256)922-2918
Fax: (256)922-2909

Hickory Venture Capital Corp.
301 Washington St. NW
Suite 301
Huntsville, AL 35801
(256)539-1931
Fax: (256)539-5130
E-mail: hvcc@hvcc.com
Website: http://www.hvcc.com

Southeastern Technology Fund
7910 South Memorial Pkwy., Ste. F
Huntsville, AL 35802
(256)883-8711
Fax: (256)883-8558

Cordova Ventures
4121 Carmichael Rd., Ste. 301
Montgomery, AL 36106
(334)271-6011
Fax: (334)260-0120
Website: http://www.cordovaventures.com

Small Business Clinic of Alabama/AG Bartholomew & Associates
PO Box 231074
Montgomery, AL 36123-1074
(334)284-3640

Arizona

Miller Capital Corp.
4909 E McDowell Rd.
Phoenix, AZ 85008
(602)225-0504
Fax: (602)225-9024
Website: http://www.themillergroup.com

The Columbine Venture Funds
9449 North 90th St., Ste. 200
Scottsdale, AZ 85258
(602)661-9222
Fax: (602)661-6262

Koch Ventures
17767 N. Perimeter Dr., Ste. 101
Scottsdale, AZ 85255
(480)419-3600
Fax: (480)419-3606
Website: http://www.kochventures.com

McKee & Co.
7702 E Doubletree Ranch Rd.
Suite 230
Scottsdale, AZ 85258
(480)368-0333
Fax: (480)607-7446

Merita Capital Ltd.
7350 E Stetson Dr., Ste. 108-A
Scottsdale, AZ 85251
(480)947-8700
Fax: (480)947-8766

Valley Ventures / Arizona Growth Partners L.P.
6720 N. Scottsdale Rd., Ste. 208
Scottsdale, AZ 85253
(480)661-6600
Fax: (480)661-6262

Estreetcapital.com
660 South Mill Ave., Ste. 315
Tempe, AZ 85281
(480)968-8400
Fax: (480)968-8480
Website: http://www.estreetcapital.com

Coronado Venture Fund
PO Box 65420
Tucson, AZ 85728-5420
(520)577-3764
Fax: (520)299-8491

Arkansas

Arkansas Capital Corp.
225 South Pulaski St.
Little Rock, AR 72201
(501)374-9247
Fax: (501)374-9425
Website: http://www.arcapital.com

California

Sundance Venture Partners, L.P.
100 Clocktower Place, Ste. 130
Carmel, CA 93923
(831)625-6500
Fax: (831)625-6590

Westar Capital (Costa Mesa)
949 South Coast Dr., Ste. 650
Costa Mesa, CA 92626
(714)481-5160
Fax: (714)481-5166
E-mail: mailbox@westarcapital.com
Website: http://www.westarcapital.com

Alpine Technology Ventures
20300 Stevens Creek Boulevard, Ste. 495
Cupertino, CA 95014
(408)725-1810
Fax: (408)725-1207
Website: http://www.alpineventures.com

Bay Partners
10600 N. De Anza Blvd.
Cupertino, CA 95014-2031
(408)725-2444
Fax: (408)446-4502
Website: http://www.baypartners.com

Novus Ventures
20111 Stevens Creek Blvd., Ste. 130
Cupertino, CA 95014
(408)252-3900
Fax: (408)252-1713
Website: http://www.novusventures.com

Triune Capital
19925 Stevens Creek Blvd., Ste. 200
Cupertino, CA 95014
(310)284-6800
Fax: (310)284-3290

Acorn Ventures
268 Bush St., Ste. 2829
Daly City, CA 94014
(650)994-7801
Fax: (650)994-3305
Website: http://www.acornventures.com

Digital Media Campus
2221 Park Place
El Segundo, CA 90245
(310)426-8000
Fax: (310)426-8010
E-mail: info@thecampus.com
Website: http://www.digitalmedia
campus.com

BankAmerica Ventures / BA Venture Partners
950 Tower Ln., Ste. 700
Foster City, CA 94404
(650)378-6000
Fax: (650)378-6040
Website: http://www.baventure
partners.com

Starting Point Partners
666 Portofino Lane
Foster City, CA 94404
(650)722-1035
Website: http://www.startingpoint
partners.com

Opportunity Capital Partners
2201 Walnut Ave., Ste. 210
Fremont, CA 94538
(510)795-7000
Fax: (510)494-5439
Website: http://www.ocpcapital.com

Imperial Ventures Inc.
9920 S La Cienega Boulevar, 14th Fl.
Inglewood, CA 90301
(310)417-5409
Fax: (310)338-6115

Ventana Global (Irvine)
18881 Von Karman Ave., Ste. 1150
Irvine, CA 92612
(949)476-2204
Fax: (949)752-0223
Website: http://www.ventanaglobal.com

Integrated Consortium Inc.
50 Ridgecrest Rd.
Kentfield, CA 94904
(415)925-0386
Fax: (415)461-2726

Enterprise Partners
979 Ivanhoe Ave., Ste. 550
La Jolla, CA 92037
(858)454-8833
Fax: (858)454-2489
Website: http://www.epvc.com

Domain Associates
28202 Cabot Rd., Ste. 200
Laguna Niguel, CA 92677
(949)347-2446
Fax: (949)347-9720
Website: http://www.domainvc.com

Cascade Communications Ventures
60 E Sir Francis Drake Blvd., Ste. 300
Larkspur, CA 94939
(415)925-6500
Fax: (415)925-6501

Allegis Capital
One First St., Ste. Two
Los Altos, CA 94022
(650)917-5900
Fax: (650)917-5901
Website: http://www.allegiscapital.com

Aspen Ventures
1000 Fremont Ave., Ste. 200
Los Altos, CA 94024
(650)917-5670
Fax: (650)917-5677
Website: http://www.aspenventures.com

AVI Capital L.P.
1 First St., Ste. 2
Los Altos, CA 94022
(650)949-9862
Fax: (650)949-8510
Website: http://www.avicapital.com

Bastion Capital Corp.
1999 Avenue of the Stars, Ste. 2960
Los Angeles, CA 90067
(310)788-5700
Fax: (310)277-7582
E-mail: ga@bastioncapital.com
Website: http://www.bastioncapital.com

Davis Group
PO Box 69953
Los Angeles, CA 90069-0953
(310)659-6327
Fax: (310)659-6337

Developers Equity Corp.
1880 Century Park East, Ste. 211
Los Angeles, CA 90067
(213)277-0300

Far East Capital Corp.
350 S Grand Ave., Ste. 4100
Los Angeles, CA 90071
(213)687-1361
Fax: (213)617-7939
E-mail: free@fareastnationalbank.com

Kline Hawkes & Co.
11726 San Vicente Blvd., Ste. 300
Los Angeles, CA 90049
(310)442-4700
Fax: (310)442-4707
Website: http://www.klinehawkes.com

Lawrence Financial Group
701 Teakwood
PO Box 491773
Los Angeles, CA 90049
(310)471-4060
Fax: (310)472-3155

Riordan Lewis & Haden
300 S Grand Ave., 29th Fl.
Los Angeles, CA 90071
(213)229-8500
Fax: (213)229-8597

Union Venture Corp.
445 S Figueroa St., 9th Fl.
Los Angeles, CA 90071

(213)236-4092
Fax: (213)236-6329

Wedbush Capital Partners
1000 Wilshire Blvd.
Los Angeles, CA 90017
(213)688-4545
Fax: (213)688-6642
Website: http://www.wedbush.com

Advent International Corp.
2180 Sand Hill Rd., Ste. 420
Menlo Park, CA 94025
(650)233-7500
Fax: (650)233-7515
Website: http://www.advent international.com

Altos Ventures
2882 Sand Hill Rd., Ste. 100
Menlo Park, CA 94025
(650)234-9771
Fax: (650)233-9821
Website: http://www.altosvc.com

Applied Technology
1010 El Camino Real, Ste. 300
Menlo Park, CA 94025
(415)326-8622
Fax: (415)326-8163

APV Technology Partners
535 Middlefield, Ste. 150
Menlo Park, CA 94025
(650)327-7871
Fax: (650)327-7631
Website: http://www.apvtp.com

August Capital Management
2480 Sand Hill Rd., Ste. 101
Menlo Park, CA 94025
(650)234-9900
Fax: (650)234-9910
Website: http://www.augustcap.com

Baccharis Capital Inc.
2420 Sand Hill Rd., Ste. 100
Menlo Park, CA 94025
(650)324-6844
Fax: (650)854-3025

Benchmark Capital
2480 Sand Hill Rd., Ste. 200
Menlo Park, CA 94025
(650)854-8180
Fax: (650)854-8183
E-mail: info@benchmark.com
Website: http://www.benchmark.com

Bessemer Venture Partners (Menlo Park)
535 Middlefield Rd., Ste. 245
Menlo Park, CA 94025
(650)853-7000
Fax: (650)853-7001
Website: http://www.bvp.com

The Cambria Group
1600 El Camino Real Rd., Ste. 155
Menlo Park, CA 94025
(650)329-8600
Fax: (650)329-8601
Website: http://www.cambriagroup.com

Canaan Partners
2884 Sand Hill Rd., Ste. 115
Menlo Park, CA 94025
(650)854-8092
Fax: (650)854-8127
Website: http://www.canaan.com

Capstone Ventures
3000 Sand Hill Rd., Bldg. One, Ste. 290
Menlo Park, CA 94025
(650)854-2523
Fax: (650)854-9010
Website: http://www.capstonevc.com

Comdisco Venture Group (Silicon Valley)
3000 Sand Hill Rd., Bldg. 1, Ste. 155
Menlo Park, CA 94025
(650)854-9484
Fax: (650)854-4026

Commtech International
535 Middlefield Rd., Ste. 200
Menlo Park, CA 94025
(650)328-0190
Fax: (650)328-6442

Compass Technology Partners
1550 El Camino Real, Ste. 275
Menlo Park, CA 94025-4111
(650)322-7595
Fax: (650)322-0588
Website: http://www.compasstech partners.com

Convergence Partners
3000 Sand Hill Rd., Ste. 235
Menlo Park, CA 94025
(650)854-3010
Fax: (650)854-3015
Website: http://www.convergence partners.com

The Dakota Group
PO Box 1025
Menlo Park, CA 94025
(650)853-0600
Fax: (650)851-4899
E-mail: info@dakota.com

Delphi Ventures
3000 Sand Hill Rd.
Bldg. One, Ste. 135
Menlo Park, CA 94025
(650)854-9650
Fax: (650)854-2961
Website: http://www.delphiventures.com

El Dorado Ventures
2884 Sand Hill Rd., Ste. 121
Menlo Park, CA 94025
(650)854-1200
Fax: (650)854-1202
Website: http://www.eldorado ventures.com

Glynn Ventures
3000 Sand Hill Rd., Bldg. 4, Ste. 235
Menlo Park, CA 94025
(650)854-2215

Indosuez Ventures
2180 Sand Hill Rd., Ste. 450
Menlo Park, CA 94025
(650)854-0587
Fax: (650)323-5561
Website: http://www.indosuezventures.com

Institutional Venture Partners
3000 Sand Hill Rd., Bldg. 2, Ste. 290
Menlo Park, CA 94025
(650)854-0132
Fax: (650)854-5762
Website: http://www.ivp.com

Interwest Partners (Menlo Park)
3000 Sand Hill Rd., Bldg. 3, Ste. 255
Menlo Park, CA 94025-7112
(650)854-8585
Fax: (650)854-4706
Website: http://www.interwest.com

Kleiner Perkins Caufield & Byers (Menlo Park)
2750 Sand Hill Rd.
Menlo Park, CA 94025
(650)233-2750
Fax: (650)233-0300
Website: http://www.kpcb.com

Magic Venture Capital LLC
1010 El Camino Real, Ste. 300
Menlo Park, CA 94025
(650)325-4149

Matrix Partners
2500 Sand Hill Rd., Ste. 113
Menlo Park, CA 94025
(650)854-3131
Fax: (650)854-3296
Website: http://www.matrixpartners.com

Mayfield Fund
2800 Sand Hill Rd.
Menlo Park, CA 94025
(650)854-5560

Fax: (650)854-5712
Website: http://www.mayfield.com

McCown De Leeuw and Co. (Menlo Park)
3000 Sand Hill Rd., Bldg. 3, Ste. 290
Menlo Park, CA 94025-7111
(650)854-6000
Fax: (650)854-0853
Website: http://www.mdcpartners.com

Menlo Ventures
3000 Sand Hill Rd., Bldg. 4, Ste. 100
Menlo Park, CA 94025
(650)854-8540
Fax: (650)854-7059
Website: http://www.menloventures.com

Merrill Pickard Anderson & Eyre
2480 Sand Hill Rd., Ste. 200
Menlo Park, CA 94025
(650)854-8600
Fax: (650)854-0345

New Enterprise Associates (Menlo Park)
2490 Sand Hill Rd.
Menlo Park, CA 94025
(650)854-9499
Fax: (650)854-9397
Website: http://www.nea.com

Onset Ventures
2400 Sand Hill Rd., Ste. 150
Menlo Park, CA 94025
(650)529-0700
Fax: (650)529-0777
Website: http://www.onset.com

Paragon Venture Partners
3000 Sand Hill Rd., Bldg. 1, Ste. 275
Menlo Park, CA 94025
(650)854-8000
Fax: (650)854-7260

Pathfinder Venture Capital Funds (Menlo Park)
3000 Sand Hill Rd., Bldg. 3, Ste. 255
Menlo Park, CA 94025
(650)854-0650
Fax: (650)854-4706

Rocket Ventures
3000 Sandhill Rd., Bldg. 1, Ste. 170
Menlo Park, CA 94025
(650)561-9100
Fax: (650)561-9183
Website: http://www.rocketventures.com

Sequoia Capital
3000 Sand Hill Rd., Bldg. 4, Ste. 280
Menlo Park, CA 94025
(650)854-3927
Fax: (650)854-2977
E-mail: sequoia@sequioacap.com
Website: http://www.sequoiacap.com

Sierra Ventures
3000 Sand Hill Rd., Bldg. 4, Ste. 210
Menlo Park, CA 94025
(650)854-1000
Fax: (650)854-5593
Website: http://www.sierraventures.com

Sigma Partners
2884 Sand Hill Rd., Ste. 121
Menlo Park, CA 94025-7022
(650)853-1700
Fax: (650)853-1717
E-mail: info@sigmapartners.com
Website: http://www.sigmapartners.com

Sprout Group (Menlo Park)
3000 Sand Hill Rd.
Bldg. 3, Ste. 170
Menlo Park, CA 94025
(650)234-2700
Fax: (650)234-2779
Website: http://www.sproutgroup.com

TA Associates (Menlo Park)
70 Willow Rd., Ste. 100
Menlo Park, CA 94025
(650)328-1210
Fax: (650)326-4933
Website: http://www.ta.com

Thompson Clive & Partners Ltd.
3000 Sand Hill Rd., Bldg. 1, Ste. 185
Menlo Park, CA 94025-7102
(650)854-0314
Fax: (650)854-0670
E-mail: mail@tcvc.com
Website: http://www.tcvc.com

Trinity Ventures Ltd.
3000 Sand Hill Rd., Bldg. 1, Ste. 240
Menlo Park, CA 94025
(650)854-9500
Fax: (650)854-9501
Website: http://www.trinityventures.com

U.S. Venture Partners
2180 Sand Hill Rd., Ste. 300
Menlo Park, CA 94025
(650)854-9080
Fax: (650)854-3018
Website: http://www.usvp.com

USVP-Schlein Marketing Fund
2180 Sand Hill Rd., Ste. 300
Menlo Park, CA 94025
(415)854-9080
Fax: (415)854-3018
Website: http://www.usvp.com

Venrock Associates
2494 Sand Hill Rd., Ste. 200
Menlo Park, CA 94025
(650)561-9580
Fax: (650)561-9180
Website: http://www.venrock.com

Brad Peery Capital Inc.
145 Chapel Pkwy.
Mill Valley, CA 94941
(415)389-0625
Fax: (415)389-1336

Dot Edu Ventures
650 Castro St., Ste. 270
Mountain View, CA 94041
(650)575-5638
Fax: (650)325-5247
Website: http://www.doteduventures.com

Forrest, Binkley & Brown
840 Newport Ctr. Dr., Ste. 480
Newport Beach, CA 92660
(949)729-3222
Fax: (949)729-3226
Website: http://www.fbbvc.com

Marwit Capital LLC
180 Newport Center Dr., Ste. 200
Newport Beach, CA 92660
(949)640-6234
Fax: (949)720-8077
Website: http://www.marwit.com

Kaiser Permanente / National Venture Development
1800 Harrison St., 22nd Fl.
Oakland, CA 94612
(510)267-4010
Fax: (510)267-4036
Website: http://www.kpventures.com

Nu Capital Access Group, Ltd.
7677 Oakport St., Ste. 105
Oakland, CA 94621
(510)635-7345
Fax: (510)635-7068

Inman and Bowman
4 Orinda Way, Bldg. D, Ste. 150
Orinda, CA 94563
(510)253-1611
Fax: (510)253-9037

Accel Partners (San Francisco)
428 University Ave.
Palo Alto, CA 94301
(650)614-4800
Fax: (650)614-4880
Website: http://www.accel.com

Advanced Technology Ventures
485 Ramona St., Ste. 200
Palo Alto, CA 94301
(650)321-8601
Fax: (650)321-0934
Website: http://www.atvcapital.com

Anila Fund
400 Channing Ave.
Palo Alto, CA 94301
(650)833-5790
Fax: (650)833-0590
Website: http://www.anila.com

Asset Management Company Venture Capital
2275 E Bayshore, Ste. 150
Palo Alto, CA 94303
(650)494-7400
Fax: (650)856-1826
E-mail: postmaster@assetman.com
Website: http://www.assetman.com

BancBoston Capital / BancBoston Ventures
435 Tasso St., Ste. 250
Palo Alto, CA 94305
(650)470-4100
Fax: (650)853-1425
Website: http://www.bancbostoncapital.com

Charter Ventures
525 University Ave., Ste. 1400
Palo Alto, CA 94301
(650)325-6953
Fax: (650)325-4762
Website: http://www.charterventures.com

Communications Ventures
505 Hamilton Avenue, Ste. 305
Palo Alto, CA 94301
(650)325-9600
Fax: (650)325-9608
Website: http://www.comven.com

HMS Group
2468 Embarcadero Way
Palo Alto, CA 94303-3313
(650)856-9862
Fax: (650)856-9864

Jafco America Ventures, Inc.
505 Hamilton Ste. 310
Palto Alto, CA 94301
(650)463-8800
Fax: (650)463-8801
Website: http://www.jafco.com

New Vista Capital
540 Cowper St., Ste. 200
Palo Alto, CA 94301
(650)329-9333
Fax: (650)328-9434
E-mail: fgreene@nvcap.com
Website: http://www.nvcap.com

Norwest Equity Partners (Palo Alto)
245 Lytton Ave., Ste. 250
Palo Alto, CA 94301-1426
(650)321-8000
Fax: (650)321-8010
Website: http://www.norwestvp.com

Oak Investment Partners
525 University Ave., Ste. 1300
Palo Alto, CA 94301
(650)614-3700
Fax: (650)328-6345
Website: http://www.oakinv.com

Patricof & Co. Ventures, Inc. (Palo Alto)
2100 Geng Rd., Ste. 150
Palo Alto, CA 94303
(650)494-9944
Fax: (650)494-6751
Website: http://www.patricof.com

RWI Group
835 Page Mill Rd.
Palo Alto, CA 94304
(650)251-1800
Fax: (650)213-8660
Website: http://www.rwigroup.com

Summit Partners (Palo Alto)
499 Hamilton Ave., Ste. 200
Palo Alto, CA 94301
(650)321-1166
Fax: (650)321-1188
Website: http://www.summitpartners.com

Sutter Hill Ventures
755 Page Mill Rd., Ste. A-200
Palo Alto, CA 94304
(650)493-5600
Fax: (650)858-1854
E-mail: shv@shv.com

Vanguard Venture Partners
525 University Ave., Ste. 600
Palo Alto, CA 94301
(650)321-2900
Fax: (650)321-2902
Website: http://www.vanguardventures.com

Venture Growth Associates
2479 East Bayshore St., Ste. 710
Palo Alto, CA 94303
(650)855-9100
Fax: (650)855-9104

Worldview Technology Partners
435 Tasso St., Ste. 120
Palo Alto, CA 94301
(650)322-3800
Fax: (650)322-3880
Website: http://www.worldview.com

Draper, Fisher, Jurvetson / Draper Associates
400 Seaport Ct., Ste.250
Redwood City, CA 94063
(415)599-9000
Fax: (415)599-9726
Website: http://www.dfj.com

Gabriel Venture Partners
350 Marine Pkwy., Ste. 200
Redwood Shores, CA 94065
(650)551-5000
Fax: (650)551-5001
Website: http://www.gabrielvp.com

Hallador Venture Partners, L.L.C.
740 University Ave., Ste. 110
Sacramento, CA 95825-6710
(916)920-0191
Fax: (916)920-5188
E-mail: chris@hallador.com

Emerald Venture Group
12396 World Trade Dr., Ste. 116
San Diego, CA 92128
(858)451-1001
Fax: (858)451-1003
Website: http://www.emeraldventure.com

Forward Ventures
9255 Towne Centre Dr.
San Diego, CA 92121
(858)677-6077
Fax: (858)452-8799
E-mail: info@forwardventure.com
Website: http://www.forwardventure.com

Idanta Partners Ltd.
4660 La Jolla Village Dr., Ste. 850
San Diego, CA 92122
(619)452-9690
Fax: (619)452-2013
Website: http://www.idanta.com

Kingsbury Associates
3655 Nobel Dr., Ste. 490
San Diego, CA 92122
(858)677-0600
Fax: (858)677-0800

Kyocera International Inc.
Corporate Development
8611 Balboa Ave.
San Diego, CA 92123

(858)576-2600
Fax: (858)492-1456

Sorrento Associates, Inc.
4370 LaJolla Village Dr., Ste. 1040
San Diego, CA 92122
(619)452-3100
Fax: (619)452-7607
Website: http://www.sorrentoventures.com

Western States Investment Group
9191 Towne Ctr. Dr., Ste. 310
San Diego, CA 92122
(619)678-0800
Fax: (619)678-0900

Aberdare Ventures
One Embarcadero Center, Ste. 4000
San Francisco, CA 94111
(415)392-7442
Fax: (415)392-4264
Website: http://www.aberdare.com

Acacia Venture Partners
101 California St., Ste. 3160
San Francisco, CA 94111
(415)433-4200
Fax: (415)433-4250
Website: http://www.acaciavp.com

Access Venture Partners
319 Laidley St.
San Francisco, CA 94131
(415)586-0132
Fax: (415)392-6310
Website: http://www.accessventure partners.com

Alta Partners
One Embarcadero Center, Ste. 4050
San Francisco, CA 94111
(415)362-4022
Fax: (415)362-6178
E-mail: alta@altapartners.com
Website: http://www.altapartners.com

Bangert Dawes Reade Davis & Thom
220 Montgomery St., Ste. 424
San Francisco, CA 94104
(415)954-9900
Fax: (415)954-9901
E-mail: bdrdt@pacbell.net

Berkeley International Capital Corp.
650 California St., Ste. 2800
San Francisco, CA 94108-2609
(415)249-0450
Fax: (415)392-3929
Website: http://www.berkeleyvc.com

Blueprint Ventures LLC
456 Montgomery St., 22nd Fl.
San Francisco, CA 94104
(415)901-4000
Fax: (415)901-4035
Website: http://www.blueprintventures .com

Blumberg Capital Ventures
580 Howard St., Ste. 401
San Francisco, CA 94105
(415)905-5007
Fax: (415)357-5027
Website: http://www.blumberg-capital.com

Burr, Egan, Deleage, and Co. (San Francisco)
1 Embarcadero Center, Ste. 4050
San Francisco, CA 94111
(415)362-4022
Fax: (415)362-6178

Burrill & Company
120 Montgomery St., Ste. 1370
San Francisco, CA 94104
(415)743-3160
Fax: (415)743-3161
Website: http://www.burrillandco.com

CMEA Ventures
235 Montgomery St., Ste. 920
San Francisco, CA 94401
(415)352-1520
Fax: (415)352-1524
Website: http://www.cmeaventures.com

Crocker Capital
1 Post St., Ste. 2500
San Francisco, CA 94101
(415)956-5250
Fax: (415)959-5710

Dominion Ventures, Inc.
44 Montgomery St., Ste. 4200
San Francisco, CA 94104
(415)362-4890
Fax: (415)394-9245

Dorset Capital
Pier 1
Bay 2
San Francisco, CA 94111
(415)398-7101
Fax: (415)398-7141
Website: http://www.dorsetcapital.com

Gatx Capital
Four Embarcadero Center, Ste. 2200
San Francisco, CA 94904
(415)955-3200
Fax: (415)955-3449

IMinds
135 Main St., Ste. 1350
San Francisco, CA 94105
(415)547-0000
Fax: (415)227-0300
Website: http://www.iminds.com

LF International Inc.
360 Post St., Ste. 705
San Francisco, CA 94108
(415)399-0110
Fax: (415)399-9222
Website: http://www.lfvc.com

Newbury Ventures
535 Pacific Ave., 2nd Fl.
San Francisco, CA 94133
(415)296-7408
Fax: (415)296-7416
Website: http://www.newburyven.com

Quest Ventures (San Francisco)
333 Bush St., Ste. 1750
San Francisco, CA 94104
(415)782-1414
Fax: (415)782-1415

Robertson-Stephens Co.
555 California St., Ste. 2600
San Francisco, CA 94104
(415)781-9700
Fax: (415)781-2556
Website: http://www.omega adventures.com

Rosewood Capital, L.P.
One Maritime Plaza, Ste. 1330
San Francisco, CA 94111-3503
(415)362-5526
Fax: (415)362-1192
Website: http://www.rosewoodvc.com

Ticonderoga Capital Inc.
555 California St., No. 4950
San Francisco, CA 94104
(415)296-7900
Fax: (415)296-8956

21st Century Internet Venture Partners
Two South Park
2nd Floor
San Francisco, CA 94107
(415)512-1221
Fax: (415)512-2650
Website: http://www.21vc.com

VK Ventures
600 California St., Ste.1700
San Francisco, CA 94111
(415)391-5600
Fax: (415)397-2744

Walden Group of Venture Capital Funds
750 Battery St., Seventh Floor
San Francisco, CA 94111

(415)391-7225
Fax: (415)391-7262

Acer Technology Ventures
2641 Orchard Pkwy.
San Jose, CA 95134
(408)433-4945
Fax: (408)433-5230

Authosis
226 Airport Pkwy., Ste. 405
San Jose, CA 95110
(650)814-3603
Website: http://www.authosis.com

Western Technology Investment
2010 N. First St., Ste. 310
San Jose, CA 95131
(408)436-8577
Fax: (408)436-8625
E-mail: mktg@westerntech.com

Drysdale Enterprises
177 Bovet Rd., Ste. 600
San Mateo, CA 94402
(650)341-6336
Fax: (650)341-1329
E-mail: drysdale@aol.com

Greylock
2929 Campus Dr., Ste. 400
San Mateo, CA 94401
(650)493-5525
Fax: (650)493-5575
Website: http://www.greylock.com

Technology Funding
2000 Alameda de las Pulgas, Ste. 250
San Mateo, CA 94403
(415)345-2200
Fax: (415)345-1797

2M Invest Inc.
1875 S Grant St.
Suite 750
San Mateo, CA 94402
(650)655-3765
Fax: (650)372-9107
E-mail: 2minfo@2minvest.com
Website: http://www.2minvest.com

Phoenix Growth Capital Corp.
2401 Kerner Blvd.
San Rafael, CA 94901
(415)485-4569
Fax: (415)485-4663

NextGen Partners LLC
1705 East Valley Rd.
Santa Barbara, CA 93108
(805)969-8540
Fax: (805)969-8542
Website: http://www.nextgenpartners.com

Denali Venture Capital
1925 Woodland Ave.
Santa Clara, CA 95050
(408)690-4838
Fax: (408)247-6979
E-mail: wael@denaliventurecapital.com
Website: http://www.denaliventure capital.com

Dotcom Ventures LP
3945 Freedom Circle, Ste. 740
Santa Clara, CA 95045
(408)919-9855
Fax: (408)919-9857
Website: http://www.dotcom venturesatl.com

Silicon Valley Bank
3003 Tasman
Santa Clara, CA 95054
(408)654-7400
Fax: (408)727-8728

Al Shugart International
920 41st Ave.
Santa Cruz, CA 95062
(831)479-7852
Fax: (831)479-7852
Website: http://www.alshugart.com

Leonard Mautner Associates
1434 Sixth St.
Santa Monica, CA 90401
(213)393-9788
Fax: (310)459-9918

Palomar Ventures
100 Wilshire Blvd., Ste. 450
Santa Monica, CA 90401
(310)260-6050
Fax: (310)656-4150
Website: http://www.palomarventures.com

Medicus Venture Partners
12930 Saratoga Ave., Ste. D8
Saratoga, CA 95070
(408)447-8600
Fax: (408)447-8599
Website: http://www.medicusvc.com

Redleaf Venture Management
14395 Saratoga Ave., Ste. 130
Saratoga, CA 95070
(408)868-0800
Fax: (408)868-0810
E-mail: nancy@redleaf.com
Website: http://www.redleaf.com

Artemis Ventures
207 Second St., Ste. E
3rd Fl.
Sausalito, CA 94965
(415)289-2500
Fax: (415)289-1789
Website: http://www.artemisventures.com

Deucalion Venture Partners
19501 Brooklime
Sonoma, CA 95476
(707)938-4974
Fax: (707)938-8921

Windward Ventures
PO Box 7688
Thousand Oaks, CA 91359-7688
(805)497-3332
Fax: (805)497-9331

National Investment Management, Inc.
2601 Airport Dr., Ste.210
Torrance, CA 90505
(310)784-7600
Fax: (310)784-7605

Southern California Ventures
406 Amapola Ave. Ste. 125
Torrance, CA 90501
(310)787-4381
Fax: (310)787-4382

Sandton Financial Group
21550 Oxnard St., Ste. 300
Woodland Hills, CA 91367
(818)702-9283

Woodside Fund
850 Woodside Dr.
Woodside, CA 94062
(650)368-5545
Fax: (650)368-2416
Website: http://www.woodsidefund.com

Colorado

Colorado Venture Management
Ste. 300
Boulder, CO 80301
(303)440-4055
Fax: (303)440-4636

Dean & Associates
4362 Apple Way
Boulder, CO 80301
Fax: (303)473-9900

Roser Ventures LLC
1105 Spruce St.
Boulder, CO 80302
(303)443-6436
Fax: (303)443-1885
Website: http://www.roserventures.com

Sequel Venture Partners
4430 Arapahoe Ave., Ste. 220
Boulder, CO 80303

(303)546-0400
Fax: (303)546-9728
E-mail: tom@sequelvc.com
Website: http://www.sequelvc.com

New Venture Resources
445C E Cheyenne Mtn. Blvd.
Colorado Springs, CO 80906-4570
(719)598-9272
Fax: (719)598-9272

The Centennial Funds
1428 15th St.
Denver, CO 80202-1318
(303)405-7500
Fax: (303)405-7575
Website: http://www.centennial.com

Rocky Mountain Capital Partners
1125 17th St., Ste. 2260
Denver, CO 80202
(303)291-5200
Fax: (303)291-5327

Sandlot Capital LLC
600 South Cherry St., Ste. 525
Denver, CO 80246
(303)893-3400
Fax: (303)893-3403
Website: http://www.sandlotcapital.com

Wolf Ventures
50 South Steele St., Ste. 777
Denver, CO 80209
(303)321-4800
Fax: (303)321-4848
E-mail: businessplan@wolfventures.com
Website: http://www.wolfventures.com

The Columbine Venture Funds
5460 S Quebec St., Ste. 270
Englewood, CO 80111
(303)694-3222
Fax: (303)694-9007

Investment Securities of Colorado, Inc.
4605 Denice Dr.
Englewood, CO 80111
(303)796-9192

Kinship Partners
6300 S Syracuse Way, Ste. 484
Englewood, CO 80111
(303)694-0268
Fax: (303)694-1707
E-mail: block@vailsys.com

Boranco Management, L.L.C.
1528 Hillside Dr.
Fort Collins, CO 80524-1969
(970)221-2297
Fax: (970)221-4787

Aweida Ventures
890 West Cherry St., Ste. 220
Louisville, CO 80027
(303)664-9520
Fax: (303)664-9530
Website: http://www.aweida.com

Access Venture Partners
8787 Turnpike Dr., Ste. 260
Westminster, CO 80030
(303)426-8899
Fax: (303)426-8828

Connecticut

Medmax Ventures, LP
1 Northwestern Dr., Ste. 203
Bloomfield, CT 06002
(860)286-2960
Fax: (860)286-9960

James B. Kobak & Co.
Four Mansfield Place
Darien, CT 06820
(203)656-3471
Fax: (203)655-2905

Orien Ventures
1 Post Rd.
Fairfield, CT 06430
(203)259-9933
Fax: (203)259-5288

ABP Acquisition Corporation
115 Maple Ave.
Greenwich, CT 06830
(203)625-8287
Fax: (203)447-6187

Catterton Partners
9 Greenwich Office Park
Greenwich, CT 06830
(203)629-4901
Fax: (203)629-4903
Website: http://www.cpequity.com

Consumer Venture Partners
3 Pickwick Plz.
Greenwich, CT 06830
(203)629-8800
Fax: (203)629-2019

Insurance Venture Partners
31 Brookside Dr., Ste. 211
Greenwich, CT 06830
(203)861-0030
Fax: (203)861-2745

The NTC Group
Three Pickwick Plaza
Ste. 200
Greenwich, CT 06830
(203)862-2800
Fax: (203)622-6538

Regulus International Capital Co., Inc.
140 Greenwich Ave.
Greenwich, CT 06830
(203)625-9700
Fax: (203)625-9706

Axiom Venture Partners
City Place II
185 Asylum St., 17th Fl.
Hartford, CT 06103
(860)548-7799
Fax: (860)548-7797
Website: http://www.axiomventures.com

Conning Capital Partners
City Place II
185 Asylum St.
Hartford, CT 06103-4105
(860)520-1289
Fax: (860)520-1299
E-mail: pe@conning.com
Website: http://www.conning.com

First New England Capital L.P.
100 Pearl St.
Hartford, CT 06103
(860)293-3333
Fax: (860)293-3338
E-mail: info@firstnewenglandcapital.com
Website: http://www.firstnewengland capital.com

Northeast Ventures
One State St., Ste. 1720
Hartford, CT 06103
(860)547-1414
Fax: (860)246-8755

Windward Holdings
38 Sylvan Rd.
Madison, CT 06443
(203)245-6870
Fax: (203)245-6865

Advanced Materials Partners, Inc.
45 Pine St.
PO Box 1022
New Canaan, CT 06840
(203)966-6415
Fax: (203)966-8448
E-mail: wkb@amplink.com

RFE Investment Partners
36 Grove St.
New Canaan, CT 06840
(203)966-2800
Fax: (203)966-3109
Website: http://www.rfeip.com

Connecticut Innovations, Inc.
999 West St.
Rocky Hill, CT 06067
(860)563-5851
Fax: (860)563-4877
E-mail: pamela.hartley@ctinnovations.com
Website: http://www.ctinnovations.com

Canaan Partners
105 Rowayton Ave.
Rowayton, CT 06853
(203)855-0400
Fax: (203)854-9117
Website: http://www.canaan.com

Landmark Partners, Inc.
10 Mill Pond Ln.
Simsbury, CT 06070
(860)651-9760
Fax: (860)651-8890
Website: http://www.landmarkpartners.com

Sweeney & Company
PO Box 567
Southport, CT 06490
(203)255-0220
Fax: (203)255-0220
E-mail: sweeney@connix.com

Baxter Associates, Inc.
PO Box 1333
Stamford, CT 06904
(203)323-3143
Fax: (203)348-0622

Beacon Partners Inc.
6 Landmark Sq., 4th Fl.
Stamford, CT 06901-2792
(203)359-5776
Fax: (203)359-5876

Collinson, Howe, and Lennox, LLC
1055 Washington Blvd., 5th Fl.
Stamford, CT 06901
(203)324-7700
Fax: (203)324-3636
E-mail: info@chlmedical.com
Website: http://www.chlmedical.com

Prime Capital Management Co.
550 West Ave.
Stamford, CT 06902
(203)964-0642
Fax: (203)964-0862

Saugatuck Capital Co.
1 Canterbury Green
Stamford, CT 06901
(203)348-6669
Fax: (203)324-6995
Website: http://www.saugatuckcapital.com

Soundview Financial Group Inc.
22 Gatehouse Rd.
Stamford, CT 06902
(203)462-7200
Fax: (203)462-7350
Website: http://www.sndv.com

TSG Ventures, L.L.C.
177 Broad St., 12th Fl.
Stamford, CT 06901
(203)406-1500
Fax: (203)406-1590

Whitney & Company
177 Broad St.
Stamford, CT 06901
(203)973-1400
Fax: (203)973-1422
Website: http://www.jhwhitney.com

Cullinane & Donnelly Venture Partners L.P.
970 Farmington Ave.
West Hartford, CT 06107
(860)521-7811

The Crestview Investment and Financial Group
431 Post Rd. E, Ste. 1
Westport, CT 06880-4403
(203)222-0333
Fax: (203)222-0000

Marketcorp Venture Associates, L.P. (MCV)
274 Riverside Ave.
Westport, CT 06880
(203)222-3030
Fax: (203)222-3033

Oak Investment Partners (Westport)
1 Gorham Island
Westport, CT 06880
(203)226-8346
Fax: (203)227-0372
Website: http://www.oakinv.com

Oxford Bioscience Partners
315 Post Rd. W
Westport, CT 06880-5200
(203)341-3300
Fax: (203)341-3309
Website: http://www.oxbio.com

Prince Ventures (Westport)
25 Ford Rd.
Westport, CT 06880
(203)227-8332
Fax: (203)226-5302

LTI Venture Leasing Corp.
221 Danbury Rd.
Wilton, CT 06897
(203)563-1100
Fax: (203)563-1111
Website: http://www.ltileasing.com

Delaware

Blue Rock Capital
5803 Kennett Pike, Ste. A
Wilmington, DE 19807
(302)426-0981
Fax: (302)426-0982
Website: http://www.bluerockcapital.com

District of Columbia

Allied Capital Corp.
1919 Pennsylvania Ave. NW
Washington, DC 20006-3434
(202)331-2444
Fax: (202)659-2053
Website: http://www.alliedcapital.com

Atlantic Coastal Ventures, L.P.
3101 South St. NW
Washington, DC 20007
(202)293-1166
Fax: (202)293-1181
Website: http://www.atlanticcv.com

Columbia Capital Group, Inc.
1660 L St. NW, Ste. 308
Washington, DC 20036
(202)775-8815
Fax: (202)223-0544

Core Capital Partners
901 15th St., NW
9th Fl.
Washington, DC 20005
(202)589-0090
Fax: (202)589-0091
Website: http://www.core-capital.com

Next Point Partners
701 Pennsylvania Ave. NW, Ste. 900
Washington, DC 20004
(202)661-8703
Fax: (202)434-7400
E-mail: mf@nextpoint.vc
Website: http://www.nextpointvc.com

Telecommunications Development Fund
2020 K. St. NW
Ste. 375
Washington, DC 20006
(202)293-8840
Fax: (202)293-8850
Website: http://www.tdfund.com

Wachtel & Co., Inc.
1101 4th St. NW
Washington, DC 20005-5680
(202)898-1144

Winslow Partners LLC
1300 Connecticut Ave. NW
Washington, DC 20036-1703
(202)530-5000
Fax: (202)530-5010
E-mail: winslow@winslowpartners.com

Women's Growth Capital Fund
1054 31st St., NW
Ste. 110
Washington, DC 20007
(202)342-1431
Fax: (202)341-1203
Website: http://www.wgcf.com

Florida

Sigma Capital Corp.
22668 Caravelle Circle
Boca Raton, FL 33433
(561)368-9783

North American Business Development Co., L.L.C.
111 East Las Olas Blvd.
Fort Lauderdale, FL 33301
(305)463-0681
Fax: (305)527-0904
Website: http://www.northamerican fund.com

Chartwell Capital Management Co. Inc.
1 Independent Dr., Ste. 3120
Jacksonville, FL 32202
(904)355-3519
Fax: (904)353-5833
E-mail: info@chartwellcap.com

CEO Advisors
1061 Maitland Center Commons
Ste. 209
Maitland, FL 32751
(407)660-9327
Fax: (407)660-2109

Henry & Co.
8201 Peters Rd., Ste. 1000
Plantation, FL 33324
(954)797-7400

Avery Business Development Services
2506 St. Michel Ct.
Ponte Vedra, FL 32082
(904)285-6033

New South Ventures
5053 Ocean Blvd.
Sarasota, FL 34242
(941)358-6000
Fax: (941)358-6078
Website: http://www.newsouth ventures.com

Venture Capital Management Corp.
PO Box 2626
Satellite Beach, FL 32937
(407)777-1969

Florida Capital Venture Ltd.
325 Florida Bank Plaza
100 W Kennedy Blvd.
Tampa, FL 33602
(813)229-2294
Fax: (813)229-2028

Quantum Capital Partners
339 South Plant Ave.
Tampa, FL 33606
(813)250-1999
Fax: (813)250-1998
Website: http://www.quantum capitalpartners.com

South Atlantic Venture Fund
614 W Bay St.
Tampa, FL 33606-2704
(813)253-2500
Fax: (813)253-2360
E-mail: venture@southatlantic.com
Website: http://www.southatlantic.com

LM Capital Corp.
120 S Olive, Ste. 400
West Palm Beach, FL 33401
(561)833-9700
Fax: (561)655-6587
Website: http://www.lmcapital securities.com

Georgia

Venture First Associates
4811 Thornwood Dr.
Acworth, GA 30102
(770)928-3733
Fax: (770)928-6455

Alliance Technology Ventures
8995 Westside Pkwy., Ste. 200
Alpharetta, GA 30004
(678)336-2000
Fax: (678)336-2001
E-mail: info@atv.com
Website: http://www.atv.com

Cordova Ventures
2500 North Winds Pkwy., Ste. 475
Alpharetta, GA 30004
(678)942-0300
Fax: (678)942-0301
Website: http://www.cordovaventures.com

Advanced Technology Development Fund
1000 Abernathy, Ste. 1420
Atlanta, GA 30328-5614
(404)668-2333
Fax: (404)668-2333

CGW Southeast Partners
12 Piedmont Center, Ste. 210
Atlanta, GA 30305
(404)816-3255
Fax: (404)816-3258
Website: http://www.cgwlp.com

Cyberstarts
1900 Emery St., NW
3rd Fl.
Atlanta, GA 30318
(404)267-5000
Fax: (404)267-5200
Website: http://www.cyberstarts.com

EGL Holdings, Inc.
10 Piedmont Center, Ste. 412
Atlanta, GA 30305
(404)949-8300
Fax: (404)949-8311

Equity South
1790 The Lenox Bldg.
3399 Peachtree Rd. NE
Atlanta, GA 30326
(404)237-6222
Fax: (404)261-1578

Five Paces
3400 Peachtree Rd., Ste. 200
Atlanta, GA 30326
(404)439-8300
Fax: (404)439-8301
Website: http://www.fivepaces.com

Frontline Capital, Inc.
3475 Lenox Rd., Ste. 400
Atlanta, GA 30326
(404)240-7280
Fax: (404)240-7281

Fuqua Ventures LLC
1201 W Peachtree St. NW, Ste. 5000
Atlanta, GA 30309
(404)815-4500
Fax: (404)815-4528
Website: http://www.fuquaventures.com

Noro-Moseley Partners
4200 Northside Pkwy., Bldg. 9
Atlanta, GA 30327
(404)233-1966
Fax: (404)239-9280
Website: http://www.noro-moseley.com

Renaissance Capital Corp.
34 Peachtree St. NW, Ste. 2230
Atlanta, GA 30303
(404)658-9061
Fax: (404)658-9064

River Capital, Inc.
Two Midtown Plaza
1360 Peachtree St. NE, Ste. 1430
Atlanta, GA 30309
(404)873-2166
Fax: (404)873-2158

State Street Bank & Trust Co.
3414 Peachtree Rd. NE, Ste. 1010
Atlanta, GA 30326
(404)364-9500
Fax: (404)261-4469

UPS Strategic Enterprise Fund
55 Glenlake Pkwy. NE
Atlanta, GA 30328
(404)828-8814
Fax: (404)828-8088
E-mail: jcacyce@ups.com
Website: http://www.ups.com/sef/sef_home

Wachovia
191 Peachtree St. NE, 26th Fl.
Atlanta, GA 30303
(404)332-1000
Fax: (404)332-1392
Website: http://www.wachovia.com/wca

Brainworks Ventures
4243 Dunwoody Club Dr.
Chamblee, GA 30341
(770)239-7447

First Growth Capital Inc.
Best Western Plaza, Ste. 105
PO Box 815
Forsyth, GA 31029
(912)781-7131

Financial Capital Resources, Inc.
21 Eastbrook Bend, Ste. 116
Peachtree City, GA 30269
(404)487-6650

Hawaii

HMS Hawaii Management Partners
Davies Pacific Center
841 Bishop St., Ste. 860
Honolulu, HI 96813
(808)545-3755
Fax: (808)531-2611

Idaho

Sun Valley Ventures
160 Second St.
Ketchum, ID 83340
(208)726-5005
Fax: (208)726-5094

Illinois

Open Prairie Ventures
115 N. Neil St., Ste. 209
Champaign, IL 61820
(217)351-7000
Fax: (217)351-7051
E-mail: inquire@openprairie.com
Website: http://www.openprairie.com

ABN AMRO Private Equity
208 S La Salle St., 10th Fl.
Chicago, IL 60604
(312)855-7079
Fax: (312)553-6648
Website: http://www.abnequity.com

Alpha Capital Partners, Ltd.
122 S Michigan Ave., Ste. 1700
Chicago, IL 60603
(312)322-9800
Fax: (312)322-9808
E-mail: acp@alphacapital.com

Ameritech Development Corp.
30 S Wacker Dr., 37th Fl.
Chicago, IL 60606
(312)750-5083
Fax: (312)609-0244

Apex Investment Partners
225 W Washington, Ste. 1450
Chicago, IL 60606
(312)857-2800
Fax: (312)857-1800
E-mail: apex@apexvc.com
Website: http://www.apexvc.com

Arch Venture Partners
8725 W Higgins Rd., Ste. 290
Chicago, IL 60631
(773)380-6600
Fax: (773)380-6606
Website: http://www.archventure.com

The Bank Funds
208 South LaSalle St., Ste. 1680
Chicago, IL 60604
(312)855-6020
Fax: (312)855-8910

Batterson Venture Partners
303 W Madison St., Ste. 1110
Chicago, IL 60606-3309
(312)269-0300
Fax: (312)269-0021
Website: http://www.battersonvp.com

William Blair Capital Partners, L.L.C.
222 W Adams St., Ste. 1300
Chicago, IL 60606
(312)364-8250
Fax: (312)236-1042
E-mail: privateequity@wmblair.com
Website: http://www.wmblair.com

Bluestar Ventures
208 South LaSalle St., Ste. 1020
Chicago, IL 60604
(312)384-5000
Fax: (312)384-5005
Website: http://www.bluestarventures.com

The Capital Strategy Management Co.
233 S Wacker Dr.
Box 06334
Chicago, IL 60606
(312)444-1170

DN Partners
77 West Wacker Dr., Ste. 4550
Chicago, IL 60601
(312)332-7960
Fax: (312)332-7979

Dresner Capital Inc.
29 South LaSalle St., Ste. 310
Chicago, IL 60603
(312)726-3600
Fax: (312)726-7448

Eblast Ventures LLC
11 South LaSalle St., 5th Fl.
Chicago, IL 60603
(312)372-2600
Fax: (312)372-5621
Website: http://www.eblastventures.com

Essex Woodlands Health Ventures, L.P.
190 S LaSalle St., Ste. 2800
Chicago, IL 60603
(312)444-6040
Fax: (312)444-6034
Website: http://www.essexwoodlands.com

First Analysis Venture Capital
233 S Wacker Dr., Ste. 9500
Chicago, IL 60606
(312)258-1400
Fax: (312)258-0334
Website: http://www.firstanalysis.com

Frontenac Co.
135 S LaSalle St., Ste.3800
Chicago, IL 60603
(312)368-0044

Fax: (312)368-9520
Website: http://www.frontenac.com

GTCR Golder Rauner, LLC
6100 Sears Tower
Chicago, IL 60606
(312)382-2200
Fax: (312)382-2201
Website: http://www.gtcr.com

High Street Capital LLC
311 South Wacker Dr., Ste. 4550
Chicago, IL 60606
(312)697-4990
Fax: (312)697-4994
Website: http://www.highstr.com

IEG Venture Management, Inc.
70 West Madison
Chicago, IL 60602
(312)644-0890
Fax: (312)454-0369
Website: http://www.iegventure.com

JK&B Capital
180 North Stetson, Ste. 4500
Chicago, IL 60601
(312)946-1200
Fax: (312)946-1103
E-mail: gspencer@jkbcapital.com
Website: http://www.jkbcapital.com

Kettle Partners L.P.
350 W Hubbard, Ste. 350
Chicago, IL 60610
(312)329-9300
Fax: (312)527-4519
Website: http://www.kettlevc.com

Lake Shore Capital Partners
20 N. Wacker Dr., Ste. 2807
Chicago, IL 60606
(312)803-3536
Fax: (312)803-3534

LaSalle Capital Group Inc.
70 W Madison St., Ste. 5710
Chicago, IL 60602
(312)236-7041
Fax: (312)236-0720

Linc Capital, Inc.
303 E Wacker Pkwy., Ste. 1000
Chicago, IL 60601
(312)946-2670
Fax: (312)938-4290
E-mail: bdemars@linccap.com

Madison Dearborn Partners, Inc.
3 First National Plz., Ste. 3800
Chicago, IL 60602
(312)895-1000
Fax: (312)895-1001
E-mail: invest@mdcp.com
Website: http://www.mdcp.com

Mesirow Private Equity Investments Inc.
350 N. Clark St.
Chicago, IL 60610
(312)595-6950
Fax: (312)595-6211
Website: http://
www.meisrowfinancial.com

Mosaix Ventures LLC
1822 North Mohawk
Chicago, IL 60614
(312)274-0988
Fax: (312)274-0989
Website: http://www.mosaixventures.com

Nesbitt Burns
111 West Monroe St.
Chicago, IL 60603
(312)416-3855
Fax: (312)765-8000
Website: http://www.harrisbank.com

Polestar Capital, Inc.
180 N. Michigan Ave., Ste. 1905
Chicago, IL 60601
(312)984-9090
Fax: (312)984-9877
E-mail: wl@polestarvc.com
Website: http://www.polestarvc.com

Prince Ventures (Chicago)
10 S Wacker Dr., Ste. 2575
Chicago, IL 60606-7407
(312)454-1408
Fax: (312)454-9125

Prism Capital
444 N. Michigan Ave.
Chicago, IL 60611
(312)464-7900
Fax: (312)464-7915
Website: http://www.prismfund.com

Third Coast Capital
900 N. Franklin St., Ste. 700
Chicago, IL 60610
(312)337-3303
Fax: (312)337-2567
E-mail: manic@earthlink.com
Website: http://
www.thirdcoastcapital.com

Thoma Cressey Equity Partners
4460 Sears Tower, 92nd Fl.
233 S Wacker Dr.
Chicago, IL 60606
(312)777-4444
Fax: (312)777-4445
Website: http://www.thomacressey.com

Tribune Ventures
435 N. Michigan Ave., Ste. 600
Chicago, IL 60611
(312)527-8797
Fax: (312)222-5993
Website: http://
www.tribuneventures.com

Wind Point Partners (Chicago)
676 N. Michigan Ave., Ste. 330
Chicago, IL 60611
(312)649-4000
Website: http://www.wppartners.com

Marquette Venture Partners
520 Lake Cook Rd., Ste. 450
Deerfield, IL 60015
(847)940-1700
Fax: (847)940-1724
Website: http://www.marquetteventures
.com

Duchossois Investments Limited, LLC
845 Larch Ave.
Elmhurst, IL 60126
(630)530-6105
Fax: (630)993-8644
Website: http://www.duchtec.com

Evanston Business Investment Corp.
1840 Oak Ave.
Evanston, IL 60201
(847)866-1840
Fax: (847)866-1808
E-mail: t-parkinson@nwu.com
Website: http://www.ebic.com

Inroads Capital Partners L.P.
1603 Orrington Ave., Ste. 2050
Evanston, IL 60201-3841
(847)864-2000
Fax: (847)864-9692

The Cerulean Fund/WGC Enterprises
1701 E Lake Ave., Ste. 170
Glenview, IL 60025
(847)657-8002
Fax: (847)657-8168

Ventana Financial Resources, Inc.
249 Market Sq.
Lake Forest, IL 60045
(847)234-3434

Beecken, Petty & Co.
901 Warrenville Rd., Ste. 205
Lisle, IL 60532
(630)435-0300
Fax: (630)435-0370
E-mail: hep@bpcompany.com
Website: http://www.bpcompany.com

Allstate Private Equity
3075 Sanders Rd., Ste. G5D
Northbrook, IL 60062-7127
(847)402-8247
Fax: (847)402-0880

KB Partners
1101 Skokie Blvd., Ste. 260
Northbrook, IL 60062-2856
(847)714-0444
Fax: (847)714-0445
E-mail: keith@kbpartners.com
Website: http://www.kbpartners.com

Transcap Associates Inc.
900 Skokie Blvd., Ste. 210
Northbrook, IL 60062
(847)753-9600
Fax: (847)753-9090

Graystone Venture Partners, L.L.C. / Portage Venture Partners
One Northfield Plaza, Ste. 530
Northfield, IL 60093
(847)446-9460
Fax: (847)446-9470
Website: http://www.portageventures.com

Motorola Inc.
1303 E Algonquin Rd.
Schaumburg, IL 60196-1065
(847)576-4929
Fax: (847)538-2250
Website: http://www.mot.com/mne

Indiana

Irwin Ventures LLC
500 Washington St.
Columbus, IN 47202
(812)373-1434
Fax: (812)376-1709
Website: http://www.irwinventures.com

Cambridge Venture Partners
4181 East 96th St., Ste. 200
Indianapolis, IN 46240
(317)814-6192
Fax: (317)944-9815

CID Equity Partners
One American Square, Ste. 2850
Box 82074
Indianapolis, IN 46282
(317)269-2350
Fax: (317)269-2355
Website: http://www.cidequity.com

Gazelle Techventures
6325 Digital Way, Ste. 460
Indianapolis, IN 46278
(317)275-6800
Fax: (317)275-1101
Website: http://www.gazellevc.com

Monument Advisors Inc.
Bank One Center/Circle
111 Monument Circle, Ste. 600
Indianapolis, IN 46204-5172
(317)656-5065
Fax: (317)656-5060
Website: http://www.monumentadv.com

MWV Capital Partners
201 N. Illinois St., Ste. 300
Indianapolis, IN 46204
(317)237-2323
Fax: (317)237-2325
Website: http://www.mwvcapital.com

First Source Capital Corp.
100 North Michigan St.
PO Box 1602
South Bend, IN 46601
(219)235-2180
Fax: (219)235-2227

Iowa

Allsop Venture Partners
118 Third Ave. SE, Ste. 837
Cedar Rapids, IA 52401
(319)368-6675
Fax: (319)363-9515

InvestAmerica Investment Advisors, Inc.
101 2nd St. SE, Ste. 800
Cedar Rapids, IA 52401
(319)363-8249
Fax: (319)363-9683

Pappajohn Capital Resources
2116 Financial Center
Des Moines, IA 50309
(515)244-5746
Fax: (515)244-2346
Website: http://www.pappajohn.com

Berthel Fisher & Company Planning Inc.
701 Tama St.
PO Box 609
Marion, IA 52302
(319)497-5700
Fax: (319)497-4244

Kansas

Enterprise Merchant Bank
7400 West 110th St., Ste. 560
Overland Park, KS 66210
(913)327-8500
Fax: (913)327-8505

Kansas Venture Capital, Inc. (Overland Park)
6700 Antioch Plz., Ste. 460
Overland Park, KS 66204
(913)262-7117
Fax: (913)262-3509
E-mail: jdalton@kvci.com

Child Health Investment Corp.
6803 W 64th St., Ste. 208
Shawnee Mission, KS 66202
(913)262-1436
Fax: (913)262-1575
Website: http://www.chca.com

Kansas Technology Enterprise Corp.
214 SW 6th, 1st Fl.
Topeka, KS 66603-3719
(785)296-5272
Fax: (785)296-1160
E-mail: ktec@ktec.com
Website: http://www.ktec.com

Kentucky

Kentucky Highlands Investment Corp.
362 Old Whitley Rd.
London, KY 40741
(606)864-5175
Fax: (606)864-5194
Website: http://www.khic.org

Chrysalis Ventures, L.L.C.
1850 National City Tower
Louisville, KY 40202
(502)583-7644
Fax: (502)583-7648
E-mail: bobsany@chrysalisventures.com
Website: http://www.chrysalisventures.com

Humana Venture Capital
500 West Main St.
Louisville, KY 40202
(502)580-3922
Fax: (502)580-2051
E-mail: gemont@humana.com
George Emont, Director

Summit Capital Group, Inc.
6510 Glenridge Park Pl., Ste. 8
Louisville, KY 40222
(502)332-2700

Louisiana

Bank One Equity Investors, Inc.
451 Florida St.
Baton Rouge, LA 70801
(504)332-4421
Fax: (504)332-7377

Advantage Capital Partners
LLE Tower
909 Poydras St., Ste. 2230
New Orleans, LA 70112
(504)522-4850
Fax: (504)522-4950
Website: http://www.advantagecap.com

Maine

CEI Ventures / Coastal Ventures LP
2 Portland Fish Pier, Ste. 201
Portland, ME 04101
(207)772-5356
Fax: (207)772-5503
Website: http://www.ceiventures.com

Commwealth Bioventures, Inc.
4 Milk St.
Portland, ME 04101
(207)780-0904
Fax: (207)780-0913

Maryland

Annapolis Ventures LLC
151 West St., Ste. 302
Annapolis, MD 21401
(443)482-9555
Fax: (443)482-9565
Website: http://www.annapolisventures.com

Delmag Ventures
220 Wardour Dr.
Annapolis, MD 21401
(410)267-8196
Fax: (410)267-8017
Website: http://www.delmagventures.com

Abell Venture Fund
111 S Calvert St., Ste. 2300
Baltimore, MD 21202
(410)547-1300
Fax: (410)539-6579
Website: http://www.abell.org

ABS Ventures (Baltimore)
1 South St., Ste. 2150
Baltimore, MD 21202
(410)895-3895
Fax: (410)895-3899
Website: http://www.absventures.com

Anthem Capital, L.P.
16 S Calvert St., Ste. 800
Baltimore, MD 21202-1305
(410)625-1510
Fax: (410)625-1735
Website: http://www.anthemcapital.com

Catalyst Ventures
1119 St. Paul St.
Baltimore, MD 21202
(410)244-0123
Fax: (410)752-7721

Maryland Venture Capital Trust
217 E Redwood St., Ste. 2200
Baltimore, MD 21202
(410)767-6361
Fax: (410)333-6931

New Enterprise Associates (Baltimore)
1119 St. Paul St.
Baltimore, MD 21202
(410)244-0115
Fax: (410)752-7721
Website: http://www.nea.com

T. Rowe Price Threshold Partnerships
100 E Pratt St., 8th Fl.
Baltimore, MD 21202
(410)345-2000
Fax: (410)345-2800

Spring Capital Partners
16 W Madison St.
Baltimore, MD 21201
(410)685-8000
Fax: (410)727-1436
E-mail: mailbox@springcap.com

Arete Corporation
3 Bethesda Metro Ctr., Ste. 770
Bethesda, MD 20814
(301)657-6268
Fax: (301)657-6254
Website: http://www.arete-microgen.com

Embryon Capital
7903 Sleaford Place
Bethesda, MD 20814
(301)656-6837
Fax: (301)656-8056

Potomac Ventures
7920 Norfolk Ave., Ste. 1100
Bethesda, MD 20814
(301)215-9240
Website: http://www.potomacventures.com

Toucan Capital Corp.
3 Bethesda Metro Center, Ste. 700
Bethesda, MD 20814
(301)961-1970
Fax: (301)961-1969
Website: http://www.toucancapital.com

Kinetic Ventures LLC
2 Wisconsin Cir., Ste. 620
Chevy Chase, MD 20815
(301)652-8066
Fax: (301)652-8310
Website: http://www.kineticventures.com

Boulder Ventures Ltd.
4750 Owings Mills Blvd.
Owings Mills, MD 21117
(410)998-3114
Fax: (410)356-5492
Website: http://www.boulderventures.com

Grotech Capital Group
9690 Deereco Rd., Ste. 800
Timonium, MD 21093
(410)560-2000
Fax: (410)560-1910
Website: http://www.grotech.com

Massachusetts

Adams, Harkness & Hill, Inc.
60 State St.
Boston, MA 02109
(617)371-3900

Advent International
75 State St., 29th Fl.
Boston, MA 02109
(617)951-9400
Fax: (617)951-0566
Website: http://www.adventinernational.com

American Research and Development
30 Federal St.
Boston, MA 02110-2508
(617)423-7500
Fax: (617)423-9655

Ascent Venture Partners
255 State St., 5th Fl.
Boston, MA 02109
(617)270-9400
Fax: (617)270-9401
E-mail: info@ascentvp.com
Website: http://www.ascentvp.com

Atlas Venture
222 Berkeley St.
Boston, MA 02116
(617)488-2200
Fax: (617)859-9292
Website: http://www.atlasventure.com

Axxon Capital
28 State St., 37th Fl.
Boston, MA 02109
(617)722-0980
Fax: (617)557-6014
Website: http://www.axxoncapital.com

BancBoston Capital/BancBoston Ventures
175 Federal St., 10th Fl.
Boston, MA 02110
(617)434-2509
Fax: (617)434-6175
Website: http://www.bancbostoncapital.com

Boston Capital Ventures
Old City Hall
45 School St.
Boston, MA 02108
(617)227-6550
Fax: (617)227-3847
E-mail: info@bcv.com
Website: http://www.bcv.com

Boston Financial & Equity Corp.
20 Overland St.
PO Box 15071
Boston, MA 02215
(617)267-2900
Fax: (617)437-7601
E-mail: debbie@bfec.com

Boston Millennia Partners
30 Rowes Wharf
Boston, MA 02110
(617)428-5150
Fax: (617)428-5160
Website: http://www.millenniapartners.com

Bristol Investment Trust
842A Beacon St.
Boston, MA 02215-3199
(617)566-5212
Fax: (617)267-0932

Brook Venture Management LLC
50 Federal St., 5th Fl.
Boston, MA 02110
(617)451-8989
Fax: (617)451-2369
Website: http://www.brookventure.com

Burr, Egan, Deleage, and Co. (Boston)
200 Clarendon St., Ste. 3800
Boston, MA 02116
(617)262-7770
Fax: (617)262-9779

Cambridge/Samsung Partners
One Exeter Plaza
Ninth Fl.
Boston, MA 02116
(617)262-4440
Fax: (617)262-5562

Chestnut Street Partners, Inc.
75 State St., Ste. 2500
Boston, MA 02109
(617)345-7220
Fax: (617)345-7201
E-mail: chestnut@chestnutp.com

Claflin Capital Management, Inc.
10 Liberty Sq., Ste. 300
Boston, MA 02109
(617)426-6505
Fax: (617)482-0016
Website: http://www.claflincapital.com

Copley Venture Partners
99 Summer St., Ste. 1720
Boston, MA 02110
(617)737-1253
Fax: (617)439-0699

Corning Capital / Corning Technology Ventures
121 High Street, Ste. 400
Boston, MA 02110
(617)338-2656
Fax: (617)261-3864
Website: http://www.corningventures.com

Downer & Co.
211 Congress St.
Boston, MA 02110
(617)482-6200
Fax: (617)482-6201
E-mail: cdowner@downer.com
Website: http://www.downer.com

Fidelity Ventures
82 Devonshire St.
Boston, MA 02109
(617)563-6370
Fax: (617)476-9023
Website: http://www.fidelityventures.com

Greylock Management Corp. (Boston)
1 Federal St.
Boston, MA 02110-2065
(617)423-5525
Fax: (617)482-0059

Gryphon Ventures
222 Berkeley St., Ste.1600
Boston, MA 02116
(617)267-9191
Fax: (617)267-4293
E-mail: all@gryphoninc.com

Halpern, Denny & Co.
500 Boylston St.
Boston, MA 02116
(617)536-6602
Fax: (617)536-8535

Harbourvest Partners, LLC
1 Financial Center, 44th Fl.
Boston, MA 02111
(617)348-3707
Fax: (617)350-0305
Website: http://www.hvpllc.com

Highland Capital Partners
2 International Pl.
Boston, MA 02110
(617)981-1500
Fax: (617)531-1550
E-mail: info@hcp.com
Website: http://www.hcp.com

Lee Munder Venture Partners
John Hancock Tower T-53
200 Clarendon St.
Boston, MA 02103
(617)380-5600
Fax: (617)380-5601
Website: http://www.leemunder.com

M/C Venture Partners
75 State St., Ste. 2500
Boston, MA 02109
(617)345-7200
Fax: (617)345-7201
Website: http://www.mcventurepartners.com

Massachusetts Capital Resources Co.
420 Boylston St.
Boston, MA 02116
(617)536-3900
Fax: (617)536-7930

Massachusetts Technology Development Corp. (MTDC)
148 State St.
Boston, MA 02109
(617)723-4920
Fax: (617)723-5983
E-mail: jhodgman@mtdc.com
Website: http://www.mtdc.com

New England Partners
One Boston Place, Ste. 2100
Boston, MA 02108
(617)624-8400
Fax: (617)624-8999
Website: http://www.nepartners.com

North Hill Ventures
Ten Post Office Square
11th Fl.
Boston, MA 02109
(617)788-2112
Fax: (617)788-2152
Website: http://www.northhillventures.com

OneLiberty Ventures
150 Cambridge Park Dr.
Boston, MA 02140
(617)492-7280
Fax: (617)492-7290
Website: http://www.oneliberty.com

Schroder Ventures
Life Sciences
60 State St., Ste. 3650
Boston, MA 02109
(617)367-8100
Fax: (617)367-1590
Website: http://
www.shroderventures.com

Shawmut Capital Partners
75 Federal St., 18th Fl.
Boston, MA 02110
(617)368-4900
Fax: (617)368-4910
Website: http://www.shawmutcapital.com

Solstice Capital LLC
15 Broad St., 3rd Fl.
Boston, MA 02109
(617)523-7733
Fax: (617)523-5827
E-mail: solticecapital@solcap.com

Spectrum Equity Investors
One International Pl., 29th Fl.
Boston, MA 02110
(617)464-4600
Fax: (617)464-4601
Website: http://
www.spectrumequity.com

Spray Venture Partners
One Walnut St.
Boston, MA 02108
(617)305-4140
Fax: (617)305-4144
Website: http://www.sprayventure.com

The Still River Fund
100 Federal St., 29th Fl.
Boston, MA 02110
(617)348-2327
Fax: (617)348-2371
Website: http://www.stillriverfund.com

Summit Partners
600 Atlantic Ave., Ste. 2800
Boston, MA 02210-2227
(617)824-1000
Fax: (617)824-1159
Website: http://www.summitpartners.com

TA Associates, Inc. (Boston)
High Street Tower
125 High St., Ste. 2500
Boston, MA 02110
(617)574-6700
Fax: (617)574-6728
Website: http://www.ta.com

TVM Techno Venture Management
101 Arch St., Ste. 1950
Boston, MA 02110
(617)345-9320
Fax: (617)345-9377
E-mail: info@tvmvc.com
Website: http://www.tvmvc.com

UNC Ventures
64 Burough St.
Boston, MA 02130-4017
(617)482-7070
Fax: (617)522-2176

Venture Investment Management Company (VIMAC)
177 Milk St.
Boston, MA 02190-3410
(617)292-3300
Fax: (617)292-7979
E-mail: bzeisig@vimac.com
Website: http://www.vimac.com

MDT Advisers, Inc.
125 Cambridge Park Dr.
Cambridge, MA 02140-2314
(617)234-2200
Fax: (617)234-2210
Website: http://www.mdtai.com

TTC Ventures
One Main St., 6th Fl.
Cambridge, MA 02142
(617)528-3137
Fax: (617)577-1715
E-mail: info@ttcventures.com

Zero Stage Capital Co. Inc.
101 Main St., 17th Fl.
Cambridge, MA 02142
(617)876-5355
Fax: (617)876-1248
Website: http://www.zerostage.com

Atlantic Capital
164 Cushing Hwy.
Cohasset, MA 02025
(617)383-9449
Fax: (617)383-6040
E-mail: info@atlanticcap.com
Website: http://www.atlanticcap.com

Seacoast Capital Partners
55 Ferncroft Rd.
Danvers, MA 01923
(978)750-1300
Fax: (978)750-1301
E-mail: gdeli@seacoastcapital.com
Website: http://www.seacoastcapital.com

Sage Management Group
44 South Street
PO Box 2026
East Dennis, MA 02641
(508)385-7172
Fax: (508)385-7272
E-mail: sagemgt@capecod.net

Applied Technology
1 Cranberry Hill
Lexington, MA 02421-7397
(617)862-8622
Fax: (617)862-8367

Royalty Capital Management
5 Downing Rd.
Lexington, MA 02421-6918
(781)861-8490

Argo Global Capital
210 Broadway, Ste. 101
Lynnfield, MA 01940
(781)592-5250
Fax: (781)592-5230
Website: http://www.gsmcapital.com

Industry Ventures
6 Bayne Lane
Newburyport, MA 01950
(978)499-7606
Fax: (978)499-0686
Website: http://
www.industryventures.com

Softbank Capital Partners
10 Langley Rd., Ste. 202
Newton Center, MA 02459
(617)928-9300
Fax: (617)928-9305
E-mail: clax@bvc.com

Advanced Technology Ventures (Boston)
281 Winter St., Ste. 350
Waltham, MA 02451
(781)290-0707
Fax: (781)684-0045
E-mail: info@atvcapital.com
Website: http://www.atvcapital.com

Castile Ventures
890 Winter St., Ste. 140
Waltham, MA 02451
(781)890-0060
Fax: (781)890-0065
Website: http://www.castileventures.com

Charles River Ventures
1000 Winter St., Ste. 3300
Waltham, MA 02451

(781)487-7060
Fax: (781)487-7065
Website: http://www.crv.com

Comdisco Venture Group (Waltham)
Totton Pond Office Center
400-1 Totten Pond Rd.
Waltham, MA 02451
(617)672-0250
Fax: (617)398-8099

Marconi Ventures
890 Winter St., Ste. 310
Waltham, MA 02451
(781)839-7177
Fax: (781)522-7477
Website: http://www.marconi.com

Matrix Partners
Bay Colony Corporate Center
1000 Winter St., Ste.4500
Waltham, MA 02451
(781)890-2244
Fax: (781)890-2288
Website: http://www.matrixpartners.com

North Bridge Venture Partners
950 Winter St. Ste. 4600
Waltham, MA 02451
(781)290-0004
Fax: (781)290-0999
E-mail: eta@nbvp.com

Polaris Venture Partners
Bay Colony Corporate Ctr.
1000 Winter St., Ste. 3500
Waltham, MA 02451
(781)290-0770
Fax: (781)290-0880
E-mail: partners@polarisventures.com
Website: http://
www.polarisventures.com

Seaflower Ventures
Bay Colony Corporate Ctr.
1000 Winter St. Ste. 1000
Waltham, MA 02451
(781)466-9552
Fax: (781)466-9553
E-mail: moot@seaflower.com
Website: http://www.seaflower.com

Ampersand Ventures
55 William St., Ste. 240
Wellesley, MA 02481
(617)239-0700
Fax: (617)239-0824
E-mail: info@ampersandventures.com
Website: http://www.ampersandventures
.com

Battery Ventures (Boston)
20 William St., Ste. 200
Wellesley, MA 02481
(781)577-1000
Fax: (781)577-1001
Website: http://www.battery.com

Commonwealth Capital Ventures, L.P.
20 William St., Ste.225
Wellesley, MA 02481
(781)237-7373
Fax: (781)235-8627
Website: http://www.ccvlp.com

Fowler, Anthony & Company
20 Walnut St.
Wellesley, MA 02481
(781)237-4201
Fax: (781)237-7718

Gemini Investors
20 William St.
Wellesley, MA 02481
(781)237-7001
Fax: (781)237-7233

Grove Street Advisors Inc.
20 William St., Ste. 230
Wellesley, MA 02481
(781)263-6100
Fax: (781)263-6101
Website: http://
www.grovestreetadvisors.com

Mees Pierson Investeringsmaat B.V.
20 William St., Ste. 210
Wellesley, MA 02482
(781)239-7600
Fax: (781)239-0377

Norwest Equity Partners
40 William St., Ste. 305
Wellesley, MA 02481-3902
(781)237-5870
Fax: (781)237-6270
Website: http://www.norwestvp.com

Bessemer Venture Partners (Wellesley Hills)
83 Walnut St.
Wellesley Hills, MA 02481
(781)237-6050
Fax: (781)235-7576
E-mail: travis@bvpny.com
Website: http://www.bvp.com

Venture Capital Fund of New England
20 Walnut St., Ste. 120
Wellesley Hills, MA 02481-2175
(781)239-8262
Fax: (781)239-8263

Prism Venture Partners
100 Lowder Brook Dr., Ste. 2500
Westwood, MA 02090
(781)302-4000
Fax: (781)302-4040
E-mail: dwbaum@prismventure.com

Palmer Partners LP
200 Unicorn Park Dr.
Woburn, MA 01801
(781)933-5445
Fax: (781)933-0698

Michigan

Arbor Partners, L.L.C.
130 South First St.
Ann Arbor, MI 48104
(734)668-9000
Fax: (734)669-4195
Website: http://www.arborpartners.com

EDF Ventures
425 N. Main St.
Ann Arbor, MI 48104
(734)663-3213
Fax: (734)663-7358
E-mail: edf@edfvc.com
Website: http://www.edfvc.com

White Pines Management, L.L.C.
2401 Plymouth Rd., Ste. B
Ann Arbor, MI 48105
(734)747-9401
Fax: (734)747-9704
E-mail: ibund@whitepines.com
Website: http://www.whitepines.com

Wellmax, Inc.
3541 Bendway Blvd., Ste. 100
Bloomfield Hills, MI 48301
(248)646-3554
Fax: (248)646-6220

Venture Funding, Ltd.
Fisher Bldg.
3011 West Grand Blvd., Ste. 321
Detroit, MI 48202
(313)871-3606
Fax: (313)873-4935

Investcare Partners L.P. / GMA Capital LLC
32330 W Twelve Mile Rd.
Farmington Hills, MI 48334
(248)489-9000
Fax: (248)489-8819
E-mail: gma@gmacapital.com
Website: http://www.gmacapital.com

Liberty Bidco Investment Corp.
30833 Northwestern Highway, Ste. 211
Farmington Hills, MI 48334

(248)626-6070
Fax: (248)626-6072

Seaflower Ventures
5170 Nicholson Rd.
PO Box 474
Fowlerville, MI 48836
(517)223-3335
Fax: (517)223-3337
E-mail: gibbons@seaflower.com
Website: http://www.seaflower.com

Ralph Wilson Equity Fund LLC
15400 E Jefferson Ave.
Gross Pointe Park, MI 48230
(313)821-9122
Fax: (313)821-9101
Website: http://
www.RalphWilsonEquityFund.com
J. Skip Simms, President

Minnesota

Development Corp. of Austin
1900 Eighth Ave., NW
Austin, MN 55912
(507)433-0346
Fax: (507)433-0361
E-mail: dca@smig.net
Website: http://www.spamtownusa.com

Northeast Ventures Corp.
802 Alworth Bldg.
Duluth, MN 55802
(218)722-9915
Fax: (218)722-9871

Medical Innovation Partners, Inc.
6450 City West Pkwy.
Eden Prairie, MN 55344-3245
(612)828-9616
Fax: (612)828-9596

St. Paul Venture Capital, Inc.
10400 Vicking Dr., Ste. 550
Eden Prairie, MN 55344
(612)995-7474
Fax: (612)995-7475
Website: http://www.stpaulvc.com

Cherry Tree Investments, Inc.
7601 France Ave. S, Ste. 150
Edina, MN 55435
(612)893-9012
Fax: (612)893-9036
Website: http://www.cherrytree.com

Shared Ventures, Inc.
6550 York Ave. S
Edina, MN 55435
(612)925-3411

Sherpa Partners LLC
5050 Lincoln Dr., Ste. 490
Edina, MN 55436
(952)942-1070
Fax: (952)942-1071
Website: http://www.sherpapartners.com

Affinity Capital Management
901 Marquette Ave., Ste. 1810
Minneapolis, MN 55402
(612)252-9900
Fax: (612)252-9911
Website: http://www.affinitycapital.com

Artesian Capital
1700 Foshay Tower
821 Marquette Ave.
Minneapolis, MN 55402
(612)334-5600
Fax: (612)334-5601
E-mail: artesian@artesian.com

Coral Ventures
60 S 6th St., Ste. 3510
Minneapolis, MN 55402
(612)335-8666
Fax: (612)335-8668
Website: http://www.coralventures.com

Crescendo Venture Management, L.L.C.
800 LaSalle Ave., Ste. 2250
Minneapolis, MN 55402
(612)607-2800
Fax: (612)607-2801
Website: http://
www.crescendoventures.com

Gideon Hixon Venture
1900 Foshay Tower
821 Marquette Ave.
Minneapolis, MN 55402
(612)904-2314
Fax: (612)204-0913

Norwest Equity Partners
3600 IDS Center
80 S 8th St.
Minneapolis, MN 55402
(612)215-1600
Fax: (612)215-1601
Website: http://www.norwestvp.com

Oak Investment Partners (Minneapolis)
4550 Norwest Center
90 S 7th St.
Minneapolis, MN 55402
(612)339-9322
Fax: (612)337-8017
Website: http://www.oakinv.com

Pathfinder Venture Capital Funds (Minneapolis)
7300 Metro Blvd., Ste. 585
Minneapolis, MN 55439
(612)835-1121
Fax: (612)835-8389
E-mail: jahrens620@aol.com

U.S. Bancorp Piper Jaffray Ventures, Inc.
800 Nicollet Mall, Ste. 800
Minneapolis, MN 55402
(612)303-5686
Fax: (612)303-1350
Website: http://
www.paperjaffreyventures.com

The Food Fund, Ltd. Partnership
5720 Smatana Dr., Ste. 300
Minnetonka, MN 55343
(612)939-3950
Fax: (612)939-8106

Mayo Medical Ventures
200 First St. SW
Rochester, MN 55905
(507)266-4586
Fax: (507)284-5410
Website: http://www.mayo.edu

Missouri

Bankers Capital Corp.
3100 Gillham Rd.
Kansas City, MO 64109
(816)531-1600
Fax: (816)531-1334

Capital for Business, Inc. (Kansas City)
1000 Walnut St., 18th Fl.
Kansas City, MO 64106
(816)234-2357
Fax: (816)234-2952
Website: http://
www.capitalforbusiness.com

De Vries & Co. Inc.
800 West 47th St.
Kansas City, MO 64112
(816)756-0055
Fax: (816)756-0061

InvestAmerica Venture Group Inc. (Kansas City)
Commerce Tower
911 Main St., Ste. 2424
Kansas City, MO 64105
(816)842-0114
Fax: (816)471-7339

Kansas City Equity Partners
233 W 47th St.
Kansas City, MO 64112

(816)960-1771
Fax: (816)960-1777
Website: http://www.kcep.com

Bome Investors, Inc.
8000 Maryland Ave., Ste. 1190
Saint Louis, MO 63105
(314)721-5707
Fax: (314)721-5135
Website: http://www.gatewayventures.com

Capital for Business, Inc. (Saint Louis)
11 S Meramac St., Ste. 1430
Saint Louis, MO 63105
(314)746-7427
Fax: (314)746-8739
Website: http://
www.capitalforbusiness.com

Crown Capital Corp.
540 Maryville Centre Dr., Ste. 120
Saint Louis, MO 63141
(314)576-1201
Fax: (314)576-1525
Website: http://www.crown-cap.com

Gateway Associates L.P.
8000 Maryland Ave., Ste. 1190
Saint Louis, MO 63105
(314)721-5707
Fax: (314)721-5135

Harbison Corp.
8112 Maryland Ave., Ste. 250
Saint Louis, MO 63105
(314)727-8200
Fax: (314)727-0249

Nebraska

Heartland Capital Fund, Ltd.
PO Box 642117
Omaha, NE 68154
(402)778-5124
Fax: (402)445-2370
Website: http://
www.heartlandcapitalfund.com

Odin Capital Group
1625 Farnam St., Ste. 700
Omaha, NE 68102
(402)346-6200
Fax: (402)342-9311
Website: http://www.odincapital.com

Nevada

Edge Capital Investment Co. LLC
1350 E Flamingo Rd., Ste. 3000
Las Vegas, NV 89119
(702)438-3343
E-mail: info@edgecapital.net
Website: http://www.edgecapital.net

The Benefit Capital Companies Inc.
PO Box 542
Logandale, NV 89021
(702)398-3222
Fax: (702)398-3700

Millennium Three Venture Group LLC
6880 South McCarran Blvd., Ste. A-11
Reno, NV 89509
(775)954-2020
Fax: (775)954-2023
Website: http://www.m3vg.com

New Jersey

Alan I. Goldman & Associates
497 Ridgewood Ave.
Glen Ridge, NJ 07028
(973)857-5680
Fax: (973)509-8856

CS Capital Partners LLC
328 Second St., Ste. 200
Lakewood, NJ 08701
(732)901-1111
Fax: (212)202-5071
Website: http://www.cs-capital.com

Edison Venture Fund
1009 Lenox Dr., Ste. 4
Lawrenceville, NJ 08648
(609)896-1900
Fax: (609)896-0066
E-mail: info@edisonventure.com
Website: http://www.edisonventure.com

Tappan Zee Capital Corp. (New Jersey)
201 Lower Notch Rd.
PO Box 416
Little Falls, NJ 07424
(973)256-8280
Fax: (973)256-2841

The CIT Group/Venture Capital, Inc.
650 CIT Dr.
Livingston, NJ 07039
(973)740-5429
Fax: (973)740-5555
Website: http://www.cit.com

Capital Express, L.L.C.
1100 Valleybrook Ave.
Lyndhurst, NJ 07071
(201)438-8228
Fax: (201)438-5131
E-mail: niles@capitalexpress.com
Website: http://www.capitalexpress.com

Westford Technology Ventures, L.P.
17 Academy St.
Newark, NJ 07102
(973)624-2131
Fax: (973)624-2008

Accel Partners
1 Palmer Sq.
Princeton, NJ 08542
(609)683-4500
Fax: (609)683-4880
Website: http://www.accel.com

Cardinal Partners
221 Nassau St.
Princeton, NJ 08542
(609)924-6452
Fax: (609)683-0174
Website: http://www.cardinalhealth
partners.com

Domain Associates L.L.C.
One Palmer Sq., Ste. 515
Princeton, NJ 08542
(609)683-5656
Fax: (609)683-9789
Website: http://www.domainvc.com

Johnston Associates, Inc.
181 Cherry Valley Rd.
Princeton, NJ 08540
(609)924-3131
Fax: (609)683-7524
E-mail: jaincorp@aol.com

Kemper Ventures
Princeton Forrestal Village
155 Village Blvd.
Princeton, NJ 08540
(609)936-3035
Fax: (609)936-3051

Penny Lane Parnters
One Palmer Sq., Ste. 309
Princeton, NJ 08542
(609)497-4646
Fax: (609)497-0611

Early Stage Enterprises L.P.
995 Route 518
Skillman, NJ 08558
(609)921-8896
Fax: (609)921-8703
Website: http://www.esevc.com

MBW Management Inc.
1 Springfield Ave.
Summit, NJ 07901
(908)273-4060
Fax: (908)273-4430

BCI Advisors, Inc.
Glenpointe Center W.
Teaneck, NJ 07666
(201)836-3900
Fax: (201)836-6368
E-mail: info@bciadvisors.com
Website: http://www.bcipartners.com

Demuth, Folger & Wetherill / DFW Capital Partners
Glenpointe Center E., 5th Fl.
300 Frank W. Burr Blvd.
Teaneck, NJ 07666
(201)836-2233
Fax: (201)836-5666
Website: http://www.dfwcapital.com

First Princeton Capital Corp.
189 Berdan Ave., No. 131
Wayne, NJ 07470-3233
(973)278-3233
Fax: (973)278-4290
Website: http://www.lytellcatt.net

Edelson Technology Partners
300 Tice Blvd.
Woodcliff Lake, NJ 07675
(201)930-9898
Fax: (201)930-8899
Website: http://www.edelsontech.com

New Mexico

Bruce F. Glaspell & Associates
10400 Academy Rd. NE, Ste. 313
Albuquerque, NM 87111
(505)292-4505
Fax: (505)292-4258

High Desert Ventures, Inc.
6101 Imparata St. NE, Ste. 1721
Albuquerque, NM 87111
(505)797-3330
Fax: (505)338-5147

New Business Capital Fund, Ltd.
5805 Torreon NE
Albuquerque, NM 87109
(505)822-8445

SBC Ventures
10400 Academy Rd. NE, Ste. 313
Albuquerque, NM 87111
(505)292-4505
Fax: (505)292-4528

Technology Ventures Corp.
1155 University Blvd. SE
Albuquerque, NM 87106
(505)246-2882
Fax: (505)246-2891

New York

Small Business Technology Investment Fund
99 Washington Ave., Ste. 1731
Albany, NY 12210
(518)473-9741
Fax: (518)473-6876

Rand Capital Corp.
2200 Rand Bldg.
Buffalo, NY 14203
(716)853-0802
Fax: (716)854-8480
Website: http://www.randcapital.com

Seed Capital Partners
620 Main St.
Buffalo, NY 14202
(716)845-7520
Fax: (716)845-7539
Website: http://www.seedcp.com

Coleman Venture Group
5909 Northern Blvd.
PO Box 224
East Norwich, NY 11732
(516)626-3642
Fax: (516)626-9722

Vega Capital Corp.
45 Knollwood Rd.
Elmsford, NY 10523
(914)345-9500
Fax: (914)345-9505

Herbert Young Securities, Inc.
98 Cuttermill Rd.
Great Neck, NY 11021
(516)487-8300
Fax: (516)487-8319

Sterling/Carl Marks Capital, Inc.
175 Great Neck Rd., Ste. 408
Great Neck, NY 11021
(516)482-7374
Fax: (516)487-0781
E-mail: stercrlmar@aol.com
Website: http://www.serlingcarlmarks.com

Impex Venture Management Co.
PO Box 1570
Green Island, NY 12183
(518)271-8008
Fax: (518)271-9101

Corporate Venture Partners L.P.
200 Sunset Park
Ithaca, NY 14850
(607)257-6323
Fax: (607)257-6128

Arthur P. Gould & Co.
One Wilshire Dr.
Lake Success, NY 11020
(516)773-3000
Fax: (516)773-3289

Dauphin Capital Partners
108 Forest Ave.
Locust Valley, NY 11560
(516)759-3339
Fax: (516)759-3322
Website: http://www.dauphincapital.com

550 Digital Media Ventures
555 Madison Ave., 10th Fl.
New York, NY 10022
Website: http://www.550dmv.com

Aberlyn Capital Management Co., Inc.
500 Fifth Ave.
New York, NY 10110
(212)391-7750
Fax: (212)391-7762

Adler & Company
342 Madison Ave., Ste. 807
New York, NY 10173
(212)599-2535
Fax: (212)599-2526

Alimansky Capital Group, Inc.
605 Madison Ave., Ste. 300
New York, NY 10022-1901
(212)832-7300
Fax: (212)832-7338

Allegra Partners
515 Madison Ave., 29th Fl.
New York, NY 10022
(212)826-9080
Fax: (212)759-2561

The Argentum Group
The Chyrsler Bldg.
405 Lexington Ave.
New York, NY 10174
(212)949-6262
Fax: (212)949-8294
Website: http://www.argentumgroup.com

Axavision Inc.
14 Wall St., 26th Fl.
New York, NY 10005
(212)619-4000
Fax: (212)619-7202

Bedford Capital Corp.
18 East 48th St., Ste. 1800
New York, NY 10017
(212)688-5700
Fax: (212)754-4699
E-mail: info@bedfordnyc.com
Website: http://www.bedfordnyc.com

Bloom & Co.
950 Third Ave.
New York, NY 10022
(212)838-1858
Fax: (212)838-1843

Bristol Capital Management
300 Park Ave., 17th Fl.
New York, NY 10022
(212)572-6306
Fax: (212)705-4292

Citicorp Venture Capital Ltd. (New York City)
399 Park Ave., 14th Fl.
Zone 4
New York, NY 10043
(212)559-1127
Fax: (212)888-2940

CM Equity Partners
135 E 57th St.
New York, NY 10022
(212)909-8428
Fax: (212)980-2630

Cohen & Co., L.L.C.
800 Third Ave.
New York, NY 10022
(212)317-2250
Fax: (212)317-2255
E-mail: nlcohen@aol.com

Cornerstone Equity Investors, L.L.C.
717 5th Ave., Ste. 1100
New York, NY 10022
(212)753-0901
Fax: (212)826-6798
Website: http://www.cornerstone-equity.com

CW Group, Inc.
1041 3rd Ave., 2nd fl.
New York, NY 10021
(212)308-5266
Fax: (212)644-0354
Website: http://www.cwventures.com

DH Blair Investment Banking Corp.
44 Wall St., 2nd Fl.
New York, NY 10005
(212)495-5000
Fax: (212)269-1438

Dresdner Kleinwort Capital
75 Wall St.
New York, NY 10005
(212)429-3131
Fax: (212)429-3139
Website: http://www.dresdnerkb.com

East River Ventures, L.P.
645 Madison Ave., 22nd Fl.
New York, NY 10022
(212)644-2322
Fax: (212)644-5498

Easton Hunt Capital Partners
641 Lexington Ave., 21st Fl.
New York, NY 10017
(212)702-0950
Fax: (212)702-0952
Website: http://www.eastoncapital.com

Elk Associates Funding Corp.
747 3rd Ave., Ste. 4C
New York, NY 10017
(212)355-2449
Fax: (212)759-3338

EOS Partners, L.P.
320 Park Ave., 22nd Fl.
New York, NY 10022
(212)832-5800
Fax: (212)832-5815
E-mail: mfirst@eospartners.com
Website: http://www.eospartners.com

Euclid Partners
45 Rockefeller Plaza, Ste. 3240
New York, NY 10111
(212)218-6880
Fax: (212)218-6877
E-mail: graham@euclidpartners.com
Website: http://www.euclidpartners.com

Evergreen Capital Partners, Inc.
150 East 58th St.
New York, NY 10155
(212)813-0758
Fax: (212)813-0754

Exeter Capital L.P.
10 E 53rd St.
New York, NY 10022
(212)872-1172
Fax: (212)872-1198
E-mail: exeter@usa.net

Financial Technology Research Corp.
518 Broadway
Penthouse
New York, NY 10012
(212)625-9100
Fax: (212)431-0300
E-mail: fintek@financier.com

4C Ventures
237 Park Ave., Ste. 801
New York, NY 10017
(212)692-3680
Fax: (212)692-3685
Website: http://www.4cventures.com

Fusient Ventures
99 Park Ave., 20th Fl.
New York, NY 10016
(212)972-8999
Fax: (212)972-9876
E-mail: info@fusient.com
Website: http://www.fusient.com

Generation Capital Partners
551 Fifth Ave., Ste. 3100
New York, NY 10176
(212)450-8507
Fax: (212)450-8550
Website: http://www.genpartners.com

Golub Associates, Inc.
555 Madison Ave.
New York, NY 10022
(212)750-6060
Fax: (212)750-5505

Hambro America Biosciences Inc.
650 Madison Ave., 21st Floor
New York, NY 10022
(212)223-7400
Fax: (212)223-0305

Hanover Capital Corp.
505 Park Ave., 15th Fl.
New York, NY 10022
(212)755-1222
Fax: (212)935-1787

Harvest Partners, Inc.
280 Park Ave, 33rd Fl.
New York, NY 10017
(212)559-6300
Fax: (212)812-0100
Website: http://www.harvpart.com

Holding Capital Group, Inc.
10 E 53rd St., 30th Fl.
New York, NY 10022
(212)486-6670
Fax: (212)486-0843

Hudson Venture Partners
660 Madison Ave., 14th Fl.
New York, NY 10021-8405
(212)644-9797
Fax: (212)644-7430
Website: http://www.hudsonptr.com

IBJS Capital Corp.
1 State St., 9th Fl.
New York, NY 10004
(212)858-2018
Fax: (212)858-2768

InterEquity Capital Partners, L.P.
220 5th Ave.
New York, NY 10001
(212)779-2022
Fax: (212)779-2103
Website: http://www.interequity-capital.com

The Jordan Edmiston Group Inc.
150 East 52nd St., 18th Fl.
New York, NY 10022
(212)754-0710
Fax: (212)754-0337

Josephberg, Grosz and Co., Inc.
633 3rd Ave., 13th Fl.
New York, NY 10017
(212)974-9926
Fax: (212)397-5832

J.P. Morgan Capital Corp.
60 Wall St.
New York, NY 10260-0060
(212)648-9000
Fax: (212)648-5002
Website: http://www.jpmorgan.com

The Lambda Funds
380 Lexington Ave., 54th Fl.
New York, NY 10168
(212)682-3454
Fax: (212)682-9231

Lepercq Capital Management Inc.
1675 Broadway
New York, NY 10019
(212)698-0795
Fax: (212)262-0155

Loeb Partners Corp.
61 Broadway, Ste. 2400
New York, NY 10006
(212)483-7000
Fax: (212)574-2001

Madison Investment Partners
660 Madison Ave.
New York, NY 10021
(212)223-2600
Fax: (212)223-8208

MC Capital Inc.
520 Madison Ave., 16th Fl.
New York, NY 10022
(212)644-0841
Fax: (212)644-2926

McCown, De Leeuw and Co. (New York)
65 E 55th St., 36th Fl.
New York, NY 10022
(212)355-5500
Fax: (212)355-6283
Website: http://www.mdcpartners.com

Morgan Stanley Venture Partners
1221 Avenue of the Americas, 33rd Fl.
New York, NY 10020
(212)762-7900
Fax: (212)762-8424
E-mail: msventures@ms.com
Website: http://www.msvp.com

Nazem and Co.
645 Madison Ave., 12th Fl.
New York, NY 10022
(212)371-7900
Fax: (212)371-2150

Needham Capital Management, L.L.C.
445 Park Ave.
New York, NY 10022
(212)371-8300
Fax: (212)705-0299
Website: http://www.needhamco.com

Norwood Venture Corp.
1430 Broadway, Ste. 1607
New York, NY 10018
(212)869-5075
Fax: (212)869-5331
E-mail: nvc@mail.idt.net
Website: http://www.norven.com

Noveltek Venture Corp.
521 Fifth Ave., Ste. 1700
New York, NY 10175
(212)286-1963

Paribas Principal, Inc.
787 7th Ave.
New York, NY 10019
(212)841-2005
Fax: (212)841-3558

Patricof & Co. Ventures, Inc. (New York)
445 Park Ave.
New York, NY 10022
(212)753-6300
Fax: (212)319-6155
Website: http://www.patricof.com

The Platinum Group, Inc.
350 Fifth Ave, Ste. 7113
New York, NY 10118
(212)736-4300
Fax: (212)736-6086
Website: http://www.platinumgroup.com

Pomona Capital
780 Third Ave., 28th Fl.
New York, NY 10017
(212)593-3639
Fax: (212)593-3987
Website: http://www.pomonacapital.com

Prospect Street Ventures
10 East 40th St., 44th Fl.
New York, NY 10016
(212)448-0702
Fax: (212)448-9652
E-mail: wkohler@prospectstreet.com
Website: http://www.prospectstreet.com

Regent Capital Management
505 Park Ave., Ste. 1700
New York, NY 10022
(212)735-9900
Fax: (212)735-9908

Rothschild Ventures, Inc.
1251 Avenue of the Americas, 51st Fl.
New York, NY 10020
(212)403-3500
Fax: (212)403-3652
Website: http://www.nmrothschild.com

Sandler Capital Management
767 Fifth Ave., 45th Fl.
New York, NY 10153
(212)754-8100
Fax: (212)826-0280

Siguler Guff & Company
630 Fifth Ave., 16th Fl.
New York, NY 10111
(212)332-5100
Fax: (212)332-5120

Spencer Trask Ventures Inc.
535 Madison Ave.
New York, NY 10022
(212)355-5565
Fax: (212)751-3362
Website: http://www.spencertrask.com

Sprout Group (New York City)
277 Park Ave.
New York, NY 10172
(212)892-3600
Fax: (212)892-3444
E-mail: info@sproutgroup.com
Website: http://www.sproutgroup.com

US Trust Private Equity
114 W.47th St.
New York, NY 10036
(212)852-3949
Fax: (212)852-3759
Website: http://www.ustrust.com/privateequity

Vencon Management Inc.
301 West 53rd St., Ste. 10F
New York, NY 10019
(212)581-8787
Fax: (212)397-4126
Website: http://www.venconinc.com

Venrock Associates
30 Rockefeller Plaza, Ste. 5508
New York, NY 10112
(212)649-5600
Fax: (212)649-5788
Website: http://www.venrock.com

Venture Capital Fund of America, Inc.
509 Madison Ave., Ste. 812
New York, NY 10022
(212)838-5577
Fax: (212)838-7614
E-mail: mail@vcfa.com
Website: http://www.vcfa.com

Venture Opportunities Corp.
150 E 58th St.
New York, NY 10155
(212)832-3737
Fax: (212)980-6603

Warburg Pincus Ventures, Inc.
466 Lexington Ave., 11th Fl.
New York, NY 10017
(212)878-9309
Fax: (212)878-9200
Website: http://www.warburgpincus.com

Wasserstein, Perella & Co. Inc.
31 W 52nd St., 27th Fl.
New York, NY 10019
(212)702-5691
Fax: (212)969-7879

Welsh, Carson, Anderson, & Stowe
320 Park Ave., Ste. 2500
New York, NY 10022-6815
(212)893-9500
Fax: (212)893-9575

Whitney and Co. (New York)
630 Fifth Ave. Ste. 3225
New York, NY 10111
(212)332-2400
Fax: (212)332-2422
Website: http://www.jhwitney.com

Winthrop Ventures
74 Trinity Place, Ste. 600
New York, NY 10006
(212)422-0100

The Pittsford Group
8 Lodge Pole Rd.
Pittsford, NY 14534
(716)223-3523

Genesee Funding
70 Linden Oaks, 3rd Fl.
Rochester, NY 14625
(716)383-5550
Fax: (716)383-5305

Gabelli Multimedia Partners
One Corporate Center
Rye, NY 10580
(914)921-5395
Fax: (914)921-5031

Stamford Financial
108 Main St.
Stamford, NY 12167
(607)652-3311
Fax: (607)652-6301
Website: http://www.stamfordfinancial.com

Northwood Ventures LLC
485 Underhill Blvd., Ste. 205
Syosset, NY 11791
(516)364-5544
Fax: (516)364-0879
E-mail: northwood@northwood.com
Website: http://www.northwoodventures.com

Exponential Business Development Co.
216 Walton St.
Syracuse, NY 13202-1227
(315)474-4500
Fax: (315)474-4682
E-mail: dirksonn@aol.com
Website: http://www.exponential-ny.com

Onondaga Venture Capital Fund Inc.
714 State Tower Bldg.
Syracuse, NY 13202
(315)478-0157
Fax: (315)478-0158

Bessemer Venture Partners (Westbury)
1400 Old Country Rd., Ste. 109
Westbury, NY 11590
(516)997-2300
Fax: (516)997-2371
E-mail: bob@bvpny.com
Website: http://www.bvp.com

Ovation Capital Partners
120 Bloomingdale Rd., 4th Fl.
White Plains, NY 10605
(914)258-0011
Fax: (914)684-0848
Website: http://www.ovationcapital.com

North Carolina

Carolinas Capital Investment Corp.
1408 Biltmore Dr.
Charlotte, NC 28207
(704)375-3888
Fax: (704)375-6226

First Union Capital Partners
1st Union Center, 12th Fl.
301 S College St.
Charlotte, NC 28288-0732
(704)383-0000
Fax: (704)374-6711
Website: http://www.fucp.com

Frontier Capital LLC
525 North Tryon St., Ste. 1700
Charlotte, NC 28202
(704)414-2880
Fax: (704)414-2881
Website: http://www.frontierfunds.com

Kitty Hawk Capital
2700 Coltsgate Rd., Ste. 202
Charlotte, NC 28211
(704)362-3909
Fax: (704)362-2774
Website: http://www.kittyhawkcapital.com

Piedmont Venture Partners
One Morrocroft Centre
6805 Morisson Blvd., Ste. 380
Charlotte, NC 28211
(704)731-5200
Fax: (704)365-9733
Website: http://www.piedmontvp.com

Ruddick Investment Co.
1800 Two First Union Center
Charlotte, NC 28282
(704)372-5404
Fax: (704)372-6409

The Shelton Companies Inc.
3600 One First Union Center
301 S College St.
Charlotte, NC 28202
(704)348-2200
Fax: (704)348-2260

Wakefield Group
1110 E Morehead St.
PO Box 36329
Charlotte, NC 28236
(704)372-0355
Fax: (704)372-8216
Website: http://www.wakefieldgroup.com

Aurora Funds, Inc.
2525 Meridian Pkwy., Ste. 220
Durham, NC 27713
(919)484-0400
Fax: (919)484-0444
Website: http://www.aurorafunds.com

Intersouth Partners
3211 Shannon Rd., Ste. 610
Durham, NC 27707
(919)493-6640
Fax: (919)493-6649
E-mail: info@intersouth.com
Website: http://www.intersouth.com

Geneva Merchant Banking Partners
PO Box 21962
Greensboro, NC 27420
(336)275-7002

Fax: (336)275-9155
Website: http://www.genevamerchantbank.com

The North Carolina Enterprise Fund, L.P.
3600 Glenwood Ave., Ste. 107
Raleigh, NC 27612
(919)781-2691
Fax: (919)783-9195
Website: http://www.ncef.com

Ohio

Senmend Medical Ventures
4445 Lake Forest Dr., Ste. 600
Cincinnati, OH 45242
(513)563-3264
Fax: (513)563-3261

The Walnut Group
312 Walnut St., Ste. 1151
Cincinnati, OH 45202
(513)651-3300
Fax: (513)929-4441
Website: http://www.thewalnutgroup.com

Brantley Venture Partners
20600 Chagrin Blvd., Ste. 1150
Cleveland, OH 44122
(216)283-4800
Fax: (216)283-5324

Clarion Capital Corp.
1801 E 9th St., Ste. 1120
Cleveland, OH 44114
(216)687-1096
Fax: (216)694-3545

Crystal Internet Venture Fund, L.P.
1120 Chester Ave., Ste. 418
Cleveland, OH 44114
(216)263-5515
Fax: (216)263-5518
E-mail: jf@crystalventure.com
Website: http://www.crystalventure.com

Key Equity Capital Corp.
127 Public Sq., 28th Fl.
Cleveland, OH 44114
(216)689-3000
Fax: (216)689-3204
Website: http://www.keybank.com

Morgenthaler Ventures
Terminal Tower
50 Public Square, Ste. 2700
Cleveland, OH 44113
(216)416-7500
Fax: (216)416-7501
Website: http://www.morgenthaler.com

National City Equity Partners Inc.
1965 E 6th St.
Cleveland, OH 44114
(216)575-2491
Fax: (216)575-9965
E-mail: nccap@aol.com
Website: http://www.nccapital.com

Primus Venture Partners, Inc.
5900 LanderBrook Dr., Ste. 2000
Cleveland, OH 44124-4020
(440)684-7300
Fax: (440)684-7342
E-mail: info@primusventure.com
Website: http://www.primusventure.com

Banc One Capital Partners (Columbus)
150 East Gay St., 24th Fl.
Columbus, OH 43215
(614)217-1100
Fax: (614)217-1217

Battelle Venture Partners
505 King Ave.
Columbus, OH 43201
(614)424-7005
Fax: (614)424-4874

Ohio Partners
62 E Board St., 3rd Fl.
Columbus, OH 43215
(614)621-1210
Fax: (614)621-1240

Capital Technology Group, L.L.C.
400 Metro Place North, Ste. 300
Dublin, OH 43017
(614)792-6066
Fax: (614)792-6036
E-mail: info@capitaltech.com
Website: http://www.capitaltech.com

Northwest Ohio Venture Fund
4159 Holland-Sylvania R., Ste. 202
Toledo, OH 43623
(419)824-8144
Fax: (419)882-2035
E-mail: bwalsh@novf.com

Oklahoma

Moore & Associates
1000 W Wilshire Blvd., Ste. 370
Oklahoma City, OK 73116
(405)842-3660
Fax: (405)842-3763

Chisholm Private Capital Partners
100 West 5th St., Ste. 805
Tulsa, OK 74103
(918)584-0440
Fax: (918)584-0441
Website: http://www.chisholmvc.com

Davis, Tuttle Venture Partners (Tulsa)
320 S Boston, Ste. 1000
Tulsa, OK 74103-3703
(918)584-7272
Fax: (918)582-3404
Website: http://www.davistuttle.com

RBC Ventures
2627 E 21st St.
Tulsa, OK 74114
(918)744-5607
Fax: (918)743-8630

Oregon

Utah Ventures II LP
10700 SW Beaverton-Hillsdale Hwy., Ste. 548
Beaverton, OR 97005
(503)574-4125
E-mail: adishlip@uven.com
Website: http://www.uven.com

Orien Ventures
14523 SW Westlake Dr.
Lake Oswego, OR 97035
(503)699-1680
Fax: (503)699-1681

OVP Venture Partners (Lake Oswego)
340 Oswego Pointe Dr., Ste. 200
Lake Oswego, OR 97034
(503)697-8766
Fax: (503)697-8863
E-mail: info@ovp.com
Website: http://www.ovp.com

Oregon Resource and Technology Development Fund
4370 NE Halsey St., Ste. 233
Portland, OR 97213-1566
(503)282-4462
Fax: (503)282-2976

Shaw Venture Partners
400 SW 6th Ave., Ste. 1100
Portland, OR 97204-1636
(503)228-4884
Fax: (503)227-2471
Website: http://www.shawventures.com

Pennsylvania

Mid-Atlantic Venture Funds
125 Goodman Dr.
Bethlehem, PA 18015
(610)865-6550
Fax: (610)865-6427
Website: http://www.mavf.com

Newspring Ventures
100 W Elm St., Ste. 101
Conshohocken, PA 19428

(610)567-2380
Fax: (610)567-2388
Website: http://www.newsprintventures.com

Patricof & Co. Ventures, Inc.
455 S Gulph Rd., Ste. 410
King of Prussia, PA 19406
(610)265-0286
Fax: (610)265-4959
Website: http://www.patricof.com

Loyalhanna Venture Fund
527 Cedar Way, Ste. 104
Oakmont, PA 15139
(412)820-7035
Fax: (412)820-7036

Innovest Group Inc.
2000 Market St., Ste. 1400
Philadelphia, PA 19103
(215)564-3960
Fax: (215)569-3272

Keystone Venture Capital Management Co.
1601 Market St., Ste. 2500
Philadelphia, PA 19103
(215)241-1200
Fax: (215)241-1211
Website: http://www.keystonevc.com

Liberty Venture Partners
2005 Market St., Ste. 200
Philadelphia, PA 19103
(215)282-4484
Fax: (215)282-4485
E-mail: info@libertyvp.com
Website: http://www.libertyvp.com

Penn Janney Fund, Inc.
1801 Market St., 11th Fl.
Philadelphia, PA 19103
(215)665-4447
Fax: (215)557-0820

Philadelphia Ventures, Inc.
The Bellevue
200 S Broad St.
Philadelphia, PA 19102
(215)732-4445
Fax: (215)732-4644

Birchmere Ventures Inc.
2000 Technology Dr.
Pittsburgh, PA 15219-3109
(412)803-8000
Fax: (412)687-8139
Website: http://www.birchmerevc.com

CEO Venture Fund
2000 Technology Dr., Ste. 160
Pittsburgh, PA 15219-3109
(412)687-3451
Fax: (412)687-8139
E-mail: ceofund@aol.com
Website: http://www.ceoventurefund.com

Innovation Works Inc.
2000 Technology Dr., Ste. 250
Pittsburgh, PA 15219
(412)681-1520
Fax: (412)681-2625
Website: http://www.innovationworks.org

Keystone Minority Capital Fund L.P.
1801 Centre Ave., Ste. 201
Williams Sq.
Pittsburgh, PA 15219
(412)338-2230
Fax: (412)338-2224

Mellon Ventures, Inc.
One Mellon Bank Ctr., Rm. 3500
Pittsburgh, PA 15258
(412)236-3594
Fax: (412)236-3593
Website: http://www.mellonventures.com

Pennsylvania Growth Fund
5850 Ellsworth Ave., Ste. 303
Pittsburgh, PA 15232
(412)661-1000
Fax: (412)361-0676

Point Venture Partners
The Century Bldg.
130 Seventh St., 7th Fl.
Pittsburgh, PA 15222
(412)261-1966
Fax: (412)261-1718

Cross Atlantic Capital Partners
5 Radnor Corporate Center, Ste. 555
Radnor, PA 19087
(610)995-2650
Fax: (610)971-2062
Website: http://www.xacp.com

Meridian Venture Partners (Radnor)
The Radnor Court Bldg., Ste. 140
259 Radnor-Chester Rd.
Radnor, PA 19087
(610)254-2999
Fax: (610)254-2996
E-mail: mvpart@ix.netcom.com

TDH
919 Conestoga Rd., Bldg. 1, Ste. 301
Rosemont, PA 19010
(610)526-9970
Fax: (610)526-9971

Adams Capital Management
500 Blackburn Ave.
Sewickley, PA 15143
(412)749-9454
Fax: (412)749-9459
Website: http://www.acm.com

S.R. One, Ltd.
Four Tower Bridge
200 Barr Harbor Dr., Ste. 250
W Conshohocken, PA 19428
(610)567-1000
Fax: (610)567-1039

Greater Philadelphia Venture Capital Corp.
351 East Conestoga Rd.
Wayne, PA 19087
(610)688-6829
Fax: (610)254-8958

PA Early Stage
435 Devon Park Dr., Bldg. 500, Ste. 510
Wayne, PA 19087
(610)293-4075
Fax: (610)254-4240
Website: http://www.paearlystage.com

The Sandhurst Venture Fund, L.P.
351 E Constoga Rd.
Wayne, PA 19087
(610)254-8900
Fax: (610)254-8958

TL Ventures
700 Bldg.
435 Devon Park Dr.
Wayne, PA 19087-1990
(610)975-3765
Fax: (610)254-4210
Website: http://www.tlventures.com

Rockhill Ventures, Inc.
100 Front St., Ste. 1350
West Conshohocken, PA 19428
(610)940-0300
Fax: (610)940-0301

Puerto Rico

Advent-Morro Equity Partners
Banco Popular Bldg.
206 Tetuan St., Ste. 903
San Juan, PR 00902
(787)725-5285
Fax: (787)721-1735

North America Investment Corp.
Mercantil Plaza, Ste. 813
PO Box 191831
San Juan, PR 00919
(787)754-6178
Fax: (787)754-6181

Rhode Island

Manchester Humphreys, Inc.
40 Westminster St., Ste. 900
Providence, RI 02903
(401)454-0400
Fax: (401)454-0403

Navis Partners
50 Kennedy Plaza, 12th Fl.
Providence, RI 02903
(401)278-6770
Fax: (401)278-6387
Website: http://www.navispartners.com

South Carolina

Capital Insights, L.L.C.
PO Box 27162
Greenville, SC 29616-2162
(864)242-6832
Fax: (864)242-6755
E-mail: jwarner@capitalinsights.com
Website: http://www.capitalinsights.com

Transamerica Mezzanine Financing
7 N. Laurens St., Ste. 603
Greenville, SC 29601
(864)232-6198
Fax: (864)241-4444

Tennessee

Valley Capital Corp.
Krystal Bldg.
100 W Martin Luther King Blvd., Ste. 212
Chattanooga, TN 37402
(423)265-1557
Fax: (423)265-1588

Coleman Swenson Booth Inc.
237 2nd Ave. S
Franklin, TN 37064-2649
(615)791-9462
Fax: (615)791-9636
Website: http://
www.colemanswenson.com

Capital Services & Resources, Inc.
5159 Wheelis Dr., Ste. 106
Memphis, TN 38117
(901)761-2156
Fax: (907)767-0060

Paradigm Capital Partners LLC
6410 Poplar Ave., Ste. 395
Memphis, TN 38119
(901)682-6060
Fax: (901)328-3061

SSM Ventures
845 Crossover Ln., Ste. 140
Memphis, TN 38117
(901)767-1131
Fax: (901)767-1135
Website: http://www.ssmventures.com

Capital Across America L.P.
501 Union St., Ste. 201
Nashville, TN 37219
(615)254-1414
Fax: (615)254-1856
Website: http://www.capitalacross
america.com

Equitas L.P.
2000 Glen Echo Rd., Ste. 101
PO Box 158838
Nashville, TN 37215-8838
(615)383-8673
Fax: (615)383-8693

Massey Burch Capital Corp.
One Burton Hills Blvd., Ste. 350
Nashville, TN 37215
(615)665-3221
Fax: (615)665-3240
E-mail: tcalton@masseyburch.com
Website: http://www.masseyburch.com

Nelson Capital Corp.
3401 West End Ave., Ste. 300
Nashville, TN 37203
(615)292-8787
Fax: (615)385-3150

Texas

Phillips-Smith Specialty Retail Group
5080 Spectrum Dr., Ste. 805 W
Addison, TX 75001
(972)387-0725
Fax: (972)458-2560
E-mail: pssrg@aol.com
Website: http://www.phillips-smith.com

Austin Ventures, L.P.
701 Brazos St., Ste. 1400
Austin, TX 78701
(512)485-1900
Fax: (512)476-3952
E-mail: info@ausven.com
Website: http://www.austinventures.com

The Capital Network
3925 West Braker Lane, Ste. 406
Austin, TX 78759-5321
(512)305-0826
Fax: (512)305-0836

Techxas Ventures LLC
5000 Plaza on the Lake
Austin, TX 78746
(512)343-0118
Fax: (512)343-1879
E-mail: bruce@techxas.com
Website: http://www.techxas.com

Alliance Financial of Houston
218 Heather Ln.
Conroe, TX 77385-9013
(936)447-3300
Fax: (936)447-4222

Amerimark Capital Corp.
1111 W Mockingbird, Ste. 1111
Dallas, TX 75247
(214)638-7878
Fax: (214)638-7612
E-mail: amerimark@amcapital.com
Website: http://www.amcapital.com

AMT Venture Partners / AMT Capital Ltd.
5220 Spring Valley Rd., Ste. 600
Dallas, TX 75240
(214)905-9757
Fax: (214)905-9761
Website: http://www.amtcapital.com

Arkoma Venture Partners
5950 Berkshire Lane, Ste. 1400
Dallas, TX 75225
(214)739-3515
Fax: (214)739-3572
E-mail: joelf@arkomavp.com

Capital Southwest Corp.
12900 Preston Rd., Ste. 700
Dallas, TX 75230
(972)233-8242
Fax: (972)233-7362
Website: http://
www.capitalsouthwest.com

Dali, Hook Partners
One Lincoln Center, Ste. 1550
5400 LBJ Freeway
Dallas, TX 75240
(972)991-5457
Fax: (972)991-5458
E-mail: dhook@hookpartners.com
Website: http://www.hookpartners.com

HO2 Partners
Two Galleria Tower
13455 Noel Rd., Ste. 1670
Dallas, TX 75240
(972)702-1144
Fax: (972)702-8234
Website: http://www.ho2.com

Interwest Partners (Dallas)
2 Galleria Tower
13455 Noel Rd., Ste. 1670
Dallas, TX 75240
(972)392-7279

Fax: (972)490-6348
Website: http://www.interwest.com

Kahala Investments, Inc.
8214 Westchester Dr., Ste. 715
Dallas, TX 75225
(214)987-0077
Fax: (214)987-2332

MESBIC Ventures Holding Co.
2435 North Central Expressway, Ste. 200
Dallas, TX 75080
(972)991-1597
Fax: (972)991-4770
Website: http://www.mvhc.com

North Texas MESBIC, Inc.
9500 Forest Lane, Ste. 430
Dallas, TX 75243
(214)221-3565
Fax: (214)221-3566

Richard Jaffe & Company, Inc,
7318 Royal Cir.
Dallas, TX 75230
(214)265-9397
Fax: (214)739-1845

Sevin Rosen Management Co.
13455 Noel Rd., Ste. 1670
Dallas, TX 75240
(972)702-1100
Fax: (972)702-1103
E-mail: info@srfunds.com
Website: http://www.srfunds.com

Stratford Capital Partners, L.P.
300 Crescent Ct., Ste. 500
Dallas, TX 75201
(214)740-7377
Fax: (214)720-7393
E-mail: stratcap@hmtf.com

Sunwestern Investment Group
12221 Merit Dr., Ste. 935
Dallas, TX 75251
(972)239-5650
Fax: (972)701-0024

Wingate Partners
750 N St. Paul St., Ste. 1200
Dallas, TX 75201
(214)720-1313
Fax: (214)871-8799

Buena Venture Associates
201 Main St., 32nd Fl.
Fort Worth, TX 76102
(817)339-7400
Fax: (817)390-8408
Website: http://www.buenaventure.com

The Catalyst Group
3 Riverway, Ste. 770
Houston, TX 77056
(713)623-8133
Fax: (713)623-0473
E-mail: herman@thecatalystgroup.net
Website: http://www.thecatalystgroup.net

Cureton & Co., Inc.
1100 Louisiana, Ste. 3250
Houston, TX 77002
(713)658-9806
Fax: (713)658-0476

Davis, Tuttle Venture Partners (Dallas)
8 Greenway Plaza, Ste. 1020
Houston, TX 77046
(713)993-0440
Fax: (713)621-2297
Website: http://www.davistuttle.com

Houston Partners
401 Louisiana, 8th Fl.
Houston, TX 77002
(713)222-8600
Fax: (713)222-8932

Southwest Venture Group
10878 Westheimer, Ste. 178
Houston, TX 77042
(713)827-8947
(713)461-1470

AM Fund
4600 Post Oak Place, Ste. 100
Houston, TX 77027
(713)627-9111
Fax: (713)627-9119

Ventex Management, Inc.
3417 Milam St.
Houston, TX 77002-9531
(713)659-7870
Fax: (713)659-7855

MBA Venture Group
1004 Olde Town Rd., Ste. 102
Irving, TX 75061
(972)986-6703

First Capital Group Management Co.
750 East Mulberry St., Ste. 305
PO Box 15616
San Antonio, TX 78212
(210)736-4233
Fax: (210)736-5449

The Southwest Venture Partnerships
16414 San Pedro, Ste. 345
San Antonio, TX 78232
(210)402-1200
Fax: (210)402-1221
E-mail: swvp@aol.com

Medtech International Inc.
1742 Carriageway
Sugarland, TX 77478
(713)980-8474
Fax: (713)980-6343

Utah

First Security Business Investment Corp.
15 East 100 South, Ste. 100
Salt Lake City, UT 84111
(801)246-5737
Fax: (801)246-5740

Utah Ventures II, L.P.
423 Wakara Way, Ste. 206
Salt Lake City, UT 84108
(801)583-5922
Fax: (801)583-4105
Website: http://www.uven.com

Wasatch Venture Corp.
1 S Main St., Ste. 1400
Salt Lake City, UT 84133
(801)524-8939
Fax: (801)524-8941
E-mail: mail@wasatchvc.com

Vermont

North Atlantic Capital Corp.
76 Saint Paul St., Ste. 600
Burlington, VT 05401
(802)658-7820
Fax: (802)658-5757
Website: http://www.northatlantic capital.com

Green Mountain Advisors Inc.
PO Box 1230
Quechee, VT 05059
(802)296-7800
Fax: (802)296-6012
Website: http://www.gmtcap.com

Virginia

Oxford Financial Services Corp.
Alexandria, VA 22314
(703)519-4900
Fax: (703)519-4910
E-mail: oxford133@aol.com

Continental SBIC
4141 N. Henderson Rd.
Arlington, VA 22203
(703)527-5200
Fax: (703)527-3700

Novak Biddle Venture Partners
1750 Tysons Blvd., Ste. 1190
McLean, VA 22102

(703)847-3770
Fax: (703)847-3771
E-mail: roger@novakbiddle.com
Website: http://www.novakbiddle.com

Spacevest
11911 Freedom Dr., Ste. 500
Reston, VA 20190
(703)904-9800
Fax: (703)904-0571
E-mail: spacevest@spacevest.com
Website: http://www.spacevest.com

Virginia Capital
1801 Libbie Ave., Ste. 201
Richmond, VA 23226
(804)648-4802
Fax: (804)648-4809
E-mail: webmaster@vacapital.com
Website: http://www.vacapital.com

Calvert Social Venture Partners
402 Maple Ave. W
Vienna, VA 22180
(703)255-4930
Fax: (703)255-4931
E-mail: calven2000@aol.com

Fairfax Partners
8000 Towers Crescent Dr., Ste. 940
Vienna, VA 22182
(703)847-9486
Fax: (703)847-0911

Global Internet Ventures
8150 Leesburg Pike, Ste. 1210
Vienna, VA 22182
(703)442-3300
Fax: (703)442-3388
Website: http://www.givinc.com

Walnut Capital Corp. (Vienna)
8000 Towers Crescent Dr., Ste. 1070
Vienna, VA 22182
(703)448-3771
Fax: (703)448-7751

Washington

Encompass Ventures
777 108th Ave. NE, Ste. 2300
Bellevue, WA 98004
(425)486-3900
Fax: (425)486-3901
E-mail: info@evpartners.com
Website: http://www.encompassventures.com

Fluke Venture Partners
11400 SE Sixth St., Ste. 230
Bellevue, WA 98004
(425)453-4590
Fax: (425)453-4675
E-mail: gabelein@flukeventures.com
Website: http://www.flukeventures.com

Pacific Northwest Partners SBIC, L.P.
15352 SE 53rd St.
Bellevue, WA 98006
(425)455-9967
Fax: (425)455-9404

Materia Venture Associates, L.P.
3435 Carillon Pointe
Kirkland, WA 98033-7354
(425)822-4100
Fax: (425)827-4086

OVP Venture Partners (Kirkland)
2420 Carillon Pt.
Kirkland, WA 98033
(425)889-9192
Fax: (425)889-0152
E-mail: info@ovp.com
Website: http://www.ovp.com

Digital Partners
999 3rd Ave., Ste. 1610
Seattle, WA 98104
(206)405-3607
Fax: (206)405-3617
Website: http://www.digitalpartners.com

Frazier & Company
601 Union St., Ste. 3300
Seattle, WA 98101
(206)621-7200
Fax: (206)621-1848
E-mail: jon@frazierco.com

Kirlan Venture Capital, Inc.
221 First Ave. W, Ste. 108
Seattle, WA 98119-4223
(206)281-8610
Fax: (206)285-3451
Website: http://www.kirlanventure.com

Phoenix Partners
1000 2nd Ave., Ste. 3600
Seattle, WA 98104
(206)624-8968
Fax: (206)624-1907

Voyager Capital
800 5th St., Ste. 4100
Seattle, WA 98103
(206)470-1180
Fax: (206)470-1185
E-mail: info@voyagercap.com
Website: http://www.voyagercap.com

Northwest Venture Associates
221 N. Wall St., Ste. 628
Spokane, WA 99201
(509)747-0728
Fax: (509)747-0758
Website: http://www.nwva.com

Wisconsin

Venture Investors Management, L.L.C.
University Research Park
505 S Rosa Rd.
Madison, WI 53719
(608)441-2700
Fax: (608)441-2727
E-mail: roger@ventureinvestors.com
Website: http://www.ventureinvesters.com

Capital Investments, Inc.
1009 West Glen Oaks Lane, Ste. 103
Mequon, WI 53092
(414)241-0303
Fax: (414)241-8451
Website: http://www.capitalinvestmentsinc.com

Future Value Venture, Inc.
2745 N. Martin Luther King Dr., Ste. 204
Milwaukee, WI 53212-2300
(414)264-2252
Fax: (414)264-2253
E-mail: fvvventures@aol.com
William Beckett, President

Lubar and Co., Inc.
700 N. Water St., Ste. 1200
Milwaukee, WI 53202
(414)291-9000
Fax: (414)291-9061

GCI
20875 Crossroads Cir., Ste. 100
Waukesha, WI 53186
(262)798-5080
Fax: (262)798-5087

Glossary of Small Business Terms

Absolute liability
Liability that is incurred due to product defects or negligent actions. Manufacturers or retail establishments are held responsible, even though the defect or action may not have been intentional or negligent.

ACE
See Active Corps of Executives

Accident and health benefits
Benefits offered to employees and their families in order to offset the costs associated with accidental death, accidental injury, or sickness.

Account statement
A record of transactions, including payments, new debt, and deposits, incurred during a defined period of time.

Accounting system
System capturing the costs of all employees and/or machinery included in business expenses.

Accounts payable
See Trade credit

Accounts receivable
Unpaid accounts which arise from unsettled claims and transactions from the sale of a company's products or services to its customers.

Active Corps of Executives (ACE)
A group of volunteers for a management assistance program of the U.S. Small Business Administration; volunteers provide one-on-one counseling and teach workshops and seminars for small firms.

ADA
See Americans with Disabilities Act

Adaptation
The process whereby an invention is modified to meet the needs of users.

Adaptive engineering
The process whereby an invention is modified to meet the manufacturing and commercial requirements of a targeted market.

Adverse selection
The tendency for higher-risk individuals to purchase health care and more comprehensive plans, resulting in increased costs.

Advertising
A marketing tool used to capture public attention and influence purchasing decisions for a product or service. Utilizes various forms of media to generate consumer response, such as flyers, magazines, newspapers, radio, and television.

Age discrimination
The denial of the rights and privileges of employment based solely on the age of an individual.

Agency costs
Costs incurred to insure that the lender or investor maintains control over assets while allowing the borrower or entrepreneur to use them. Monitoring and information costs are the two major types of agency costs.

Agribusiness
The production and sale of commodities and products from the commercial farming industry.

Americans with Disabilities Act (ADA)
Law designed to ensure equal access and opportunity to handicapped persons.

Annual report
Yearly financial report prepared by a business that adheres to the requirements set forth by the Securities and Exchange Commission (SEC).

Antitrust immunity
Exemption from prosecution under antitrust laws. In the transportation industry, firms with antitrust immunity are permitted under certain conditions to set schedules and sometimes prices for the public benefit.

Applied research
Scientific study targeted for use in a product or process.

Assets
Anything of value owned by a company.

Audit
The verification of accounting records and business procedures conducted by an outside accounting service.

Average cost
Total production costs divided by the quantity produced.

Balance Sheet
A financial statement listing the total assets and liabilities of a company at a given time.

Bankruptcy
The condition in which a business cannot meet its debt obligations and petitions a federal district court either for reorganization of its debts (Chapter 11) or for liquidation of its assets (Chapter 7).

Basket clause
A provision specifying the amount of public pension funds that may be placed in investments not included on a state's legal list (see separate citation).

BDC
See Business development corporation

Benefit
Various services, such as health care, flextime, day care, insurance, and vacation, offered to employees as part of a hiring package. Typically subsidized in whole or in part by the business.

BIDCO
See Business and industrial development company

Billing cycle
A system designed to evenly distribute customer billing throughout the month, preventing clerical backlogs.

Blue chip security
A low-risk, low-yield security representing an interest in a very stable company.

Blue sky laws
A general term that denotes various states' laws regulating securities.

Bond
A written instrument executed by a bidder or contractor (the principal) and a second party (the surety or sureties) to assure fulfillment of the principal's obligations to a third party (the obligee or government) identified in the bond. If the principal's obligations are not met, the bond assures payment to the extent stipulated of any loss sustained by the obligee.

Bonding requirements
Terms contained in a bond (see separate citation).

Bonus
An amount of money paid to an employee as a reward for achieving certain business goals or objectives.

Brainstorming
A group session where employees contribute their ideas for solving a problem or meeting a company objective without fear of retribution or ridicule.

Brand name
The part of a brand, trademark, or service mark that can be spoken. It can be a word, letter, or group of words or letters.

Bridge financing
A short-term loan made in expectation of intermediateterm or long-term financing. Can be used when a company plans to go public in the near future.

Broker
One who matches resources available for innovation with those who need them.

Budget
An estimate of the spending necessary to complete a project or offer a service in comparison to cash-on-hand and expected earnings for the coming year, with an emphasis on cost control.

Business and industrial development company (BIDCO)
A private, for-profit financing corporation chartered by the state to provide both equity and long-term debt capital to small business owners (see separate citations for equity and debt capital).

Business birth
The formation of a new establishment or enterprise. The appearance of a new establishment or enterprise in the Small Business Data Base (see separate citation).

Business conditions
Outside factors that can affect the financial performance of a business.

Business contractions
The number of establishments that have decreased in employment during a specified time.

Business cycle
A period of economic recession and recovery. These cycles vary in duration.

Business death
The voluntary or involuntary closure of a firm or establishment. The disappearance of an establishment or enterprise from the Small Business Data Base (see separate citation).

Business development corporation (BDC)
A business financing agency, usually composed of the financial institutions in an area or state, organized to assist in financing businesses unable to obtain assistance through normal channels; the risk is spread among various members of the business development corporation, and interest rates may vary somewhat from those charged by member institutions. A venture capital firm in which shares of ownership are publicly held and to which the Investment Act of 1940 applies.

Business dissolution
For enumeration purposes, the absence of a business that was present in the prior time period from any current record.

Business entry
See Business birth

Business ethics
Moral values and principles espoused by members of the business community as a guide to fair and honest business practices.

Business exit
See Business death

Business expansions
The number of establishments that added employees during a specified time.

Business failure
Closure of a business causing a loss to at least one creditor.

Business format franchising
The purchase of the name, trademark, and an ongoing business plan of the parent corporation or franchisor by the franchisee.

Business license
A legal authorization issued by municipal and state governments and required for business operations.

Business name
Enterprises must register their business names with local governments usually on a "doing business as" (DBA) form. (This name is sometimes referred to as a "fictional name.") The procedure is part of the business licensing process and prevents any other business from using that same name for a similar business in the same locality.

Business norms
See Financial ratios

Business permit
See Business license

Business plan
A document that spells out a company's expected course of action for a specified period, usually including a detailed listing and analysis of risks and uncertainties. For the small business, it should examine the proposed products, the market, the industry, the management policies, the marketing policies, production needs, and financial needs. Frequently, it is used as a prospectus for potential investors and lenders.

Business proposal
See Business plan

Business service firm
An establishment primarily engaged in rendering services to other business organizations on a fee or contract basis.

Business start
For enumeration purposes, a business with a name or similar designation that did not exist in a prior time period.

Cafeteria plan
See Flexible benefit plan

Capacity
Level of a firm's, industry's, or nation's output corresponding to full practical utilization of available resources.

Capital
Assets less liabilities, representing the ownership interest in a business. A stock of accumulated goods, especially at a specified time and in contrast to income received during a specified time period. Accumulated goods devoted to production. Accumulated possessions calculated to bring income.

Capital expenditure
Expenses incurred by a business for improvements that will depreciate over time.

Capital gain
The monetary difference between the purchase price and the selling price of capital. Capital gains are taxed at a rate of 28% by the federal government.

Capital intensity
The relative importance of capital in the production process, usually expressed as the ratio of capital to labor but also sometimes as the ratio of capital to output.

Capital resource
The equipment, facilities and labor used to create products and services.

Catastrophic care
Medical and other services for acute and long-term illnesses that cost more than insurance coverage limits or that cost the amount most families may be expected to pay with their own resources.

CDC
See Certified development corporation

Certified development corporation (CDC)
A local area or statewide corporation or authority (for profit or nonprofit) that packages U.S. Small Business Administration (SBA), bank, state, and/or private money into financial assistance for existing business capital improvements. The SBA holds the second lien on its maximum share of 40 percent involvement. Each state has at least one certified development corporation. This program is called the SBA 504 Program.

Certified lenders
Banks that participate in the SBA guaranteed loan program (see separate citation). Such banks must have a good track record with the U.S. Small Business Administration (SBA) and must agree to certain conditions set forth by the agency. In return, the SBA agrees to process any guaranteed loan application within three business days.

Channel of distribution
The means used to transport merchandise from the manufacturer to the consumer.

Chapter 7 of the 1978 Bankruptcy Act
Provides for a court-appointed trustee who is responsible for liquidating a company's assets in order to settle outstanding debts.

Chapter 11 of the 1978 Bankruptcy Act
Allows the business owners to retain control of the company while working with their creditors to reorganize their finances and establish better business practices to prevent liquidation of assets.

Closely held corporation
A corporation in which the shares are held by a few persons, usually officers, employees, or others close to the management; these shares are rarely offered to the public.

Code of Federal Regulations
Codification of general and permanent rules of the federal government published in the Federal Register.

Code sharing
See Computer code sharing

Coinsurance
Upon meeting the deductible payment, health insurance participants may be required to make additional health care cost-sharing payments. Coinsurance is a payment of a fixed percentage of the cost of each service; copayment is usually a fixed amount to be paid with each service.

Collateral
Securities, evidence of deposit, or other property pledged by a borrower to secure repayment of a loan.

Collective ratemaking
The establishment of uniform charges for services by a group of businesses in the same industry.

Commercial insurance plan
See Underwriting

Commercial loans
Short-term renewable loans used to finance specific capital needs of a business.

Commercialization
The final stage of the innovation process, including production and distribution.

Common stock
The most frequently used instrument for purchasing ownership in private or public companies. Common stock generally carries the right to vote on certain corporate actions and may pay dividends, although it rarely does in venture investments. In liquidation, common stockholders are the last to share in the proceeds from the sale of a corporation's assets; bondholders and preferred shareholders have priority. Common stock is often used in firstround start-up financing.

Community development corporation
A corporation established to develop economic programs for a community and, in most cases, to provide financial support for such development.

Competitor
A business whose product or service is marketed for the same purpose/use and to the same consumer group as the product or service of another.

Consignment
A merchandising agreement, usually referring to secondhand shops, where the dealer pays the owner of an item a percentage of the profit when the item is sold.

Consortium
A coalition of organizations such as banks and corporations for ventures requiring large capital resources.

Consultant
An individual that is paid by a business to provide advice and expertise in a particular area.

Consumer price index
A measure of the fluctuation in prices between two points in time.

Consumer research
Research conducted by a business to obtain information about existing or potential consumer markets.

Continuation coverage
Health coverage offered for a specified period of time to employees who leave their jobs and to their widows, divorced spouses, or dependents.

Contractions
See Business contractions

Convertible preferred stock
A class of stock that pays a reasonable dividend and is convertible into common stock (see separate citation). Generally the convertible feature may only be exercised after being held for a stated period of time. This arrangement is usually considered second-round financing when a company needs equity to maintain its cash flow.

Convertible securities
A feature of certain bonds, debentures, or preferred stocks that allows them to be exchanged by the owner for another class of securities at a future date and in accordance with any other terms of the issue.

Copayment
See Coinsurance

Copyright
A legal form of protection available to creators and authors to safeguard their works from unlawful use or claim of ownership by others. Copyrights may be

acquired for works of art, sculpture, music, and published or unpublished manuscripts. All copyrights should be registered at the Copyright Office of the Library of Congress.

Corporate financial ratios
The relationship between key figures found in a company's financial statement expressed as a numeric value. Used to evaluate risk and company performance. Also known as Financial averages, Operating ratios, and Business ratios.

Corporation
A legal entity, chartered by a state or the federal government, recognized as a separate entity having its own rights, privileges, and liabilities distinct from those of its members.

Cost containment
Actions taken by employers and insurers to curtail rising health care costs; for example, increasing employee cost sharing (see separate citation), requiring second opinions, or preadmission screening.

Cost sharing
The requirement that health care consumers contribute to their own medical care costs through deductibles and coinsurance (see separate citations). Cost sharing does not include the amounts paid in premiums. It is used to control utilization of services; for example, requiring a fixed amount to be paid with each health care service.

Cottage industry
Businesses based in the home in which the family members are the labor force and family-owned equipment is used to process the goods.

Credit Rating
A letter or number calculated by an organization (such as Dun & Bradstreet) to represent the ability and disposition of a business to meet its financial obligations.

Customer service
Various techniques used to ensure the satisfaction of a customer.

Cyclical peak
The upper turning point in a business cycle.

Cyclical trough
The lower turning point in a business cycle.

DBA (Doing business as)
See Business name

Death
See Business death

Debenture
A certificate given as acknowledgment of a debt (see separate citation) secured by the general credit of the issuing corporation. A bond, usually without security, issued by a corporation and sometimes convertible to common stock.

Debt
Something owed by one person to another. Financing in which a company receives capital that must be repaid; no ownership is transferred.

Debt capital
Business financing that normally requires periodic interest payments and repayment of the principal within a specified time.

Debt financing
See Debt capital

Debt securities
Loans such as bonds and notes that provide a specified rate of return for a specified period of time.

Deductible
A set amount that an individual must pay before any benefits are received.

Demand shock absorbers
A term used to describe the role that some small firms play by expanding their output levels to accommodate a transient surge in demand.

Demographics
Statistics on various markets, including age, income, and education, used to target specific products or services to appropriate consumer groups.

Demonstration
Showing that a product or process has been modified sufficiently to meet the needs of users.

Deregulation
The lifting of government restrictions; for example, the lifting of government restrictions on the entry of new businesses, the expansion of services, and the setting of prices in particular industries.

Disaster loans
Various types of physical and economic assistance available to individuals and businesses through the U.S. Small Business Administration (SBA). This is the only SBA loan program available for residential purposes.

Discrimination
The denial of the rights and privileges of employment based on factors such as age, race, religion, or gender.

Diseconomies of scale
The condition in which the costs of production increase faster than the volume of production.

Dissolution
See Business dissolution

Distribution
Delivering a product or process to the user.

Distributor
One who delivers merchandise to the user.

Diversified company
A company whose products and services are used by several different markets.

Doing business as (DBA)
See Business name

Dow Jones
An information services company that publishes the Wall Street Journal and other sources of financial information.

Dow Jones Industrial Average
An indicator of stock market performance.

Earned income
A tax term that refers to wages and salaries earned by the recipient, as opposed to monies earned through interest and dividends.

Economic efficiency
The use of productive resources to the fullest practical extent in the provision of the set of goods and services that is most preferred by purchasers in the economy.

Economic indicators
Statistics used to express the state of the economy. These include the length of the average work week, the rate of unemployment, and stock prices.

Economically disadvantaged
See Socially and economically disadvantaged

Economies of scale
See Scale economies

EEOC
See Equal Employment Opportunity Commission

8(a) Program
A program authorized by the Small Business Act that directs federal contracts to small businesses owned and operated by socially and economically disadvantaged individuals.

Electronic mail (e-mail)
The electronic transmission of mail via phone lines.

E-mail
See Electronic mail

Employee leasing
A contract by which employers arrange to have their workers hired by a leasing company and then leased back to them for a management fee. The leasing company typically assumes the administrative burden of payroll and provides a benefit package to the workers.

Employee tenure
The length of time an employee works for a particular employer.

Employer identification number
The business equivalent of a social security number. Assigned by the U.S. Internal Revenue Service.

Enterprise
An aggregation of all establishments owned by a parent company. An enterprise may consist of a single, independent establishment or include subsidiaries and other branches under the same ownership and control.

Enterprise zone
A designated area, usually found in inner cities and other areas with significant unemployment, where businesses receive tax credits and other incentives to entice them to establish operations there.

Entrepreneur
A person who takes the risk of organizing and operating a new business venture.

Entry
See Business entry

Equal Employment Opportunity Commission (EEOC)
A federal agency that ensures nondiscrimination in the hiring and firing practices of a business.

Equal opportunity employer
An employer who adheres to the standards set by the Equal Employment Opportunity Commission (see separate citation).

Equity
The ownership interest. Financing in which partial or total ownership of a company is surrendered in exchange for capital. An investor's financial return comes from dividend payments and from growth in the net worth of the business.

Equity capital
See Equity; Equity midrisk venture capital

Equity financing
See Equity; Equity midrisk venture capital

Equity midrisk venture capital
An unsecured investment in a company. Usually a purchase of ownership interest in a company that occurs in the later stages of a company's development.

Equity partnership
A limited partnership arrangement for providing start-up and seed capital to businesses.

Equity securities
See Equity

Equity-type
Debt financing subordinated to conventional debt.

Establishment
A single-location business unit that may be independent (a single-establishment enterprise) or owned by a parent enterprise.

Establishment and Enterprise Microdata File
See U.S. Establishment and Enterprise Microdata File

Establishment birth
See Business birth

Establishment Longitudinal Microdata File
See U.S. Establishment Longitudinal Microdata File

Ethics
See Business ethics

Evaluation
Determining the potential success of translating an invention into a product or process.

Exit
See Business exit

Experience rating
See Underwriting

Export
A product sold outside of the country.

Export license
A general or specific license granted by the U.S. Department of Commerce required of anyone wishing to export goods. Some restricted articles need approval from the U.S. Departments of State, Defense, or Energy.

Failure
See Business failure

Fair share agreement
An agreement reached between a franchisor and a minority business organization to extend business ownership to minorities by either reducing the amount of capital required or by setting aside certain marketing areas for minority business owners.

Feasibility study
A study to determine the likelihood that a proposed product or development will fulfill the objectives of a particular investor.

Federal Trade Commission (FTC)
Federal agency that promotes free enterprise and competition within the U.S.

Federal Trade Mark Act of 1946
See Lanham Act

Fictional name
See Business name

Fiduciary
An individual or group that hold assets in trust for a beneficiary.

Financial analysis
The techniques used to determine money needs in a business. Techniques include ratio analysis, calculation of return on investment, guides for measuring profitability, and break-even analysis to determine ultimate success.

Financial intermediary
A financial institution that acts as the intermediary between borrowers and lenders. Banks, savings and loan associations, finance companies, and venture capital companies are major financial intermediaries in the United States.

Financial ratios
See Corporate financial ratios; Industry financial ratios

Financial statement
A written record of business finances, including balance sheets and profit and loss statements.

Financing
See First-stage financing; Second-stage financing; Thirdstage financing

First-stage financing
Financing provided to companies that have expended their initial capital, and require funds to start full-scale manufacturing and sales. Also known as First-round financing.

Fiscal year
Any twelve-month period used by businesses for accounting purposes.

504 Program
See Certified development corporation

Flexible benefit plan
A plan that offers a choice among cash and/or qualified benefits such as group term life insurance, accident and health insurance, group legal services, dependent care assistance, and vacations.

FOB
See Free on board

Format franchising
See Business format franchising; Franchising

401(k) plan
A financial plan where employees contribute a percentage of their earnings to a fund that is invested in stocks, bonds, or money markets for the purpose of saving money for retirement.

Four Ps
Marketing terms referring to Product, Price, Place, and Promotion.

Franchising
A form of licensing by which the owner-the franchisor- distributes or markets a product, method, or service through affiliated dealers called franchisees. The product, method, or service being marketed is identified by a brand name, and the franchisor maintains control over the marketing methods employed. The franchisee is often given exclusive access to a defined geographic area.

Free on board (FOB)
A pricing term indicating that the quoted price includes the cost of loading goods into transport vessels at a specified place.

Frictional unemployment
See Unemployment

FTC
See Federal Trade Commission

Fulfillment
The systems necessary for accurate delivery of an ordered item, including subscriptions and direct marketing.

Full-time workers
Generally, those who work a regular schedule of more than 35 hours per week.

Garment registration number
A number that must appear on every garment sold in the U.S. to indicate the manufacturer of the garment, which may or may not be the same as the label under which the garment is sold. The U.S. Federal Trade Commission assigns and regulates garment registration numbers.

Gatekeeper
A key contact point for entry into a network.

GDP
See Gross domestic product

General obligation bond
A municipal bond secured by the taxing power of the municipality. The Tax Reform Act of 1986 limits the purposes for which such bonds may be issued and establishes volume limits on the extent of their issuance.

GNP
See Gross national product

Good Housekeeping Seal
Seal appearing on products that signifies the fulfillment of the standards set by the Good Housekeeping Institute to protect consumer interests.

Goods sector
All businesses producing tangible goods, including agriculture, mining, construction, and manufacturing businesses.

GPO
See Gross product originating

Gross domestic product (GDP)
The part of the nation's gross national product (see separate citation) generated by private business using resources from within the country.

Gross national product (GNP)
The most comprehensive single measure of aggregate economic output. Represents the market value of the total output of goods and services produced by a nation's economy.

Gross product originating (GPO)
A measure of business output estimated from the income or production side using employee compensation, profit income, net interest, capital consumption, and indirect business taxes.

HAL
See Handicapped assistance loan program

Handicapped assistance loan program (HAL)
Low-interest direct loan program through the U.S. Small Business Administration (SBA) for handicapped persons. The SBA requires that these persons demonstrate that their disability is such that it is impossible for them to secure employment, thus making it necessary to go into their own business to make a living.

Health maintenance organization (HMO)
Organization of physicians and other health care professionals that provides health services to subscribers and their dependents on a prepaid basis.

Health provider
An individual or institution that gives medical care. Under Medicare, an institutional provider is a hospital, skilled nursing facility, home health agency, or provider of certain physical therapy services.

Hispanic
A person of Cuban, Mexican, Puerto Rican, Latin American (Central or South American), European Spanish, or other Spanish-speaking origin or ancestry.

HMO
See Health maintenance organization

Home-based business
A business with an operating address that is also a residential address (usually the residential address of the proprietor).

Hub-and-spoke system
A system in which flights of an airline from many different cities (the spokes) converge at a single airport (the hub). After allowing passengers sufficient time to make connections, planes then depart for different cities.

Human Resources Management
A business program designed to oversee recruiting, pay, benefits, and other issues related to the company's work force, including planning to determine the optimal use of labor to increase production, thereby increasing profit.

Idea
An original concept for a new product or process.

Import
Products produced outside the country in which they are consumed.

Income
Money or its equivalent, earned or accrued, resulting from the sale of goods and services.

Income statement
A financial statement that lists the profits and losses of a company at a given time.

Incorporation
The filing of a certificate of incorporation with a state's secretary of state, thereby limiting the business owner's liability.

Incubator
A facility designed to encourage entrepreneurship and minimize obstacles to new business formation and growth, particularly for high-technology firms, by housing a number of fledgling enterprises that share an array of services, such as meeting areas, secretarial services, accounting, research library, on-site financial and management counseling, and word processing facilities.

Independent contractor
An individual considered self-employed (see separate citation) and responsible for paying Social Security taxes and income taxes on earnings.

Indirect health coverage
Health insurance obtained through another individual's health care plan; for example, a spouse's employersponsored plan.

Industrial development authority
The financial arm of a state or other political subdivision established for the purpose of financing economic development in an area, usually through loans to nonprofit organizations, which in turn provide facilities for manufacturing and other industrial operations.

Industry financial ratios
Corporate financial ratios averaged for a specified industry. These are used for comparison purposes and reveal industry trends and identify differences between the performance of a specific company and the performance of its industry. Also known as Industrial averages, Industry ratios, Financial averages, and Business or Industrial norms.

Inflation
Increases in volume of currency and credit, generally resulting in a sharp and continuing rise in price levels.

Informal capital
Financing from informal, unorganized sources; includes informal debt capital such as trade credit or loans from friends and relatives and equity capital from informal investors.

Initial public offering (IPO)
A corporation's first offering of stock to the public.

Innovation
The introduction of a new idea into the marketplace in the form of a new product or service or an improvement in organization or process.

Intellectual property
Any idea or work that can be considered proprietary in nature and is thus protected from infringement by others.

Internal capital
Debt or equity financing obtained from the owner or through retained business earnings.

Internet
A government-designed computer network that contains large amounts of information and is accessible through various vendors for a fee.

Intrapreneurship
The state of employing entrepreneurial principles to nonentrepreneurial situations.

Invention
The tangible form of a technological idea, which could include a laboratory prototype, drawings, formulas, etc.

IPO
See Initial public offering

Job description
The duties and responsibilities required in a particular position.

Job tenure
A period of time during which an individual is continuously employed in the same job.

Joint marketing agreements
Agreements between regional and major airlines, often involving the coordination of flight schedules, fares, and baggage transfer. These agreements help regional carriers operate at lower cost.

Joint venture
Venture in which two or more people combine efforts in a particular business enterprise, usually a single transaction or a limited activity, and agree to share the profits and losses jointly or in proportion to their contributions.

Keogh plan
Designed for self-employed persons and unincorporated businesses as a tax-deferred pension account.

Labor force
Civilians considered eligible for employment who are also willing and able to work.

Labor force participation rate
The civilian labor force as a percentage of the civilian population.

Labor intensity
The relative importance of labor in the production process, usually measured as the capital-labor ratio; i.e., the ratio of units of capital (typically, dollars of tangible assets) to the number of employees. The higher the capital-labor ratio exhibited by a firm or industry, the lower the capital intensity of that firm or industry is said to be.

Labor surplus area
An area in which there exists a high unemployment rate. In procurement (see separate citation), extra points are given to firms in counties that are designated a labor surplus area; this information is requested on procurement bid sheets.

Labor union
An organization of similarly-skilled workers who collectively bargain with management over the conditions of employment.

Laboratory prototype
See Prototype

LAN
See Local Area Network

Lanham Act
Refers to the Federal Trade Mark Act of 1946. Protects registered trademarks, trade names, and other service marks used in commerce.

Large business-dominated industry
Industry in which a minimum of 60 percent of employment or sales is in firms with more than 500 workers.

LBO
See Leveraged buy-out

Leader pricing
A reduction in the price of a good or service in order to generate more sales of that good or service.

Legal list
A list of securities selected by a state in which certain institutions and fiduciaries (such as pension funds, insurance companies, and banks) may invest. Securities not on the list are not eligible for investment. Legal lists typically restrict investments to high quality securities meeting certain specifications. Generally, investment is limited to U.S. securities and investment-grade blue chip securities (see separate citation).

Leveraged buy-out (LBO)
The purchase of a business or a division of a corporation through a highly leveraged financing package.

Liability
An obligation or duty to perform a service or an act. Also defined as money owed.

License
A legal agreement granting to another the right to use a technological innovation.

Limited Liability Company
A hybrid type of legal structure that provides the limited liability features of a corporation and the tax efficiencies and operational flexibility of a partnership. Depending on the state, the members can consist of a single individual (one owner), two or more individuals, corporations or other LLCs.

Limited liability partnerships
A business organization that allows limited partners to enjoy limited personal liability while general partners have unlimited personal liability

Liquidity
The ability to convert a security into cash promptly.

Loans
See Commercial loans; Disaster loans; SBA direct loans; SBA guaranteed loans; SBA special lending institution categories Local Area Network (LAN) Computer networks contained within a single building or small area; used to facilitate the sharing of information.

Local development corporation
An organization, usually made up of local citizens of a community, designed to improve the economy of the area by inducing business and industry to locate and expand there. A local development corporation establishes a capability to finance local growth.

Long-haul rates
Rates charged by a transporter in which the distance traveled is more than 800 miles.

Long-term debt
An obligation that matures in a period that exceeds five years.

Low-grade bond
A corporate bond that is rated below investment grade by the major rating agencies (Standard and Poor's, Moody's).

Macro-efficiency
Efficiency as it pertains to the operation of markets and market systems.

Managed care
A cost-effective health care program initiated by employers whereby low-cost health care is made available to the employees in return for exclusive patronage to program doctors.

Management Assistance Programs
See SBA Management Assistance Programs

Management and technical assistance
A term used by many programs to mean business (as opposed to technological) assistance.

Mandated benefits
Specific treatments, providers, or individuals required by law to be included in commercial health plans.

Market evaluation
The use of market information to determine the sales potential of a specific product or process.

Market failure
The situation in which the workings of a competitive market do not produce the best results from the point of view of the entire society.

Market information
Data of any type that can be used for market evaluation, which could include demographic data, technology forecasting, regulatory changes, etc.

Market research
A systematic collection, analysis, and reporting of data about the market and its preferences, opinions, trends, and plans; used for corporate decision-making.

Market share
In a particular market, the percentage of sales of a specific product.

Marketing
Promotion of goods or services through various media.

Master Establishment List (MEL)
A list of firms in the United States developed by the U.S. Small Business Administration; firms can be selected by industry, region, state, standard metropolitan statistical area (see separate citation), county, and zip code.

Maturity
The date upon which the principal or stated value of a bond or other indebtedness becomes due and payable.

Medicaid (Title XIX)
A federally aided, state-operated and administered program that provides medical benefits for certain low income persons in need of health and medical care who are eligible for one of the government's welfare cash payment programs, including the aged, the blind, the disabled, and members of families with dependent children where one parent is absent, incapacitated, or unemployed.

Medicare (Title XVIII)
A nationwide health insurance program for disabled and aged persons. Health insurance is available to insured persons without regard to income. Monies from payroll taxes cover hospital insurance and monies from general revenues and beneficiary premiums pay for supplementary medical insurance.

MEL
See Master Establishment List

Merchant Status
The relationship between a company and a bank or credit card company allowing the company to accept credit card payments

MESBIC
See Minority enterprise small business investment corporation

MET
See Multiple employer trust

Metropolitan statistical area (MSA)
A means used by the government to define large population centers that may transverse different governmental jurisdictions. For example, the Washington, D.C. MSA includes the District of Columbia and contiguous parts of Maryland and Virginia because all of these geopolitical areas comprise one population and economic operating unit.

Mezzanine financing
See Third-stage financing

Micro-efficiency
Efficiency as it pertains to the operation of individual firms.

Microdata
Information on the characteristics of an individual business firm.

Microloan
An SBA loan program that helps entrepreneurs obtain loans from less than $100 to $25,000.

Mid-term debt
An obligation that matures within one to five years.

Midrisk venture capital
See Equity midrisk venture capital

Minimum premium plan
A combination approach to funding an insurance plan aimed primarily at premium tax savings. The employer self-funds a fixed percentage of estimated monthly claims and the insurance company insures the excess.

Minimum wage
The lowest hourly wage allowed by the federal government.

Minority Business Development Agency
Contracts with private firms throughout the nation to sponsor Minority Business Development Centers which provide minority firms with advice and technical assistance on a fee basis.

Minority Enterprise Small Business Investment Corporation (MESBIC)
A federally funded private venture capital firm licensed by the U.S. Small Business Administration to provide capital to minority-owned businesses (see separate citation).

Minority-owned business
Businesses owned by those who are socially or economically disadvantaged (see separate citation).

Mission statement
A short statement describing a company's function, markets and competitive advantages.

Mom and Pop business
A small store or enterprise having limited capital, principally employing family members.

Multi-employer plan
A health plan to which more than one employer is required to contribute and that may be maintained through a collective bargaining agreement and required to meet standards prescribed by the U.S. Department of Labor.

Multi-level marketing
A system of selling in which you sign up other people to assist you and they, in turn, recruit others to help them. Some entrepreneurs have built successful companies on this concept because the main focus of their activities is their product and product sales.

Multiple employer trust (MET)
A self-funded benefit plan generally geared toward small employers sharing a common interest.

NASDAQ
See National Association of Securities Dealers Automated Quotations

National Association of Securities Dealers Automated Quotations
Provides price quotes on over-the-counter securities as well as securities listed on the New York Stock Exchange.

National income
Aggregate earnings of labor and property arising from the production of goods and services in a nation's economy.

Net assets
See Net worth

Net income
The amount remaining from earnings and profits after all expenses and costs have been met or deducted. Also known as Net earnings.

Net profit
Money earned after production and overhead expenses (see separate citations) have been deducted.

Net worth
The difference between a company's total assets and its total liabilities.

Network
A chain of interconnected individuals or organizations sharing information and/or services.

New York Stock Exchange (NYSE)
The oldest stock exchange in the U.S. Allows for trading in stocks, bonds, warrants, options, and rights that meet listing requirements.

Niche
A career or business for which a person is well-suited. Also, a product which fulfills one need of a particular market segment, often with little or no competition.

Nodes
One workstation in a network, either local area or wide area (see separate citations).

Nonbank bank
A bank that either accepts deposits or makes loans, but not both. Used to create many new branch banks.

Noncompetitive awards
A method of contracting whereby the federal government negotiates with only one contractor to supply a product or service.

Nonmember bank
A state-regulated bank that does not belong to the federal bank system.

Nonprofit
An organization that has no shareholders, does not distribute profits, and is without federal and state tax liabilities.

Norms
See Financial ratios

North American Free Trade Agreement (NAFTA)
Passed in 1993, NAFTA eliminates trade barriers among businesses in the U.S., Canada, and Mexico.

NYSE
See New York Stock Exchange

Occupational Safety & Health Administration (OSHA)
Federal agency that regulates health and safety standards within the workplace.

Operating Expenses
Business expenditures not directly associated with the production of goods or services.

Optimal firm size
The business size at which the production cost per unit of output (average cost) is, in the long run, at its minimum.

Organizational chart
A hierarchical chart tracking the chain of command within an organization.

OSHA
See Occupational Safety & Health Administration

Overhead
Expenses, such as employee benefits and building utilities, incurred by a business that are unrelated to the actual product or service sold.

Owner's capital
Debt or equity funds provided by the owner(s) of a business; sources of owner's capital are personal savings, sales of assets, or loans from financial institutions.

P & L
See Profit and loss statement

Part-time workers
Normally, those who work less than 35 hours per week. The Tax Reform Act indicated that part-time workers who work less than 17.5 hours per week may be excluded from health plans for purposes of complying with federal nondiscrimination rules.

Part-year workers
Those who work less than 50 weeks per year.

Partnership
Two or more parties who enter into a legal relationship to conduct business for profit. Defined by the U.S. Internal Revenue Code as joint ventures, syndicates, groups, pools, and other associations of two or more persons organized for profit that are not specifically classified in the IRS code as corporations or proprietorships.

Patent
A grant made by the government assuring an inventor the sole right to make, use, and sell an invention for a period of 17 years.

PC
See Professional corporation

Peak
See Cyclical peak

Pension
A series of payments made monthly, semiannually, annually, or at other specified intervals during the lifetime of the pensioner for distribution upon retirement. The term is sometimes used to denote the portion of the retirement allowance financed by the employer's contributions.

Pension fund
A fund established to provide for the payment of pension benefits; the collective contributions made by all of the parties to the pension plan.

Performance appraisal
An established set of objective criteria, based on job description and requirements, that is used to evaluate the performance of an employee in a specific job.

Permit
See Business license

Plan
See Business plan

Pooling
An arrangement for employers to achieve efficiencies and lower health costs by joining together to purchase group health insurance or self-insurance.

PPO
See Preferred provider organization

Preferred lenders program
See SBA special lending institution categories

Preferred provider organization (PPO)
A contractual arrangement with a health care services organization that agrees to discount its health care rates in return for faster payment and/or a patient base.

Premiums
The amount of money paid to an insurer for health insurance under a policy. The premium is generally paid periodically (e.g., monthly), and often is split between the employer and the employee. Unlike deductibles and coinsurance or copayments, premiums are paid for coverage whether or not benefits are actually used.

Prime-age workers
Employees 25 to 54 years of age.

Prime contract
A contract awarded directly by the U.S. Federal Government.

Private company
See Closely held corporation

Private placement
A method of raising capital by offering for sale an investment or business to a small group of investors (generally avoiding registration with the Securities and Exchange Commission or state securities registration agencies). Also known as Private financing or Private offering.

Pro forma
The use of hypothetical figures in financial statements to represent future expenditures, debts, and other potential financial expenses.

Proactive
Taking the initiative to solve problems and anticipate future events before they happen, instead of reacting to an already existing problem or waiting for a difficult situation to occur.

Procurement
A contract from an agency of the federal government for goods or services from a small business.

Product development
The stage of the innovation process where research is translated into a product or process through evaluation, adaptation, and demonstration.

Product franchising
An arrangement for a franchisee to use the name and to produce the product line of the franchisor or parent corporation.

Production
The manufacture of a product.

Production prototype
See Prototype

Productivity
A measurement of the number of goods produced during a specific amount of time.

Professional corporation (PC)
Organized by members of a profession such as medicine, dentistry, or law for the purpose of conducting their professional activities as a corporation. Liability of a member or shareholder is limited in the same manner as in a business corporation.

Profit and loss statement (P & L)
The summary of the incomes (total revenues) and costs of a company's operation during a specific period of time. Also known as Income and expense statement.

Proposal
See Business plan

Proprietorship
The most common legal form of business ownership; about 85 percent of all small businesses are proprietorships. The liability of the owner is unlimited in this form of ownership.

Prospective payment system
A cost-containment measure included in the Social Security Amendments of 1983 whereby Medicare payments to hospitals are based on established prices, rather than on cost reimbursement.

Prototype
A model that demonstrates the validity of the concept of an invention (laboratory prototype); a model that meets the needs of the manufacturing process and the user (production prototype).

Prudent investor rule or standard
A legal doctrine that requires fiduciaries to make investments using the prudence, diligence, and intelligence that would be used by a prudent person in making similar investments. Because fiduciaries make investments on behalf of third-party beneficiaries, the standard results in very conservative investments. Until recently, most state regulations required the fiduciary to apply this standard to each investment. Newer, more progressive regulations permit fiduciaries to apply this standard to the portfolio taken as a whole, thereby allowing a fiduciary to balance a portfolio with higher-yield, higher-risk investments. In states with more progressive regulations, practically every type of security is eligible for inclusion in the portfolio of investments made by a fiduciary, provided that the portfolio investments, in their totality, are those of a prudent person.

Public equity markets
Organized markets for trading in equity shares such as common stocks, preferred stocks, and warrants. Includes markets for both regularly traded and nonregularly traded securities.

Public offering
General solicitation for participation in an investment opportunity. Interstate public offerings are supervised by the U.S. Securities and Exchange Commission (see separate citation).

Quality control
The process by which a product is checked and tested to ensure consistent standards of high quality.

Rate of return
The yield obtained on a security or other investment based on its purchase price or its current market price. The total rate of return is current income plus or minus capital appreciation or depreciation.

Real property
Includes the land and all that is contained on it.

Realignment
See Resource realignment

Recession
Contraction of economic activity occurring between the peak and trough (see separate citations) of a business cycle.

Regulated market
A market in which the government controls the forces of supply and demand, such as who may enter and what price may be charged.

Regulation D
A vehicle by which small businesses make small offerings and private placements of securities with limited disclosure requirements. It was designed to ease the burdens imposed on small businesses utilizing this method of capital formation.

Regulatory Flexibility Act
An act requiring federal agencies to evaluate the impact of their regulations on small businesses before the regulations are issued and to consider less burdensome alternatives.

Research
The initial stage of the innovation process, which includes idea generation and invention.

Research and development financing
A tax-advantaged partnership set up to finance product development for start-ups as well as more mature companies.

Resource mobility
The ease with which labor and capital move from firm to firm or from industry to industry.

Resource realignment
The adjustment of productive resources to interindustry changes in demand.

Resources
The sources of support or help in the innovation process, including sources of financing, technical evaluation, market evaluation, management and business assistance, etc.

Retained business earnings
Business profits that are retained by the business rather than being distributed to the shareholders as dividends.

Return on investment
A profitability measure that evaluates the performance of a business by dividing net profit by net worth.

Revolving credit
An agreement with a lending institution for an amount of money, which cannot exceed a set maximum, over a specified period of time. Each time the borrower repays a portion of the loan, the amount of the repayment may be borrowed yet again.

Risk capital
See Venture capital

Risk management
The act of identifying potential sources of financial loss and taking action to minimize their negative impact.

Routing
The sequence of steps necessary to complete a product during production.

S corporations
See Sub chapter S corporations

SBA
See Small Business Administration

SBA direct loans
Loans made directly by the U.S. Small Business Administration (SBA); monies come from funds appropriated specifically for this purpose. In general, SBA direct loans carry interest rates slightly lower than those in the private financial markets and are available only to applicants unable to secure private financing or an SBA guaranteed loan.

SBA 504 Program
See Certified development corporation

SBA guaranteed loans
Loans made by lending institutions in which the U.S. Small Business Administration (SBA) will pay a prior agreed-upon percentage of the outstanding principal in the event the borrower of the loan defaults. The terms of the loan and the interest rate are negotiated between theborrower and the lending institution, within set parameters.

SBA loans
See Disaster loans; SBA direct loans; SBA guaranteed loans; SBA special lending institution categories

SBA Management Assistance Programs
Classes, workshops, counseling, and publications offered by the U.S. Small Business Administration.

SBA special lending institution categories
U.S. Small Business Administration (SBA) loan program in which the SBA promises certified banks a 72-hour turnaround period in giving its approval for a loan, and in which preferred lenders in a pilot program are allowed to write SBA loans without seeking prior SBA approval.

SBDB
See Small Business Data Base

SBDC
See Small business development centers

SBI
See Small business institutes program

SBIC
See Small business investment corporation

SBIR Program
See Small Business Innovation Development Act of 1982

Scale economies
The decline of the production cost per unit of output (average cost) as the volume of output increases.

Scale efficiency
The reduction in unit cost available to a firm when producing at a higher output volume.

SCORE
See Service Corps of Retired Executives

SEC
See Securities and Exchange Commission

SECA
See Self-Employment Contributions Act

Second-stage financing
Working capital for the initial expansion of a company that is producing, shipping, and has growing accounts receivable and inventories. Also known as Second-round financing.

Secondary market
A market established for the purchase and sale of outstanding securities following their initial distribution.

Secondary worker
Any worker in a family other than the person who is the primary source of income for the family.

Secondhand capital
Previously used and subsequently resold capital equipment (e.g., buildings and machinery).

Securities and Exchange Commission (SEC)
Federal agency charged with regulating the trade of securities to prevent unethical practices in the investor market.

Securitized debt
A marketing technique that converts long-term loans to marketable securities.

Seed capital
Venture financing provided in the early stages of the innovation process, usually during product development.

Self-employed person
One who works for a profit or fees in his or her own business, profession, or trade, or who operates a farm.

Self-Employment Contributions Act (SECA)
Federal law that governs the self-employment tax (see separate citation).

Self-employment income
Income covered by Social Security if a business earns a net income of at least $400.00 during the year. Taxes are paid on earnings that exceed $400.00.

Self-employment retirement plan
See Keogh plan

Self-employment tax
Required tax imposed on self-employed individuals for the provision of Social Security and Medicare. The tax must be paid quarterly with estimated income tax statements.

Self-funding
A health benefit plan in which a firm uses its own funds to pay claims, rather than transferring the financial risks of paying claims to an outside insurer in exchange for premium payments.

Service Corps of Retired Executives (SCORE)
Volunteers for the SBA Management Assistance Program who provide one-on-one counseling and teach workshops and seminars for small firms.

Service firm
See Business service firm

Service sector
Broadly defined, all U.S. industries that produce intangibles, including the five major industry divisions of transportation, communications, and utilities; wholesale trade; retail trade; finance, insurance, and real estate; and services.

Set asides
See Small business set asides

Short-haul service
A type of transportation service in which the transporter supplies service between cities where the maximum distance is no more than 200 miles.

Short-term debt
An obligation that matures in one year.

SIC codes
See Standard Industrial Classification codes

Single-establishment enterprise
See Establishment

Small business
An enterprise that is independently owned and operated, is not dominant in its field, and employs fewer than 500 people. For SBA purposes, the U.S. Small Business Administration (SBA) considers various other factors (such as gross annual sales) in determining size of a business.

Small Business Administration (SBA)
An independent federal agency that provides assistance with loans, management, and advocating interests before other federal agencies.

Small Business Data Base
A collection of microdata (see separate citation) files on individual firms developed and maintained by the U.S. Small Business Administration.

Small business development centers (SBDC)
Centers that provide support services to small businesses, such as individual counseling, SBA advice, seminars and conferences, and other learning center activities. Most services are free of charge, or available at minimal cost.

Small business development corporation
See Certified development corporation

Small business-dominated industry
Industry in which a minimum of 60 percent of employment or sales is in firms with fewer than 500 employees.

Small Business Innovation Development Act of 1982
Federal statute requiring federal agencies with large extramural research and development budgets to allocate a certain percentage of these funds to small research and development firms. The program, called the Small Business Innovation Research (SBIR) Program, is designed to stimulate technological innovation and make greater use of small businesses in meeting national innovation needs.

Small business institutes (SBI) program
Cooperative arrangements made by U.S. Small Business Administration district offices and local colleges and universities to provide small business firms with graduate students to counsel them without charge.

Small business investment corporation (SBIC)
A privately owned company licensed and funded through the U.S. Small Business Administration and private sector sources to provide equity or debt capital to small businesses.

Small business set asides
Procurement (see separate citation) opportunities required by law to be on all contracts under $10,000 or a certain percentage of an agency's total procurement expenditure.

Smaller firms
For U.S. Department of Commerce purposes, those firms not included in the Fortune 1000.

SMSA
See Metropolitan statistical area

Socially and economically disadvantaged
Individuals who have been subjected to racial or ethnic prejudice or cultural bias without regard to their qualities as individuals, and whose abilities to compete are impaired because of diminished opportunities to obtain capital and credit.

Sole proprietorship
An unincorporated, one-owner business, farm, or professional practice.

Special lending institution categories
See SBA special lending institution categories

Standard Industrial Classification (SIC) codes
Four-digit codes established by the U.S. Federal Government to categorize businesses by type of economic activity; the first two digits correspond to major groups such as construction and manufacturing, while the last two digits correspond to subgroups such as home construction or highway construction.

Start-up
A new business, at the earliest stages of development and financing.

Start-up costs
Costs incurred before a business can commence operations.

Start-up financing
Financing provided to companies that have either completed product development and initial marketing or have been in business for less than one year but have not yet sold their product commercially.

Stock
A certificate of equity ownership in a business.

Stop-loss coverage
Insurance for a self-insured plan that reimburses the company for any losses it might incur in its health claims beyond a specified amount.

Strategic planning
Projected growth and development of a business to establish a guiding direction for the future. Also used to determine which market segments to explore for optimal sales of products or services.

Structural unemployment
See Unemployment

Sub chapter S corporations
Corporations that are considered noncorporate for tax purposes but legally remain corporations.

Subcontract
A contract between a prime contractor and a subcontractor, or between subcontractors, to furnish supplies or services for performance of a prime contract (see separate citation) or a subcontract.

Surety bonds
Bonds providing reimbursement to an individual, company, or the government if a firm fails to complete a contract. The U.S. Small Business Administration guarantees surety bonds in a program much like the SBA guaranteed loan program (see separate citation).

Swing loan
See Bridge financing

Target market
The clients or customers sought for a business' product or service.

Targeted Jobs Tax Credit
Federal legislation enacted in 1978 that provides a tax credit to an employer who hires structurally unemployed individuals.

Tax number
A number assigned to a business by a state revenue department that enables the business to buy goods without paying sales tax.

Taxable bonds
An interest-bearing certificate of public or private indebtedness. Bonds are issued by public agencies to finance economic development.

Technical assistance
See Management and technical assistance

Technical evaluation
Assessment of technological feasibility.

Technology
The method in which a firm combines and utilizes labor and capital resources to produce goods or services; the application of science for commercial or industrial purposes.

Technology transfer
The movement of information about a technology or intellectual property from one party to another for use.

Tenure
See Employee tenure

Term
The length of time for which a loan is made.

Terms of a note
The conditions or limits of a note; includes the interest rate per annum, the due date, and transferability and convertibility features, if any.

Third-party administrator
An outside company responsible for handling claims and performing administrative tasks associated with health insurance plan maintenance.

Third-stage financing
Financing provided for the major expansion of a company whose sales volume is increasing and that is breaking even or profitable. These funds are used for further plant expansion, marketing, working capital, or development of an improved product. Also known as Third-round or Mezzanine financing.

Time management
Skills and scheduling techniques used to maximize productivity.

Trade credit
Credit extended by suppliers of raw materials or finished products. In an accounting statement, trade credit is referred to as "accounts payable."

Trade name
The name under which a company conducts business, or by which its business, goods, or services are identified. It may or may not be registered as a trademark.

Trade periodical
A publication with a specific focus on one or more aspects of business and industry.

Trade secret
Competitive advantage gained by a business through the use of a unique manufacturing process or formula.

Trade show
An exhibition of goods or services used in a particular industry. Typically held in exhibition centers where exhibitors rent space to display their merchandise.

Trademark
A graphic symbol, device, or slogan that identifies a business. A business has property rights to its trademark from the inception of its use, but it is still prudent to register all trademarks with the Trademark Office of the U.S. Department of Commerce.

Trend
A statistical measurement used to track changes that occur over time.

Trough
See Cyclical trough

UCC
See Uniform Commercial Code

UL
See Underwriters Laboratories

Underwriters Laboratories (UL)
One of several private firms that tests products and processes to determine their safety. Although various firms can provide this kind of testing service, many local and insurance codes specify UL certification.

Underwriting
A process by which an insurer determines whether or not and on what basis it will accept an application for insurance. In an experience-rated plan, premiums are based on a firm's or group's past claims; factors other than prior claims are used for community-rated or manually rated plans.

Unfair competition
Refers to business practices, usually unethical, such as using unlicensed products, pirating merchandise, or misleading the public through false advertising, which give the offending business an unequitable advantage over others.

Unfunded accrued liability
The excess of total liabilities, both present and prospective, over present and prospective assets.

Unemployment
The joblessness of individuals who are willing to work, who are legally and physically able to work, and who are seeking work. Unemployment may represent the temporary joblessness of a worker between jobs (frictional unemployment) or the joblessness of a worker whose skills are not suitable for jobs available in the labor market (structural unemployment).

Uniform Commercial Code (UCC)
A code of laws governing commercial transactions across the U.S., except Louisiana. Their purpose is to bring uniformity to financial transactions.

Uniform product code (UPC symbol)
A computer-readable label comprised of ten digits and stripes that encodes what a product is and how much it costs. The first five digits are assigned by the Uniform Product Code Council, and the last five digits by the individual manufacturer.

Unit cost
See Average cost

UPC symbol
See Uniform product code

U.S. Establishment and Enterprise Microdata (USEEM) File
A cross-sectional database containing information on employment, sales, and location for individual enterprises and establishments with employees that have a Dun & Bradstreet credit rating.

U.S. Establishment Longitudinal Microdata (USELM) File
A database containing longitudinally linked sample microdata on establishments drawn from the U.S. Establishment and Enterprise Microdata file (see separate citation).

U.S. Small Business Administration 504 Program
See Certified development corporation

USEEM
See U.S. Establishment and Enterprise Microdata File

USELM
See U.S. Establishment Longitudinal Microdata File

VCN
See Venture capital network

Venture capital
Money used to support new or unusual business ventures that exhibit above-average growth rates, significant potential for market expansion, and are in need of additional financing to sustain growth or further research and development; equity or equity-type financing traditionally provided at the commercialization stage, increasingly available prior to commercialization.

Venture capital company
A company organized to provide seed capital to a business in its formation stage, or in its first or second stage of expansion. Funding is obtained through public or private pension funds, commercial banks and bank holding companies, small business investment corporations licensed by the U.S. Small Business Administration, private venture capital firms, insurance companies, investment management companies, bank trust departments, industrial companies seeking to diversify their investment, and investment bankers acting as intermediaries for other investors or directly investing on their own behalf.

Venture capital limited partnerships
Designed for business development, these partnerships are an institutional mechanism for providing capital for young, technology-oriented businesses. The investors' money is pooled and invested in money

market assets until venture investments have been selected. The general partners are experienced investment managers who select and invest the equity and debt securities of firms with high growth potential and the ability to go public in the near future.

Venture capital network (VCN)
A computer database that matches investors with entrepreneurs.

WAN
See Wide Area Network

Wide Area Network (WAN)
Computer networks linking systems throughout a state or around the world in order to facilitate the sharing of information.

Withholding
Federal, state, social security, and unemployment taxes withheld by the employer from employees' wages; employers are liable for these taxes and the corporate umbrella and bankruptcy will not exonerate an employer from paying back payroll withholding. Employers should escrow these funds in a separate account and disperse them quarterly to withholding authorities.

Workers' compensation
A state-mandated form of insurance covering workers injured in job-related accidents. In some states, the state is the insurer; in other states, insurance must be acquired from commercial insurance firms. Insurance rates are based on a number of factors, including salaries, firm history, and risk of occupation.

Working capital
Refers to a firm's short-term investment of current assets, including cash, short-term securities, accounts receivable, and inventories.

Yield
The rate of income returned on an investment, expressed as a percentage. Income yield is obtained by dividing the current dollar income by the current market price of the security. Net yield or yield to maturity is the current income yield minus any premium above par or plus any discount from par in purchase price, with the adjustment spread over the period from the date of purchase to the date of maturity.

Index

Listings in this index are arranged alphabetically by business plan type, then alphabetically by business plan name. Users are provided with the volume number in which the plan appears.